THE POWER OF
ROBERT SIMPSON

THE POWER OF
ROBERT SIMPSON

A BIOGRAPHY

DONALD MACAULEY

Copyright © 2013 by Donald Macauley.

Library of Congress Control Number: 2013902834
ISBN: Hardcover   978-1-4797-9438-6
              Softcover   978-1-4797-9437-9
              eBook   978-1-4797-9439-3

All rights reserved. No part of this book may be reproduced or transmitted in any form or by any means, electronic or mechanical, including photocopying, recording, or by any information storage and retrieval system, without permission in writing from the copyright owner.

Print information available on the last page.

Rev. date: 07/14/2015

To order additional copies of this book, contact:
Xlibris
800-056-3182
www.Xlibrispublishing.co.uk
Orders@Xlibrispublishing.co.uk

TABLE OF CONTENTS

Page 6	Foreword
Page 9	Remember Who And What You Are (Family History)
Page 20	The Bolshiest Brat They Ever Had (A Salvation Army Childhood, 1921-1939)
Page 34	A Frightful Crew Of Toughs (1940-1945)
Page 47	I'll Marry Her, Then! (1946-1950)
Page 55	The Envy Of The Whole Civilised World (1951-1952)
Page 70	A Great Lady And A Great Artist (1953-1958)
Page 83	Composed By An Orang-Utan When I Wasn't Looking (1959-1965)
Page 92	I'm Not Going To Die – I've Just Bought A New Pair Of Trousers! (1966-1971)
Page 115	A Nose-Bleed In The Brain (1972-1976)
Page 133	The End Is C Sharp (1977-1980)
Page 140	That Lot Ought To Be Taught A Lesson (1981-1985)
Page 170	A Cathedral In Sound (1986-1988)
Page 191	It Scares The Living Daylights Out Of Me (1989-1990)
Page 199	I'd Rather Not Be An Interesting Case (1991-1997)
Page 213	A Practical Idealist
Page 232	Music And Musicians
Page 258	Friends
Page 303	Afterword
Page 307	Simpson Antagonistes
Page 315	Appendices

Thou has left behind

Powers that will work for thee; air, earth, and skies;

There's not a breathing of the common wind

That will forget thee; thou has great allies;

Thy friends are exultations, agonies,

And love, and man's unconquerable mind.

(From: To Toussaint L'Ouverture, by William Wordsworth)

DEDICATION: To Petra Tonderová, fellow Reading survivor, painter, and muse.

Author's note: Where possible, I have ascribed quotes from the composer. Where no attribution is given, they derive either from conversations with him, or from third parties whose truthfulness I have no reason to doubt.

The interviews with Lewis Foreman and Julian Budden cited in the text are accessible in the back numbers of "Tonic" on the Robert Simpson Society website, along with much other material.

ACKNOWLEDGEMENTS

My thanks are due above all both to Robert Simpson's widow, Angela (who also made a very generous contribution toward the production costs), and his sister, Miriam MacEwan, for providing much information and photographs and for their support and encouragement, to Elisabeth Benians for her account of the composer's formative years and many valuable extracts from his letters to her, to the late Terry Hazell, former chairman and archivist of the Robert Simpson Society, for suggesting the biography in the first place and for background information on Salvation Army matters, to Martin Holmes of the Bodleian music Library, where the Simpson archive now resides, to Gordon Taylor and colleagues at the Salvation Army heritage centre, to Philip Ashworth for additional information about Robert Simpson senior's activities during and after world war 1, to Jurgen Schaarwëchter, RSS chairman, for advice regarding potential publishers, to Peter Bendall, who proof-read the manuscript, to Sarah Dimmock, who typed it on to disc, and to Petra Tonderová and her daughter Tamsin Ronan, who translated the review of the Czech performance of the fifth Symphony. I would also like to thank Ronald Stevenson, David Willcocks, Colin Davis, Oliver Knussen, Hugh Wood, Patric Standford, Jane Manning, and Andre Previn for permission to quote from their letters to Robert Simpson. My thanks are also due to Rex Roberts and Peter Musgrave for certain of the later photographs.

FOREWORD

Robert Simpson 1921 - 1997

Ultimately, the creative process remains mysterious: nobody has yet satisfactorily explained why certain individuals feel compelled to compose music, paint pictures or write poetry, and to continue doing so throughout their adult lives, often in the teeth of critical and public indifference, even hostility. One can, I think, rule out hope of eventual fame and fortune as the driving force: to reverse Johnson's dictum, nobody but a blockhead would nowadays enter the creative arts in the expectation of making money. Other than incidental music for films and TV, composition has long since ceased to be a feasible way of making even a modest living.

Additionally, in music (as also in the visual arts, although less so in literature) there is the "modernist" problem. Not that modern, in truth: since Beethoven's day, and the supplanting of generally accepted norms by individual modes of expression, most new work has received, at best, a mixed reception: at worst, baffled incomprehension or outright hatred. Alienation has, over the last century, been deepened by various experimental techniques: in such an atmosphere, it has become even more difficult for a composer to gain a sympathetic hearing, even though the work in question may be in no way iconoclastic, nihilistic, or plain silly. While there is an extensive discography, public performances of Simpson's music are a rarity: I have no doubt that built-in suspicion of anything "new" on the part of both audiences and programme planners has been a factor here.

While composing is, in itself, a solitary activity, musicians have the further disadvantage of being reliant upon others to perform their works – well or ill – while success or failure in painting is entirely down to the individual. As Robert Simpson said "At least nobody can interfere with your work – I'm dependant on my interpreters". First performances, especially, can vary wildly in quality: Simpson considered that the first decent premiere of any of his symphonies was that of the Fifth, under Andrew Davies, reflected not merely in a terrific response from the concert-goers, and very favourable press reviews, but a standing ovation from the orchestra – a rare event! A shambolic premiere can, on the other hand, blight the reputation of a piece for many years, if not forever.

Gustave Flaubert observed, to George Sand: "The man is nothing; the work, all". A fair point – we know hardly anything of Shakespeare's life, and this has, most likely, spared us countless volumes of pointless speculation about the correlation between events in his personal domain and the play he happened to be writing at the time. The two can, in any case, as often seem to contradict as to tally. While Nielsen's heart attack surely influenced the development of his Sixth symphony, Beethoven composed his brilliant and confident Second at a time when realisation of his approaching total deafness had plunged him into suicidal depression.

Simpson was, moreover, the least illustrative of composers. Only a handful of his works have any admitted extra-musical inspiration, and even in those the source is usually psychological rather than concrete. The composer described the second movement of his Third symphony as "Nature music, in a sense – the only piece of mine which has an origin in some external situation…" Put programmatically, the situation is this: a sleeper wakes in the early morning, his mind passively receptive; the first bird-songs begin, gradually becoming the dawn chorus; the mind quietly absorbs and reflects until at last a tremendous sense of excitement is experienced, "an energy that cannot be repressed". (From a sleeve note by Hugh Ottaway). The second (scherzo) movement of the Eighth quartet (Eretmapodites gilletti) gives an impression of the "formidable delicacy" of the mosquito – the subtitle refers to Professor Gillett, discoverer of the species, to whom the quartet is dedicated. Asked if the music of this piece is what the insects sound like, the Professor replied, "No – but it's what they behave like". (from a sleeve note by Lionel Pike)

The soft chord which opens the Fifth symphony, links the five movements, and ends the work, represents, in the composer's words "the part of the mind which quietly watches you, regardless of the sort of experiences you are having". The Sixth symphony is the dedicated to Professor Ian Craft, the pioneer of in vitro fertilization, who suggested the idea of a symphony whose growth from initial melodic germs might parallel the emergence of life from a fertilized cell. The character and form of the Eighth were suggested, in general terms, by the work's dedicatees, Anthony and Daphne Dorrell, following the composer's requests as to the kind of symphony they would like to hear. The hard, bleak ending of the Seventh caused some listeners to liken it to the aftermath of a nuclear holocaust, or to sense frustrated rage or despair, to all of which he replied "the end is C sharp". He did, however, add "Here we have facts to face, not pleasant ones. Is the end a picture of people not facing a fact that stares them in the face? Melting away in front of it?… Being active in the peace movement has made me horribly aware of the way people bury their heads in the sand – don't want to know – would rather turn away, often with hostility. What you hold up before them they don't even see… That's the part of my experience (this symphony) seems to reflect".

All very much in tune with Beethoven's comments on his Pastoral that it was "more the expression of feelings than painting", although I suspect that Simpson would have shied away from referring even to feelings, preferring to describe his own work in purely technical terms.

One should not, however, conclude that the life of a determinedly "absolute" musician is of no interest or significance. Don't, by any means, get it the wrong way round: learn to appreciate the music first, and only then come to consider the influences, personal and external, which helped to shape it. Bruckner's works were hardly played in this country until in the 1960s and, even then, often got a sniffy reception. I feel sure that part of the reason for this was the seemingly endless supply of anecdotes portraying him as a sort of rustic semi-halfwit. Fortunately, listeners soon came to pay more heed to the music than to the stories, and his symphonies are now firmly established in the repertory. Robert Simpson understood this well: his Radio Three series, "The Innocent Ear", made a point of not announcing the composer's name until after the work had been played.

And yet, we are what made us – from our parents' relayed genetic inheritance to our formative influences, and the events in our subsequent lives which leave a lasting psychological impression. As Gustav Mahler said: "We do not compose – we are composed". The keen-eyed will have deduced from some of my comments that I am a painter, not a musician: as far as the latter discipline is concerned, I am no more than a listener – although, I like to think, a good one. You will thus find here no technical analysis, merely a straightforward account of the composer's life. This is not to say that opinions, his and others, will not be voiced: he was a man of decided views, which often provoked a vigorous response for and against which is all to the good; too much consensus can be stultifying.

If this book helps in any way to generate further understanding and appreciation of a body of work which I consider to be both of exceptional quality and grossly underexposed, it will have served its purpose.

Donald Macauley

"REMEMBER WHO AND WHAT YOU ARE"

FAMILY HISTORY

Robert Simpson once observed "I haven't got a drop of English blood in me – my father was Scottish, and my mother was half Welsh and half Dutch". Something of an over-simplification: there is, as we shall see, an American connection, and indeed an extant family branch in the USA, ironic in view of his generally dismissive attitude towards "the Yanks" – prompted more, I think by dislike of American foreign policy than any personal animosity.

One factor here, I believe, was his socialist and pacifist principles, acquired early and deeply held, which led him to distrust any form of nationalism. He rejected Churchill's romantic patriotism (describing him as "that old swine") and refused to take up arms during the Second World War, although he certainly put his life equally at risk driving a Mobile Surgical Unit for ARP during the blitz as he would have done in front-line service. Among other reasons, his move to Eire during the 1980s was encouraged by the Irish tradition of neutrality. He even came to view English people as innately aggressive though he was, in my estimation (and in the best sense) one of the most profoundly English people I have known – whatever that may mean.

For all that, it would be difficult to identify any specifically English character, to his music: while Parry, Elgar, Vaughan Williams, Holst, Rubbra and Tippett all hint at their nationality from time to time – if not directly, by folk-song quotation, then in some other, less readily definable flavour – one would be hard put to place Simpson's work in a more precise context than North European.

The question of how far genetics may determine the quality of an artist's achievement is a knotty, even dangerous one, as evinced by those Nazi clowns who decided that Mendelssohn (and not he alone) couldn't be a great composer because he was Jewish, and took down his statue in Leipzig.

Robert Simpson's grandfathers were both gifted musicians, and the young Simpson may well have been spurred by their example: he may equally well have found his own way there. History provides far more instances of isolated achievers than it does of dynastic tradition. The painters Giovanni and Gentile Bellini (brothers), the two Pieter Breughels (father and son), Camille and Lucien Pissarro (likewise), and Augustas and Gwen John (brother and sister) were undoubtedly related, but from whence sprang the peculiar genius of (to name a few at random) Caravaggio, Samuel Palmer, Constable, Soutine or Francis Bacon?

Similarly in music: one can readily understand why four of JS Bach's sons chose to make composition their career, while remaining baffled as to the provenance of Berlioz, Janáček or Havergal Brian.

The Salvation Army, the organisation in which Robert Simpson grew up, places much emphasis on music – brass bands and choirs – and so some at least of the tools of the trade were to hand from an early age.

For the remainder of this chapter, I shall refer to the composer as RS – not out of affectation, but simply because there were no less than seven previous Robert Simpsons!

RS's earliest ancestor to have been traced to date is George, of Kinross, whose dates and spouse are unknown, but who had the honour (or otherwise) of being listed as a Covenanter in 1664 – which confirms the Scottish origins. (Note: A person upholding the National Covenant of 1638 or the solemn league and covenant of 1643 between Scotland and England to establish presbyterianism). His son Robert, who died in 1738 (age not known) married, on 8th August 1718, Janet Coventry. Whether they had any other children is unclear, but the direct line continues with another Robert (born 1721/2), died 1774 who married Christiana Lowe, the daughter of Robert Lowe of Balcanguhal (died 1754) and Helen Dick. The couple had eight children, and there seems to have been a strong army link in this generation: James, a soldier, died at the battle of Saratoga (1777). George, another soldier died in the West Indies, while John fathered two sons, both of whom died serving in the Royal Artillery. While RS would hardly have approved of the military connexion, he might have appreciated the adventurous streak which took them so far abroad. Robert the third, a doctor (born in February 1746/47, died 21st December 1817) moved to England in 1779 and married, at Birstal on 16th August 1780, Sarah Lee, the daughter of Abraham Lee and Sarah his wife, nee Stott. Again, there were eight children of this union: our story continues with the sixth child, William Skinner Simpson, (born 27th September 1775, died 21st July 1868). He married, in 1817, or 1818, Mary Levick (born 28th April 1795, died February 1867), and the couple founded the American branch of the family by emigrating to Petersburg, Virginia, in 1819. Robert, the eldest of their four children (born 5th April 1829, death date unknown) married Annie Levick (1830-1874) and, at an undetermined date, reversed his father's decision and emigrated to England.

I hope the above does not read too much like one of those less compelling chapters in the Old Testament, with seemingly endless lists of who begat whom, but the facts need to be recorded. For the curious, full family trees may be seen at appendices 1-2. The Levick family originated from Nottinghamshire. The first generation for whom I have details are George Levick (born 4th January 1764, died c. 1840) who married, on 2nd March

1794. Mary Edmonds, born 12th February 1772, in Grays Inn Road. George is known to have been Secretary of the London Corn Exchange. Mary Levick, who married William Skinner Simpson, was the eldest of their eight children, while Annie (who married Robert Simpson the fifth) was the daughter of one of their sons, Frederick (3rd July 1803-1867) and Mary Homer, for whom no dates are known.

There was a business, as well as a marital link, between the two families. Frederick became, in 1844, manager of the Blania Ironworks in Monmouthshire. His original partner having died in the 1850s, he gave his nephew Robert a share in the business, and they traded as Levick and Simpson. Following Frederick's death, the business closed for two years, and was purchased by a Mr James Carlton of Manchester. Frederick's son, of the same name, carried on the manufacturing tradition – in 1870, aged thirty-three, he became manager of the Carlton Ironworks. The firm was successful, soon expanded, and in 1873 he became manager of the London office. Later, mismanagement by the sons led him to sever his connections with the company. He carried on business in London as an iron and steel broker and merchant, and by his retirement (1911) had established a large overseas trade. He lived to be ninety-five.

Robert and Annie had a daughter and two sons. The middle child, Wilfred Levick Simpson, was born on 1st March 1862, dying 28th July 1937. He married, on 14/10/1885, Rose Berry, born 25th February 1862, died 7th January 1946.

A word here on the Salvation Army, of which Robert Simpson was a third generation member. In 1865 the Reverend William Booth, an itinerant Preacher formerly of the Methodist New Connection, started preaching in the East End of London naming his organisation The Christian Mission. In 1878 the name was changed to The Salvation Army, becoming both a church and a provider of social facilities. This organisation is deemed the last great religious revival of the Victorian age and rapidly spread throughout the world. It is a puritanical sect with quasi-military ranks and terminology – members are forbidden to use alcohol or tobacco – but has always maintained a strong musical tradition, with brass bands and choirs to the fore.

The Salvation Army link begins with Wilfred as an orphan. He had been a scholar at Christ's College School (a Bluecoat Boy) and in 1880 heard William Booth's wife, Catherine, speak at Steinway Hall*. He was inspired to become a Salvationist and was appointed an officer in November of that

---

* His attendance may have been on account of the fact that his cousin Florence was married to Bramwell Booth, William's son. Florence's maiden name, Levick, survived as Wilfred's and Wallace's middle name, and the third Christian name of our composer, Robert.

year, in the Whitechapel corps. He spent twenty-five years playing E flat tuba in the International Staff Band (of which he was Leader) and had a successful and responsible career as an Army officer, rising to the rank of Commander in 1905. He was also widely travelled spending time in South Africa, South America and the West Indies as well as Europe. One of his positions was Manager of the Army's Hadleigh Farm Colony. Wilfred became blind in his latter years, but his faith remained unshaken. He is buried in Camberwell New Cemetery near to his son Wallace, who pre-deceased him. Rose had close connections to the founder's family, and Bramwell Booth officiated at their wedding.

In 1929 a crisis occurred in the Salvation Army when a group of officers met to try to prevent Bramwell Booth, (who was in poor health) from appointing his own successor as the next General (International Leader) of the SA as they wanted to end what appeared to be nepotism in the Booth family. A group of seven officers, including Wilfred Simpson, insisted on calling together the first High Council which was appointed to find a successor to Bramwell and to ask for his resignation. The modernisers won the day – the High Council has elected the General ever since – but it must have been a painful experience for Wilfred, since his cousin Florence was married to Bramwell and his son's father-in-law, Gerrit Govaars, supported Bramwell's position.

The couple had five children: (Wilfred) Gordon (born 12th July 1886, died 1st May 1969), Wallace (Levick) (May 1890 - 1934), Robert Warren (born 27th January 1892, died 19th February 1974), Maude (Rose) (June 1900-1957) and Kenneth (Homer) born March 1904, died 7th November 1922).

The free spirit already apparent in the military adventures of the eighteenth-century Simpson family was not quashed by Salvationism. Wilfred's travels have already been noted: prosetylisation at home and abroad was expected of the faithful, and you went where you were posted – this at a time when few English people other than the rich travelled extensively. In Gordon's case, this manifested itself in his choice of life partner: in 1932, he married a Latvian lady, Fransiska (Frances) Balshaitis, a gifted speaker, writer and linguist. Forty-six seems an advanced age for a man to marry for the first time: not, however, when one learns that Gordon was previously in love with Miriam Booth. She could not make up her mind about him and died, after a long illness, in 1917, throughout which her suitor stood by her. A romantic at heart. then, despite his somewhat stern appearance; he had, as Mim (Miriam Simpson) put it, "a big personality." Gordon, like his father Wilfred, attained the rank of Commissioner, the highest Salvation army rank other than General, and the equivalent of Bishop in the C. of E. Maude was in charge of the Salvation Army Childrens' Home in Strawberry Hill, Liverpool.

Robert Warren, RS's father, also had an ill-starred romance prior to marriage. He was a teacher before going into training from Hadleigh Farm Colony (which Wilfred managed) on 10th August 1911. As a single officer, he asked permission to correspond with Amy Halliday, a nurse and soldier at Leamington Spa: the engagement was broken, for reasons unknown, in 1917.

During the same year, Robert resigned as a Salvation Army officer to drive an ambulance on the Western Front. The SA, as an international organisation, did not wish to be too closely identified with the allied cause, and their part in the war effort was restricted to supplying sixty ambulances and drivers. Robert served only from 5th June to 29th August, but was awarded both the British War Medal and the Allied Victory Medal. Red Cross records show a Reverend Robert Simpson acting as chaplain at the Thornton Military Hospital in Surrey from October 1917 to 1919. Robert's period of service coincided with the battle of Passchendaele, one of the bloodiest of the war – rain turned the battlefield to mud, and both sides lost an estimated 250,000 men killed and missing. It's conceivable that Robert was wounded, convalesced at Thornton Hospital, and volunteered to act as chaplain before rejoining the Salvation Army, although this cannot be confirmed – no citations were issued with general awards of this kind (women nurses as well as male civilians sometimes received them) and, as Miriam said, in a letter to the author dated 22nd July 2010, "He never talked of his experiences of that time."

On 22nd April 1920, a Robert married Helena Hendrika Govaars, who had served as a V.A.D. (Voluntary Aid Detachment) Red Cross nurse at Brighton Pavilion, tending wounded soldiers returning from the Western Front.

On the Dutch side of the family, I have rather less information. RS's maternal grandfather was Gerrit Jurianne Govaars, born 19th April 1866, died 20th October 1954, the first Salvationist convert in the Netherlands, and founder of the Dutch equivalent, the Leger Des Heils. The family name changed over the years: Joannes Goyars (1557), Joannes Goyaerts (1624), Joannes Govaarts (Amsterdam, 1768) and Josephus Govaars (1799). (Note: Govaars family were originally from Belgium and It's believed that one was a cathedral organist). He was twelve years old when his father died: by gaining a free six-year scholarship he was able to attend teacher training college, and became a schoolmaster. He spoke English, German and French and was evidently very musical: he played violin and organ* and the Salvation Army published four of his songs: one of these remains in the standard SA songbook under the title "Govaars". He spent some time working as a medical missionary in the Dutch East Indies, which no doubt influenced his grandson's early ambitions in this direction.

He married in 1889, Mary Jane Wilson, born 16th October 1864. There were five children of the union: Gerrit (born August 1889), Richard (September 1890), Victor (February 1892), William (April 1895) and Hendrika (1896). Gerrit retired early from the Salvation Army, perhaps because of differences regarding Bramwell Booth's successor.

Gerrit Govaars received the Order of the House of Orange from Queen Wilhelmina of the Netherlands for his work in setting up the Salvation Army in Holland, and his missionary activities in Java and Celebes (where head-hunting was still practised at this time!) He founded, and administered for a few years, a colony for lepers.

Gerrit Govaars (1866-1954)
In youth, middle years, and old age

He received an equivalent award from King Peter of Serbia for his relief work. After beating back two attempts at invasion by Austro-Hungary, a third attack was made in October 1915; this time, the Austro-Hungarians were reinforced by German troops, while Bulgaria attacked from the east. The Serbian army was defeated, and the survivors made their way through the mountains of Montenegro and Albania to the Dalmatian coast, from whence they were evacuated by boat to Salonika, where the Allies had a bridgehead. Govaars organised a convoy loaded with food and medical supplies and travelled via France and Italy to reach the stricken Serbs. He continued relief work on their behalf, on and off, until 1919. He was awarded the Royal Order of St Sava and the Grand Cross of the Serbian Red Cross.

Serbia suffered dreadfully in this war, with a million killed, one-sixth of the population. World War II was even worse, with a million and a half casualties. We should remember this when considering the decidedly one-sided media presentation of the Yugoslav civil wars during the 1990s, wherein the Serbs were almost invariably cast as the villains.

Colonel and Mrs Govaars moved to Holland on 3rd January 1931, settling at Soest, near Utrecht, where their English relatives frequently stayed with them during the pre-war decade. Mrs Govaars died in March 1933: Gerrit was apparently on the receiving end of some ill-treatment later at the hands of the occupying Germans. He died on 20th October 1954: there is a typewritten biography of him by his daughter in the SA archives entitled "Salvationist of the Netherlands".

Wilfred Levick Simpson (1862-1937)

Rose Simpson (nee Berry) 1862-1946

The Simpson Family c 1920
Back row: Robert Warren, Edith, Gordon, Wallace
Middle row: Wilfred and Rose
Front row: Helena (nee Govaars) and Maude

(Wilfred) Gordon Simpson (1886-1969)

*(centre, back row) with Fransiska (nee Balshaitis), fellow SA officers
and Latvian in-laws in national costume, c. 1932*

Robert Simpson as a baby with his parents, Robert Senior and Helena, 1921

As a toddler, with his parents and sister Miriam, 1924

"THE BOLSHIEST BRAT THEY EVER HAD"
A SALVATION ARMY CHILDHOOD (1921 - 1939)

Robert Wilfred Levick Simpson (Bob) was born at 21 Rosefield Street, Leamington Spa on 2nd March 1921. These were officers' (ministers) quarters – the SA corps (church) were based in nearby Park Street. The family then moved to Sutton, Surrey, where they had a second child, Mary, who lived only a few days. A further move took them to Upper Norwood, where Miriam Jane Simpson (Mim) was born on 21st February 1924. For the remainder of these chapters dealing with their early life, I shall use the diminutives. Much of the material comes from Mim's reminiscences and also those of Elisabeth Benians (nee Matthews) who was to be his first love, while some of the composer's own recollections have been quoted.

A Mrs Olive Murphy wrote on 20/10/74:

"Dear Dr. Simpson,

On two occasions I have been curiously interested in reading articles in the Press (together with pictures), of your work in connection with the music of Havergal Brian's compositions.

May I ask – are you the son of former Salvation army Officers, who were in charge of the Chelmsford Corps of the Salvation army many years ago? If this is so, may I lay claim to the privilege of, at one time, teaching both you and your sister as small children, in my Sunday School class at Chelmsford?

If my assumption is correct your musical background may rest with your grandfather, Commissioner Govaars, who gave us the lovely tune GOVAARs, which is published in our songbook.

As one of the older soldiers of the Chelmsford Corps, such happy memories bring much joy."

The composer replied on 31st October:

"Dear Mrs Murphy

I was very touched to get your letter –it is true – I am the little chap you remember. I think when we lived in Chelmsford. I was six and my sister was three. She is now a grandmother and her husband is a clergyman. They are shortly moving to the Durham area where he will have a vicarage. My parents both passed away some while ago.

I think you are quite right – my music probably does come from my Dutch grandfather, whom I revered greatly; in fact I still carry his photograph around in my pocket – he was one of the most magnificent men I ever knew.

Thank you so much for your kind letter."

Bob once observed "My parents should never have married", without elaborating. While Salvation Army marriages were not formally arranged, they were the next thing: It was a very rank-conscious organisation, and an officer was only permitted to marry another officer. Temperamentally, the two were very different: Robert was upright and reserved, taking the motto "Remember who and what you are" seriously, while Helena was more outgoing and often temperamental. She would entertain the children with stories of her early life and travels as a child schooling in Switzerland and Germany, and later of her experiences nursing during the Great War.

The family were very poor: officers' pay was low, and failure to sell enough copies of the War Cry on Saturday (the vendor received a cut) could mean an empty table on Sunday. Helena having been diagnosed with a heart condition, the doctor advised Robert against further pregnancies, and there were no more children. Robert also seems to have suffered from intermittent poor health: there is a letter on file in the SA archives from Wilfred requesting dispensation on the grounds of his son's tendency to rheumatism. After the outbreak of the Second World War the parents effectively separated, and were later to divorce – rare enough at the time outside the upper classes, but almost unheard of in Salvation Army circles.

Despite this, says Mim, their childhood was a happy one: Bob was always a "fun person"; a cheerful, lively, intelligent boy, always very supportive of his sister although, like most siblings, they fought as youngsters. Of her parental family, she can recall her grandfather's blindness in his last years, and grandmother Rose as "very strict". Uncle Gordon, known as "The Intrepid Aviator" – was Commissioner in charge of Territories, and often sent photographs home of himself boarding or alighting from aircraft in some foreign field: his portraits indicate a man of commanding presence. All the Simpsons were immensely proud of their supposed descent from Sir James Simpson Bart., the pioneer of chloroform as an anaesthetic, although no link has ever been established.

In a letter to Lionel Pike (4th September 1991) the composer observed: "The supposed relationship was in any case further back than 'great-uncle' – an extra 'great' would be needed if the dates mean anything at all. But a cousin of mine has been absorbed for years in the 'family tree' and now insists that there is no connection with Sir JYS. I must be content with an undistinguished lineage." In some ways, the children were closer to their Dutch relatives, of which more later.

In August 1927, after a three-month furlough, Robert was transferred to the Salvation Army Assurance Society, which occasioned their last move as a family, to 21 Manwood Road, Crofton Park SE4, a brick-built late nineteenth century terraced house. Mim remembers (aged three) waiting impatiently for her dolls' pram to be unloaded from the removal van. Robert joined the SAAS Songsters following his transfer.

Music was often heard at home, too: Helena played piano and guitar. The parents sang duets – he bass, she soprano, and Helena would serenade the children to bed, singing in German. Bob's first instrument was the cornet, which he learned at the age of seven, later specialising in the soprano cornet in E flat. He added: "I went on playing in the brass band. I played every instrument in a brass band except the trombone and that because I never really bothered to learn the shifts of the slide." *Later, at Westminster City School, he played trumpet and French horn in the school orchestra, and the interest in, and masterly understanding of, brass instruments never left him, as witness the late brass band scores, several of which have been used as test pieces in national competitions. As he said in a (dictated) letter to a Miss Stark, 2/4/94: "I always enjoy writing for brass band – it's in my blood." In a letter to the author dated 24/1/08, Mim added: "Bob had piano lessons but was very unenthusiastic and had to be bribed to practice. So he never got to like the instrument or be happy with it." Elisabeth adds: "He tried the cello, but couldn't stand the noise he made." (Note: Interview with Lewis Foreman(1980).

21 Manwood Road, London SE4, Robert SImpson's home from 1927 to 1946

Helena was a great 'organiser', which Mim ascribes to her Dutch origins. On birthdays a special chair would be decked and brought to the table. Mim remembers emerging from the bedroom on her thirteenth birthday to find the stairs decked with pink roses, which her mother had spent many evenings painstakingly making.

Both parents could paint, mainly copies: Helena favoured Dutch scenes, while Robert often used postcard views as a basis for Christmas cards and the like. He also produced some original work, notably a strong self-portrait painted during his post-war service in Germany.

One of Bob's boyhood passions, and one which stayed with him for life, was cricket – no other sport excited him. They would play as a family side on the recreation ground against other locals. Mim was allowed to field, but not bowl; Bob also went to matches at Lords with his father. Much later, while working for the BBC, he and Deryck Cooke would often take the opportunity if they were at the Maida Vale studios to slip across to Lords, which is a short distance away.

A youthful hero was Albert Schweitzer, that remarkable polymath and holder of four doctorates (music, medicine, divinity and philosophy), who devoted most of his life to working as a medical missionary in Lamberéné, West Africa. Bob had similar ambitions, no doubt spurred by his Dutch grandfather's example, but these soon faded.

Another early idol was, rather surprisingly, Larry Adler, the harmonica virtuoso, Bob always carried a mouth-organ (about the last instrument one would associate with the composer in later life!) and the children would cycle to Chislehurst woods: Bob would climb a tree and play his harmonica, while his sister picked violets.

He loved the film comedies of Charlie Chaplin and Laurel and Hardy; later, Benny Hill would become another favourite, however politically incorrect.

While the children were expected to behave impeccably at functions, they often compensated for this when let out to play: in fact, some of Bob's amusements would be considered downright reprehensible in the present "Health and Safety" obsessed day.

He would place pennies and bangers on the Catford – Blackfriars loop line which ran at the back of their home to see what happened: he owned a chemistry set and, like most boys, delighted in causing explosions, on one occasion almost wrecking the kitchen. He was highly imaginative, often telling his sister bedtime stories, and always being called upon to write her school essays. The leading character in one of his tales was called Agamemnon Motherspoon Waterbiffle! He drew well, mostly cartoons or pictures of fighter aircraft. The composer described himself, in a letter to

Dennis Brookes (30/10/89) as "the bolshiest brat they ever had. Miracle I wasn't expelled. I just hope the present head doesn't do a bit of research." He had been called upon to present the prizes at his old school, and the above musings were prompted by his recollection that he had once thrown a stink bomb into the Headmaster's study while the beak was there. Another time, he and some other boys explored a manhole in the school yard: after crawling through a tunnel they emerged from another manhole on the main road, with buses speeding by only a few feet away. The Headmaster was not amused. Bob was also wont to grab the tailboard of lorries while on his bike, and freewheel behind. His sister adds: "As children, Bob to me was completely without fear, perhaps that's being a normal boy!"

The date of his first original music is uncertain: at various times he gave his age as nine, ten or twelve. We know what it was: "My first attempt at composition was variations on "Annie Laurie" for the cornet, and I couldn't write an accompaniment for the piano because I just didn't know how. So I got a chap to play Annie Laurie by ear on the piano, over and over again, while I played all the twiddly bits on the cornet." (Ibid).

Aged eleven, Bob won a scholarship to Westminster City School, which was in part fee-paying. Mim recalls "I can remember being so proud of him. It's hard to believe now that a child of twelve would travel by train every day to the city of London by himself. Once there, he had a music teacher whom he admired greatly, and he was a big influence on Bob. He also, I think, was an encouragement to Bob in his young new appreciation of classical music and playing in an orchestra. The school orchestra was such a great thing for Bob and it certainly made his school days "bearable". He went off to school with either a trumpet or a French horn tucked under his arm. I think, and am pretty sure, that the teacher's name was Mr Lobb – *(Letter to Terry Hazell 3/8/06)* "Lobb's main subject was mathematics (and in fact Bob's school report does not include music as a subject). It has been claimed that maths and music are closely related; along with chess, they are the only activities which produce child prodigies.

Apropos the orchestra, the composer recalled: "There used to be a competition for school orchestras every year. I don't know if there still is, but there used to be then. We used to either win it or come second every year. It was always held at the Queen's Hall. I played horn and trumpet as required. We actually broadcast once – my first time in Maida Vale Number 1 studio at the age of about 15 – and I played the horn and the trumpet in that same concert. In fact, I was terrified, because the concert started with the Trumpet Voluntary which I had to play right at the very beginning". The Queen's Hall, the original venue for the Henry Wood Promenade Concerts, was situated near Broadcasting House; it was destroyed during the blitz, and only a fragment of wall survives.

The young Simpson's knowledge of the classical repertoire was greatly enhanced when his parents hired a radiogram – not that they shared his interest to the same degree. In the Lewis Foreman interview from 1980, he recalled:

"I had to sit with my head inside the radiogram because my family were sitting there talking and telling me to turn it down. And so I eventually crept round the back of the cabinet with my hand on the volume control, and emerged like a sort of crippled octopus at the end of it."

It was via the radiogram that classical music made its first real impact. In Bob's words: "My first great musical experience occurred when I was fourteen, hearing Beethoven's Sixth Symphony on the radio from a Promenade Concert; I didn't know what had hit me, and went out of the house and walked around in a daze for hours." *(Appendix 10)*

Bob's best friend at school was David MacEwan (born 24th December 1920), who sat at the same desk. The two helped each other – Bob was better at maths, while David had more of a flair for languages. They remained friends for life. Bob was very fond of Richmal Crompton's "William" stories, seeing himself as the leading character. Fred Grant, who billeted with Robert, recalls him announcing to his son on his fourteenth birthday: "Now you're old enough to wash yourself!" which suggests that, like his literary hero (and most prepubertal boys) personal hygiene was not a burning concern. David, despite having grown up in the North-East, had acquired a rather plummy voice through his education and was nicknamed "Billy Bunter", a role to which he readily played up, although he was nowhere near in girth to the Fat Owl of the Remove. He married Mim shortly after the end of the war.

Mim has observed: "In some ways, ours was quite an ordinary childhood; when you are young you never imagine your brother is going to turn out to be so clever." Well, perhaps not that ordinary – few English families at that time had relatives in continental Europe, and foreign travel was largely unknown to all but the well-to-do. As has already been stated, Bob was close to his Dutch grandfather, who stimulated his interest in both music and astronomy (another lifelong passion), giving him a telescope on a stand for his thirteenth birthday.

Helena and the children often visited their relatives during the inter-war years, although Robert rarely came. Mim remembers her grandmother, Mary, as a tiny Welsh lady, and very vague. She had the same answer to everything: on seeing that Bob had removed her precious china from the cabinet and balanced it in various unsafe places: "Very nice, dear." Another time, Bob dared his sister to jump over a large cow-pat: she failed, and returned to the house covered in dung. "Very nice, dear!"

There were many cousins, and snowball fights at Christmas. Once, three sledges were hitched to the back of grandfather Gerrits car, and some sixteen children climbed aboard: they then drove around the town waving to the populace. Gerrit, however, drove a shade too fast and Ben Govaars fell off, fortunately without sustaining serious injury. Another time, Bob and Mim borrowed a double scooter and scootered into neighbouring Amersfoort.

Some of the Dutch relatives were wealthy, with business interests in the East Indies, and often helped Helena financially. Come independence (1945) they were expelled with what they could carry – the only one who managed to salvage some of his assets was Will Govaars, who had owned the only company in what was to become Indonesia which imported and sold motor vehicles: he managed to get some money home via relatives.

There was also a German cousin, Rudolf Varwig, with whom Bob stayed and got on well. Communication ceased with the outbreak of war, but they met again afterwards. Rudolf said that the day he was taken prisoner was the happiest of his life: when in action he would deliberately aim wide for fear of shooting his English cousin, unaware that Bob had registered as a conscientious objector.

In Rotterdam, waiting for the bus, with Lt Col or uncle Joss Govaars c 1930

Back row: Will Govaars, Ben and Gertie Govaars, Gerrit Govaars
Middle row: Helena Simpson, Mary Govaars, Miriam Simpson, great-aunt Mina Govaars
Front row: Robert Simpson Again, c 1930

At the seaside, c 1931

Miriam and Bob, c 1929

In uniform, with cornet (and sister), c 1930

On the beach—undated, but seemingly somewhat earlier

Westminster City School

LOWER SCHOOL.
AUTUMN TERM, 1932.

Report on **Robert Simpson** Age **11.9**
of Form **Lower III Shell** Average Age **11.7**

Subject	No. in Form or Set	Position in Form or Set	Remarks
Scripture	19	5	Good. G.N.
English	19	1	Very good. Can improve the appearance of his handwriting. E.H.
Latin			
French	19	2	Very gone work. J.D.M.
German			
History	19	3	Very fair work. E.H.D.
Geography	19	10	Satisfactory.
Arithmetic / Algebra	19	4	Very good work. G.P.
Geometry	19	7	Moderate. G.P.
Physics	19	1	Excellent. G.P.
Chemistry			
Nature Study	19	5	Good. L.M.P.
Art	19	4	Very good. M.P.
Woodwork	19	6	Very good. G.P.
Physical Training			Good.

Times Late **2**
Times Absent **0**
Conduct **Very good**

_____ Form Master.
_____ Headmaster.

Spring Term 1933 begins Friday, January 20th, and ends Thursday, April 13th.
Summer Term 1933 begins Friday, May 5th, and ends Friday July 28th.
Autumn Term 1933 begins Tuesday, Sept. 19th, and ends Thursday, Dec. 21st.

Bob Simpson's first report from Westminster City School. Thirty years later, masters were still making similarly laconic comments. No music section, but worth noting that the eleven-year-old Simpson topped the form in both English and Physics.

The family holidayed in England, too. In a letter to the author dated 24th January 2008, Mim wrote:

"Summer holidays were spent in Westgate of Folkestone. The last days, the treat was a visit to the funfair "Dreamland". Bob would spend most of his time and his allowance on the "Big Dipper". Nothing less other than the Ghost Train. Not for me. Just before the war he was thrilled that Dad had arranged a holiday sailing in the Norfolk Broads. Dad as a boy had sailed with his brothers, so he reckoned he knew about sailing. My mother wasn't too keen. Her expectations were fulfilled. Several occasions we had problems. One morning we woke to the tide having gone out and we were grounded for hours. Putting up sails in a wind which would come from an unexpected quarter. Berthing was like parking a double-decker bus.

One day Bob took out the dinghy and was trying to put up the sail in the middle of one of the broads. My father shouts "Boy, don't do it, you'll fall in!" He took a step back and he himself fell in. All was well. Bob got his sail up and Dad came up safely still with his glasses on. We threw him a rope and he climbed up looking very sheepish!

"This experience of boating was for Bob a new enthusiasm. He took a couple of holidays with like-minded friends. Then, when he moved to Chearsley, he bought a boat and had it moored on the Thames. Then moving to Ireland he bought a sea-going motor boat. However, that was sad, because he was never able to go out in it. It was needing quite a bit of work on it. Then during that time he had the stroke and that was the end to boating, and a lot of other good things."

In October 1937 Bob registered at Chelsea Polytechnic (later Chelsea College), studying Botany and Zoology for six hours a week, possibly as part of a course "Biology for Secondary School Pupils." In October 1938 he registered at the same institution for a Pre-Medical course, studying Biology, Chemistry, Physics and Mechanics for thirty hours weekly. This was very much Robert and Helena's wish rather than his own: "My parents had continually been saying "You are going to be a doctor. "His first year exam results were undistinguished." I found myself writing music during the lectures." (Ibid). Mim adds, in a letter to Terry Hazell (3rd August 2006): "He hated dissection, and couldn't muster any enthusiasm for bodies." At one point, his parents were summoned to the Principal's office and asked bluntly what he was doing there – the books in his possession were all musical, not medical. Despite its uncongeniality, he stuck at the course for two years before abandoning his medical studies.

During the same year, Bob met Elisabeth Grant Matthews, who became his first love. Here is her own account of the meeting from a letter to the author dated 18th March 2009:

"I am a Scot born in Glasgow in 1920 (8th September). My sister was delicate so we came South hoping she would benefit from a milder climate. Owing to my long period of no schooling I realised I wasn't ready for the scholarship I badly needed financially (Grants were not so prevalent in those days as today). So I opted for a Teacher's Training Course and was accepted on the strength of my Matric at Avery Hill T.C., Eltham. My father had met Robert's father on one occasion, thinking, I imagine, that if I needed advice I could approach him. This was 1938: the political situation was very worrying and the generation of parents who had lived through the First World War were apprehensive for the young and immature who were leaving home for the first time. So I received an invitation from Robert's parents for lunch and that was it. I vividly remember meeting a young man who was obviously bored with the appearance of yet another girl (he claimed to be a misogynist). However, when it was revealed that I played the violin (very mediocre), I was immediately involved in listening to records of the Sibelius Violin Concerto and the Elgar Cello.

"We were engaged. I don't know where the idea originated that my parents were opposed to the marriage. My mother was very fond of Robert though she had reservations about a too speedy marriage. We were both young and I had little experience of life. I had a very serious illness in my teens and perhaps I had been somewhat sheltered and my Mother was concerned lest I or we should embark on an early start with much hardship. So R. was prepared to wait. I have a letter from him to my Mother which clearly demonstrates that he was prepared to enable us to make a successful marriage in the future, i.e. wait and live in a one-bedroom flat if need be.

"I owe Robert a tremendous debt. He did so much to further and develop my love and knowledge of music. Met me at Liverpool Street Station on my birthday with a bound copy of Beethoven Sonatas (I was a very mediocre pianist), then followed the Violin Sonatas. We had a little wind-up gramophone and records were posted to me on loan from the London Library, mainly Bach played on the organ by Schweitzer. He educated me in the best possible way, for my concert-going had been limited, geographically and financially."

Bob's sister Mim never actually met Elisabeth, although she lived with her parents at the time; she was aware that he had a girlfriend in Kettering, and heard that the relationship had ended. As she said in a letter to the author (15th October 2010): "Brothers don't always tell their sisters everything."

Salvation Army Senior Band Uniform, c 1936

Miriam, Helena and Robert, 1936

"A FRIGHTFUL CREW OF TOUGHS"

(1940-1945)

Following the outbreak of war, the Simpsons, father and son, both volunteered as Air Raid Wardens. The extracts from his letters to Elisabeth which follow give a vivid picture of wartime life both inside and outside the A.R.P. unit in Lewisham to which he was assigned as a stretcher-bearer in a mobile surgical unit.

The latter were a little-known but vital part of the Civil Defence (Air Raid Precautions) system: during the Blitz hospitals were under intense pressure, and the MSUs – essentially large vans with an operating table, a doctor and two nurses, as well as the driver/orderly (Simpson's job) – no doubt saved many lives by performing surgery on the spot. Also among the ARP staff were Harry Newstone, later a celebrated conductor, and Bessie Fraser (Squibs) who became the composer's first wife. Robert Simpson recalled one occasion when he swapped shifts with a colleague – that night, there was a direct hit on the shelter and the man was killed. Naturally, if irrationally, Simpson was guilt-stricken. Perhaps the least enviable task in ARP was "Heavy rescue" – digging the injured and dead out of bombed buildings, at which the composer took his turn.

In 1940 Robert Simpson made the momentous decision to abandon medicine in favour of music. Up until the last moment, he seems to have had every intention of taking his second year exams, saying to Elisabeth in a letter from July:

"I'm working at home this week and getting through piles of work. I should get 75% in biology, chemistry and physics, but maths is all up the pole." Not just maths – he later told Elisabeth that he walked out of the classroom after half an hour.

His parents were not best pleased. "I had a glorious row with my parents and gave it up, and took to music." * His father was less than enthusiastic about his chosen career, observing "There's no money in music, my boy!" Much later in life, his mother was to ask: "Why don't you write a nice tune, Bobby?", to which the composer replied: "Because I haven't got a nice tune in my head!" Abandoning medicine brought a great sense of release; as he wrote to Elisabeth: "Glorious to be free of lectures and exams. I'm going out on an errand to an old lady whose daughter has just died, and she seems to have got some encouragement out of me in the past." Much later in life, Simpson was to write:

---

*   *Interview with Lewis Foreman, 1980*

"All you can do now is point out that giving up medicine was my greatest gift to the human race, if one considers the number of people who are walking around now who wouldn't be if I'd been a doctor. On the other hand, if I'd been Thatcher's doctor, I might have been able to save my compatriots a lot of misery by the administration of certain drugs or insisting that she needed drastic brain surgery." (Letter to Lionel Pike, 4/9/91).

Simpson's decision rendered him liable for call-up (medicine was a "reserved" occupation, music was not) and he was summoned to a tribunal to explain his refusal to take up arms. By his own account, he had become a pacifist at the early age of nine, while attending a Salvation Army meeting with his parents. The speaker was a man who had served in the trenches during the Great War. He related a distressing experience: while on watch one night, he was distracted by a dreadful screaming emanating from no-man's land. He tried to shut it out, but eventually could stand no more, and crawled over in the direction of the noise. He found a German soldier in a shell-hole: the man had a severe abdominal wound. Medical assistance was out of the question – the German was clearly going to die, and the best he could do was to try and make the enemy soldier more comfortable. Unbuttoning the German's tunic, he saw that he was wearing a Salvation Army jersey, and unfastened his own to reveal a similar garment. As he reflected "It might have been me that shot him; I was firing in that direction earlier." The young Simpson thought it so absurd that two members of the same avowedly Christian organisation should be doing their best to kill each other that he vowed there and then that he would never fight in a war, later signing the Peace Pledge. Michael Tippett took a more extreme position, refusing to aid the war effort in any way, and received a three-month Jail term. Oddly enough, Tippett was later offered, and accepted, a knighthood, the C.B.E. and the Order of Merit.

Simpson described his encounter with the tribunal in a letter to Alan Noble dated 9/4/91:

"Chairman: Are your objections religious?

RS: No.

CH: On what grounds are they based?

RS: Humanitarian and logic. Are you a Christian?

CH: Yes.

RS: Then you must believe that Christ on the cross refrained from using the power that he had to destroy those who were crucifying him?

CH: Yes, but Christ had divine power behind him. You don't.

RS: How do you know that?

No reply, or further discussion. I was directed to stay with the Mobile Surgical Unit I was already attached to in the London "Blitz".

Robert Simpson's letters to Elisabeth indicate that life in an A.R.P. unit was at first something of a culture shock.

2nd June 1940. "I've settled down comfortably at the Stretcher Party. They are a frightful crew of toughs and the air is blue with invective for 24 hours on end. I've never heard such consummate mastery of the art of sustained blasphemy. It's really ghastly. After I told one or two (after some moments of jaw-grinding courage) that their language was extremely jarring and would they moderate it occasionally, they were very decent and have not sworn in my presence again.

I've been placed second in charge of the Stretcher Squad.

I'm on Fatigue Squad today, unpleasant but necessary.

I'm badly in need of some sort of stabilising force as I've been having a rough time lately."

Mim mentioned in conversation that her brother was sometimes bullied by other members of the unit, on one occasion being thrown into a water tank. The roughnecks took a dislike to him because he was "different", and no doubt his short stature (5'5" – as Mim said, "He never grew") was an added inducement.

August. "We hired a car to take my Mother for a change and some fresh air. Caught in an air raid over East Grinstead. Donned our A.R.P. kit. (There followed a vivid account of fighter planes five miles up). It seemed like a crazy nightmare, so unreal and unbelievable, and so much destruction of the charming villages nearby."

A Prom concert took an unusual turn, effectively a musical "lock-in":

24th August. "The Prom continued until the All Clear went at 4am. We had quartets, trios, sonatas etc. Members of the audience gave items. I played my jolly old Nocturne, although I played it abominably. I was as nervous as a cat. Still, you can't do justice to a thing at 2 am. I never expected to play at the Queen's Hall to 2,000 people. But it went down well. People were lying around all over the floor: a delightful night, marvellous substitute for Anderson Shelter. One member of the audience gave an excruciatingly funny imitation of Sir Thomas Beecham, Sit Bones Teach 'Em, as he called himself; we rocked with laughter. I feel I need some comfort. I feel terribly lonely and miserable. Things at the Depot are much as usual. I seem to have become quite popular in spite of my sad lack of language and my

Christian Principles. I have had a lot of trouble with the leader of the Squad. He gave me an order couched in the most obscene and revolting terms. I told him that I definitely would not obey any order unless it was completely free from language that was offensive to me. He got a bit obstreperous but climbed down and apologised afterwards. He said he knew I never swore and could understand that I didn't like being sworn at, although it was purely unconscious on his part. We are good friends now."

November. "Changing to meet you at 6am at the Depot from a filthy uniform and no hot water, afraid of disturbing 200 sleeping men, is very difficult."

8th November. "A crowd of garrulous nurses; conversation changes about every third sentence. It's amazing the lack of concentration women always show in their babblings."

12th November. "I'm on duty again today. When this duty is finished I'll have done 72 hours straight off. I volunteered yesterday to relieve a man for 24 hours of my Mother's Mobile Unit (she was a very efficient trained nurse who was in complete charge of a Mobile Unit) and her Orderly is ill." (There followed a vivid description of his Mother and the Doctor amputating the leg of a young boy on the concrete in the open during a raid: they had to amputate the second leg and they were covered in blood, but alas the boy died).

The war disrupted many families, the Simpsons among them. Robert and Helena effectively separated: the former was promoted to Brigadier in 1941 and was evacuated, with the other SAAS staff, from Victoria to Rosehill Park, Reading. His wife (despite her heart condition she had been furnished by her GP with a certificate declaring her fit for service – she had previously helped him on a voluntary basis, and was much in demand for assisting at deliveries) following her ARP service was appointed Matron-in-Chief with the Netherlands Womens Royal Auxiliary Corps (UHK) Medical Team and, after the D-day invasion, went to Holland to help feed starving children, driving three-ton lorries among other duties! The Salvation Army frowned on this since it was not SA employment, however useful.

Mim was evacuated with her school in 1939, but returned in time for Christmas. Later, she joined her father at Rosehill. Bob always refused to go into the shelter during air-raids: saying "I'm staying in my bed!" and using it instead to store his precious gramophone records. He had a narrow escape one night when a glass splinter pierced the pillow only inches from his head.

During the war years Simpson continued, as best he could, his work as a composer and as a writer on other people's music. The following extracts from his letters to Elisabeth give a fascinating insight into his activities at this time.

16th August 1940. "It's Beethoven night and there is not a work I don't know backwards.

(Musical extract of Elisabeth's portrait.) Try on the fiddle melodic line is no more important than harmonic. The most subtle I've ever written.

The prom. on Friday was superb. On Tuesday I bought a record, only 6/-, of the Haydn Trumpet Concerto, the one I orchestrated and I find to my delight that my score tallies marvellously with Haydn's original. There are bound to be differences here and there but I'm quite proud of the fact that I've orchestrated it almost exactly as he did. I'd not previously heard the original so it was pure musicianship though I say it!

I may have a try at Inter Mus. Bach. when I can afford it. The chap who advised me to do it, my schoolmaster friend Frank Birkill, very generously offered to pay all my fees. Overwhelmed by such a magnanimous gesture. I felt I couldn't accept."

30th December. "On Saturday I'm going to lecture on Bruckner. I wish you could come and give moral support. I feel like a salesman or apostle when I lecture on Bruckner's music. I shall probably give them the whole of the 7th and part of the 4th. I'm working at composition now. My symphony, probably No. 1 if it is completed before the one in G maj. which is also on the stocks, is progressing favourably although it is so harsh and uncompromising that I hardly know whether to like it or not. As Vaughan Williams said of his 4th, "I don't know whether I like it, but that's what I meant."

"Here's the main theme on full brass (quotation included) it appears through a fiery curtain of fearful discord of tremolo strings. The second subject of the 1st is most weird and strange also on string tremolo but beginning on oboe pianissimo.

"The whole of the movement is complete and fully scored and so is half the slow movement. The symphony shows the influence of the times, harsh and unrelenting. I hope it doesn't sound too hideous but it expresses a side of me. We all have some savagery in our hearts. It is better to let people shudder at it in your music than to inflict it on them in your behaviour. The other symphony in G, no. 1, has no key, is sweet and jolly. It reverts more or less to the classical of Mozart and Schubert with, I hope, some small touches of individuality. The critics will condemn no. 1 with a sense of shock and disgust as an attempt to be too original, and the G major as being too conventional and not discordant enough. On the other hand no critic may hear either of them."

Prescient words: along with the Nocturne and Elisabeth's musical portrait, these early works have been destroyed. In character they sound very much like a first attempt at the Fourth and Fifth Symphonies of thirty years later.

January 1941. "Slight diffidence and anxiety caused inspiration to dry up but analysis of Bruckner's 9th is finished, with which I am fairly pleased. The essay on Brahms and Bruckner is approaching completion and contains some really original ideas, tho' I say it what shouldn't.

"I'm going to learn German. I can already master the pronunciation of any German word. I can read a page of German with perfect pronunciation without having the slightest idea of what it all means.

I've seen Major Ward and he is very impressed to say the least with my essays. He thinks they should be published and is having them typed to be sent to some influential people at the B.B.C. and R.A. He asked to see some of my music and I've sent him a mass of stuff with explanations. I hope this will impress him equally, though I doubt it, for I've had no systematic musical training. My counterpoint would be much more facile for a strict course of training. Perhaps the B.B.C. nobs will give me advice. I must have individual teaching, correspondence courses are not much good for counterpoint, harmony and composition. Not that anyone can teach a fellow to compose. It either flows through the brain or it doesn't. My methods being self-evolved and self-taught are somewhat laborious."

February. "I've done three big essays in two days. Analyses of Bruckner's 7th, Beethoven 3, the Eroica, and Brahms 4. Also I've finished the great thesis on Brahms and Bruckner symphonies. Major Ward has the lot as well as a whole mass of music and some orchestration of Haydn and Busoni, not everything complete. I must prepare the Bruckner lecture, not the whole symphony, they couldn't stand that, odd movements and the like illustrating the different characteristics of B's music. I shall fill in a couple of hours.

"Got a complete recording of the B Mi. Mass at the Gramophone Exchange for half price. On Saturday 30th St. Matthew Passion. Everyone should hear one of the greatest works in the whole world of music.

"I wrote to the Guildhall about trumpet lessons but it's been bombed out. Major Ward had a letter from Dennis Wright, who seems impressed with my efforts and is sending them to a higher authority."

June 1942. "I was playing records of the B Mi. Mass and tried to sing at sight the bass parts. My voice is an incredible instrument of torture so I daren't sing if I thought anyone were listening. But I enjoyed myself croaking some of the colossal passages and very good exercise in reading; far superior to my singing.

"Symphony progressing very slowly. An orchestral score is a very complex and laborious process. Don't expect a work half finished when I bring it to you on the 26th. I may possibly have completed the Exposition of the 1st Movement. But I'm not going to skip anything. If I'm not sure of myself I don't put anything down. I simply wait until the idea crystallises itself in my imagination. Then I know there's nothing commonplace or trivial in my music. Yesterday I worked about 5½ hours on the Eroica essay. I'm halfway through the analysis of the Finale and have reached page 85 and 96 music quotations – of a real piece of hard labour. It represents the greatest effort of thought I've ever made and I think I've succeeded in penetrating a little into the vastness of Beethoven's mind. It is not really a descriptive analysis like those other little ones of mine you've seen – it is also technical and truly analytical. I'm thinking of adding another chapter on the orchestration and general characteristics; an infinite number of wonders in my beloved Eroica. What a marvellous work it is. Beethoven must have had the greatest and most profound mind the world has ever known. The truth and beauty of such a stupendous work cannot be surpassed; not even the life and utterances of Jesus. Truth is truth and nothing can ever alter or surpass it."

In 1942 Robert Simpson began lessons with Herbert Howells. "I didn't know how to get the kind of lessons I needed to have a go at the B. Mus., and I couldn't afford to go to a music college full-time... So I wrote to the Registrar of the Royal College of Music, asking if he could tell me who might give me private lessons (not too expensive). He suggested either Herbert Howells or Gordon Jacob. I had heard more of Howell's music, and so I approached him." (Note: See Friends Chapter) He studied with Howells from 1942[1] to 1944, although some sources have claimed that it was actually for four years rather than two.

8th June. "I've seen Howells today. He paid me a great compliment. He was discussing the ornamental harmonisation of chorales and remarked that most people find the process extremely difficult. I showed him a couple I had done and he was very pleased with them indeed. He asked if I found any great difficulty with them and when I said "No" he said: "Well of course it wouldn't naturally be very hard for a musician like you." In his opinion most students aren't musicians, they only learn the stuff for exam purposes. That's the first time I've been seriously called a musician. Oh boy!!

The Beethoven Mass in C is the first and lesser of the Masses. His religious beliefs were of an extremely simple and sketchy kind. Sometimes he did not know what he believed. He most certainly did not believe in the divinity of Christ. He classed Jesus with Shakespeare as the two greatest men who ever lived. But he believed in the omnipotence of God, not in the mercy and loving kindness but in the sheer might and universal scope. I think there was only one thing in life of which he was certain, Beauty and Truth as expressed through his natural medium – music. I don't think the most inspired parts of the Mass are inspired by the text. It is his musical inspiration as in the Gloria which raises him to the heights, not any firm belief in the text. Words can be set to music even if one has no sympathy with them. It is artistically possible to write a most moving and beautiful love song without being in love. Holst was an agnostic, but his Hymn of Jesus is most moving and some of his settings of the psalms are the finest extant. In almost any setting of the Mass there is a change of mood at Homo Factus Est. The doctrine is unfathomable in its mystery."

June 1942. "The symphony has now reached bar 27, beginning of second subject. You might like me to quote the main theme (which he did).

"The tempo is Allergro non troppo ma deciso, crotchet at 96, begins percussion with muted strings. I doubt very seriously whether it will astound the world. I'm concerned largely with completing it to my own satisfaction. Then I can say that there is some stuffing in me. To me the most important thing is the achievement of a large-scale creation to prove my mettle. Anyone can conquer a natural desire but not everyone can conquer their physical body's fatigue, unwillingness or weakness in order to create something. I'm out of touch with concerts and broadcasts of late because I'm preoccupied with my work. It's a queer thing with creative work, you are not only working the actual time when you are putting things on paper. You often spend hours of intense mental concentration before you put anything down. I'm constantly working in the streets, on duty, in bed, even at the cinema if the film isn't very interesting.

"Get an exercise book, divide it into sections and write down everything you hear, bad as well as good, so you can form sound judgments. True appreciation of art is brought about by a willingness to be bored. I did this for a year and amassed over 200 different symphonies. That is why my musical knowledge is always at my fingertips. I discontinued it because I lost the book, now I've found it I shall continue for all types of music. Always write to tell me what works you hear for the first time. I like to watch your progress as closely as possible."

July 1942. "Having lessons from Howells. Thinking of joining Toynbee Hall or orchestra, my trumpet playing is good enough for that. Howells thought the ground had already been covered with Eroica but he is going to look at it during the summer holidays. I'm convinced of its merit though I'm sure he will find much to criticise."

Elisabeth attended one of the lessons, and the experience is related in the Howells section of the "Friends" chapter.

In time, the engagement of Robert and Elisabeth was amicably ended. Her own account follows:

He wrote: "We mustn't allow our love to become old and tarnished. If we find it is losing its perfection we must do what I believe a compassionate God would have done with humanity, annihilate it utterly." A typically uncompromising view! She continues:

"That view explains, I think, his unwillingness later to consider a slight cooling-off period. We had family problems and I felt I was needed. I also began to realise that Robert had developed enormously and I began to have doubts as to whether I could keep up with him intellectually. Once he had written:

"We are vastly different. You are more the cautious steady-going straightforward type. I'm impetuous, ready to take advantage of any situation, not worrying about convention."

He wasn't a bit clothes-conscious, while I was most guided by my mother and older sister. We didn't drift apart but we were both profoundly affected by being the victims of living in an age of unbearable suffering and wickedness. I felt I needed a breathing space and suggested we should reduce our contact a little, have a sort of platonic friendship for a few months, but to that R. wouldn't or couldn't agree.

But we never lost that indescribable sense of oneness with each other. Years later I occasionally wrote regarding musical problems and had a reply by return of post. We met at the BBC and he took me out to lunch. He told me of his marriage, how he had met a dejected young lady sitting on a tombstone, both parents had been killed, and his sorrow that she wasn't well enough to entertain visitors. Things were very difficult for him at that time. Later my husband and I met him again when he gave a lecture at Norwich, unfortunately his hospitality had been fixed so he couldn't stay with us. Then some years later I introduced my son to him at Yalding house. Always there was a strong awareness that we still had a very strong bond. I think of him often with much affection and appreciation."

Elisabeth married Martin Benians, and in a letter to the author dated 18/3/09 she gives an account of her later life:

"I made good friends at Avery Hill though I didn't really like the course for although I took history in some depth as my main subject, I found the other compulsory subjects tedious. However, I finished the course, to my surprise got a glowing testimonial so had no difficulty in obtaining a teaching post and decided to work for a London Hons. Degree External. I was teaching at the East Anglian School for Girls, a sister school for Culford Boys School when Martin was appointed Chaplain to both schools. Martin came from Cambridge: his father was Master of St. John's College and Vice-Chancellor 1939-41; his mother had been a brilliant member of Girton. We were married in 1949 and had 59½ wonderfully happy years together. Martin was a most gracious, charming, caring person (the opinion of all who met him), at ease with "all sorts and conditions of men." He was the epitome of Chaucer's Parish Priest as described in the Prologue to The Canterbury Tales which our son read at the Thanksgiving. We retired to Sheringham in 1989 after we found a property which could house his beloved model railways. He continued to care for people, helping out when needed and acting as a Voluntary Chaplain at Norwich Cathedral, enjoying meeting visitors from all over the world. He had a stroke three years ago and although our activities became restricted, we still shared our loves of books, music and the garden."

After the end of his engagement to Elisabeth, Bob took his sister to classical concerts at the Royal Albert Hall. He was always very considerate, joining the queue for tickets hours before the concert started, and making sure that she got one of the few seats available, since she had been on her feet all day training as a nurse.

In 1944, no doubt buoyed by Howells' advice and support he took his Bachelor of Music degree. He phoned his sister at her place of work to tell her the good news. His father, despite his earlier misgivings, was also very proud of his son's achievement. I quote from his letter of 19th October to his brother Gordon:

"You will be glad to know that Bob was successful with his Examination and he is now a Bachelor of Music (Mus. Bac. Durham University). They tell him at the University that he is the youngest in living memory to take the degree and also the only one to have passed the examination at the first attempt. All the other candidates (17) were up for their second or third attempt and only five passed!

"Bob is certainly very gifted and should go far in the musical world. I think he has ambitions to conduct at the Albert Hall! He will take his Doctor of Music degree in five years time. It is apparently a rigid rule of all Universities that five years must elapse between the two degrees.

"However – there are plenty of musical celebrities who remain Mus. Bac.s – the higher degree of D. Mus is not easily attained – but I don't think it is beyond Bob's capacity or reach."

By this stage in the war, air raids on Britain by manned aircraft had pretty much ceased, although havoc continued to be wrought by unmanned flying bombs – V1 "Doodlebugs" and later V2 rockets. With parents and sister all elsewhere, there was plenty of spare room at the house in Manwood Road.

Bessie Fraser (Squibs) was bombed out of her home and both parents killed, and Bob offered her accommodation there – he already knew her as a co-worker in ARP. She had always found it difficult to make friends, and he was effectively her only one. Harry Newstone, a fellow pupil of Herbert Howells, also joined ARP as a driver/orderly and likewise moved in.

Portrait c. 1940 – the lapel badge is probably Civil Defence

Aged 18

On obtaining his Bachelor of Music

Circa 1944

"I'LL MARRY HER, THEN!"

(1946 - 1950)

Robert Layton, a lifelong friend who later played piano at some of the Exploratory Concert Society recitals and contributed to the two-volume Pelican symposium The Symphony (chapters on Prokofiev, Shostakovich, Martinu and the Czech Tradition, and Vagn Holmboe and the Later Scandinavians) gave, in his essay for the 1971 birthday booklet, a portrait of the composer at this time:

"I first met him at the Friends House, Barking, only a few weeks after the end of the war where he was beginning a WEA music class. He was then in his mid-twenties, bespectacled, quiet-spoken, scholarly and unassuming; in short he looked not a little unlike the photos one sees of the young Shostakovich but without the tenseness. For all the somewhat spartan atmosphere of the cold autumn nights and the temperamental gramophone, he rapidly established these Monday evenings as the highlight of the week. These were the days when music was not so readily available as it is now and when people saved up to buy recordings of a work one 78 at a time. They were the days too when Bruckner and Mahler were cast into outer darkness and Nielsen was barely a name to the average musician. They were not the only composers he spoke about; there were illuminating analyses of the great classics, Beethoven and Mozart, as well as studies of Reger, Medtner, Tchaikovsky and others. If I dwell on these evenings it is only because his talk about music was as distinctive as his writing. His style, whether of the spoken or written word, seems to me to possess a Sibelian quality; the argument is cogent and the insights revealing; he knows exactly what he wants to say and equally exactly how he wants to say it. Hence his writing is as direct as he is himself and as free from artifice as is his music."

In November 1946 Robert senior was appointed to the European Relief Department Overseas (Control Commission) and posted to Budapest, where he had the job of interviewing Polish soldiers who had been Soviet POWs, with the aim of identifying potential spies. Since the house in Crofton Park was Salvation Army property he had to clear and vacate it: while doing so, he remarked to his son that some of the neighbours had been gossiping about the unusual situation of an older woman sharing a house with two young men. "Right I'll marry her, then!" was the composer's typically forthright reply, and so he did.

Bessie Fraser was born in Mitcham, Surrey on 12th August 1902. Her father was Seymour, a builder's labourer. I have no other knowledge of her life pre-war. The pair were married on the 26th April 1946 at Lewisham Registry Office, on which occasion she rather naughtily stated her age as thirty-five.

The couple initially lived at 276 Verdant Lane, SE6. This was the house of Squib's aunt, which had sustained bomb damage but by 1947 was once more habitable.

The marriage caused some consternation amongst family and friends. When he told Miriam and David, themselves recently married, that she was now his wife, they thought at first that he was joking. Dick Edwards, a fellow Bruckner aficionado who had some 78rpm sets of the symphonies acquired during his army service in Germany and unavailable in the UK, had a similar reaction: "When he introduced us, I wasn't sure whether she was his wife or his mother!" But then, says Miriam, her brother was never one to care much about what other people thought.

Though possessive she was, thinks his sister, good for the composer in many ways: since she was past child-bearing age there would be no family to distract him from his work; in fact, if the phone rang while he was composing she would tell the caller that he could not take it. She was, recalled Dick Edwards, very small, a chain-smoker, and did not walk very well – "Just a simple housewife." She was a good cook, and prepared him enormous meals – the composer always enjoyed his food. Miriam recalls the food as "Very rich – lots of cream."

Bob Simpson and his first wife, Squibbs. Undated, probably 1960s

As far as music went, she was more in tune with Beethoven and other classics than with her husband's work, though she was wont to say that "Bob is a genius, you know."

The first work which Simpson allowed to survive, the Piano Sonata of 1946, is dedicated to his first wife, although he was inspired to write it by Harold Truscott's playing. Simpson himself owned "I'm a bad pianist" and Truscott, in a personal memoir, wrote: "The piano he did not play, although I once caught him fighting his way through some of the first movement of that Schubert unfinished C major Sonata, rather in the manner of someone forcing their way through thick jungle."

The work is in E major, with three movements: Allegro molto moderato, Molto adagio et tranquillo, and Allegro vivace, and plays for some 23½ minutes. It was premiered by Truscott in 1947 at an Exploratory Concert Society recital, of which more later. Charles W. Simons, who attended the concert, recalled that Simpson also played a trumpet work by Purcell; presumably not the famous "Voluntary", often now attributed to Jeremiah Clark, which would hardly need such exposure. The work has rarely been played since. Ronald Smith gave it a broadcast recital on 13/9/54, with the Music for Cello and Piano (Thomas Rajna) and the 1st Quartet Op. 21 by Allan Hawthorne Baker. It had further airing on 21/9/73 in a concert at the Queen Elizabeth Hall by Albert Ferber, who also played Beethoven's Salieri Variations and the Schubert A major Sonata. It was recorded by Raymond Clarke with the rest of Simpson's piano output, a disc issued in 1996. Although he spared the work and allowed it to be published, the composer's later opinion of the sonata was not high. "It was the first thing I took at all seriously. I took it a great deal more seriously when it was published than I do now."[1]

Lengnicks, now no more, were Simpson's major publisher from an early date. From Lewis Foreman Interview.

"LF: How did you get introduced to Lengnicks in the first place?

RS: Back in the early days in the 50s - 51 or so – I met Bernard de Nevers, who was then in charge of the firm, he owned it. He heard my Piano Sonata and wanted to publish it. Then he did everything else after that. Then he retired."

During the later 1940's Simpson continued to write on musical subjects. His articles were published in The Music Review, Disc and a short-lived arts journal Gangrel. Most of them have recently been reprinted in Tonic, the Robert Simpson Society magazine. They are still well worth reading and his youthful opinions provocative, sometimes perhaps deliberately so. He also founded, with Harold Truscott and Donald Mitchell the Exploratory

Concert Society already referred to. The Society had the patronage of Herbert Howells. The object was to give the public the opportunity to hear worthwhile music which did not form part of the mainstream repertoire, a mission which he pursued throughout his years with the BBC, especially in his programme "The Innocent Ear", where the composer's name was only given after the work had been played. As well as Dick Edwards, he met Anthony Dorrell, "My best friend for thirty years" and Professor (later Sir) David Gillette, later the first Robert Simpson Society Chairman, by way of these concerts. One of the recitals took place at St. Martins School of Art, Charing Cross Road, on 15th November 1947. Harold Truscott (piano) and Henry Holst (violin) played Nielsen's Chaconne (twice), the Theme and Variations in D minor, both for solo piano, and the Second Violin Sonata. The programme ends with an appeal which vividly illustrates the decline in value of our currency over succeeding years.

"N.B. In order that the expenses of this concert may be met, an individual contribution of not less than 2/6 (12½p) is requested. Please be as generous as you can."

In 1948 Simpson followed his Sonata with the Variations and Finale on a Theme of Haydn, also for piano. The theme is the palindromic minuet from Haydn's 47th Symphony in G and his 41st Piano Sonata, a theme which Simpson also used as the basis for his massive thirty-two variation Ninth Quartet of 1982. The work (there are twelve variations and the playing time is a little under twenty-three minutes) is dedicated to Harold Truscott, who recalled that when introducing the first (broadcast)

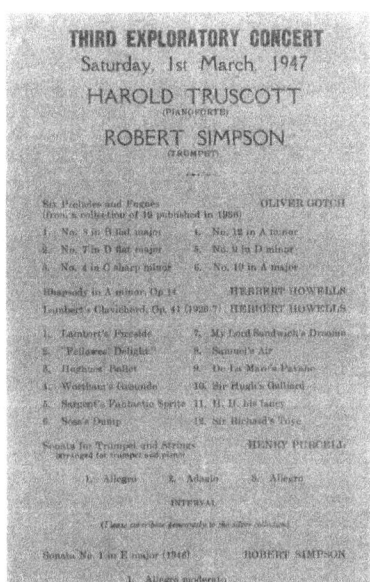

Exploratory Concert Society Leaflet

performance the composer "talked about [the variations] first, referred to my sight-reading and his attempts to beat it, and admitted that he never succeeded." Lamar Crowson gave this premiere (on 14/12/55) and the other works were the Piano Trio Op. 35 by Salzedo and Kenneth V. Jones's Second Wind Quintet. The first public performance took place, unusually enough, at the Lecture Hall of the Detroit Institute of the Arts, where it was played by Caroline Jewell as part of a programme of contemporary British music on 25 November 1957.

The UK public première was a McNaughten Society concert in the Great Drawing Room, Arts Council of Great Britain, on 23/1/59, played by Eric Parkin. The other works were "A Scarlatti Suite", Kodaly's Cello Sonata, Kenneth Regan's Legend, Elizabeth Maconchy's Variations on a Theme from Job (by Vaughan Williams) and John Ireland's Piano Sonata.

The Daily Telegraph (24/1/59, "M.C.") described Simpson's work as "An academic joke which often yields interesting results." "C.G-F."* (Musical Opinion, March 1959) found it "undeniably original." It was given again at the same venue on 6/2/61 by Lamar Crowson, in the Company of David Dorward's 1958 String Quartet and "Stray Birds" by Harry Hancock, under the auspices of the Society for the Promotion of New Music. The anonymous Times reviewer (7/2/61) considered that the work "contains much ingenious and attractive music which presents no problems other

---

*   Clinton Gray-Fiske.

than purely technical ones for the performer." It was recorded by Raymond Clarke on the disc already referred to following a recital at the Royal College of Music, Manchester, on 23rd January 1993.

There is an undated arrangement of the Haydn Variations for Piano Trio in the British Library.

In 1949 the Simpsons moved to their first home of their own, 18 Grand Avenue, N10, an end-of-terrace red-brick house of late 19th of early 20th century vintage. Not quite their own, in the first place: Simpson could not afford to take on the whole mortgage himself – while preparing to take his doctorate he had been receiving a grant, which he supplemented by working illegally for the Post Office, and when this came to light, he was obliged to repay the grant. Thus, he made a joint purchase with another man, who occupied the first floor while Bob and Squibs lived below. Unfortunately, the co-owner turned out to be a pederast, in the habit of bringing boys home and entertaining them in his quarters while their bicycles remained downstairs. Although the gentleman concerned was eventually persuaded to leave, his behaviour greatly upset Squibs and, Miriam believes, triggered a nervous breakdown (at one point she threatened her husband with a carving knife) and she was confined in Friern Barnet Hospital for two years. Various treatments, including ECT, were tried without success, and by the end of the period there was no discernible improvement. The doctors then suggested the kill-or-cure procedure of a

Robert Simpson's home from 1949 to 1961, 18 Grand Avenue N10

lobotomy. The composer agonised over his decision, describing it as the worst day of his life. Happily, the operation was a success, and Squibs was able to return home.

During the later 1940s, as well as working towards his Doctorate, Robert Simpson continued to compose. The two piano works from this era have already been dealt with, and in 1946 he began what was to become his First Symphony, a work which will receive detailed treatment in the following chapter. As previously mentioned, nothing written before the Piano Sonata has survived. The composer described his other (non-symphonic) early efforts thus: "I wrote a lot of songs at one time – I tried to. Mostly to German poems, I couldn't really cope with English poetry. I've always had a bit of a block with words. Then I also wrote chamber music of various kinds – all sorts of things I attempted. But none of it exists. I got rid of it all *(from the 1980 interview with Lewis Foreman)*". An interview with C.B. Rees (London Musical Events, July 1959) makes intriguing mention of an Overture and a Fantasia for Strings, otherwise unknown. Were these also works that Simpson eventually discarded, or did Rees simply get it wrong?*

In 1950 Robert Simpson began his thirty-year association with the BBC, which forms a natural beginning to the next chapter. I will round off this one with a brief account of the later fortunes of the composer's immediate family.

Robert Simpson Senior, regarded with some disapprobation by the Salvation Army on account of his marital difficulties, was appointed, in May 1948, Advisory Officer, General Relief and Welfare Work, and was posted to Australia. On the boat there, he met a lady called Eileen, whom he found highly congenial. Although they lived on opposite sides of this vast country – he ran an Approved School in Perth, while she was assistant head of a private girls' school in Sydney – they continued to see each other. He resigned as a Salvation Army Officer in December 1951, and later Helena was outraged to receive a letter from her estranged husband asking for a divorce. "But we thought you didn't want to be with him anyway!" remonstrated the children, to which she replied: "No, but he did promise that he would never divorce me!" She agreed, nevertheless, and he married Eileen: sadly, they only had some eight years together before she died of cancer. Following this, Robert returned briefly to England (he had, by then contracted Parkinson's disease) and announced to his son and daughter that he had proposed to Eileen's best friend Jessie – she had turned him down. Should he persist? "Go for it!" they advised – he did, they married, and Jessie looked after him until his death, on 19th February 1974. As Miriam says, "He was a sad man, but he found happiness in the end."

---

* *A string quartet in D major, dated 26th March 1945, has recently been discovered in the archives of the University of Durham. This pre-dates the Piano Sonata (his first acknowledged work) by only a year. It has yet to be performed*

As previously noted, Miriam married David MacEwan, Bob's best friend from school. They had three children, Janet, Richard and Helen. Having served in the Signals Corps during the war, David worked subsequently in telecommunications but, at age forty-eight, decided to fulfil a long-standing ambition, and took holy orders as a Church of England vicar. Despite their divergent beliefs – the composer had by then long been a convinced atheist – they continued to be friends, swapping endless (sometimes risqué) jokes, and each asking the other how someone of their intelligence could, or could not, be a believer. A note from Cedar Cottage, undated but clearly from 1981, the year that "The Proms and Natural Justice" was published, conveys the flavour of their friendship:

Dear David

"Hope you're surviving! Thought you might like to see the enclosed. I'll now be pariah dog No. 1 in the BBC's corridors of power. Buggerum omnium!

As ever

Bob"

David died of a massive heart attack on 19th February 1989, having stepped out of his church in Wigston for some fresh air prior to a service.

Helena lived with Miram and David for her last sixteen years, and for the final three suffered from senile dementia. She drove an NHS three-wheel electric invalid cart, and became disoriented after the move to Wigston – her doctor advised that, if he saw her on the road, he would make sure that he left his own car in the garage! She died on 10th February 1973.

"THE ENVY OF THE WHOLE CIVILISED WORLD'
(1951 - 1952)

Robert Simpson's first work for the BBC, in 1950, was not as an established member of staff. "I was in and out. I was doing a contract job analysing the first four years of the Third Programme. * Leonard Isaacs, Head of the Music Division, was clearly impressed by his work and wrote, in an internal memo dated 26th July 1950: "This man is first class – his reports are helpful and he has an informed mind. Any chance of keeping him permanently?" His wish was granted, and Simpson joined the BBC as a producer in 1951. First posted to Birmingham, he returned to London after two years to become second-in-command in programming. The Birmingham connection endured over the years: the first three String Quartets were premiered by the Element Quartet, the Violin Concerto was written for Ernie Element, and the Third Symphony was first performed by the CBSO. Isaacs remained a friend for life; after retirement, he emigrated to Canada, where he died in 1995.

The atmosphere of the Third Programme in those early years suited Robert Simpson down to the ground. "When I first started, the Third Programme was four years old, and there was still a feeling of great excitement about it. We could now have a programme that was especially for the arts, especially for things which required concentrated listening from a particular audience: this had never been done in the world before. It was the envy of the whole world, and I think the BBC is forever to be congratulated for having started such a thing. We all had a wonderful feeling of freedom. We could do all sorts of works which had never been performed and which nobody would dream of performing in public. They couldn't afford to put them on in public, and so we did." (Ibid) From the early 1950s, Simpson also worked as a record reviewer writing for the Monthly Letter (A Critical Review of Recent Recordings), published by the gloriously-named EMG Hand-Made Gramophones Ltd, who had a small shop in Soho Square. Simpson was the sole reviewer for many years, later as one of a panel.** From the later 1950s a number of review copies were passed on to Angela Musgrave (later Simpson), Bob's secretary, and formed the basis of her record collection. At Soho Square Bob first met Ted Perry, who was working behind the counter, and who decades later founded the Hyperion company, which recorded the bulk of Simpson's output. Despite a long life (first issued in 1930), the Newsletter eventually disappeared: EMG themselves went into liquidation

---

*   Interview with Lewis Foreman, 1980
**   The company was named after its founder, E.M. Gomme, Esq. Basil Lam also contributed reviews from an early stage, covering earlier music in particular Bach.

in July 1980). After a lapse of 5 months, the magazine was revived by the Sir Thomas Beecham Trust, but ceased publication a couple of years later, no doubt ousted by flashier productions. Robert Simpson's reviews are still lively reading, especially for those of us who have stubbornly not junked our LP collections.

It was at the BBC that Simpson first saw Havergal Brian's music – an essay from 1947 (Orchestral Style) indicates that he knew Brian's name but had not heard a note of the music, the senior composer having suffered almost total neglect since the 1920s. "When I first joined the BBC, one of the things I did was to look up all the neglected names, particularly of British music, that one knew but had never heard. I got hold of masses of scores, piles of them, I was nearly up to my neck in them: Cyril Scott, Bantock and Holbrooke, and Brian – all those people. Out of them all, Brian was the only one to strike sparks out of me. I thought "I can't really lay my hand on my heart and say I've got to make a crusade on behalf of Bantock, say." But Brian I did feel was something outstanding, and not merely because of his guts in carrying on in spite of everything.")[1]. Simpson told me an amusing story, which he heard from Brian, about Josef (originally Joseph) Holbrooke, who seems to have been a man of considerable ego. One evening there came a knock at the door of Brian's London home, and in stumbled Holbrooke, battered and bruised – he had been struck by a cab. Brian and Hilda cleaned up the composer, gave him a brandy, and saw him safely on his way. In the morning paper was a news item "Famous composer injured in road accident" – only then did they realise that Holbrooke, being an inveterate publicity-hound, had telephoned the newspaper to report the incident before seeking help. It was Brian's Eighth Symphony (written 1949) which grabbed Simpson's attention, and he arranged for numbers 8,9,10,11 and 12 to be broadcast over the following years, the intention being to cover Brian's entire oeuvre in time. This project was scotched in 1960, when William Glock (who had no time for Brian's music) was appointed Controller, and it was not until the 1970s that the whole of the elder composer's (by then massive) symphonic output could be aired. Brian and Simpson remained friends until the end of the former's long life, with frequent visits and letters (Brian's have survived, but not Simpson's). Robert Simpson's opinion of Brian was far from uncritical: "I still think he's an incredibly uneven composer. Some of his music I think is really bad, terrible. But at his best he's got tremendous originality and that's what I was looking for."

1951 saw two important events in the composer's life, as well as his joining the BBC: the completion of his First Symphony and the award of his Doctorate of Music; in fact, the first was instrumental in the achievement of the second. The First was actually Simpson's fifth essay in this form. The

---

* *Interview with Lewis Foreman, 1980*

previous four, including the two on which he was working simultaneously in 1942 no longer exist. In a 60th birthday interview with Michael Oliver he said: "It was a long time before I actually threw them away. It was actually after I had written what is now No.1, and I thought it was such an advance on what I had done before that I didn't want anybody to see those." In an earlier interview with Christopher Ford (Guardian, October 23rd 1974) he gave a somewhat different account of the fate of one of them, a 12-note work written at the age of sixteen. Asked what had happened to it, he replied: "Exactly what should have happened to it. It went on the fire. I burned it within six months of writing it. At that age, if I thought it bad it must have been bad." Either way, we shall never see the publication of these early efforts, unlike those of Dvořák, who withdrew, but did not actually destroy, his first four. The symphony was begun in 1946. Harold Truscott, in a personal memoir, gave an account of the origins of some of the symphony's material. "When I first met Bob, he had been working slowly on an orchestral piece which he called, tentatively, "Cathedral Music." He also began a second piano sonata for Truscott: the latter found the opening bars not merely orchestral, but symphonic. Eventually, the beginning of the sonata became the symphony's opening, while "cathedral music" found its "rightful place" in the slow central section. By 1947 the work was two-thirds finished. Then, the composer first heard recordings of Carl Nielsen's music, the Wind Quintet and the Third Symphony, "Espansiva". "I was hit by the first movement of the Espansiva, which knocked me for six, I just didn't know what to do, I thought: "Well, someone's done it. I've been wasting my time. But then it all came back; and I think the last movement of that symphony does, perhaps, show the influence of Nielsen more than the rest." The symphony was resumed in 1950, and finished the following year.

The First Symphony is in a single movement, with three sections - moderate, slow and fast - written over a single pulse. In the Hyperion recording the work lasts nearly 29 minutes. It is dedicated to Sir Adrian Boult. Simpson observed in a programme note: "The three stages in the Symphony pass from what might be described as conflict, through consideration, to resolution." Nevertheless, he added, "This is not a "programme" symphony, nor is it romanticism."

The work won Simpson his Doctorate; like his B. Mus. this was taken at Durham, although for the academic work he went to Hull. In the same note, he says: "With some trepidation I submitted it as a thesis for a D.Mus. degree, having been too lazy to perspire over an "academic" work. Fortunately, the examiners were indulgent, and accepted it."

The next step was to get the symphony performed. Simpson submitted it to a BBC panel who were less than enthusiastic - in fact, it is worth quoting from the notes of their meeting (July 1952, BBC Archives) which has a rare flavour of querulous sourness. Conductor Clarence Raybould said "… sorry I can't find any interest in it from a purely musical point of view… I feel it has no "life". I hope I am wrong, but I must say "no"."

Composer Gordon Jacob added: "I find this far too contrived and manufactured in spite of its obvious ability. I agree with Raybould that it fails to give real musical satisfaction. In spite of its sound and fury (in places) it relies too much on mere cleverness and not enough on musical conviction." Finally, Mosco Carner, critic: "My impression is that this composer has not yet reached the stage of what I would call "symphonic maturity"… "there is little feeling of organic growth about this work and it relies too much on external effects … shows talent, but too immature as a symphony to be recommended."

Nothing daunted, Simpson tried elsewhere. "I then sent it to Danish Radio, to Launy Grøndahl [whom he had presumably met while researching his book "Carl Nielsen, Symphonist"] who actually did the first performance in Copenhagen." [1]. This was a broadcast on 11th June 1953 – the Danish State Radio Orchestra under Grøndahl – the other works in the programme being the Vaughan Williams "Wasps" overture, and Nielsen's "Saga-Drøm". Simpson continued: "I wasn't there, I couldn't go because I didn't have any money… then they sent me a recording of it… 78 discs because tape was still then not really going. They sent me some acetate discs of it which I then sent to the BBC and they listened to it and reversed (their decision)." (Ibid).

Sir Adrian Boult was entrusted with the British première. "He did a marvellous job on it. It was really superb…" The performance was broadcast on 23rd September 1954 - BBCSO, Boult – and the programme also included Haydn's 104th (London) Symphony and Debussy's Saxophone Rhapsody.

Hugh Ottaway (Musical Opinion, November 1954) was hugely enthusiastic. "The most encouraging work by a young Englishman… that I have heard for several years"; "vitally inspired and surely executed"; "No exercise"; "If Robert Simpson can develop the promise of this work and the more recent string quartet… then he will make an impact on the concert audience such as nobody after Vaughan Williams and the younger Walton has quite achieved." Later, in 1956, Ottaway wrote a two-page analysis of the symphony for the Musical Times.

The first public performance came on 8th June 1956 at the Royal Festival Hall (LPO, Boult) along with Arnold's overture "Tam O'Shanter", Elgar's Introduction and Allegro, and Vaughan Williams's Fourth Symphony.

C.G-F, writing in Musical Opinion (August 1956), said: "The symphony as a whole is a solid, substantial achievement that seems likely to improve on further acquaintance." Noel Goodwin (Daily Express, 9/6/56) bizarrely observed: "Stocky Robert Simpson – with a huge red tie – got a tepid welcome for the first public performance of his Symphony No.1, a 23-minute work which gained a music-doctor's degree for the 35-year-old composer from Leamington.

"It sounded like it … studious, carefully worked out ideas, promising techniques – but cold as ice."

Quite what relevance the composer's choice of neckwear had is unclear – as Lionel Pike has observed, had Bob been a woman, his vital statistics would no doubt have been recorded.

Percy Cater (Daily Mail, 9/6/56) thought: "It is strong, it has something to say, and knows how to say it. It has style. The orchestra is boldly handled, the colour is effective, in moods of subtlety and power.

"This is a composer who writes according to inspiration, without worrying about the ruling vogues."

However, he qualified this by adding that he felt it "impaired … by its over-engrossed concern with scholarship … there is too much working out of technical problems "in public"."

Astonishingly enough, Stephen Williams wrote a review for the New York Times; he felt it "shows an able grasp of the symphonic form and the faculty of raising and victoriously solving important problems. It seems at first music to admire rather than to love; but no doubt, like all worthwhile art, it will reward further study."

A recording followed in 1957, the first of any of Simpson's music, with the LPO under Boult, on a ten-inch HMV long-player, with a sleeve-note by Deryck Cooke, funded by the British Council. Reviews were, on the whole, favourable. Gramophone, April 1957 (A.P.): "I would urge this symphony on all who have any interest in contemporary music."

Birmingham Post, 6/5/57 (J.F. Waterhouse): "This is an altogether outstanding first symphony by a young man who has begun his formal training later than most. This record and score of it should be possessed by everyone who has the slightest interest in the immediate future of British music."

Edmund Rubbra (EMG Monthly Letter, April 1957 – Simpson could obviously not review his own work!): "Let it be said at once that this is a most remarkable work not merely as a <u>first</u> symphony but <u>as</u> a symphony

… there is in it not a trace of diffidence in facing the issues of symphonic thought."

John Warrack (Daily Telegraph, 27/5/57): "Beyond doubt this work is a major achievement." Times, 8/6/57 (Anon): "This is strong, but not pugnacious or outrageous music, cogently expressed."

Desmond Shawe-Taylor (Observer, 9/6/57) noted the influence of Nielsen, "but the work stands firmly on its own feet as a lucid, original and often very beautiful essay in symphonic form." Others were less taken; Scott Goddard (Gramophone Record Review, May 1957): "It will undoubtedly interest the more intellectual listener and will puzzle those who are foreign to British music, since Robert Simpson shows little affinity to any recognisable local influences."

Buxton Orr (Record News, May 1957): "My imagination fails to respond: I see only flatness in the material; the transformations have little meaning, and the contrapuntal movement lacks both interaction and inevitability." No doubt Simpson considered himself suitably admonished. On a more positive note: John Amis (Radio Times, 26/7/57: "This is powerful, stimulating music, closely argued, but not difficult to follow."

Desmond Shawe-Taylor (New Statesman, 27/7/57):" *striking and beautiful work."

Dyneley Hussey (Listener, 8/7/57) found it "Neither bright nor brisk, but of a deep unsmiling seriousness that nevertheless contains, as its central feature, a serene contemplation of ideal beauty such as none of this composer's contemporaries has imagined."

A Prom performance came on 2nd August 1957 at the Royal Albert Hall, with Sir Adrian again conducting the LPO. An all-Beethoven first half; Leonora No.1 Overture, Second Symphony and the Fifth (Emperor) Piano Concerto, with Lamar Crowson as soloist. Elgar's "Cockaigne" Overture completed the second half.

Mervyn Vicars (Musical Times, October 1957) rubbished the symphony impatiently: "This over-announced work reminded one of the music written for existentialist films between the wars." He must have been thinking (if that is the word) of expressionist films.

The symphony received another performance at the Royal Festival Hall on 10th March 1970. Simpson conducted the LPO in his own work, while Charles Mackerras directed the Elgar Cello Concerto (Leonard Rose, soloist) and Brahms's Third Symphony.

Alan Blyth (Times, 11/3/70) observed: "Robert Simpson's 19-year-old First should, in the context of today's music, be as dead as a dodo, or at least dormant – as are so many of its contemporaries – yet it came up alive and kicking at last night's LPO concert."

Martin Cooper (Daily Telegraph, 11/3/70) referred to its "vitality of thought."

Neville Cardus (Guardian, 11th March) was more grudging. "An acute brain is obviously in action but nothing strikingly memorable remains, except the technical know-how." He may, of course, still have been smarting over one of Simpson's most effective put-downs.

On 28th January 1967, the Guardian published a lengthy article by Cardus entitled Point and Counterpoint. I will quote the last paragraph:

"Criticising the second-rate

"It is while dealing with the second-rate that criticism can usually arrive at unanimity of opinion. There can be no two critical evaluations of, say, Saint-Saëns, Rimsky-Korsakov, and others similarly expertly endowed technically, and fully in control of what little they have to say. Such excellent professionals are not ravaged by a creative demon that impels them to the heights and also leads them to ineffectualities, divine futilities and subsidences, as happen to the Beethovens, the Shakespeares, the Goethes of the world, but seldom to the accomplished and versatile Stravinskys.

"So far I have discussed here the problems put to the critic by the works performed, by the composers. It might be thought that we arrive on firmer ground when we consider performances. Surely, we can get near to "objective" truth now. But, as we have seen, from the above quotations from this newspaper and the "Times", the opinions of two experts were at variance while considering a palpable fact in time and space – whether during performance Yehudi and Hepzibah Menuhin maintained much the same pace or tempo. Obviously; a photo-finish was called for. A critic's aesthetic reactions necessarily involve subtle psychological analysis; but how could two trained minds, four trained ears, go wrong on a point of togetherness, there to be "objectively" perceived, under your very nose?

"A critic once protested that he couldn't hear a Fürtwängler pianissimo. "He should change his seat," retorted Fürtwängler, "it is too far back." Recently, learned colleagues resorted trustfully to the authority of Beethoven's metronome indications. At a rehearsal, Georg Szell and Schnabel argued on this same point. "But, Artur, your tempo is wrong," persisted Szell, "I have seen Beethoven's metronome markings in his own handwriting, in original manuscript." "Maybe," retaliated Schnabel, from the piano, "and I have seen Beethoven's metronome and it never could have been in order." So, as Bishop Bloughram puts it, "we call the check-board white, we call it black." But there was no need for critics to protest overmuch at Mr Bean's playful sport with them. Criticism of music, or of the arts in general, is not as serious as all that. Nobody will be a penny the worse if a critic pronounces the most unjust verdict. He is not sentencing anybody to death. I am all for a little more humour, even flippancy, in music criticism."

The penultimate sentence is simply untrue; there seems no doubt that vitriolic criticism from Eduard Hanslick played a part in driving Hugo Wolf insane and to his subsequent premature death. Simpson felt the same way, as his reply from 31st January indicates:

"Sir Neville's View

Dear Sir

I would dearly love the opportunity to house-train a few music critics.

faithfully

Robert Simpson"

Cardus, for all his eminence, had some decided eccentricities; despite being (presumably!) a lover of classical music, he defended the BBC's then practice of suspending musical broadcasts in favour of cricket commentaries, he considered Sibelius's Third and Sixth Symphonies "anaemic", and I well remember a review in which, after bragging that he had been one of the few to recognise Bruckner's genius in the bad old days, he proceeded to rip the beautiful and powerful Sixth Symphony to pieces (the work itself, not the rendition).

The Boult recording was reissued in 12-inch format in 1966 in the HMV 20 series, coupled with Peter Racine Fricker's Second Symphony (RLPO under John Pritchard). Hyperion issued a modern recording with the Royal Philharmonic conducted by Vernon Handley (coupled with Simpson's Eighth Symphony) in 1996.

As far as I know, the First has not received a public performance since 1970. This is a great shame: the work still makes a powerful impact and, if the Ninth (also written over a single pulse) surpasses it in depth and imaginative range, this does not render it negligible. One can well understand why Simpson said in a 1988 interview: "… the whole piece is a complete unity in that sense. At least, I hope it is, and I still think that it is now after 35 years. I think it is really as good a piece as I could have made at that time: I think I could do better nowadays, but that's another thing!"

If you can locate a copy of the Boult recording, grab it: it has the edge, I think, over the (very good) later recording, and even the sound stands up well.

The first recording of Simpson's music (1957)

His first book, published 1951

Those interested in the oddities of creative inspiration will be intrigued to learn that the minor third on two trumpets which opens the symphony was suggested by the sound of the wartime air raid siren which the composer heard so many times in the course of his duties.

Robert Simpson's first book, "Carl Nielsen – Symphonist", was published by Dent in 1952. Although Nielsen had conducted a concert of his own music, including the Fourth Symphony, at the Queen's Hall in 1923, nothing further was heard in this country until a visit by the Danish Radio Symphony Orchestra, who played the Fifth Symphony at the Edinburgh Festival in 1950, and the Fourth at the Royal Festival Hall the following year. Simpson already knew some of Nielsen's music from gramophone records – as previously noted, hearing the "Espansiva" halted work on his own First for three years. An article in the Monthly Musical Record by "G.A." (February 1953) asserts: "The present vogue of Nielsen in England dates from just after the liberation of Denmark, when Mr Laurence Gilliam, the BBC's Director of Features, brought back from that country a number of recordings including one of Nielsen's symphonies which was heard by Sir William Walton and other British musicians, who were deeply impressed. Then came broadcasts …"

Simpson comments, in his preface to the revised edition of the book (completed 1979, published by Kahn and Averill): "By (1951) I was familiar with most of Nielsen's major works and was sure of his permanent value; I had also been corresponding with his friend and pupil Jørgen Bentzon, from whom I got a number of scores and much help. When I visited Copenhagen for the first time at Christmas 1951 he had, alas, just died; so I never met him, but will always be grateful to him.

"It was just before this that a group of musicians and others in London had decided to arrange, if we could get the money from somewhere, a Nielsen Festival. Sir Thomas Beecham was interested and agreed to conduct all the symphonies in a series of Festival Hall concerts; this fired everyone concerned, and it was proposed that I should write a book to be published at the time of the festival, which was intended for some time in 1952. So the book had to be done quickly – in nine weeks to be precise, including a trip to Copenhagen to meet Danish musicians involved in Nielsen's music as friends, pupils, composers, or performers, and, especially, to contact his two daughters, Irmelin Eggert and Anne Marie Telmanyi, who were able to show me many manuscripts and tell me much about their father's nature. In the meantime, strenuous efforts were being made to get funds for the projected festival – hopes rose and fell, and finally fell; the festival didn't happen. But the book did." One conversation failed to find its way into the book; on learning that Sibelius had been a frequent visitor to the Nielsen household, Simpson mused to one of the daughters: "There must have been some wonderful conversations about music." "No!" she replied, "Sibelius was always drunk!"

"Carl Nielsen – Symphonist" concentrates on these works, after a some preliminary observations entitled "The Growth of the Artist", with a sizeable chapter devoted to each and, at the end of each chapter, a list of works by other composers contemporaneous with the symphony. There then follow chapters on the three concertos, other orchestral works, chamber music, keyboard music, and vocal works, including Nielsen's two operas.

After a chapter entitled "General Observations" comes a biographical appendix by Torben Meyer, a chronological list of works, and a list of recordings available in Britain at the time. The book was reviewed, on the whole favourably, by a wide variety of journals, including the splendidly-titled "Northern Whig and Belfast Post", which sounds like an invention of Peter Simple. I should mention that at this time Simpson used a press cuttings agency and some weird and wonderful things found their way into the scrapbooks. It is also worth noting that "Peter Simple" (Colm Brogan and Michael Wharton, who took turns writing the column.) quoted approvingly from Robert Simpson's 1959 article "On Composing" in his Telegraph column, although I suspect that the right-wing satirist and the "fierce left-winger" would have agreed about little else.

Richard Capell (Daily Telegraph, 3/1/53), in a piece entitled "The use and abuse of literary titles – Carl Nielsen's practice questioned" deviated somewhat from the theme of the book. "Why should the composer have attempted a translation of the gist of his message when his own language, music, was so incomparably eloquent?" and was glad that "he spared the finest, No 5 of that remarkable series."

Martin Cooper (Spectator, 9/1/53) thought that "The book is, in fact, the work of an apostle and states a maximalist case" comparing Cecil Gray's promotion of Philip Heseltine (Peter Warlock). He found Simpson "impatient" in his mentions of Sibelius and Vaughan Williams, and queried the specifically Danish character which Simpson found in some of the music ("outwardly Brahmsian but inwardly and serenely Danish.")

An anonymous reviewer in the Listener (15/1/53) felt that "His enthusiasm is laudable, though it sometimes leads him into excesses. We are told that in the finale of the Third Symphony there is a "thumping honest tune" … but why try to make things better by saying that it "makes Holst's Jupiter seem cold and mirthless by comparison"?"

Desmond Shawe-Taylor (New Statesman, 31/1/53) was enthusiastic, but criticised the brief treatment of the operas. The Scotsman (Anon, 12/3/53) found it "A valuable interim assessment … which will no doubt be mercilessly pillaged by writers of sleeve-notes" and also thought it "adjective-happy ... but the titles of some of his symphonies ... do invite this sort of treatment."

Rosemary Hughes (Tablet, 24/5/53) liked the book, but found it "curiously lop-sided in its proportions", and unsurprisingly took exception to Simpson's comparison between the slow movement of the Second Symphony and Elgar's prelude to part 2 of The Dream of Gerontius: "Nielsen, the blunt, logical man of the soil . . . Elgar, the dreamy, religious romantic", and set the author to rights:

"Mysticism means direct contact with reality, not escape from it." We had best take her word for it.

Mosco Carner (Time and Tide, 13/6/53) thought the book "Helpful and informative, but unnecessarily interlarded with quasiphilosophical asides."

"J.G." in Tempo (no date) found the bias towards the symphonies understandable for reasons of space, but considered that "His sentences, particularly the metaphorous (sic) purple ones, run better without their heavy load of descriptive adjectives." I am unclear as to what other kind of adjectives there are.

The reviewer added "Of course the qualities of Nielsen, like those of any love-object, are overstated by Doctor Simpson but, though he is counsel for the defence rather than the judge, it is still our duty, as members of the jury, to listen attentively to what he has to say." Absolutely.

Simpson's association with Nielsen and with Denmark itself endured over the years. He took a great liking to the warm, laid-back Danes and their self-deprecating humour (he once told me the Danes described their own very guttural language as a disease of the throat) and often holidayed there in later years, travelling in a red VW camper van. He made three particular friends in addition to the conductor Mogens Wöldike, pianist Arne Skjold Rasmussen, organist Svend Aage Spange, to whom he dedicated his sole organ work, Eppur si muove, and the greatly admired Vagn Holmboe, fellow (and perhaps only strictly comparable) composer, about whom he wrote an article for the Listener as early as 1955.

A Nielsen Festival in Copenhagen held between 31st August and 4th September 1953 included talks and a short essay by Robert Simpson. In 1956 the Danish government awarded Simpson the Carl Nielsen Gold Medal in recognition of his work on behalf of their greatest composer. As late as 1990 he gave an illustrated talk at Ronne on the island of Bornholm. Above any medal he no doubt valued the gift of Nielsen's gold-plated propelling pencil (engraved with the composer's name and the date 9 June 1925, his sixtieth birthday) which was given to him by Nielsen's daughter in 1952. In a letter to a Mrs Wall (15/4/85) he said "I've worked with it ever since ... so it's composed for me six symphonies, eight quartets and plenty of other music, unworthy of it, maybe, but privileged nonetheless. It's one of my greatest treasures." Angela Simpson passed the pencil on to Robert Simpson's friend and protegé, composer and conductor Matthew Taylor, although sadly leads of the appropriate size are no longer available.

Recordings were also pursued. In 1969 Simpson produced, for Unicorn Records, an LP of the Fifth Symphony and the tone-poem Saga Drøm with the NPO under Jascha Horenstein, who had first conducted the symphony in 1927, rehearsing it for Wilhelm Fürtwängler at the ISCM Festival, Frankfurt, in the composer's presence. This was followed, in 1974, by the first integral set of all six symphonies, also for Unicorn. Simpson again produced and the LSO were conducted by Ole Schmidt. The set contained an extra disc with a short talk about each work by his fellow composer.

As previously mentioned, "Carl Nielsen – Symphonist" had been revised by 1979. Most of the amendments are minor, although there is an additional chapter, "Sibelius, Nielsen and the Symphonic Problem" closely based on an excellent booklet published by the BBC in 1965. One of the original chapters was, however, completely rewritten – that on the Sixth Symphony. Simpson originally felt that, after a first movement which he considered a tragic masterpiece, the rest of the work was a disappointment; that the composer's judgement had been clouded by knowledge of the heart condition that was to kill him, leading him into bitterness and subjective expression. Gradually, he came to take a different view. "All this time I was becoming convinced by the symphony, yet could not explain why, and this was still true in 1974 (the year of the recorded set) ... the truth began to dawn ... that for twenty years I had been simply looking for the wrong clue." I will not go into technicalities (for those, read the book!) but the gist of it is that, while in most of Nielsen's previous work, there is a gradual progression towards the home key, in the Sixth the key of B flat is deliberately avoided until the very end: an unpleasant fact which is finally faced, indeed treated as a joke, as one might one's own mortality.

Nielsen's standing as a composer has changed immeasurably since Simpson first wrote his volume: his works are now firmly established in the repertory, and in 1982 the dream of the pioneers from the early 1950s was finally realised, with all six symphonies played at the Barbican by the CBSO under Simon Rattle, in tandem with Sibelius's seven directed by Colin Davis (LSO) – a memorable series of concerts.

How far Robert Simpson's book contributed to this is difficult to assess. It does have its faults, I think, which can be attributed to the speed at which it was written, and I would say that some of the references to other composers are unnecessarily dismissive. The Essence of Bruckner has, I think, greater depth, especially in the revision – but then it was written fifteen years later, so this should hardly surprise. The title is as blunt as the man's music (and his photographs) and this is probably as it should be. It certainly helped me in my budding acquaintance with a composer whom I initially reacted against (to my present shame I recall thinking, on hearing the opening of the Second Symphony on the radio "What a racket!"). Simpson's advocacy was a powerful incentive to persist. For what it may be worth – probably not much – I never had a problem with the Sixth, but then I was no doubt insensitive to subtleties which another composer would notice. Above all, Simpson was big enough to admit he got it wrong the first time round ("It took me thirty years to understand that symphony"), as he was with Bruckner's Third and Fourth. As he wrote in the preface to the second edition: "where my opinion has changed it has invariably been for the better, and this I am sure is a greater tribute to the staying power of Nielsen's music than to the inflexibility of my mind. If in crabbed middle age I love it more than in the first flush of youthful enthusiasm, that is because its qualities are even deeper and rounder than I knew. Sibelius has also stood up to this test, which many more spectacular composers have spectacularly failed. It has not been necessary to rewrite more of this book – had it been so, I might have tempered some of the eloquence but would certainly not have lowered one single estimate."

Amen to that.

"A GREAT LADY AND A GREAT ARTIST'

(1953 - 1958)

It makes sense, I think, to consider Robert Simpson's first three string quartets together: they were written in succession, and the composer observed, in a programme note:, "Although they were not consciously designed as a group, they nevertheless seem to fall into a natural sequence." The First Quartet is dedicated to George Enescu, the Second to the Element Quartet, and the Third to Dorothy Hemmings, the violist, whom Ernie Element was wont to describe as "a great lady and a great artist" when he wanted to bum a fag off her, according to Simpson. She and the composer were, in Angela's words, "<u>very</u> good friends." The other members of the original Quartet were Sylvia Cleaver (violin) and Norman Jones (cello). The Quartet split up in 1955 but re-formed the same year, with Kenneth Page and Oliver Brookes taking the place of Cleaver and Jones.

The First Quartet was written in 1952, and is in two movements:1) Allegro moderato, semplice 2) Andante, grave – allegro – tempo 1.

It lasts about 24½ minutes.

Simpson wrote quite a detailed programme for the première: "The idea behind this work is very simple. It is a study in human character in which a person is shown trying (at first unconsciously, then consciously) to achieve or win something of deep human value. The process is expressed by means of two keys, E flat and A, which are at opposite poles, and the music strives to move away from E flat to its real goal, the desirable and apparently remote region of A. The two movements show the two phases in this process – the unconscious or instinctive, and the consciously realised effort." By 1955 he had dropped this in favour of a technical description, although he did describe the coda as "a naive and gentle dance". In the sleeve-note to the first recording he adds: "I remember composing the whole of that coda lying on my stomach on a sunny day in Regents Park, feeling very pleasant. Maybe there's a touch of wistfulness in it, hence the marking "Poco pensoso"."

The first performance was given at the Midland Institute, Birmingham on 30th March 1953, in company with the Mozart C major K465 and Arthur Bliss's Clarinet Quintet.

J.F. Waterhouse (Birmingham Post, 31/3/53) found it "A genuinely impressive piece of musical thinking", while Barbara Jones (Evening Despatch, Birmingham, same date) thought it "Vigorous, cleverly organised, and uses the string ensemble with skill."

The quartet received its first broadcast performance on 24th May 1953, along with the Sibelius "Voces Intimae" and Nielsen's Fourth Quartet. The same programme was given in the London premiere at the Wigmore Hall on 29th June 1953, and a further broadcast on 7th February 1955.

The Times (30/6/53) was favourable but lukewarm: "Both its two movements ... seem a little too long", but "R.C.", writing in the Daily Telegraph on the same date, was far more enthusiastic:

"Anything but banal, it is the composition of a strenuous thinker with abundant contrapuntal resource." Eric Blom (Observer, 5/7/53) again felt the quartet "Overlong for what it has to give, and a little diffuse in style, but contains music of character and much genuine quartet texture." The strangest comments came from M. Montagu-Nathan, writing in The Strad, March 1955: "What a relief to be able to recommend a composition of our early fifties to the notice of progressive amateur quartet parties desirous of ascertaining the reaction of their musical sensibilities, and of their technique, to a modernistic example! For that purpose such a work as Robert Simpson's Quartet No.1, composed in 1951-52 and recorded by the Element Quartet, seems to me to be just the thing. It would be most interesting, and perhaps gratifying, to hear of any response to this challenge." The composer seems to have been equally flummoxed to hear his work described as "modernistic", adding a series of exclamation marks to the quote. The quartet was recorded by the Aeolian Quartet (Emanuel Hurwitz and Raymond Keenlyside (violins), Margaret Major (viola) and Derek Simpson (cello) who were joined by Bernard Walton for the coupling, the Clarinet Quintet of 1968. The disc was issued by Unicorn in 1971, with sleeve notes by Hugh Ottaway. Records and Recording (July 1971) thought it an "impressive early work ... performances ... are very fine indeed." Martin Cooper (Daily Telegraph, undated) found it "Strongly individual music, with a mind as well as a sound of its own" while R.L.(Robert Layton) in Gramophone (August 1971) considered it "A strong work whose musical rewards are lasting."

The quartet was re-recorded for Hyperion in 1990 by the Delmé Quartet (Galina Solodchin and John Trusler (violins), John Underwood (viola) and Jonathan Williams (cello), coupled with the Fourth Quartet.

The Second Quartet followed in 1953. It is in a single movement lasting a little over 15 minutes and, like the First Symphony (and later the Ninth), it is written over a single basic pulse. Simpson wrote in his programme note: "There are three themes. The first is a simple dancing measure heard immediately on first violin. This is fiercely attacked by a tattoo of repeated notes. The third idea is a contrasting cantabile... The essence of the piece is in the attempts of the cheerful tune to recover itself after having run into trouble. At the height of a wild climax it fails, and the end is in darkness."

The premiere was given at the Midland Institute, Birmingham, on 11th June 1954, by the Element Quartet, along with the First Quartet by Wilfred Mellors, and the Fourth by Mary Chandler. J.F. Waterhouse (Birmingham Post, 12/6/54) wrote: "Doctor Simpson's struck me as at once the most originally inventive, the most consistent in style, and (very decidedly) the most assured technically in what it sought to say."

The first broadcast performance was on 28th October 1954, again by the Element, who also played the Beethoven F major Op 18 No 1, and the London premiere on 11th February 1955, when the same ensemble gave all three early quartets in the Great Drawing Room, Arts Council of Great Britain, 4 St James's Square.

The first recording was by the Delmé Quartet, on a Hyperion disc issued in 1989, coupled with the Fifth Quartet.

The Third Quartet was written in 1954, and is in two movements: 1) Con duolo a tenerazza (Adagio) 2) Allegro deciso. It lasts slightly under twenty minutes in performance. As noted above, the first performance was at Arts Council HQ. Simpson wrote in his programme note: "The opening slow movement is set in C major, but grief is its strongest feeling… the Allegro deciso shows a change of temper. In a large sonata form… There is a long coda, driving to an affirmative finish in E major.

J.F. Waterhouse (Birmingham Post, 12/2/55) commented: "With the Third, Doctor Simpson would seem to have established his genius", adding: "Doctor Simpson's quartets are music of the high intellectual imagination, owing nothing whatever to current fashions, and uniting head and heart to a degree most rare in our time. On their progressive evidence, I will lay a wager that well within ten years their composer will be recognised as one of the finest and most truly original creative artists of his generation." The Times (Anon, 12/2/55) found the works as a whole "impressive", though with some reservations about the Third. The first broadcast was on 7th April 1955, with the Mozart Divertimento K136.

The re-formed Element Quartet gave their first recital at the Midland Institute on 23rd April 1955 – Simpson's Third, Mozart's C major K465 and Schubert's "Death and the Maiden" quartet. A review by Mosco Carner (Time and Tide, 19/2/55) which opined "Even without the composer's explanatory notes the listener gained the clear impression of a triptych, the central theme of which could be summed up as Conflict – Attempt at Reconciliation – Failure and Relinquishment." drew a bewildered comment from Simpson in the form of two exclamation and two question marks. He also scrawled "who played 'em?" in the margin, Carner having failed to name the quartet.

Even J.F. Waterhouse (Birmingham Post, 25/4/55), one of Simpson's earliest champions, drew some metaphorical flak for referring to the Birmingham premiere of the Third as "somewhat inferior" to the previous London one: "No: performance was better, even" growled Simpson in another marginal note. The composer was always fiercely defensive of musicians he admired.

A more serious spat occurred when Donald Mitchell (Musical Times, April 1955) commented at the end of his review: "Doctor Simpson's inspiration, which may yet prove valuable, would doubtless benefit from less critical self-examination during periods of creative activity. His technique is so good that he should forget it, not flourish it." This drew a withering response from Simpson: "Evidently he has his own ideas about the value of perceptive criticism; these prevent him from blundering into it himself. I am most grateful to him for a hint that in future I shall act upon. Henceforth I shall be as self-critical as possible, but not perceptively." This provoked an even more savage comment from fellow composer Kaikhosru Sorabji (evidently no friend of Mitchell's) in a postcard dated 31st May: "Heartiest congratulations on dealing so faithfully with that pompous, pretentious windbag, that dreary prig!"

Like the Second, the Third Quartet had to wait a long time for its first recording, until 1989, when the Delmé recorded it for Hyperion coupled with the Sixth Quartet. Acetate recordings by the Element of the three early quartets, previously in the composer's private collection, were transferred to CD and issued by the Pearl label in 1998.

After Ernie Element's death, in October 1991, Robert Simpson wrote a heartfelt tribute:

"All musicians who worked with Ernest Element agree that he was a great artist. For me he was one of the greatest quartet players, and the quartet that bore his name was, in my view, the finest Britain ever produced. This was never appreciated as widely as it should have been, but I remember with awe some of his performances of Mozart, Haydn and late Beethoven (especially a miraculous Op.132 in Lichfield Cathedral – the Heilige Dankgesang seemed to float marvellously in mid-air, as if no one was playing it). All Ernie really wanted to do was play quartets at home, with friends, not appear in public. In him was a pure and profoundly naive spirit: of all the men I have known he was the most lovable and approachable, and this naturally made him a great teacher. He must have changed many lives in his quiet unassertive way and with his rich humour. I can speak only of my own, and I know it was transformed by his friendship and by his and

Elsie's kindness to me at a difficult time. But most of all I remember what this man showed me without effort – the supreme value of selflessness in art."

Does the "difficult time" refer to Squibs's mental breakdown? After number three, Simpson wrote no further quartets until the 4th, 5th and 6th of 1973-75, modelled on Beethoven's Razumovskys. The Third, however, produced an early offspring in the form of the Allegro Deciso for Strings of 1954, an arrangement (suggested by Walter Goehr) of the second movement, lasting some eleven minutes. The première was given at the Cheltenham Festival (Town Hall) on 11th July 1958, by the Twentieth Century Ensemble conducted by Hans-Hubert Schönzeler, the other works being Carlo Martelli's Serenade, Martinů's Concertino for Piano Trio and Strings, and Hindemith's Four Temperaments.

Dyneley Hussey (Daily Telegraph, 12/7/58) thought it "an assured and mature piece", William Mann (Times, same date) "strikingly individual in effect for all its plainness of language." For Felix Aprahamian (Sunday Times, 13/7/58) it was a "welcome addition to the repertoire, as brisk and assured as its title, maintaining its musical strength and interest from first note to last." Desmond Shawe-Taylor New Statesman, 19/7/58) was, surprisingly, less keen: "The argument holds our interest, but the music is too square-toed to provoke a more enthusiastic response." A review of several new pieces premiered at the Festival by Colin Mason (Guardian, 14/7/58) evidently baffled the composer: "It is twelve minutes of very determined and unrelenting thorough development of three short fragments of theme." The last five words are underscored and adorned by three exclamation marks.

A second performance was given at the Edinburgh Festival the same year (precise date unknown) by the Eric Roberts String Orchestra at Adam House, with Purcell's Fantasia on One Note. "B.O.", in The Scotsman (9/9/58) considered it "An impulsive, gusty piece that strides along filling its lungs with keen fresh air."

The Allegro Deciso has been performed several times under Matthew Taylor's baton, notably at a MANA (Musicians Against Nuclear Arms) concert at Blackheath Halls on 7th March 2001 and also at a concert in St John's Smith Square on 29th January 2002, which also saw the London premiere of the Variations and Fugue on a Theme of J.S. Bach, but still awaits a recording.*

---

*　*The Allegro Deciso has now been recorded on the SOMM label, along with arrangements for string orchestra by David Matthews of the quartets by Walton and Arnold. The St Pauls Orchestra is conducted by Ben Palmer.*

In 1956 Robert Simpson participated, in a small way, in the first of Gerard Hoffnung's comical concerts, the Hoffnung Music Festival Concert, held at the Royal Festival Hall on 13th November. Simpson and other members of the BBC Music Division (Harry Croft-Jackson, George Willoughby and Desmond Orland) adorned the Andante of Haydn's 94th ("Surprise") Symphony by blowing into cider and stone hot-water bottles, in an arrangement by Donald Swann, conducted by Laurence Leonard. No doubt Simpson would have got on well with Hoffnung, with their shared pacifist and anti-nuclear views, and very much musicians' sense of humour. Hoffnung organised only two further Festivals before his premature death (the Interplanetary and the Astronomical): I still find them hilariously funny, and can thoroughly recommend the EMI recordings.

Robert Simpson's Second Symphony was composed in 1955-56. It is dedicated to Anthony Bernard, conductor of the London Chamber Orchestra, and Mary Bernard, and is, not surprisingly, written for a smaller orchestra than the First: the same size as late Haydn or early Beethoven although, as Simpson once remarked, "I can make quite a lot of noise with a small orchestra!" It is in three movements: 1) Allegro grazioso 2) Largo cantabile 3) Non troppo allegro, ma con brio. It lasts slightly over twenty-eight minutes in performance. Simpson's programme note describes the processes thus: "The symphony is in the key of B minor – major, with G and E flat playing crucial intermediate roles; in the first movement, which begins actively but quietly, the first stage culminates in E flat and the eventual climax is in G, before the music subsides into its shadowy B minor. The slow movement, a set of variations on an unharmonised viola theme, is entirely dominated by the keys of E flat and G, the theme itself swinging slowly from one tonality to the other, so that each variation does the same. The middle variations are all pianissimo, a kind of still heart to this sometimes disturbed piece. Except for the gentle little coda at the end, the whole movement, beside being variations, is a palindrome, so the oscillation between the keys is reversed halfway through. The energetic stamping finale restores the original tonic, with the first stage running into E flat and the recapitulation occurring in G. An eventful coda is needed to bring back G major; when this is effected the movement finishes abruptly with no more ado." The symphony received its first performance at the Cheltenham Festival on 16th July 1957, played by the Hallé Orchestra under Sir John Barbirolli, in the Town Hall. The other works in the programme were Walton's Johannesburg Festival Overture, Mendelssohn's Fourth ("Italian") Symphony, and three pieces by Chabrier: Marche Joyeuse, Habanera, and Rhapsody (Espana). Hugh Ottaway, who later contributed an article on Nielsen and an afterward 'Prospect and Perspective' to the symposium The Symphony, published an article in The Listener on Simpson's oeuvre to date to mark the broadcast of the first performance, headed Humanism and Tonality, in which he quoted a sentence from Constant Lambert's Music Ho!, written in 1934, but as apt in 1957 and today as it was then: "The glamour of the anarchist and the mystery of the sphinx have begun to pall, and we are faced with the unenviable task of making constructive effort and plain statement appear interesting."

J.F. Waterhouse (Birmingham Post, 12/7/57) found in the slow movement "a rare, serene beauty", but the other movements had "so tough, eruptive a texture that the ear had great difficulty in apprehending and keeping pace with their arguments."

Peter Heyworth (Observer, 21/7/57): "Robert Simpson is clearly a symphonist by nature ... (his) traditionalism is essentially active and creative", although he didn't care for the last movement as much as the other two. Anthony Milner (Musical Times, September 1957) felt it "a truly stirring and exciting experience which, it is to be hoped, we will be able to hear again soon."

Colin Mason (Spectator, 26/7/57) found the work "very ambitious in conception ... highly charged with Nordic intensity ... very ably written, except for some monotony in Simpson's orchestration." Mosco Carner (Time and Tide, 27/7/57) commented: "Simpson's symphony is closely reasoned, its discourse has strength, cogency and a clear sense of direction." He qualified this by saying that invention in the finale "did not seem to me to reach quite the same level as the two preceding movements." An amusing example of how the same work may strike two listeners quite differently: "A.K.H." (Liverpool Post, 17/7/57) found it "a symphony by one of our angry young men" while Dyneley Hussey (Listener, 27/7/57) flatly contradicted this: "Yet austere and somewhat grim though it is, Simpson's Second Symphony is neither pessimistic nor ill-tempered. It is eminently serious, and for that we may be grateful in a world of angry young men and frivolous entertainment."

The sourest review was that by Noel Goodwin (Truth, 26/7/57) who grumbled: "It suffers ... from insufficiently memorable thematic material to sustain his argument and from an oratorical over-insistence of repeated fragments and emphasised rhythms, tiresomely hammered home." I hope the poor man took a powder. The first broadcast came on 15th September 1957, with the dedicatee, Anthony Bernard, conducting the London Chamber Orchestra. Also in the programme were Mozart's Serenade in D K320, the Clarinet Concerto in F minor op.5 by Bernard Crusell, and Dvořák's Nocturne in B. It was broadcast again on 31st August 1958, with the BBC Scottish Symphony Orchestra conducted by Colin Davis, in the company of Douglas Lilburn's Festival Overture and Hindemith's Music for Brass and Strings.

The Second returned to Cheltenham Town Hall on 4th July 1962, played this time by the City of Birmingham Symphony Orchestra under Hugo Rignold. The concert also included Berg's Violin Concerto (Ralph Holmes, soloist) and Kodály's Symphony in C. Wilfred Mellers (New Statesman, 20/7/62) had reservations, but considered that "it remains gripping and intensely dramatic." Noel Goodwin (Daily Express, 5/7/62) observed "He puts tradition to new creative purpose", while W.A. Chislett (Oxford Mail, 5/7/62) thought: "Unlike many composers today, Dr Simpson is able and willing to think in terms of long phrases, and he says what he has to say in very agreeable terms." The Second has turned out to be the most frequently performed of Simpson's symphonies, and I will not mention every airing here, only those of particular note. In 1967, the Prague Chamber Orchestra visited England. The composer takes up the story: "When I first heard that the Prague Chamber Orchestra were going to play my Second Symphony without a conductor, I must confess to a certain apprehension (although I ought not to have felt this, after the experience of hearing the New Philharmonia play it for me while I stood in front of them.) But when I heard those remarkable Czechs rehearsing it in the Birmingham studios I was amazed. It was like a string quartet." He went on to praise the leader in particular. "He proved highly sensitive and full of understanding of the music. After the recording, he said simply "Are you really satisfied? If not we'll do it all again – and we won't want any more money." Musicians like that are worth more than we poor composers can say."

The composer conducted his own Second Symphony at St Paul's Church, Birmingham, on 23rd September 1968, along with Beethoven's Eroica and Mozart's 23rd Symphony.

The United States première came on 10th November 1968, when Simpson's old friend Harry Newstone conducted the Sacramento Symphony Orchestra. Also in the programme were Berwald's Overture, Estralla de Soria and Chopin's Second Piano Concerto. Richard Simon (Sacramento Union, 11/11/68) thought it "a strikingly original work", while the Sacramento Bee (!) of the same date found it "a work of commanding vigour and eloquence." The Nord Deutscher Rundfunks Orchestra played the Second with Hans Schmidt-Isserstedt, although I have no date for this concert.

Jascha Horenstein conducted the Second with the New Philharmonia along with Simpson's Entr'acte from the incidental music to The Pretenders and Nielsen's Fifth Symphony in a concert broadcast on 18th April 1971, and again with the Bournemouth SO, in a concert also featuring Beethoven's Leonora No.2 overture and Schumann's Third (Rhenish) Symphony broadcast on 30th June 1971. On 1st November 1984 the Second Symphony was played at the Royal Festival Hall by the London

Philharmonic under Vernon Handley. The other works in the programme were Bax's Cortege Concertante for Three Woodwinds and Orchestra, and John McCabe's Second Piano Concerto, with the composer as soloist. Simpson gave a preconcert talk about his symphony, and the concert was one in a series of six devoted to works written between 1925 and 1975 under the collective title of the Great British Music Festival, funded by the Greater London Council.

On 14th October 1989 the Thames Sinfonia, conducted by Matthew Taylor, played the Second Symphony at St James Piccadilly, along with Beethoven's Prometheus Overture and the Fifth ("Emperor") Piano Concerto with Raymond Clarke as soloist. The Lyrita company proposed recording the First and Second Symphonies in the early 1980s; the composer was none too happy, feeling that he would rather have had some of his later music recorded – plus, of course, the First had already been recorded once. The plan was dropped in 1983. The Second finally appeared on record in 1992 in Hyperion's series, with Vernon Handley conducting the Bournemouth Symphony Orchestra, coupled with the Fourth Symphony.

1956, the year in which Robert Simpson completed his Second Symphony, was also the year in which he met Angela Musgrave, who was, twenty-five years later, to become the composer's second wife. Angela Mary Musgrave was born in Putney on 24th February 1933. Upon the outbreak of hostilities, the family moved to Cranleigh, to avoid the expected bombing of London. Her mother, Ethel May (usually known as Doris – calling people by other than their given names was a common practice among that generation) was originally a model and married three times. Percy Eric Musgrave, father of Angela and her set designer and photographer brother Peter, was her second husband. His family owned a wholesale fish business in Billingsgate. During the war he was an Army Paymaster, with the rank of Major, and left Doris for another woman. He subsequently became director of a financial advice company which was not a success – he was bankrupted, and committed suicide in about 1950, after which Doris remarried. As Angela says, "I hardly knew my father, and I can't tell you much about my mother!" She attended Putney High School and, later, St Catherine's, a private school in Bramley. She freely admits "I was a bad pupil", only interested in music and literature. Although she had wanted to study the former, she had to earn an income, and took a series of secretarial jobs while living in London bedsits. In 1955, she joined the BBC, working in Central Operations, which dealt with foreign reports, including those of Alistair Cooke. It was a year before she was allowed to apply for another vacancy. The job of secretary to Peter Crossley-Holland (Third Programme Music Organiser) was advertised – she applied but was unsuccessful, the post going to the existing incumbent (although she got a good testimonial).

Luckily, Bob's secretary (he was by then Assistant Third Programme Music Organiser) went on maternity leave, and she was appointed Production Assistant, acting as his secretary for the next twenty-five years.

She greatly enjoyed the job, with gave the opportunity to hear very various musical programmes, until resigning in 1980. She had come to feel that it was time for a change, and decided to train as a speech therapist, first having to take the A levels she had not had the opportunity to sit in her youth.

Robert Simpson's next work was the Canzona for Brass (orchestral, not brass band) written in 1958. This short work (a little over five minutes) is dedicated to David Cox and John Manduell, two BBC colleagues who later contributed to Simpson's symposium "The Symphony" – Cox on Elgar, Vaughan Williams, Bax and Walton, Manduell on Franck, Borodin and Roussel. The Canzona was first performed at a BBC Overseas Service Thursday concert on 27th March 1958 by the Philip Jones Brass Ensemble, along with Beethoven's Three Equali and the Brahms D minor Violin Sonata, played by Manoug Parikian and Lamar Crowson. The first public performance followed on 16th June the same year at Cecil Sharp House – the Wind Music Society conducted by Bryan Fairfax, who also played Constant Lambert's Piano Concerto (soloist, Christopher Wood), Hugo Cole's Octet, and Vaughan Williams's Household Music (from The Wasps)* and the scherzo from the Eighth Symphony. A further performance followed at Westminster Central Hall on 16th May 1959, with an unnamed (presumably ad hoc) Symphony Orchestra again conducted by Fairfax. The programme also included music by Gabrieli, as well as Bruckner's F minor Mass and motet "Ecce Sacerdos Magnus".

The work has been recorded three times:, by Decca, again by RCA in 1977 on a disc called "Jubilant Brass British Music for Symphonic Brass Ensemble", the artists being the Locke Brass Consort conducted by James Stobart; Hyperion recorded it again in 1998 – Corydon Brass Ensemble conducted by Matthew Best, coupled with the motets "Media Morte in Vita Sumus" and "Tempi" and the organ work "Eppur si Muove". Simpson re-used the Canzona as the Entr'acte in his incidental music for Ibsen's play "The Pretenders" (1965).

The next work seems somewhat out of character – Variations and Fugue for Recorder and String Quartet (1959). The recorder is about the last instrument one would associate with Robert Simpson (I might add that some of us still shudder when recalling our siblings' youthful attempts to play English Country Gardens) and he did have some doubts as to whether he would be able to produce a satisfactory piece. It was requested by the

---

*   Billed as such - actually March-past of the Kitchen Utensils from Aristophanic Suite "The Wasps".

recorder virtuoso Carl Dolmetsch, who had earlier tried unsuccessfully to persuade Peter Racine Fricker and Malcolm Arnold to write a work for him. Simpson wrote, on 23rd December 1958: "Many thanks for your letter and the leaflet. Those red letters scared the life out of me – almost. I hope it will be good enough. As so often with me, I find the work is turning out a bit different (in character), more serious than originally intended…" The reference here is to the poster advertising the concert, which was partially printed in red. The dedication is to Horace Dann, in memorium, a BBC colleague. Simpson added: "The dedication is to you, but the music is (or will be) a tribute to one of my dearest friends, who has just died very tragically. But don't worry, it won't be funeral music, or anything like it. I'm now almost two-thirds through the whole thing and I hope to finish it over Xmas. It should be about 12 mins – or maybe a bit longer, even 15. [almost 13 as recorded]. I'm full of trepidation that it shouldn't be good enough for you, but you have moved me at least to take the recorder very seriously as an expressive instrument, even though my invertion should fail to meet your artistry." Simpson wrote again to Dolmetsch on 8th January 1959: "My apologies for having been so long with the enclosed. An attack of 'flu put me right back. I hope the parts are all right and totally legible - I haven't had time to do a proper decent score, and perhaps the pencil one will do for a rough guide. The parts are more accurate and up-to-date than the score, as I made little changes while doing them. I do hope it's all right! Some of it may be pretty difficult, especially the very fast pianissimo fugue that should go like the wind, but at a whisper. Please let me know if there's anything downright impossible, then perhaps we could meet over it when you're next in town. I'm afraid it's turned out as a real quintet – how it would come over with string orchestra I'm not sure. You'd need a pretty good orchestra, I think. However … we shall see. I almost dread hearing it, having done it in such a rush, and with so many things buzzing around my head. I hope it isn't too bad." For the première, Simpson requested some extra tickets for Horace Dann's widow and daughter. "He retired from here about 18 months ago – no finer gentleman ever breathed." (Letter dated 14th January 1959). Dann was also a composer, and the depth of Simpson's regard for him is evident in the programme note: "(his) recent sudden death was grievously felt by all who knew him at the BBC and elsewhere. The music, though serious and even elegiac in part, is by no means funereal, and the Fugue is light in texture, swift in pace."

The first performance took place on 9th February 1959 at the Wigmore Hall, with Carl Dolmetsch and the Martin Quartet. The programme also included Recorder Concertos by Albinoni and Scheibe, Sonatas and Solos by Handel, Purcell, Locatelli and Couperin, and Sammartini's Trio in G. Simpson's work was well received: The Times, 10/2/59 (Anon) "Never heavily funereal, it is nevertheless shot through with the sharpness, and sometimes the bleakness, of sorrow." "D.M." in the Telegraph, same day, found it "Solemn and deeply felt", while for "R.H.", writing in the Musical Times, April 1959, it was "A deeply-felt but not oppressive elegy."

After the premiere, the piece disappeared off the radar for over forty years. The full score had disappeared (it was never published) but the parts survived in the Dolmetsch family archive, and on 5th December 2000 John Turner and the Camerata Ensemble played it at the Royal Northern College of Music. John Turner has also recorded it, on an Olympia disc intriguingly titled "Thirteen Ways of Looking at a Blackbird" released in 2001, and also including music by David Forshaw, Leonard Bernstein, Richard Arnell, David Ellis, Beth Wiseman, Matyas Seiber and Philip Wood.

Undated portrait, probably 1950s

"COMPOSED BY AN ORANG-UTAN WHEN I WASN'T LOOKING"
(1959 - 1965)

Robert Simpson next produced the Violin Concerto, his first work in concerto form, begun 1957 and completed in 1959. It was written for Ernest Element, and is in three movements, the second and third of which are linked: 1) Con ira, ma maestoso 2) Largo 3) Cantando con allegrezza. It lasts about twenty-nine minutes. Simpson wrote an unusually long and detailed programme note, something which he later eschewed, with some observations about the change in the nature of the concerto form during the nineteenth century. "The opening tutti of a Mozart, Beethoven or Brahms concerto gives the soloist something to attack, approach or influence; it makes sure that the ensuing process will be on a high plane, where the soloist's display must be supremely necessary." He contrasts this with "another, easier type of concerto ... in which the orchestra is reduced to being no more than a frame, or background, for the soloist's brilliance. In this type of essentially decorative concerto, the soloist is usually allowed to dominate from the very start..." He continues with an uncharacteristically metaphorical description of his own work. "Imagine a great crowd (the orchestra), angry, turbulent, without direction, confused, yet not wanting in human dignity (Con ira, ma maestoso). Addressing it is an individual who can see clearly the way ahead; he is humane, rational, insistent in varying degrees of intensity, persuasive in his very intensiveness. At first the situation seems irreconcilable. The crowd is unable to see its way out of the key of D, but the enlightened character persists (in many different ways) in speaking of the key of E, where hope and reason lie. After many upheavals and changes of dominance, the first movement ends with the problem unresolved.

"In the second movement (Largo) the process continues ... This time his persuasions are more successful and he gradually rouses the orchestra from its lethargy and, at last, from its fixation on the key of D. A climax is naturally generated; when it dies away, E is fully established and the soloist expresses his calm satisfaction in a long singing passage (molto sereno) over a shifting but sympathetic harmonic background. He has won his fellows over and the music drifts directly into a finale that is quite decidedly in the key of E. At first it strolls and sings contentedly (Cantando con allegrezza) and laughter is never far off ... Then it becomes wild and dance–like, mainly in seven-eight time, and the orchestra breaks out with a fierce excitement very different from its upheavals in the first movement. But the finale is not by any means just a celebration. The earlier struggles are not forgotten and the stride of this movement is intentionally muscular and powerful. Someone once described a certain concerto as being for violin against orchestra; this one could be said to be between violin and orchestra."

The première took place at Birmingham Town Hall on 25th February 1960. Naturally, the soloist was Ernest Element, with the City of Birmingham Symphony Orchestra conducted by Sir Adrian Boult. The other works in the programme were Rossini's Semiramide Overture and the Brahms Fourth Symphony. Reactions were mixed: Donald Mitchell (Daily Telegraph,22/2/60) praised the concerto's "seriousness and integrity". "This new concerto represents his music at its most characteristic … only the laboured and protracted finale…seems to fall below his own high level of achievement."

J.F. Waterhouse (Birmingham Post, 26/2/60) thought that "Of the seven major works by Doctor Simpson so far known to me, this new concerto is certainly the finest, and that also means a great deal." Waterhouse followed this a few days later with an article in which he analysed the concerto in greater depth. "I know of nothing lovelier in contemporary music than the sustained meditation of the slow movement, growing organically out of that wonderful slow canon for muted strings." He did, however, chide Simpson for being "when he writes or broadcasts… sometimes… almost as silly about serialism as are those who would condemn his music as "out of date."" The Musical Times, February 1960, Anon, found that "This novel scheme gives rise to a cogently argued work, with a very beautiful slow movement."

Colin Mason (Guardian, 26/2/60) took a somewhat historicist view, remarking, of "progressive tonality": "This no longer ranks as a very "progressive" idea, and the concerto is strongly conservative in thought and language. Today, in spite of the composer's inventiveness within his chosen limits, it has less claim on our interest.

In other respects, if it is accepted on its own terms, it is an impressive work, though still open to serious objections."

He concluded his review by saying that it was "a work that in spite of its weaknesses contains much attractive music."

The Birmingham premiere was followed by a broadcast performance on 17th November 1960, with the same forces, but with Vaughan Willliams's "Wasps" Overture and Holst's Egdon Heath as companion pieces. 'J.W.' in the Daily Telegraph, (26/11/60) clearly had reservations: "But at a single hearing the formal control which has distinguished him as a symphonist seems relaxed here, while the personality which should be more fully divulged is shadowy. It seriously disappoints by its poor response to the very attractive and promising theme for the finale."

The concerto never received, so far as I know, a further performance, nor was it ever published. It may be that Simpson grew dissatisfied with it at an early stage. In an interview with Lewis Foreman (3rd November 1980) he said that he thought the concerto was "my least satisfactory piece." Asked for an explanation he added: "It's the basic idea behind it – I don't think it works. I don't think I've extracted from the material what is in it. I think it's an entirely unsatisfactory piece … in the case of the fiddle concerto I don't think anything can save it except starting at square one again. And I think that is the only work of mine that I do want to get at." He never did recompose the work, and in a letter to Sally Willison dated 19th August 1989 he was even more scathing: "I've taken out the violin concerto, as this work is now withdrawn, having been composed by an orang utan when I wasn't looking." In the same year, he was approached by Ruggiero Ricci with a view to writing a second concerto. The celebrated violinist had been impressed by the writing for his instrument while listening to a broadcast of the Eighth Quartet. Nothing further was heard from Ricci, and the piece never materialised. Despite the low opinion he came to have of the concerto, Simpson never destroyed the score, and tapes of Element playing it do exist. Having finally heard one, I have to say that, although the composer's later comment seems to me excessively harsh, I feel that the structure is not quite right for the material, and I can understand why he withdrew it; the slow movement is, however, very fine. In 1960 Robert Simpson journeyed to Bolzano, Italy, to attend the 12th International Piano Competition of Ferrucio Busoni; he always greatly admired the Italian-German master. The following year, Simpson and his wife moved to Cedar Cottage, Chearsley, a village in Buckinghamshire some twelve miles from Aylesbury. This was a new house and, as the name suggests, of all-timber construction – the buyer selected their preferred design from a catalogue supplied by the builders, Colt.*

The Third Symphony, completed in 1962, is a further milestone in Simpson's output. It was a Feeny Trust commission, is dedicated to Havergal Brian, and plays for almost thirty-one minutes. The symphony is in two movements: 1) Allegro ma non troppo 2) Adagio. Simpson, in his programme note, states: "Its two-movement form is determined by contention between two tonal centres, B flat and C. The first movement, though it begins with a sustained C, is firmly rooted in B flat. It is a large sonata design, deliberate in pace, dark and massive in nature." "The second movement has an unusual but simple plan. In essence it is a composed accelerando; that is to say, the gradual increase in speed from Adagio to Presto is made, not by asking the conductor to beat faster and faster, but by regulating the pace of the thought

---

* At Lionel Pike's suggestion, and with Angela Simpson's blessing, Matthew Taylor has revised the Violin Concerto, shortening it by some ten minutes. The revision is to be published by Peters, and Martin Anderson intends to record it on his Toccata label.

itself and by relating all the tempi." "The symphony began with a high C that was undermined; now it ends on a low C that is firmly rooted. There is no matter not arising from it." "It is scored for normal orchestra, except that the three flutes are all asked to double with piccolos." In a sense, the Third has a programme, though it only occurred to the composer afterwards. "The second movement of the Third Symphony wasn't composed with anything in mind, but afterwards I recalled

An aerial view of Cedar Cottage, Chearsley, Bucks., Robert Simpson's home from 1961 to 1986.
Note the observatory.

an experience of waking up in the morning and hearing life gradually gather itself together. The little birds singing and so on – the dawn chorus. And a sudden explosive feeling of vitality when I just couldn't lie in bed any longer, I just had to get up."

The first performance was at Birmingham Town Hall on 14th March 1963, by the City of Birmingham Symphony Orchestra under Hugo Rignold. The other works in the programme were Mozart's Symphony K199, Brigg Fair by Delius, and Tchaikovsky's Violin Concerto (Endre Wolff, soloist).

The London première came shortly afterwards, on 10th April 1963 at the Royal Festival Hall, by the same team, but with the Berlioz Roman Carnival Overture, Strauss's Don Juan, and the Brahms Violin Concerto played by

Hendryk Szerying. Reviews of both performances were mostly thoroughly unenthusiastic when not downright dismissive. There even seemed to be some confusion as to the nature of the work: Deryck Cooke, in a Listener article the following year recalled that the symphony was "defiantly praised by one eclectic intellectual critic despite its unfashionable musical language, while one ordinary music-lover of a musical journalist could protest that it was "A long way out – a gala night for the avant-garde."

Tony Loftus (Wolverhampton Express and Star, 15/3/63) thought that "It imposed as severe a test on the listener's imagination as that of the more extreme expressions of avant-garde music … ingeniously worked but hardly worth remembering." Percy Cater (Daily Mail, same date) provides a vivid example of why Simpson had such a low opinion of critics: beside his review, headed "I can't see a rush to play this work" the composer has noted "This gentleman was seen to leave the concert before the symphony". It takes some brass neck to comment on a work that one has not actually heard, but I suppose that's show business. Richard Last (Daily Herald, 11/4/63) at least found it "Freakish but attractive." Not so Noel Goodwin (Daily Express, same date) who groused about "Musical ideas that often sound so stodgy as to produce a kind of numb torpor in the audience … the results sound more artificial to modern ears than the most "advanced" modern music." Ronald Crichton (Financial Times, same date) thought "It is unassuming, there is no lip-service to fashion, but nothing positive to put in its place." For Sydney Edwards (Evening Standard, same date again) it was "So impersonal it might have been taken out of a deep-freeze." Nigel Fortune (Musical Times, May 1963) found it "A disappointing successor to his first two." David Drew (New Statesman and Nation, 26/4/63) took a more thoughtful approach, comparing Simpson's Third with Walton's Second, which had appeared three years earlier. Simpson's was "a platonic exercise, scholarly, logical and sceptical. Ultimately the symphony is a failure for the most honourable reasons – it sets its intellectual sights too high… whereas a less weighty and much more organically defective work like Walton's 2nd Symphony manages to get a little way off the ground." He did however add: "But … Simpson reaffirms a principle that is vital to the continuance of music … to your own inner ear be true." He also noted that the performance seemed "uncertain". Drew's comments brought a furious response from Simpson, who evidently knew Drew, but felt that he had been completely misunderstood (letter dated 26th April): "having read with glassy-eyed fascination your review of No.3, there are a few things that I mustn't let you get away with…" He continued later: "The intellect has a part to play in this, but it is for me a subordinate one, the more so because I've never thought of myself as a formidable intellect; I merely enjoy the sensation of letting a beast loose and then trying to ride him. More often than not, I come a hard cropper, but I can always get on again.

That's why your review reads to me like so much Chinese – it bears no relevance to the processes I experience when I try to compose." He ends the letter: "So – if, as you rather dogmatically say, the work "is a failure", it's for reasons other than you describe. I'll try to improve – but, then I'm always doing that. Dear sir, in reply to your request, you are forgiven – for the time being.

As ever,"

By the time of its next performance – Royal Festival Hall, 18th January 1967, London Philharmonic Orchestra conducted by Charles Groves, along with Haydn's 96th ("Miracle") Symphony and Dvořák's Cello Concerto with Paul Tortelier as soloist, it seems that the Third had improved out of all recognition – or perhaps the presentation had. The Strad (March 1967, Anon) recalled the tentative first performance (a problem with much new music), found this one much better, and considered that Simpson "Openly thinks orchestrally in the best old-fashioned sense." For David Cairns (Financial Times, 19/1/67) it was "impressive", for the anonymous reviewer in the Glasgow Herald, 31/1/67 "A remarkable and very individual symphony." Edward Greenfield (Guardian, 19/1/67) found that "The two-movement form is both ingenious and satisfying … there are not many symphonies by British composers of Simpson's generation to match this in confidence and strength of purpose."

The Times (Anon, same date) also thought the performance "much more polished, clear-cut and dramatic than the earlier ones" and praised the work's "unusual logic". "M.R.C." (Daily Telegraph, also same date) considered that "The work springs from a genuine symphonic vision, shows organic growth and coherence, and moreover, suggests that the composer knew exactly what he wanted to say, and how to say it." Charles Reid (Spectator, 27/1/67) thought that "Simpson clearly has the true symphonist's vision and imaginative span." There had to be one sourpuss, and on this occasion it was Felix Aprahamian (Sunday Times, 22/1/67) for whom the basic material remained "obstinately unmemorable." Groves repeated this triumph at a Prom concert on 22nd August the same year, conducting the Royal Philharmonic Orchestra – Simpson's Third was, somewhat bizarrely, coupled with some Monteverdi madrigals.

Matthew Quinn (Morning Star, 23/8/67) considered that Simpson showed us "What an ass fashion is", adding "Such courage and commitment seem to me to be absent in much music from our new composers, Mr Simpson's work is particularly welcome." I have to report also that Anthony Payne (Times, same date), who has achieved eminence by producing performing versions of Elgar's last unfinished works, found it "a difficult symphony" (Times, 23/8/67).

Better yet was to come for the Third. On 25th May 1970 Jascha Horenstein conducted the London Symphony Orchestra at the Royal Festival Hall in a programme which also included Strauss's Tod und Verklärung, Mendelssohn's Midsummer Night's Dream Overture, and the Mozart D minor Piano Concerto, with Clifford Curzon as soloist. The superlatives continued to fly. Stephen Walsh (Times, 28/5/70) thought that "Horenstein's magnificently sustained performance … left no room for doubt on the vitality and self-sufficiency of Simpson's thought." Gillian Widdecombe (Financial Times, same date) found the music "better than its reputation is broad" and "forceful to the point of strong originality", but then rather strangely ticked off the composer: "His fault as much as ours, for he buries his composition beneath a full-time administrative post in the BBC Music Division." Well, we all have to earn a living, and if Ms Widdecombe knew the secret of making money out of classical music, I've no doubt that Simpson would have been pleased to hear it. Peter Stadlen (Daily Telegraph, 28/5/70) commented: "If, in retrospect, the symphony as a whole seems more impressive than some of its parts, it is thanks to the powerfully-built climax, abandoned with an elegant, almost valedictory gesture."

I quote these comments at some length to illustrate the point that the reviewers of 1963 and those of 1967 and 1970 hardly seem to be referring to the same work, and show the huge difference that the performance can make to the music's reputation and, indeed, to whether it has a future.

Horenstein recorded the symphony with the LSO, and the disc was issued the same year, on the Unicorn label, at mid-price because, rather than lose sound quality by squashing the work onto one side, they preferred to allow a side for each movement.

Connoisseurs of the curious may care to note that the Italian pirate company, Intaglio, issued a double CD set in 1992, with Horenstein's shattering 1970 Prom performance of Bruckner's Eighth Symphony (since issued legitimately on the BBC's own label) and, as filler, a rehearsal of Simpson's Third – only the date is given as 5th May 1966, and the orchestra the Royal Philharmonic. I know of no performance that year – was Horenstein intending to conduct it, but prevented from doing so by illness? It is certainly authentic – the composer's voice is also audible from time to time. It gives an excellent idea of Horenstein's meticulous preparation, and I wonder where on earth Intaglio found it.

The LP record (which features on the sleeve, quite appropriately, the celebrated photograph of the Earth from Apollo 11) also received rave reviews. Burnett James (Hi-fi News, November 1970) found it "A powerful and individual document". "E.G." (Gramophone, September 1970) thought the Third "A fine and powerful symphony… an impressive specimen which fully deserves the sort of close study possible on the gramophone." For "J.McC." (Records and Recording, same month) "It is a work of massive strength... it hardly needs saying that the performance is superb."

The Third was one of Simpson's first works that I was able to get to know thoroughly, and it made (and still makes) in this performance an awesome impression – the climax practically blows your head off. Unicorn reissued their recording on CD some years later, coupled with the Clarinet Quintet (1968), and there is a fine modern recording on Hyperion – Royal Philharmonic Orchestra conducted by Vernon Handley, coupled with the Fifth, and released in 1995.

Considering the enthusiasm of the reception in 1967, it seems strange that it has hardly been heard since. The LSO intended to play it in Ghent, Bucharest, Cluj and Brno during 1970, but sadly this never happened. The only further performance of which I know was the American première by the Oklahoma City Symphony under Ainslee Cox, as long ago as 8th December 1974.

With the London Symphony Orchestra, 1970
(Third Symphony recording)

Jascha Horenstein's stunning 1970 recording

During the five years following the completion of the Third Symphony Robert Simpson produced very little music; in fact, only his incidental music to Ibsen's The Pretenders, in 1965. This was written for a Canadian radio production, first broadcast in 1966, with Simpson's old friend Harry Newstone conducting an unnamed orchestra. The first UK broadcast came on 18th April 1971, of the Entr'acte only. As previously noted, this is actually the Canzona from 1958. The other music consists of a prelude for brass and chorus, fanfares, choruses and Gregorian-like chanting at various strategic points throughout the play, and a single soprano solo. The brooding, mesmeric character of the Canzona is maintained throughout, and is well suited to the play, with its themes of power struggle and martial and other intrigue. The work has not been published, and remains in manuscript.

Did the hostile reception given to the Third during its first performances dishearten the composer for a while? Angela thinks it unlikely, and yet from personal experience those of us who seem indifferent to hostile criticism are not entirely so – after all, who would not prefer a bouquet to a brickbat (whatever that may be)?

"I'M NOT GOING TO DIE – I'VE JUST BOUGHT A NEW PAIR OF TROUSERS!"*
(Havergal Brian's indignant reply when Simpson playfully remarked to his wife "Keep him alive until the Gothic!")

(1966 - 1971)

At any rate, Simpson had plenty else on his plate during those years; as well as his literary work (writing The Essence of Bruckner and editing the two-volume Pelican symposium The Symphony) his full-time job with the BBC included, among many other things, producing Havergal Brian's huge Gothic Symphony. Simpson's previous efforts on behalf of, and during his friendship with Brian, have already been mentioned, and during the sixties and seventies he continued to press for performances of the latter's music. The Musical Times for November 1959 carried an article by him on the later works, to accompany broadcasts of the Eleventh and Twelfth Symphonies. His next priority was to secure the première of the mighty "Gothic" (Symphony No.1 in D minor, an earlier symphony having been broken up and partially lost.) Brian wrote the Gothic between 1919 and 1927. It lasts approximately 100 minutes and is in two parts; part 1 consists of three purely orchestral movements, said to have been inspired in a general way by Goethe's Faust: part 2 is an hour-long setting of the Te Deum. Hearing this, one half-expects the music to be intensely Germanic, but not a bit. Simpson takes up the story in an article published January 1961:

"There were legends about a gigantic Gothic Symphony, vaguely heard of, that had never been performed, and it was not unnaturally assumed that this must be an attempt – of course, laughable – to outblow Strauss and Mahler. Very few people took the trouble to hunt out the score; and even for those who did, one look at the colossal list of resources required – enormous orchestra, four extra brass choirs (bands), quadruple chorus and a children's choir – was enough." Later, he writes: "The Gothic Symphony is in no way romantic, at least not in the usual sense of the word, nor is it "Gothic" in any Victorian sense. It is fantastic and gigantic, not in any egotistical would-be sense, but in reality.

"Anyone who has read the score with real application – and this score is too huge to read easily – has discovered that this is remarkably disciplined music, despite its dimensions. Its dimensions are, in fact, real and necessary for the expression of a mighty thought. Gothic architecture, not the "Gothic" novel, come to mind."

Having got to know this vast work over the years, I would add that not merely is it in no way Teutonic, but that the only other composer with whom it seems to have a certain kinship is Berlioz in his great blockbusters - the Requiem, Te Deum, and Funeral and Triumph Symphony – and, even then, not stylistically but in its daring imaginative scope.

Harty, Beecham, Goossens and Wood had all wanted to perform the Gothic, but could never get the finance. Simpson's article was written as part of a fund-raising exercise to give the work its first hearing, and the performance duly took place on 24th June 1961, with largely amateur forces conducted by Bryan Fairfax, of the Wind Music Society, at Westminster Central Hall. I have never heard this performance and I think one can assume that it left a good deal to be desired in terms of precision, but it was a brave pioneering effort, and the composer was delighted enough to dedicate his next symphony, the Eighteenth, to Fairfax.

A professional performance was the logical next step, but here Simpson came up against the decidedly unsympathetic attitude of the Controller, Sir William Glock. Glock grudgingly agreed that Brian's 90th birthday should be marked by a Prom performance, but even then insisted on programming the Twelfth Symphony, which he believed to be the shortest (in fact, the Twenty-Second is even shorter!). On the Gothic he would not budge, and Simpson, realising that he would get nowhere by himself, persuaded all the senior BBC producers, some of whom had radically different tastes to his own (Hans Keller, for example, was an ardent Schoenbergian), to read the score and give their opinions. All agreed, and said so in writing, that the Gothic should be given a public hearing: Glock capitulated, and the performance took place at the Royal Albert Hall on 30th October 1966, with the BBC Symphony Orchestra, BBC Chorus and Choral Society, augmented by the City of London Choir, Hampstead Choral Society, Emmanuel School Choir and Orpington Junior Singers, the soloists Honor Sheppard (soprano), Shirley Minty (contralto), Ronald Dowd (tenor) and Roger Stalman (bass), conducted by Sir Adrian Boult, in the composer's presence. Brian agreed to slight reductions in the size of the orchestra (four brass bands down to two larger ones) simply for reasons of space. The Hall was packed, and the venerable composer got a tremendous ovation. "You never really knew what he was thinking," said Simpson of Brian, and expanded, in a telephone interview with Stephen Johnson (1990): "Oh, he was thrilled to bits, obviously, but the comic thing was that, at the Boult performance, I was sitting with him in the stalls, and the audience just erupted at the end, it was an enormous reception, I mean everyone stood, there must have been six or seven thousand people in the Hall, and the din was colossal, and I bellowed in his ear, I said "Come on, you've got to come round the back and get on the platform". So he got up, we went round the back, and as soon as the door closed behind us we could hear each other speak, and he said to me "Cor," he said, "it's good to get up on your feet after sitting there all that long time", he said, "it gets you behind the knees". That was his first reaction! And then when I got him onto the platform, I sort of gave him a little push, and he sort of walked on, he didn't know what to do with himself; there was all this terrific row going on, fantastic applause, and he just stood there and scratched his head. And then Adrian came across and put his arm round him and took him in hand, you know, and practically tilted him over to make a bow, and everybody went wild – it was the most moving occasion; he was 90 then." Robert Simpson described this production as his "greatest pride" in his CV for Victor Gollancz. After only being available in pirated form for many years, the Boult Gothic was recently issued legitimately, on the Testament label.

It should not occasion surprise that a number of critics took a "de haut en bas" attitude, in Simpson's words, refusing to accept that the work could be of any interest if it had been neglected for so long. In 1969 Simpson, with John Anderson of CBC, visited Brian at home, and conducted a lengthy interview. This makes fascinating reading, but since it mainly concerns the older composer I have not included it as an appendix – it may be accessed in the archives of the Havergal Brian Society.

In 1972 came the first recording of Brian's music, on the enterprising Unicorn label, produced by Simpson and featuring the Tenth and Twenty-First Symphonies played by the Leicestershire Schools S.O. conducted by James Loughran and Eric Pinkett. Sadly, the composer did not live to see the record released the following year, although he did attend the recording sessions. Simpson wrote a perceptive sleeve-note, part of which I quote: "Its consistency is that of Brian himself. As a person you could take him or leave him – it was all the same to him: so it is with his music. Yet as he communes with himself we sense a profound human sensibility and a courage of altogether unusual depth; as we learn our way into this music it grows more and more significant until we discover that we are face to face with a great composer, and this is the point at which the depths are seen to be unfathomable."

The retirement in 1974 of Sir William Glock, and the appointment of the more sympathetic (or at least less hostile) Robert Ponsonby, opened the way for broadcasts of Brian's remaining unheard symphonies. Of particular note was the Centenary Festival in 1976, with four splendid concerts, three at Alexandra Palace: the New Philharmonia under Harry Newstone playing Brian's Preludio Tragico and Thirteenth Symphony, Strauss's Four Last Songs, Berlioz's Royal Hunt and Storm from The Trojans and Funeral March for the last scene of Hamlet, and Beethoven's Three Equali (24th September). On the 29th Stanley Pope conducted the NPO in Brian's Fifth Symphony (Wine of Summer) with Brian Rayner Cook as soloist, Wagner's Lohengrin Prelude, and Bruckner's Seventh Symphony. The same orchestra, this time with Vernon Handley directing, played Brian's 20th and 26th Symphonies, The Oceanides by Sibelius, and Vaughan Williams's Fifth Symphony on 5th October and, to round off the celebrations, Charles Groves conducted the NPO at the Albert Hall on October 10th, playing Brian's In Memoriam and Part 1 of the Gothic – after the interval came Berlioz's setting of the Marseillaise and his Funeral and Triumph Symphony.

Some hack in the Guardian (25th September), whom one wonders had ever heard a note of Brian's music, attempted limp-wristed mockery:

"FORGET-ME-NOT BY TURNING UP

The late Havergal Brian is said to be England's most neglected composer. He wrote countless symphonies, scarcely any of which he heard, never mind the rest of us, and his advocates project him as a difficult, lonely, not to say Gothic genius. Thus the story so far. For four nights the centenary of his birth is being marked by concerts including some of his previously unplayed works. Fittingly, three are at the forgotten Alexandra Palace. Most people have heard of it, few know where it is. A day before the first concert only about a sixth of the 3,000 tickets had been sold, which was again appropriate. If the concerts were a sell-out how then could Brian keep his reputation as the great neglected? The fewer who hear him, the better the legend. What a pity that the BBC have let the side down by broadcasting the concerts live: 11 o'clock of a Monday morning, VHF only, during next summer's Test series would have been more apt. A reputation like Havergal Brian's requires suitably sensitive treatment."

Tee-hee. Simpson was quick to demolish the would-be joker (letter published 28th September:

"For the sake of those readers who may have been misled by the wisely anonymous attempt at sixth–form wit in the rump of your leading article, it should amiably be remarked that the current Havergal Brian Festival is being mounted not by a fringe group of myth-mongers, but jointly by the BBC, the GLC, and the New Philharmonia Orchestra.

"About a year ago the BBC hired the Great Hall of Alexandra Palace for a recording of Brian's Fourth Symphony, without intending to have an audience. It was suggested to the producer (myself) that there should be an invited audience. After arguing that any such audience would be absurdly outnumbered by the performers, I was finally persuaded. The BBC's ticket unit was informed; it was announced a few times on Radio; the GLC circulated its mailing list and notified the local press. Between three and four thousand people turned up.

"This, together with the fact that Brian's Gothic Symphony had in the past been sold out, was why the responsible bodies were encouraged to mount this festival in Brian's centenary year."

On 25th May 1980 the BBC again mounted the Gothic Symphony at the Royal Albert Hall, with Robert Simpson producing, this time with the London Symphony Orchestra and Chorus (and soloists Jane Manning, Shirley Minty, John Mitchinson and David Thomas) conducted by Ole Schmidt, who had worked with Simpson on the integral set of Nielsen's symphonies. I was able to attend this one, and found it stunning: Schmidt and his team managed to negotiate a fiendishly difficult passage in the Judex Crederis which had momentarily stopped Boult's forces in 1966; the conductor later admitted that he didn't know how they had done it, and that they probably couldn't do it again!

In 1990 the Gothic was commercially recorded by Marco Polo, with the CSR Symphony (Bratislava) and Slovak Philharmonic (and no fewer than seven choirs!) conducted by Ondrej Lenard. Simpson had been a bit miffed not to be invited to the recording sessions (as the man who had twice produced the work before) but was hugely enthusiastic about the result. In the interview with Stephen Johnson already referred to (broadcast by Radio Three prior to the recording being heard), he said: "It's astonishing, really, what they managed to do; marvellous, it's the best performance it's had, certainly." He added later: "Well, right at the end I said to him "What do you think's the best thing you've ever done"; he said "The Gothic". No hesitation, not a moment's thought – "The Gothic."" It would be good to be able to record that Simpson's advocacy secured Brian his rightful place in the repertoire, but this has yet not happened. Of the major companies, EMI recorded four of his symphonies, Lyrita two and Hyperion one, but nothing else for nearly twenty years now. Marco Polo intended a complete cycle of Brian's orchestral output, but this project fizzled out during the 1990s. Live performances remain as rare as hens' teeth. Planned recordings of some of Brian's more approachable pieces by the small independent companies Toccata and Dutton may help tip the scales – let's hope so. In addition, the Gothic was played at the Proms on 17th July 2011 – perhaps the tide has finally turned. (Note; Now recorded by Hyperion)

During 1967 Robert Simpson was appointed an Honorary Fellow of the Royal Astronomical Society and also took part in the construction of an observatory at Winchenden Hill, Long Crendon, in the Chiltern Hills, along with other members of the Aylesbury Astronomical Society, although he modestly described his own role as "holding a few spanners."

The two-volume Pelican symposium The Symphony, edited by Simpson, was published in 1966 (Haydn to Dvořák) and 1967 (Elgar to the present day). The volumes replaced the original Pelican The Symphony, edited by Ralph Hill and first published in 1940. One piece was reprinted from the older book, Humphrey Searle's article on Liszt. Both volumes are dedicated in memoriam to Julius Harrison, who contributed articles on Mendelssohn, Schumann, Brahms and Dvořák. In a letter from Angela Simpson to Nicholas Woods (20/11/95) she comments that Bob had told her that Harrison "knew more about the orchestra than anyone else he knew" and had been a great help to him. Simpson prefaces each volume with a closely-argued introduction: in the first he makes "an attempt to show the origins of symphony and (an attempt) to define its essence." Not an easy task! In volume 2 he says: "Now it is my task to indicate why some admirable composers have not found their way into the scheme of this book, even though they have published works called symphonies. Since some of these works are widely performed, their omission will justly require some sort of apologia for my decisions. I must begin by reassuring my readers that none of these omissions is made with intent to disparage; so far as I am concerned, the matter is one of careful classification. No intelligent bat would take offence at the omission of his species from a book on birds; but he may well feel that his "wings" entitle him to be mentioned, if only to show that he may deserve another book to himself. The title "symphony" is in some respects even looser terminology than "wings" in respect of a bat. To discuss this is valuable, so here goes." I will not attempt to summarise Simpson's arguments; far better to read the introductions, which I have reprinted as appendices 4 and 5. Suffice it to say that Stravinsky, Schoenberg, Hindemith and Britten were all excluded for various reasons. The editor later came to feel that he had been wrong in respect of Hindemith, but stuck to his guns as far as Stravinsky was concerned. Naturally enough, Simpson himself is not included. He rounds off the second introduction by saying "The number of composers that could be dealt with has also been limited by space; here it has been necessary to stop somewhere in our own time. This unfortunately meant the exclusion of gifted figures.

"To mention only some British composers, the symphonies of Malcolm Arnold, Peter Racine Fricker, Daniel Jones, Alan Rawsthorne, Humphrey Searle and William Wordsworth all deserve detailed consideration. The fact that there is still a notable body of music that has had to be crowded out is at least evidence that the idea of composing symphonies is far from dead. But I must leave the reader to speculate upon what he would have included here, or excluded; perhaps he will charitably observe that the two volumes cover a very wide range of music. If anything in them makes him cross, let us hope it will sharpen his enthusiasm as well as his temper."

Simpson contributed one chapter himself, an essay on Rachmaninov, in which he wrote with particular enthusiasm about the First Symphony. The exclusions were bound to annoy the fans of those left out: I well remember a radio reviewer who snarlingly dismissed the "bat v. bird'" argument as "disingenuous" and went on to play an excerpt from Messiaen's sprawling Turangalila "Symphony", an illustration which, I would have thought, confirmed rather than confounded Simpson's point. Stanley Sadie in The Times drew a stinging rebuke from the editor: "Stanley Sadie, in reviewing the Pelican "The Symphony", is so anxious to propagate his own personal views that he totally fails to give the reader any idea of the book's format, what it contains, the kind of contributors it has, etc. etc. This is an example of the worst kind of egotistical criticism, for the points with which he disagrees are confined to the introductions and the first chapter of these two considerable volumes. Did he bother to look any further, I wonder?"

An anonymous reviewer in the Times Educational Supplement (14/7/67) was more favourable: "Even those who think they know their symphony backwards will find much of interest", although he did take issue with Peter Jona Korn's debunking of the then fashionable Charles Ives: "A brash example of contemporary American musicology." Korn thought that Ives was not merely not a great composer, but not even a very good one. His vogue certainly seems to have diminished since the 1960s.

Sir Jack Westrup wrote a long and decidedly nit-picking review of the symposium for Music and Letters. He took exception to most of the contributors (Julius Harrison apart), feeling that the editor had allowed too free a rein. Here, to give a flavour, are a couple of paragraphs:

"The other writers are in the main either dull dogs or clever dogs. The dull dogs tend to write more or less conventional programme notes, enlivened occasionally by traditional generalizations, e.g. on the slow movement of Franck's symphony: "The Parisian academicians spluttered with indignation at the first performance in 1889. No 'real' symphony would employ a cor anglais, protested the reactionaries!" This derives from a passage in D'Indy's 'César Franck'. After the first performance of the symphony in 1889 he asked one of the teachers at the Conservatoire what he thought of the work. The reply was: "Ça, une symphonie? Mais, cher Monsieur, à-t-on jamais vu ecrire du cor anglais dans une symphonie?" This was the opinion of a single individual: there is nothing in D'Indy's account to suggest that others held the same view, though he does mention that most of the orchestra disliked the work and the subscribers did not understand it. Similarly, in the chapter on Elgar we are told of Dent's reference (in an Italian symposium) to "the chevalresque rhetoric which badly covers up his essential vulgarity", but no indication is given of the context in which this remark was made.

"Both here and in his contribution to Adler's 'Handbuch' Dent made the point that 'academic' musicians in England had a horror of Liszt's music, the influence of which he saw in Elgar. His remarks are far less severe than Constant Lambert's in 'Music Ho!': "Much of Elgar's music, through no fault of its own, has for the present generation (i.e. in 1934) an almost intolerable air of smugness, self-assurance and autocratic benevolence". The clever dogs are naturally inclined to show that they are clever. There are perky parentheses which cry aloud for the editor's blue pencil. There are lordly remarks about the world in general. Why do we need formal description?

"The answer is – insecurity, an insecurity which is only partly of our time, inasmuch as it is part of our general artistic crisis, in the course of which we have arrived at a state of bewilderment which makes us welcome anything that replaces rather than explains our waning musical experiences, until we are glad to be told what we ought to feel."

This sounds impressive, once it has been disentangled; but who are 'we'? Elsewhere there is a reference to "our age's collective neurosis", in which apparently Einstein participated when he was unwise enough to say that Tchaikovsky "filled his purely instrumental music... with a programme of feeling". And there are the inevitable epigrams, e.g.: "Only bad composers write chronically good music" – which is too silly to be worth saying. The 'musicologists' and the 'academics' receive the expected attention. "Certain academics, looking everywhere rather than at the music itself... "My dear sir, academics spend their lives looking at music – and listening to it, and performing it. Those mysterious volumes known as 'textbooks' are not spared. We read, on the finale of Tchaikovsky's fourth symphony: "In the textbooks... the movement is described as a 'set of free variations'. What textbooks, and where?"

And so on. Simpson's answer, in a letter dated 31st January 1968, is short and to the point.

"Dear Sir Jack, I have just seen your review of the Pelican book on "The Symphony" and it reminds me that in addition to the categories of clever dogs and dull dogs, there is also another even more common one – the dog in the manger.

Yours sincerely,

Robert Simpson"

The books remain an invaluable "rough guide" to the subject, although it is certainly time for an update, and now Simpson himself could have a chapter.

The Essence of Bruckner, published in 1967 by Victor Gollancz, was evidently the fruit of many years love of, and study of the music. Simpson became acquainted with the composer at an early stage; in a 1991 interview with Simon Cargill he recalled those early years: "You could get scores of the Bruckner Symphonies, but only in the butchered versions. I couldn't afford to buy complete recordings – 16 sides at six bob a time* (30p) – so I got them gradually. When it finished a side in the middle of a movement, I would feverishly read the score to discover what was coming next. That was a marvellous way of coming to read scores."

A recording of the Seventh was played at one of Exploratory Concert Society's events, and once working for the BBC Robert Simpson lost little time in programming Bruckner's work; a broadcast of the Seventh was accompanied by a Listener article on 17th December 1953. In 1959 came a Bruckner Festival at St Pancras Town Hall: Brian Fairfax conducted an ad hoc orchestra and the Goldsmith's Choral Union in the Fifth, Sixth and Eighth Symphonies and the E minor Mass, all comparatively little-known works at the time, with introductory talks by Simpson. In 1963 and 1964 the BBC programmed all ten symphonies (including number 0) at roughly monthly intervals, beginning with the Ninth at the Royal Festival Hall, conducted by Dean Dixon. Simpson's brief article for the Radio Times is, I think, worth quoting in full: "In this country before the war it was difficult to find a music critic, or even a musician, with a good word to say about Bruckner, or, for that matter, about Mahler. Nowadays Mahler has assumed the aspect of a super-Tchaikovsky. The cause of Bruckner has also advanced immeasurably, although the complete absence of sensationalism from his vast symphonies is always likely to protect him from the more dangerous kind of vogue.

"As Tovey said, Bruckner will never show signs of wear; the deep reason for this is that the more closely we study him and the more intimately we understand him through humility and patience, the more does he enhance our own stature by strengthening the mind's fibre. For Bruckner is concerned to compose himself and us – to achieve an expression valid not only for his own times or his own personal problems, but for any time and situation. We may be sure that when he does not succeed, it is not because he is subjectively distraught; it is because an architectural problem has defeated him.

---

*   30p

"Although we can recognise in Bruckner's music many things that could have occurred in no other epoch, he shares with the greater masters, such as Bach and Beethoven, a timeless quality, a certain natural majesty that is very rare, and uncorrupted."

To coincide with the series, Simpson wrote a booklet "Bruckner and the Symphony" (BBC Publications, 3s 6d). A sympathetic but anonymous review in Music and Musicians, December 1963, reveals a close kinship with Simpson's view. "The time has long passed when Mahler and Bruckner were automatically paired off as a couple of colossal bores. How they ever came to be linked together in the first place is one of those quirks of the English mind that defies explanation, but even so late as 1955 Messrs Dent could still publish a combined Bruckner and Mahler volume in their "Master Musicians" series and get away with it. Since then Mahler has crested a wave of popular acclaim and has been recognised as a composer of genius in his own right, as well as a seminal force in the development of music in our century. Bruckner, on the other hand, has made slower progress along the path of misunderstanding or indifference to wider

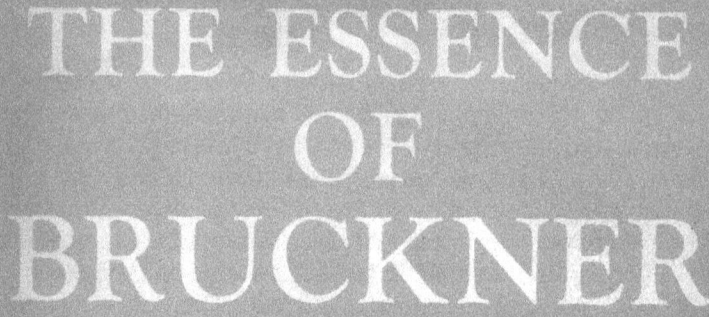

The front cover of Simpson's definitive Bruckner study, published 1967

recognition." He ends his review: "Here are all the resources of late-Romantic harmony put to the service of an essential simplicity of purpose and effect. It is not music for the temperamentally impatient, but even Stravinsky, who finds the overall pace of Bruckner too slow, could find it in his heart to praise the Adagio of the Ninth Symphony. Bruckner's musical imagination was conditioned by the countryside of upper Austria, which he loved, by the unhurried rhythm of rural life and by the solemn splendour of Baroque churches and their ceremonial. It is his gentle experience of this which he invites us to share; that is all."

Well, perhaps not all! Simpson's full-length book was published by Victor Gollancz, with whom he got on well. He was required to complete a sort of CV for the publishers, and could not resist a joke: to the question "When and what did you first start writing?" he replied: "To Father Xmas, at the age of 4". Asked to give the names of people whose advance opinions about the book might help it find a larger audience, he suggested Deryck Cooke, Sir John Barbirolli, Sir Adrian Boult, Rudolf Kempe, Eugene Ormandy and Otto Klemperer, adding that, although he had met Kempe and Klemperer, he didn't know them well.

The Essence of Bruckner is sub-titled, on the dust-jacket, "An examination of Anton Bruckner's musical mind, by way of his music, and an analysis of the nine great symphonies" below a rather endearing silhouette of Bruckner conducting by Otto Bohler. On the title page it is more shortly described as "An essay towards the understanding of his music." The dedication is to Jascha Horenstein "who interprets Bruckner with love and authority." There is a preface, a first chapter called "Emergence", which discusses Bruckner's background, his early music and later choral works and his sole mature piece of chamber music, the String Quintet. The nine numbered symphonies get a chapter each, followed by a final chapter, "Reflections". In the preface, the author states: "This book attempts to consider Bruckner through the ears of a composer; I am no musicologist, nor biographer, nor (in the common meaning of the term) critic. It is my belief that the inner processes of music reveal themselves most readily to another sympathetic composer, and since Bruckner's music has moved and fascinated me for some twenty-five years, I feel at last able to try to describe some of the things I have found in it." Nor can he resist a side-swipe at the critics. "Now that the "climate" has changed (in other words, now that all the old journalists are dead or retired, and new ones have taken over with different views), the risk is no longer serious and the number of Bruckner performances is rapidly increasing. We can only hope that the present incumbents will have long and preferably silent lives."

I will quote some of his keener observations from "Reflections": "...the religious man will say that the infidel who is profoundly moved by Bruckner is touched by religious instincts he is unprepared to admit, while the heretic will reply that the other is placing a religious or mystical interpretation on matters that originate elsewhere. I have already indicated which side I am on. Ignoring my own sympathies, it seems to me an incontrovertible fact that neither side is able to prove to the other that it derives the deeper and more satisfactory experience from the music, and I cannot help wondering how much of this argument would have flourished if nothing had been known about Bruckner's personal life."

"The quality most notable in the search for such an expression is patience, and this is what I think Bruckner's music really defines. In emphasizing the need for patience in both understanding and performing Bruckner, and for pointing out that this quality is indeed one of the chief things his music expresses, I have been accused of a somewhat priggish form of special pleading ("Pecksniffian" was the kindly term employed). But patience is a state of mind, and I doubt if there is any state of mind music cannot express. Love music demands from its hearers a knowledge (and preferably the experience) of what love is. Patience is, if you like, an aspect of love."

"There used to be a legend that Bruckner's symphonies were not only very long but were scored for a Götterdämmerung-sized orchestra. In actual fact, he was very slow to absorb Wagner's influence. It was not until the last three symphonies that he brought himself to use Wagner tubas … In his attitude to sonorities Bruckner has more in common with a seventeenth-century master like Giovanni Gabrieli than he has with his own romantic contemporaries." "Bruckner belonged to the romantic era only so far as he happened to live in it…" Simpson was perhaps overoptimistic in assuming that the battle for Bruckner's recognition had been won. Certainly there were more performances, but they were still rare enough for me in my youth to travel to London from Cambridge or Reading specifically to hear the Fifth, Sixth, Eighth and Ninth Symphonies. It is difficult to believe now that the music is securely established in the mainstream repertoire, but at the time of publication there were still plenty of pundits who regarded Bruckner as a long-winded, incompetent, Teutonic dullard. The anonymous reviewer of the book in Musical Events (January 1968) could include the astounding comment: "Is Bruckner really necessary? The affirmative is taken for granted by Doctor Simpson, yet the answer is not so simple." He concludes his review with ineffable pomposity: "This is an illuminating book which doubtless has its several uses." Thanks a bundle. Other reviewers, though they may have had reservations, were more perceptive. The Birmingham Post (Anon, 19/8/67) criticised the short treatment of the church music, but found it "A most sensible and most useful study." William Mann (source and date unknown) considered that "It is a work of real knowledge and affection", although he was critical of Simpson's "scathing" comments on the finale of the Third. Neville Cardus (Guardian, 13/10/67) enthused: "At last a book on Bruckner has been written which gets to the heart of the matter." Deryck Cooke (Musical Times, January 1968): "Here at last we have the authoritative book we have been waiting for… (R.S.'s) claim to present "The Essence of Bruckner" is no idle one." He also found the comments on the Third Symphony harsh, but added "Such readiness to be frank about what the author believes to be Bruckner's weaknesses should give the reader the confidence to accept his conviction of the greatness of Bruckner's music." Desmond Shawe-Taylor thought it "Required reading for all serious students." Jack Diether (American Record Guide, May 1969) observed: "The already-confirmed Brucknerite should enjoy this book even more than the as-yet predominantly curious or uncertain." Simpson already held the Kilenyi Bruckner Medal of Honor (USA), although I have been unable to find out when this was awarded.

In 1984 Robert Simpson began to revise The Essence of Bruckner. Publication of the revised version was delayed (to the author's annoyance) because the American agents still had some stocks of the first edition, but it was finally issued in 1992, as a Gollancz paperback. The main differences are that the String quintet now has a chapter to itself, while those on the Third and Fourth Symphonies are completely rewritten, for different reasons. To quote the author: "Since this book was written in 1966 the first versions of Bruckner's Third, Fourth and Eighth Symphonies have become available; this has prompted much rewriting. The earlier scores of No. 4 and 8 were referred to in the Appendix to the second edition (1977) and seem to be inferior to Bruckner's final versions… The case of the Third Symphony is completely different; the first version, which came to hand only after the printing of that appendix, made nonsense of everything hitherto written about the work in this book. Not knowing the 1873/74 score and assuming it to be, like the other preliminary versions of the Fourth and Eighth, a relatively diffuse attempt (a guess reinforced by Fritz Oeser's introduction to his edition of the 1877/78 version), I treated the Third as the somewhat bungled transitional work it seemed, an unsatisfactory version in 1878 made worse by a desperate revision in 1889/90. But it turned out that in 1873/4 Bruckner had largely achieved the work and that the later scores were a progressive ruination of it, brought about by loss of confidence and pressure from self-appointed assistants."

So, from being "the weakest of the numbered symphonies", the Third became "a near-masterpiece" – as with Nielsen's Sixth, an illustration of how Simpson was always ready to change his mind in the face of new evidence.

In the case of the Fourth, the new evidence was a particular performance. In the first edition, Simpson had been highly critical of the finale, finding the structure deficient, and being particularly unkind about the lyrical C major theme, calling it a "crackjaw platitude". Hearing a "revelatory performance" under Sergiu Celibidache utterly changed his view. The conductor "has magnificently shown that the whole of this finale is really an Adagio, and by maintaining the slow tempo through the next theme in the major made nonsense of my derisory remarks in the first edition of this book ("an empty cigarette packet picked up in Pompeii"). We are used to hearing this music played at twice its proper tempo!" Celibidache's performance has since been made (legally) available on an EMI disc – during his lifetime the conductor refused to do studio recordings, or allow his live performances to be issued on record – and I cannot recommend it too highly; the coda to the finale is utterly awesome.

Simpson did consider adding an appendix to the book: in a letter to Richard Wigmore of Victor Gollancz (7th August 1991) he said: "I've been thinking about the idea of adding material to the Bruckner book about recordings, etc, and have come to the conclusion that it would be difficult to get through it by the end of this month as I have such a mass of composition to do – two more big works before the end of the year. In any case I'd suppose that the reader who can cope with the analyses in this book will find plenty of hints about interpretation in the course of them…" Bemoaning the lack of a wholly satisfactory recording of the Sixth, he mentions a broadcast performance under Jascha Horenstein: "he instinctively solved all the problems of No. 6 as finely as those in any of the others." Simpson himself had no tape of this broadcast – to anyone who does manage to find one, eternal fame. A review of all available versions in the early 1990s would have been a far larger task than considering the few discs of Nielsen's music which could be bought forty years earlier – although he did send a prompt and courteous reply to me after I had written to him in the late 1960s asking which recordings he would recommend.

Robert Simpson was himself asked to "complete" the finale of Bruckner's Ninth: he declined (although he did travel to Vienna in 1987 to discuss the matter) and his comments in the revised book explain why. "If Bruckner had finished it, it would have been in his own terms, in the language he was conditioned to use in his own time. For later composers or scholars it is a problem of pastiche, since they perforce are conditioned by a different epoch. We may be steeped in Bruckner, but unlike him we are also steeped in everything else that has happened since he lived, including elements that were, fortunately for him, entirely beyond his imagination. If we are to try to put ourselves in Bruckner's shoes, we must go through the unnatural process of ridding ourselves of every kind of prejudice except his – and how can we experience that? I have nothing but admiration for the intrepidity, skill and patience of those who have made the attempt out of dedicated love for the composer. Two Italian musicians, Nicola Samale and Guiseppe Mazzuca, have made a conjectural score; that of the American, William Carragan, has been recorded with the rest of the symphony. These versions, full of intelligent and imaginative ingenuities, will no doubt be widely performed and will be followed by many other experiments. But discussion of them in detail cannot evade the essential fact that even if Bruckner in his last moments had the end of his Ninth Symphony in his mind, it cannot enter ours."

In the revised preface, there are some touching reflections on a conundrum which Simpson often mused about in later life. "On the face of it you would suppose that when for the first time in history the human species is capable of abrupt self-extinction, few people would find the patience for Bruckner. But this very threat has provoked many reactions, not least the vast and growing demand for a stop to the insane accumulation of weapons of mass destruction. The mere existence of such technology and its probable proliferation (despite the apparent end of the 'cold war') evokes a widening call for a halt to this ultimate gamble with human life by people who can no longer claim humanity, whose activities now have terminal implications if violence is not decisively abrogated. Bruckner could be said to typify the pacific strain in humankind, in default of which the race is now certainly doomed. His art could have, and perhaps already has, a special appeal in our time to our urgent need for calm and sanity, for a sense of deep stability in the world, whatever our beliefs, religious or other. He may be said to be a peace movement in himself."

Both versions of the book end with an intensely moving tribute from one master musician to another:

"Yet within this oddly humble and puzzled little man was hidden a majesty which he discovered for himself with infinite patience and a sublime conscientiousness typical of a great artist. His surroundings and he himself have vanished, and many a sparkling and scornful intellect can bewilder and plague him no more. Though there are Hanslicks still with us, they can no longer trouble him. The frothing tide that often threatened his work and his sanity has long drained into crevices in the soft earth, but the hard and jagged rock of his life's achievement is still there. It has survived all seeming odds. The cracks in the stone are honourable scars on its mighty face."

I cannot recommend The Essence of Bruckner too highly, I read it at a time when I was first getting to know the master's ouevre, and it deepened my understanding immeasurably. All Bruckner lovers should have a copy. I cannot resist one more quote, this time regarding the Scherzo of the Sixth Symphony:

"Quiet though much of it is, and delicate, it nevertheless creates a sense of suppressed power. We are out in the night with owls and blown leaves, and the sharp tiny glint of unthinkably alien stars. We sense a soft drumming in the earth. A door flies wide with a flare of light and din; there is the smith and the anvil. At all events, there is no nightmare in this music – only wonder."

Reading descriptive writing of this quality is almost as good as hearing the symphony (although I've no doubt that the author would have disagreed fiercely): and, of course, we do hear the music in our minds at the same time.

With the books behind him, Simpson could now devote more time to his own work, and his next major piece was the Piano Concerto of 1967. The Concerto was commissioned by the Cheltenham Festival at the request of John Ogdon, that most adventurous-minded of virtuosi, whose playing Simpson greatly admired. It was written in three weeks. The work is in a single movement, lasting just under twenty minutes, falling into several sections: a heavy, dissonant opening with massive piano writing, a chorale, a faster section leading to a big climax, then a delicately Haydnesque minuet, and finally a fast and furious finale. The première took place at Cheltenham Town Hall on 14th July 1967, with the City of Birmingham Orchestra conducted by Hugo Rignold. Ogdon was, of course, the soloist, and also in the programme was music by Strauss and Stravinsky and Richard Rodney Bennett. Reactions to the work varied wildly: Noel Goodwin (Daily Express, undated), in a review headed "I fancy it was meant as a joke", wrote: "It sounded like a spoof of all piano concertos both ancient and modern. There were passages when Ogdon battered the piano so hard that I feared for the floorboards. Yet his efforts were drowned out by the orchestra playing even louder. There were other passages when the pianist planted soft chords at long intervals separated by silences not so much pregnant as dormant. The composer was laughing when he took his bow. I think I understand why." Stephen Walsh (Observer, also undated) thought that "The concerto's attractions are real" but felt that the piano writing "leaves little feeling that the solo instrument has been anything but a hindrance to Simpson's way of composition." William Mann (14/7/67, source unknown) said "The concerto is enjoyable – and that's a mot I'm surprised to find juste for such an earnest composer." Edward Greenfield (Guardian, 15/7/67) referred to its "Massiveness" and added: "This is an ambitious piece that presents its ideas with no apology and no inhibitions about having its arguments tightly compressed." A hostile review by Stewart Dean in Country Life, 27th July, referred to the concerto's "inconsistency of style", and Dean pronounced himself "bewildered and disappointed." Simpson was not one to let this go, nor did he. In a letter to the editor he states: "I am not interested in "style", for it is the curse of our time. "What style do you compose in?" is a question that rouses me, amiable fellow that I am, near to the pitch of homicidal mania. The trouble is that critics have never liked being shocked, and still less do they enjoy being shocked by a refusal to be shocking all the time, or to indulge in the easily-achieved narrow "consistency" they seem to admire these days."

Ogdon played the concerto again the same year, with the BSO under Constantin Silvestri. It then languished a long time before the London première; at St John's Smith Square on 6th March 1993, with Raymond Clarke as soloist and Matthew Taylor conducting the Royal Holloway Orchestra, the companion pieces being Borodin's Overture Prince Igor, the Sibelius Impromptu for Strings, and Schumann's Fourth Symphony. There followed something of a revival in the concerto's fortunes; it was played again at a Prom concert on 6th August 1998 by Piers Lane with the BBC Concert Orchestra under Barry Wordsworth, along with Walton's Suite "Henry 5th", Three Mantras by John Foulds, and Elgar's Enigma Variations. Matthew Rye (Telegraph, 7th August) said of the work after the Proms performance that it "combines delicate wit with earthy power in a single-movement span, its formal ingenuities balanced by the integrity with which Simpson shapes his bold and memorable material." Another BBC performance followed on 5th March 2001 (a live broadcast from Maida Vale) with the BBCSO conducted by Grant Llewellyn. Raymond Clarke was again the soloist, and there was a somewhat heterogenous group of other works in the concert: Debussy's La Plus Que Lente, "Entourages" by Robert Keeley, and George Antheil's First Piano Concerto. The second Ogdon performance was issued on CD in the BBC Carlton Classics series, with Alan Rawsthorne's 2nd Piano Concerto and his Concerto for Two Pianos now deleted. One reviewer commented that "Simpson… bends the instrument to his will, making it deliver a sense of Brahmsian cussedness and intransigence."

It has yet to receive a modern recording. The Piano Concerto was the first of Simpson's works which I heard; I found it exhilarating at first hearing, and still do.

1967 also saw the production of a new chamber work by Robert Simpson, his first since the Third Quartet of 1954: the Trio for Clarinet, Cello and Piano. Simpson's sleeve-note is short, so I will quote it in full: "This one-movement work was composed for and dedicated to Bernard Walton, Eileen Croxford and David Parkhouse. It begins with a short slow introduction, leading to an Allegro non troppo. This goes straight into a slow central section, developing long lines of rising and falling melody, eventually becoming static. It is then abruptly interrupted by the final Allegro molto e furioso, in which considerable technical demands are made on all three players. The ending is mysterious, on a soft chord of E flat minor."

The work lasts about twenty-four minutes. The première was given at the Queen Elizabeth Hall on 18th June 1968, not by the dedicatees, but by Gervase de Peyer (clarinet), William Pleeth (cello) and Peter Wallfisch (piano), and the programme also included the Beethoven B flat Trio, Phyllis Tate's Sonata for Clarinet and Cello, and the Brahms A minor Trio. A broadcast performance followed on 2nd January 1969, but as far as I know the piece has not been played since. It is also the only chamber work by Simpson which has yet to be recorded.

In 1968 Robert Simpson produced a major new chamber piece, the Quintet for Clarinet and Strings. It is in a single movement, subdivided as follows: 1) Adagio, non troppo lento 2) Allegro ma non troppo 3) Adagio molto 4) Prestissimo 5) Lento grazioso e tranquillo 6) Allegro molto 7) Andantino 8) Poco meno mosso. Here is the composer's programme note:

"Composed for the Melos Ensemble and dedicated to Gervase de Peyer, this quintet was first performed in New York. It is continuous, and its five sections all grow from the material of the opening, a classical slow introduction. This leads to a quick movement which at once begins development. It is abruptly supplanted by a remote slow movement, Adagio molto. A central scherzo interrupts it (the transitions between the sections are all sudden), this Prestissimo is extended and gives the material new forms. It vanishes, and the next slow section follows; it is a free variant of the earlier slow movement, with more elaborate counterpoint. At length it is invaded by fast music, largely a variant of the scherzo but also developing in the manner of the first Allegro, though faster. It is thus doubly recapitulatory, and eventually gives way to a quiet coda, where the basic material is much simplified.

"Everything in the work is derived from the introduction. It is strictly a quintet – the clarinet is treated as part of the whole, not as a solo instrument."

The work lasts about 34½ minutes in performance. As stated, it was premièred in New York, on 1st November 1968, at the Grace Rainey Rogers Auditorium in the Metropolitan Museum of Art, by the Melos Ensemble, who also played Beethoven's Op.16 for Piano and Winds and Schumann's Piano Quintet Op.44. Peter G. Davis (New York Times, 2/11/68) thought it "A satisfyingly proportioned and charming work, if not one of overpowering originality." The Melos Ensemble gave the British première at the Queen Elizabeth Hall on 26th November 1968.

The Quintet did not have to wait long for a recording: Unicorn released an LP in 1971 which coupled it with the First Quartet. The players on this occasion were Bernard Walton (clarinet) and the Aeolian Quartet. The disc was well received: the anonymous reviewer in Records and Recording (July 1971) said that "The Clarinet Quintet is an exceptionally satisfying work, laid out with power and strength … it is good to have these moving, personal and richly rewarding pieces on record." "R.L." in the Gramophone (August 1971) thought it "a work of very considerable substance and achievement, and shows him at his most searching." The composer's rather dry description gives little idea of the almost hypnotic power of the slow sections, or the ferocious energy of the fast ones. It is worth quoting from Hugh Ottaway's sleeve-note; referring to the endings of both works, he says: "The feeling is different, but in each case the simple tune is candid and direct, quite without undertones of cynicism or parody. In the present musical climate these genuine simplicities are sometimes misunderstood. The ultra-sophisticated would do well to bear in mind Simpson's own comment, which is similarly candid and direct: "If I write a tune, I bloody well mean it!" The Quintet was reissued on CD by Unicorn-Kamchana, coupled with Horenstein's stunning performance of the Third Symphony. It received a second recording on the Hyperion label in 1997, with Thea King (clarinet) and the Delme Quartet, coupled with the Thirteenth String Quartet and the Second String Quintet, Simpson's last completed work.

In 1969 Robert Simpson lent his knowledge and pen to an ultimately ill-fated project by the publishers Fabbri and Partners, a series called The Great Musicians, in which a booklet with an essay about the music was issued containing an LP recording of the work, under the generic slogan "Understand the man and you'll understand the music." A publicity photo showed the conductor Charles Groves with Robert Simpson, both wearing avuncular smiles, with the caption: "Robert Simpson says its a book. Charles Groves says its a record." Simpson handled the issues devoted to Beethoven, and also, presumably, selected the recordings, which included a fine new performance of the "Pastoral" under Groves, and Horenstein's classic 1956 version of the Ninth. Simpson's contributions were of the expected high standard, but the series laboured under certain disadvantages from the outset - the choice of the 10-inch format meant that the longer works, such as the Symphonie Fantastique, had to be split over two discs, and some of the publicity had a decidedly sensational flavour. "Brahms – woman-hater, Tchaikovsky – homosexual" and so on. Private Eye mercilessly lampooned this with epithets of their own, such as "Schubert - a roaring poof" and "Scarlatti – he killed "for kicks"". It has to be said also that some of the recorded performances were not of the highest standard. Still, it was a brave attempt to bring classical music to a wider audience, although I suspect that most buyers were already classical fans.

In 1971 Robert Simpson reached the age of fifty, and the occasion was marked by the issue of a limited-edition book of essays edited by Edward Johnson, and published by Triad Press. There was a foreword by Jascha Horenstein and contributions from Robert Layton, Hans Keller, Hugh Ottaway, Peter Dobson, and Ainslee Cox, who later directed the American première of the Third Symphony. Something new to me, until I read a copy of the booklet kindly supplied by Angela Simpson, is that, by Robert Layton's account, Egon Wellesz said, upon hearing the First Symphony: "Here is a real composer" - Wellesz himself (1885-1974) was also a man of principle: he left Austria following the Anschluss, although as a Gentile he had no compulsion to do so. The Nazis admired his music, and wanted to play it, but he refused permission for all but one work; a string quartet based on Jewish themes! The conductor Erich Kleiber showed similar backbone: begged to return to Germany by, among others, Hermann Goering, he finally agreed to do so, but only on condition that his first concert would be an all-Mendelssohn programme.

In 1971 Simpson also produced "Energy – Symphonic Study for Brass Band", his first work for the medium, although there is the earlier Canzona, for orchestral brass. It was commissioned as the test piece for the 1971 World Championship, and premiered at the Albert Hall on 9th October that year. It is dedicated to "Eric Ball, for old times' sake." It lasts a little under ten minutes. The composer wrote, in The Conductor, October 1971: "So far as Energy is concerned, I don't see why I shouldn't make a few observations on the shape of the piece; it can scarcely do harm, or give advantage, to anybody!

"The first thing to say, I suppose, is that it's as serious a piece as any other I've composed; the only concessions it makes to the brass band medium are entirely concerned with the medium itself, and are concessions only in the sense that one has to make such to whatever medium is being employed (i.e. one has to concede that there are things unsuitable for, say, a string quartet, or the piano, or the orchestra).

"In other words, there is in this piece no attempt to "write down" out of a snobbery which (having been brought up in a brass band) I couldn't feel as some people seem to. If the idiom is a little more popular and easily accessible than some of my nastier pieces, that's intended as a compliment to the brass band movement!

"The title refers to the gradual accumulation of momentum throughout the piece; the whole thing is a huge accelerando in effect, but composed; the continual increase in energy is made, not by asking the conductor to whip it up, but by crowding more and more musical activity into the score as it goes along. The opening chorale and the figure in the first bar that introduces it are thematically the germs of the whole work; you'll find very little that isn't somehow derived from one or other, and sometimes they are brought together."

The actual tempo indications are: 1) Adagio maestoso 2) Andante tranquillo 3) Allegro grazioso 4) Allegro molto 5) Presto vivo. The champions that year were the wonderfully-named GUS (Footwear) Band, conducted by Stanley Boddington. They recorded it for Columbia later. Energy was again the test piece for the Boosey and Hawkes National Brass Band Championships in 1991, and in the same year the Desford Colliery Caterpillar Band under James Watson re-recorded it for Hyperion on their disc of Simpson's complete brass band music.

There followed something of a jeu d'esprit in Simpson's output. On 9th November 1970 Andre Previn, then chief conductor of the London Symphony Orchestra, wrote to the composer: "On 28th March 1972, the LSO and I are giving Sir William Walton a concert to celebrate his 70th birthday. The programme will consist of his new "Improvisation on an Impromptu of Britten", the Viola Concerto with Mr Menuhin as soloist and "Balthasar's Feast".(sic) Of course, Sir William will be there and it will undoubtedly be quite an occasion.

"At the end of the programme I would like to propose the following idea: could you, along with perhaps four or five other major composers, write an approximately one-minute version of the tune "Happy Birthday to You"? We would love to hear these various birthday greetings to Sir William played at the end of the concert as a gesture of affection. Needless to say, if you would be willing to conduct your contribution, that would be even more exciting.

If you can find the time, and if you are willing to participate in this small venture, could you please let me know?"

Simpson duly obliged, and the concert went ahead as planned. To quote Stanley Sadie's review (The Times, 29/2/72): "Three of them (the variations on Happy Birthday) borrowed from Sir William. Malcolm Arnold's used the Popular Song from Façade, in a bright and glossy little piece with a hint of the film studio (not out of place). Façade was also quoted in Nick Maw's mock waltz; though I thought the humour here a shade earnest.

"Richard Rodney Bennett's setting had suitably tinselly textures and warmly swooning strings. I especially liked Thea Musgrave's: an absolutely characteristic piece with real harmonic tensions; and colourful, too. Robert Simpson's, easily the wittiest, started as if it were to be an hour-long symphony jointly composed by Beethoven, Bruckner, Sibelius and Nielsen; but ended promptly, the theme having been symphonically developed and paced to a delicate little motif. Finally, Peter Maxwell Davies hilariously took us from march (Crown Imperial) to foxtrot – a nice resonance of the days when Walton made his name as an enfant terrible."

Martin Cooper (Daily Telegraph, same date) also praised Simpson, "who turned the opening of the first symphony to witty topical use." Previn wrote to him afterwards (letter dated 30th March): "Dear Robert – thank you so much for your Walton birthday piece. It was a fine addition to a quite memorable evening. William was truly pleased and touched by every note of the whole concert. Thought your variation was genuinely witty (and difficult!) and the orchestra was totally captivated by it, as I was." Previn expressed great admiration for Simpson's more serious effusions, and said that he would very much like to conduct one of the symphonies, but nothing ever came of it. The same happened (or rather failed to) with Leonard Slatkin and Herbert Blomstedt – a shame, since the endorsement of any of these high-profile conductors would have been a tremendous boost.

"A NOSE-BLEED IN THE BRAIN"

(1972 - 1976)

1972 was a momentous year for Robert Simpson, during which he completed his Fourth and Fifth Symphonies - a remarkable achievement for a man with a responsible full-time BBC job. He also had a serious illness, from which he fortunately made an almost complete recovery.

The Fourth Symphony was begun in 1970 and completed "after various interruptions" in February 1972. The composer's programme note is a long one, so I will quote it only in part.

"The strongest influence on it is that of Beethoven, and it is a large classical E flat symphony in four movements, even to the extent that its middle movements are in dominant and subdominant keys. The interval of the fourth informs most of the themes, clearly shown in the opening phrase; this interval is also used harmonically, creating at times complex but directly functional sounds. A fourth inverted is a fifth, and another frequent effect is of identical chords placed a fifth (and three or four octaves) apart, so that the upper one sounds like harmonics of the lower; occasionally, whole passages are written thus in parallel. These technical descriptions appear forbidding – but the music is genial and expansive."

The opening Allegro moderato "has a steady pace and is rather transparently scored." To this I would add that, although this gently ruminative piece has been compared to the first movement of Nielsen's Sixth, there is nothing comparable to the rending climax which tears apart the Dane's pastoral idyll, only the occasional muted swell from the orchestra to hint at latent power.

The scherzo (Presto-allegro-presto) is a huge, pounding movement which greatly impressed me at first hearing (Radio Three broadcast): "Like Beethoven on speed driving the wrong way up the M11", as Bob Hill once put it. Simpson's description is more sober: "The main part is in fully developed sonata form and the tempo is that of a typical fast triple-time scherzo. The trio is based on a quotation from the first movement of Haydn's Symphony No. 76 in E flat ... The energy of the scherzo returns – but wholly recomposed; only the subject-matter is the same." The Haydn theme, which Simpson described as "the most innocent thing I'd ever heard. I thought, let's subject it to stress and see what happens." (Guardian interview with Christopher Ford, 23/10/74) does indeed get a fearful battering from the full orchestra, but continues blithely on its way until the return of the scherzo. The slow movement as originally written was an Adagio "in straightforward ternary (ABA) form with two broad melodies." I will deal with the differences between the original and revised versions later.

The finale, Allegro vivace, "is mobile, vigorous, and expansive, starting abruptly in a remote key. Rather more than half of this movement is a strongly animated transformation of the whole first movement which now, far from evaporating, gathers energy for a tumultuous coda that begins with a new theme (still founded on fourths). Elements of the scherzo add fuel to the fire, and with stretchings and flexings of the muscles (that's to say, broadenings and tightenings of phrase-rhythms and harmony) the final climax is generated. The symphony ends in E flat with fierce joy, and a tense rhythmic metamorphosis of the phrase that began the whole work." This finale, in a first-rate performance, has a thrilling momentum, and the final bars should practically blow the roof off.

The work lasts slightly over forty-seven minutes. It was originally dedicated to "my friend and fellow Beethovenian James Loughran."

The première was given at the Free Trade Hall, Manchester, by the Hallé Orchestra under Loughran, on 26th April 1973, the rest of the programme comprising, aptly enough, Beethoven's Prometheus Overture and his Fifth ('Emperor') Piano Concerto, with John Lill as soloist. Simpson was later to describe the performance of his own work "a disaster, best forgotten" (letter to Jim Pattison, 7/11/90). He amplified this in conversation, saying that he had "never sensed such cold hostility from an orchestra." For all that, the Fourth got some very favourable reviews. "M.K." (Daily Telegraph, headed "Beethoven as model") said: "There is much more to this fine work than its influences, it repays close study." Stephen Walsh (Observer, 6/5/73) found it "Huge, Olympian and immensely enjoyable." Joan Chissell (Times, 27/4/73) was more cautious: "Certainly Simpson deserves credit for determination to keep the classical spirit alive." Brian Newbould (Guardian, 28/4/73) thought it "A classical symphony in essence, not incidentals… reassures one at every turn that its composer is in full command of his resources." Most enthusiastic was Desmond Shawe-Taylor (Sunday Times, 29/4/73), who commented: "A remarkable and heartening work to appear at a time when so many composers allow their music to come about through vaguely directed performers' whims, or compose sounds that hover on the brink of silence. Simpson's symphony has bone and muscle." Max Loppert (Financial Times, 4/5/73) preferred the Fifth, premièred shortly after, finding the Fourth "altogether less impressive" and felt that "The emotional world explored seems small in dimension, easy in an ultimately limited sense." Michael Nyman (Listener, 3/5/73) was critical, but called it an "immediately appealing work" and praised its "rugged individualism", adding that it was "not so much Beethovenian as solidly conceived within the Beethoven tradition." He also compared the slow movement's cello solo to Walford

Davies's "Solemn Melody" (which I doubt would have pleased Simpson much) and candidly admitted his own identification with the minimalist school of composition. The London première followed at the Royal Festival Hall on 23rd October 1974, this time with Andrew Davis conducting the BBC Symphony Orchestra, but again with companion works by Beethoven; the second Leonora Overture and the Third Piano Concerto, played by Stephen Bishop.

Again, Simpson was less than enamoured of this performance, to the extent that he wrote to the orchestra's general manager on 30th October. "First, the sight-reading astounded me; it was better than the "finished" performance of the same work by the Halle last year. It was, in fact, so good that I was convinced that here was the basis for a real performance. That was in the first two rehearsals.

"The next rehearsal was, however, another matter; it quickly became apparent that the orchestra, having ascertained that it could play the notes, was not prepared to go much further. After an hour and a half the playing had deteriorated to well below the sight-reading standard and was worsening. Andrew Davis and I both agreed that there was nothing to be gained by continuing, and sent the orchestra home." Later he adds: "It was only Andrew's magnificent conducting that wrung something like a real performance from the orchestra at the concert." He continues: "…I was sad to find that what is potentially as good an orchestra as one could find is no more than a very efficient sight-reading machine. I am sure that this <u>must</u> be due to the amount of sight-reading of the sort of music their principal conductor is mainly interested in, and to his constant insistence on mechanical accuracy, to which his performances frequently testify all too well.* My impression is that this talented orchestra is frozen, cynical, faceless, and that Rudolf Kempe will be a Godsend to them, though I can't say I envy him his task." On the cynical aspect, it may be noted that Davis's youthful appearance sometimes provoked rather childish abuse from players, along the lines of "Isn't it your bedtime yet, sonny?" (*The reference is to Pierre Boulez, chief conductor 1971-1974.)

For all the composer's reservations, the performance was generally well received. Hugh Ottaway (source and date unknown) observed: "The large-scale scherzo and trio is the most daring part of this courageous symphony, for it positively insists that we <u>think</u> of Beethoven and, in the trio, of Haydn too", adding "The slow movement… is a deeply lyrical expression of a kind that the composer has not hitherto permitted himself. I found this made such a strong impression that I soon lost the thread of the finale." Felix Aprahamian (Sunday Times, 27/10/74) was more grudging: "…difficult to discern …a more specifically personal or even national (?) quality in this well-made and often exciting work." Hugo Cole (Guardian) found that "He knows well where he is going and what he is doing" and that the "scherzo… has immense dynamic energy" while considering the slow movement "over-long". Martin Cooper (Daily Telegraph, 24/10/74) praised the work's "coherent thought" and added: "Robert Simpson is unquestionably one of the few [symphonists]". Max Loppert (Financial Times, same date) remained underwhelmed: "Admirable music, difficult to love." Alan Blyth (Times, same date) also found the Fourth "More diffuse, less serious than its successor… it inhabits very much its own world", and found the inner movements the more successful.

Some nine years after composing the symphony, Simpson radically revised the slow movement, quickening the tempo from Adagio to Andante, altering the contours of the opening cello tune, and making the climax hushed rather than forte. The outcome did not please all his admirers; I recall Bob Hill saying he felt the original movement to be one of the best things Simpson had written, to which the composer replied "I think it's better now." A fuller exchange was printed in Tonic, Summer 1982. In a letter headed "Simpson Revisionistes?" Nicholas Woolven wrote:

"As is well known, Bruckner's First Symphony exists in two versions, the earlier of which now has the popular soubriquet "Linz". In RS's book The Essence of Bruckner, he reprimands the later composer for tinkering with the work of the earlier on the grounds that the original "Linz" version continues to be a valid representation of Bruckner's musical thought at the time of its composition.

"I hear that, almost ten years after its composition, RS has completely rewritten the "Linz" slow movement of his Fourth Symphony. Accordingly, I respectfully wonder if RS stands outside the passage of time."

Simpson replied: "Bruckner, it is well known, did most of his late revision of earlier works under pressure from well-intentioned but misguided friends, who encouraged him to shove his music in a disastrously inapt Wagnerian direction. I must assure Mr Woolven that any revisions I undertake will be under no kind of duress, except that of my own artistic conscience. That is not to say that Bruckner's artistic conscience was lacking – but its confusions caused him much externally induced trouble. Even so, he was careful to preserve his original scores "for 50 years' time". Being more fortunate in my friends, I can guarantee that my work is, for better or worse, all my own, and that "original versions" will be prevented from surviving into the week following their revision, let alone for 50 years." The revised version was first performed by the BBC Welsh SO under Bryden Thompson in 1986.

The question remains why Simpson became so dissatisfied with his original slow movement, while he made only minor adjustments to most of his scores, mainly for practical reasons after hearing them premièred, as he did with the other three movements of the Fourth. He did, of course, come to disown the Violin Concerto, but this is from a much earlier period in his career. Stephen Johnson, in his contribution to the Tonic memorial book, provides a clue: "Long pause, then – "It was Arne Skjold Rasmussen..." Pardon? Bob then told me how he had played the tape of the Fourth Symphony, not long after the first performance, to the Danish pianist. The first two movements had met with approval, but then, as the slow movement began, Rasmussen exploded: "No! No! You must not write like Mahler!" Bob didn't exactly say so, but I gather he was deeply wounded. Is that why the original slow movement had to go?" Would Simpson have been so affected by the opinion of even a respected fellow musician, or did it perhaps confirm something he already half-felt, that in this movement he had given a little too much away, emotionally speaking? Having heard both, my own preference is for the original; unlike Rasmussen, I don't find it at all Mahleresque; it seems to me to have more kinship with the Andante malinconico (melancholic temperament) of Nielsen's Second Symphony, with a similar grinding power at the climax. It is perhaps worth noting that in the very fine performance by the BBC SO under Nicholas Kok (a live broadcast on 17th May 2001, which also included Pfitzner's "Palestrina" Preludes and Peter Maxwell Davies's "Prolation" under the general title The Old in the New) the tempo seems to this layman more Adagio than Andante, and I think the music gains as a result. As well as revising the slow movement, Simpson let it be known, in the letter to Jim Pattison already quoted, that "the dedication has been quietly dropped." Did he feel so strongly about the inadequacies of the first performance as to do this? I know of no personal falling-out - in conversation he would always refer affectionately to the conductor as Jimmy - so his reasons remain a mystery.

The only other public performance of the Fourth which I have been able to trace was given by the Kensington Symphony Orchestra under Russell Keable at the Queen Elizabeth Hall on 13th January 1995, which concert also included Walton's overture Portsmouth Point, Keable's "Attend!" and the Shostakovich Second Piano Concerto (Julian Bolton, soloist). Simpson was sent a tape of this performance, and greatly enjoyed it: to quote from his dictated letter: "I found the performance amazingly good, full of vitality and excitement. It is the best string playing I've heard from an amateur orchestra – quite astonishing, especially the accuracy in the high registers." Praising the horn player and principal cellist in the slow movement, he ends: "I thought perhaps the tempo of the finale was almost beyond what was possible but the players rose to it." (27/2/95)

There is an excellent recording, coupled with the Second, which Hyperion released in 1992 – Bournemouth SO under Vernon Handley, with financial assistance from the Rex Foundation – but is it not high time that this friendliest, most approachable and most classical of Robert Simpson's symphonies got a Prom hearing?

There could be no greater contrast than that between Simpson's Fourth Symphony and his Fifth, completed the same year, but written much more quickly. The Fourth is a classical four-movement symphony, predominantly genial in character, although some have found the energy of the finale "aggressive". The Fifth is, to use the composer's own term, a "blockbuster", often extremely dissonant. It was commissioned by the London Symphony Orchestra and is dedicated to them. The composer's programme note is again quite a long one, so I will not quote it in full.

"…this one-movement symphony is divided into sections. At the beginning and the end are weighty fast movements. In the centre is a short scherzino, while on either side of that are canonic slow movements. The soft string chord sustained at the opening of the symphony is basic to the work, structurally and emotionally; it is like that part of you that coldly observes yourself no matter what happens." On another occasion, a seminar in Killelton, Simpson referred to this objective part of the mind as "essential to sanity" and said that the only other music in which he had found such a thing was certain of Havergal Brian's works – the Tenth Symphony springs to mind.

The first section, marked simply Allegro, "is tempestuously disturbed, but it at length starts to break up": the soft chord is heard, then follows Canone 1: Comodo e tranquillo. "The music is quietly reflective (marked grazioso ma non espressivo); the static chord shows a life of its own, utterly removed from emotional or physical stress.

From this quietness a rhythm grows, initiating the brief but aggressive Scherzino; this is the form that used to be known as a "patrol" – essentially a crescendo-diminuendo, like a band approaching, passing and receding.

Then comes Canone 2: Adagio. "The subject is a long crescendo diminuendo and the answer is inverted; this is a canon without note-counterpoint – each voice, when it has finished the subject, sticks to the original note so that the chord shall be built." Last comes the finale: Molto allegro e con fuoco. "A harsh crescendo brings in the fast finale, largely a metamorphosis of the first allegro, plus a long coda. The temper is rough, and the coda drives to a massively resonant climax; then the music, as in the first movement, begins to fragment. At length all that remains is The Chord, and even that fades away note by note, until only the highest C is left." The symphony plays for almost exactly forty minutes.

Robert Simpson had completed the first three sections of his Fifth Symphony when he was taken gravely ill. He and Squibs were visiting Havergal and Hilda Brian in Shoreham-by-Sea. They decided to eat at an Indian restaurant; while there, Bob complained of feeling unwell, and made his way to the gents lavatory, where he collapsed. An ambulance was called, and he was admitted to the local hospital, later being transferred to the Atkinson Morley, Wimbledon, which had a specialist neurology department) and lastly to Stoke Mandeville near his home. He was told that he had suffered a sub-arachnoid haemorrhage (which he described as "a nose-bleed in the brain") and would not be able to move his head for three weeks lest the vessel ruptured again. Rather inconsiderately, of a man recovering from a potentially fatal illness, the LSO management enquired anxiously whether the Fifth would be completed in time for the projected première. It was, and the composer made a full recovery, apart from the permanent loss of his sense of smell. As he said, philosophically: "It could have been much worse; I might have died, been left paralysed, or lost my sight or hearing." If you have to lose a sense, that of smell is clearly the most dispensable: indeed, as the composer observed, there are places where the lack of it can be a positive advantage. At the time of being treated for the emergency, he was also diagnosed with late-onset diabetes – his eyesight had been deteriorating for some time, and he was obliged to buy a special outsized music paper also used by Michael Tippett. Insulin injections greatly improved his vision. The use of oversize paper was suggested by Jack Ludd, who had been working for Michael Tippett, and offered to do the same for Simpson after hearing of his plight.

The première duly took place at the Royal Festival Hall on 3rd May 1973, with the LSO conducted by Andrew Davis. The other works in the concert were the Brahms Tragic Overture and Mozart's last Piano Concerto, K595, with Stephen Bishop as soloist. For once, the first performance was worthy of the music, and superlatives abounded in the reviews. The anonymous Daily Express writer (4/5/73) in a piece headed The Gritty Voice of Today, described it thus: "Quietly mysterious chords open and close this forty-minute symphony… in between the composer takes us through a varied landscape, boisterous, witty and delicate by turns." Edward Greenfield (Guardian, same date) considered that "His structures emerge naturally out of the material, without ever seeming, even in the most ingenious moments, to be working to a forced pattern." "The performance was one of the finest premieres I can remember of a major orchestral work, fearless in its physical impact." Alan Blyth (Times, same date) thought that "Perhaps his Fifth … shows even more strongly than his Fourth that there is life in the old form yet" and again found it "a brilliant performance". Ivon Adams (Evening News, same date) reckoned that it must have been "the loudest symphony played here for some time", but went on to say "But Simpson, whose genius is now coming to be recognised, is such a craftsman, so knowledgeable in his ways round an orchestra, that the excitement never palls." Martin Cooper (Daily Telegraph, 4th May again) wrote: "One day we shall outgrow our present sensationalism and again ask for new music that is both an intellectual structure and also a qualitative comment on human existence. Then, no doubt belatedly, Simpson's stature as a composer of just such music will be fully recognised." "Under Andrew Davis the orchestral playing showed an exceptional virtuosity worthy of the music."

Max Loppert (Financial Times), who hadn't cared for the Fourth much, commented rather prissily that "Both Dr Simpson's programme note and his recent Listener article ... manage the disconcerting feat of outlining the work exactly without characterising it in the least." He went on to assert that "The historians and biographers will one day tell us about the terrible crisis, physical or spiritual, which shocked this work into being" adding: "I feel for the composer of such a work and in my impatience to get to know it more deeply." Sorry to disappoint this caring man, but 1 know of no "terrible crisis" which impelled Simpson to write the Fifth. He was, of course, taken seriously ill three-fifths of the way through and, during the Killelton seminar, remarked of the second canon: "There's a lot of pain in this music", but denied that his condition was a determining factor, saying that he had already decided on the form and character of the canon before the haemorrhage.

Desmond Shawe-Taylor (Sunday Times, 6th May), in a piece headed "Power of Robert Simpson" (a phrase 1 took the liberty of using for the title of this book) also detected "some shattering personal crisis" and observed that the 4th and 5th "compel all but the most rigidly advanced of listeners to take a closer look at this remarkable composer." He also preferred the later work, finding the Fourth "perhaps over-expansive", and found the Fifth "bolder, tougher and more mysterious in substance", once again praising the "grasp and conviction of the performance." Hugh Ottaway (source unknown) found it "Compelling from first to last" and "almost certainly Simpson's biggest achievement so far", also praising the "magnificent performance under Andrew Davis." Only Stephen Walsh (source also untraced) was somewhat more sniffy, calling the symphony "A passably modern (i.e. dissonant) essay in psychological stress, fierce and energetic, perhaps a trifle over-composed."

Few, if any, new works can have received such rave reviews at their first performance; it seems strange, therefore, that the Fifth has had so few airings since, and half of these have been outside the UK.

It was performed in what was then Czechoslovakia in 1975 by the Moravian Philharmonic under Jaromír Nohejl; I quote a translation of the review in Hudebni Rozhledy (Musical Overview) from 20th August:

"The most important event of the next February concert (12/2/75) was the Czechoslovak premiere of the Fifth Symphony by the English composer and writer Robert Simpson, who was present at the concert. The composition, with a suitably deep philosophical sub-text, is divided into five related parts, of which the odd numbered movements are characterised by rhythmic movement and a powerful (or loud, or tense) full orchestra.

"The even numbered are canonically constructed with single instrument solos. The symphony contains a whole string of wonderful compositional and instrumental ideas (especially of a rationalistic character), with especially prominent fortissimo verging on the painful. The aggressive rhythm is, however, somewhat one-sided. The conductor Jaromír Nohejl and the orchestra treated the work with a great deal of care and the demanding woodwind solos (especially the piccolos in the second part) and greatly deserved the enthusiastic response from the public."

Andrew Davis followed his initial triumph with another powerful rendition at the Royal Festival Hall on 29th March 1984, as part of the Great British Music Festival. Davis conducted the Philharmonia, and the remainder of the concert comprised A Song of Summer by Delius and Alan Rawsthorne's Second Piano Concerto with John Ogdon as soloist, returning to public performance after a lengthy mental illness.

The Fifth received its Danish première on 29th November 1984, with the Aarhus Symphony Orchestra conducted by Simpson's old friend Ole Schmidt. It was played at St John's Smith Square by the Young Musicians Symphony Orchestra under James Blair on 14th May 1988, again with the composer present.

Andrew Davis conducted the Fifth a third time at a Prom concert on 9th August 1990 – the BBC Philharmonic preceded the Simpson with Mozart's 36th ("Linz") Symphony and Elgar's Violin Concerto in the arrangement for viola by Lionel Tertis and, rather oddly, followed it with Beethoven's Second Leonora Overture.

Having attended the 1984 performance, I had high hopes of this one, and urged a number of musical friends to attend, much to my later embarrassment. I found the performance formless and gutless, more like a play-through than anything, while the player of the important side-drum part looked as if he would have been more at home in a dance-band, quite failing to make this rattlesnake of the orchestra hiss and spit as it should. Having written to the composer along these lines, I received his own comments in a letter dated 21st October: "That 'performance' of No.5 – I heard a tape of it and wasn't surprised it was like that. Thereby hangs a tale – Faber's, who publish No.9, had been trying to get Drummond to put it in a Prom for its first London performance. He temporised and messed about (he had himself turned it down flat when offered it by the Bournemouth orchestra for the previous season) but eventually told them to send the score to A. Davis. I at once predicted that this lazy and cynical egotist would opt to do the one he'd done twice before rather than learn another. So it was. I then wrote to Andrew quite amiably, wondering if he could possibly reconsider, and have a London première of a better symphony. No reply, nor to a second letter (I have means of knowing he got both!). So I informed them I wouldn't be at the concert, not being able to tolerate that kind of boorish arrogance. It would have been astonishing if he'd taken any trouble over the performance."

To be fair, not everybody took a similarly low opinion: Fellow-composer Patric Standford wrote in a letter dated 15th August:

"Dear Bob,

I must tell you with what immense delight I listened to your 5th Symphony at the Proms. I had not heard it before, and it unfolded as a wonderfully energetic surprise. Its architectural strength and logic I admire and like a fourth division player I derive learning as well as enjoyment from your first division display. Very many good wishes Patric. The Fifth received its US première(s) on 26th and 27th March 2004 by the Concord Orchestra at Concord, Mass., along with the Brahms First Piano Concerto played by Russell Sherman. Finally (to date) it was played at an invitation concert at the Maida Vale Studios by the BBCSO under Reinbert de Leew on 25th November 2005 (broadcast on 9th December the same year), the companion piece being Two Other Movements for Orchestra by Wolfgang Rihm. The Fifth was recorded by the Royal Philharmonic Orchestra conducted by Vernon Handley, coupled with the Third, and released by Hyperion in 1995.

To end this section on the Fifth, I will quote a letter from Patrick Piggott, dated 27th December 1976:

"Dear Bob,

I have now been able to listen several times to your 5th Symphony and I cannot wait until January 12th to tell you about the <u>immense</u> impression it has made on me. It is, quite simply, a masterwork. Though I knew very well the importance of your music I have to confess that I had no idea you could <u>feel</u> like that. And with the feeling goes the very great skill – several great skills: construction, scoring, the unending <u>interest</u> in the detail, and other splendid qualities. I do congratulate you most sincerely and I want to express my gratitude to you for letting me have this tape, to which I shall often listen. In fact, I propose to transfer it to my cassette recorder so that I can sometimes listen to it on headphones in the watches of the night. In this way I shall get to know it even better. And it certainly is a work one must hear often to appreciate to the full, though it hit me for six first go. What puzzles me is why it is not regularly played. What a strange race we are! If you were a Finn or a Czech, your 5th Symphony would be not only regularly performed at home but it would be taken abroad by native orchestras and conductors. I wonder, has the Philharmonic Society ever put on one of your symphonies? I can't remember it happening. I propose to write to the committee to call its attention to this absurd state of affairs.

You are quite right in your own estimation of the symphony as a rather frightening work. It is frightening, but not because it is outré in any way: it alarms because it deals with the universal subconscious, the violence that is somewhere in everybody. In this connection I found the introductory talk very valuable. Your idea of the 'still centre' in all of us, the 'observation platform' from which we see our own behaviour, being symbolised by the initial string chord - it was helpful and very interesting to know about this."

Piggott's remarks regarding the British neglect of their homegrown talents is particularly pertinent, and a theme to which I shall return in the penultimate chapter, Afterword.

Robert Simpson next returned to quartet writing after a nineteen-year break. The Fourth, Fifth and Sixth Quartets must certainly be considered a group: in the words of the composer's note to the published version of all three scores:

"The Fourth, Fifth and Sixth Quartets constitute a close study of Beethoven's three Rasumovsky Quartets, Opus 59; that is to say, the attempt to understand these great works resulted not in a verbal analysis, but in music. The hope is that anyone studying intelligently the musical analogies offered here will find the experience of benefit in approaching and entering Beethoven's masterpieces. To try to describe such analogies in words would defeat the object. Some of them are obvious, of the kind that Brahms would say any fool can see. Others are much less so and reflect subtleties that defy language. They may be perceived only by those with ears to hear them. If these three string quartets enhance understanding of the genius of Beethoven at their own expense, their purpose will have been served."

The project had its origin in a BBC2 TV programme on 7th October 1973 in which Simpson gave an illustrated talk about the Third Rasumovsky. "People asked me after the programme, which seemed to have gone down quite well, why I didn't write a book on the Beethoven quartets, and on the Rasumovskys in particular. But I don't really want to write any more books. Words seemed to be rather an inadequate means of expression. More and more, as I was looking into the Rasumovsky Quartets, which I have known since I was a boy, I felt that somehow I could learn something about composing from them in a positive way, by taking them as models.

"The interesting thing is that while each of my Quartets started off in a way which is obviously similar to the Beethoven, each began to develop along lines of its own, and the nature of the material itself dictated the nature of the work, so that in the end what I produced are not attempts to recapture the moods of Beethoven's quartets – heaven forbid that anyone should attempt to do that! – but I took the Rasumovskys as their starting point, then allowed the music to develop, keeping an eye on the model all the time and seeing the interesting, fascinating, compelling things that can happen to one during this process. And so you find the proportions of the work are much the same as those of the Beethoven. But the material itself is different, therefore producing different results, different developments, different modulations, different key distributions in places, and so, in the end, different works. It is the differences, rather than the similarities, between my Quartets and Beethoven's masterpieces which should shed light on both of us – I hope.

"The Fourth Quartet (1973) is dedicated to Basil Lam. It is in four movements: 1) Allegro 2) Presto 3) Andante sostenuto 4) Assai vivace. It lasts approximately forty-one minutes. The Fifth (1974) is dedicated to Angela Musgrave, and lasts about forty-four minutes. Again it is in four movements: 1) Allegro molto 2) Adagio, sempre semplice 3) Allegretto vivace 4) Prestissimo.

Number 6 (1975) is dedicated to Barry Gavin and lasts a little over thirty-eight minutes. Classical four-movement form again: 1) Adagio – vivacissimo 2) Con moto: grazioso ed intensivo 3) Molto tranquillo – allegro grazioso – tempo 1 4) Molto rapido. The three were premièred in broadcast performances by the Gabrieli Quartet, along with the Beethoven models, on 27th January 1980, 3rd February 1980 and 10th February. After hearing the Fourth, Bayan Northcott (Sunday Telegraph, 3/2/80) wrote: "If, on one level, this amounts to the analysis of music by music, on another it has enabled Simpson to recapture that sustained sense of growth and momentum which so many more note splitting 20th-century composers seem to have lost the feel for", and announced his "keenest anticipation to hear the rest." There were, inevitably, accusations of plagiarism. A propos of this, Malcolm Macdonald asked at the end of a series of broadcast Interviews, 1980. "Can you imagine ever doing the same kind of thing again with a masterwork by another great composer?", to which Simpson ruefully replied: "I doubt it, but I don't know. It's possible but I think if I did it again, I wouldn't declare my guilt, I wouldn't confess. I'd just do it and see whether anybody noticed it." These discussions make fascinating reading:* I would, however, recommend listening thoroughly to the quartets before reading them, playing them in conjunction with the Beethoven models. They were recorded by the Delmé Quartet, coupled with the first three quartets, released by Hyperion in 1990. The recordings were subsidised to the tune of £7000 by an anonymous benefactor. Before completing the quartet cycle, Simpson produced two works of a very different order. The incidental music to Milton's Samson Agonistes was written in 1974 for a production to mark the three-hundredth anniversary of the poet's death. The composer was a great admirer of Milton's verse, and compared the devastating climax in the first movement of Bruckner's Ninth Symphony to a passage from Paradise Lost. The work received its first performance at Chalfont St Giles on 14th November 1974, by the Kneller Hall Brass Players conducted by Anthony Watts. It remains in manuscript.

In 1975 came the motet Media Morte in Vita Sumus. His mental block when it came to word-setting has already been mentioned, and this is one of only two surviving vocal pieces. The title means "In the midst of death we are in life", a reversal of the gloomier Christian dictum. Here is the composer's programme note: "This motet for mixed chorus, brass and timpani was composed for the Aylesbury Choral Society and dedicated to Charles Pope, "a necessary man". The text (the composer's own) is set in a Latin version by David Nightingale. It embodies a simple morality that has nothing to do with religion, and explains itself:-

In semine durat genus

Quae sub oculis hominum agunt homines, haec per saecula manent.

Omnem vitam omnis vita mutat, et sic per saecula.

Mutatia malefica genus tollit.

Nihil recordantur mortui; plurimi in oblivionem evanescent.

Tamen omnis contendere debet recordationem merere.

Sic vivificabit saecula rerum immemoria quae venient.

In vita igitur mors superari potest.

The race continues in the seed.

All perceived human acts endure through the generations.

---

* They are reprinted in full in Robert Simpson, Composer: Essays, Interviews, Recollections (see bibliography).

Among his fellows no man can vanish utterly, not even in death.

All human lives change others, and so through the generations.

Malignant change will kill the race.

The dead remember nothing, and multitudes must be forgotten.

Even so, every man must strive to deserve remembrance.

Thus will he vivify the unremembering generations after him.

So in life can death be overcome.

The motet takes the form of a prelude and fugue, corresponding to the two sections of the text, with a short instrumental interlude between the two."

The work lasts some 14½ minutes in performance. The premiere was given in Aylesbury on 3rd April 1976 by the forces for whom it was written, and was followed by Beethoven's Ninth Symphony – the brass complement is the same. The first London performance came on 7th September 1994, in a late-night Prom concert by the Corydon singers and Orchestra conducted by Matthew Best, in the very suitable company of Bruckner's motet Ecce Sacerdos Magnus and his E minor Mass, and Edmund Rubbra's Veni Creator Spiritus. It was recorded by the same players for Hyperion, coupled with Tempi (Simpson's other motet), the Canzona for Brass, and the sole organ work Eppur si muove, a record issued in 1998. Robert Simpson's next work was also an unusual one; the Quartet for Horn, Violin, Cello and Piano, written in 1975. The composer takes up the story: "This work for horn and piano trio was written for the Music Group of London, who could find nothing for this combination. The first movement is a study in the gradual increase of activity, with a constant pulse underlying everything. The opening is broad and intense, at first seeming something like a fugue, and the first idea is constantly transformed as more and more animation enters the music. At length the tempo is a very fast triple-time – about the same as in a typical Beethoven scherzo. After that, the action eases, and in a quiet coda the final forms of the basic material are heard. Like the first movement, the ensuing variations are in D, based on a theme of great simplicity in the plainest D major. There are four variations of increasing elaboration (a parallel to the increase of activity in the first movement), followed by a tranquil coda containing another variation. In different ways the two movements are cumulative, finally relaxing."

The movements are headed 1) Moto crescente 2) Tema semplice con variazioni, and the quartet plays for some 31½ minutes. As first written, it comprised only the opening movement – the second was added after the première. This took place in Hong Kong, and the first London performance followed at St John's Smith Square on 9th May 1977. The players were (naturally) from the Music Group of London – Alan Civil (horn), Frances Mason (violin), Eileen Croxford (cello) and David Parkhouse (piano). The group also played Ravel's Piano Trio.

Arthur Peacock (Listener, 26/5/77) felt that the first movement was (like some Beethoven) "almost written against the instruments", but that the second had "a serene, elusive beauty. I feel confident that this work will prove to be of permanent value." Edward Greenfield (Guardian, 10/5/77) commented that there were "not many composers in this country who can handle large-scale form with such confidence", while for "R.L.H." (Daily Telegraph, same date) it had "an almost Beethovenian feeling of inevitability and self-generation."

The quartet was recorded by Hyperion and released in 1994, coupled with Simpson's Horn Trio: the players are Richard Watkins (horn), Pauline Lowbury (violin), Caroline Dearnley (cello) and Christopher Green-Armytage (piano).

On 30th December 1976, Robert Simpson wrote a gently ironic letter to Barrie Iliffe, of the Arts Council:

"Dear Barrie

I notice that 1977 will include the twentieth anniversary of the first and last time that the British Council did anything for my music. Don't you think the occasion ought to be celebrated?

Happy New Year to you.

Yours sincerely

Robert Simpson"

The reference is to the grant for the recording of the First Symphony. A lively correspondence ensued, which Simpson wound up on 26th January 1977, with a letter to Richard Lawrence, Arts Council Music Officer:

"My somewhat jocular note to Barrie Iliffe tried to treat with good humour a question that might well have been otherwise dealt with. It was the first time in my life I had approached any official body on behalf of my own music, and I won't repeat the experiment. The responses from both him and you merely confirm my own belief that the only sensible thing a composer can do is to get on with his work without worrying about anything else. I doubt if the negligibility of mine is quite sufficient to warrant the almost ostentatious neglect of the British Council in the last twenty years, and I note that neither of you is tactless or rash enough to comment on this aspect of the matter. Leaving me out of it, I would urge you to review the British Council's sponsorship over this period and see whether or not it is true that comparable neglect has been suffered by other substantial composers who have declined to be either modishly conformist or merely eclectic – Edmund Rubbra, Kenneth Leighton, Arnold Cooke, Franz Reizenstein, Ronald Stevenson, for example. Such composers have only quiet independence and integrity in common."

The dispute had a positive outcome: Simpson's next symphony was commissioned by the London Philharmonic Orchestra with funds provided by the Arts Council, who later sponsored the recording of the Sixth and Seventh, and also contributed to a number of later commissions.

1977, like 1972, was a momentous year for Simpson's symphonic output. The genesis of both the Sixth and Seventh was decidedly unusual. I quote from the composer's programme note for the former:

"Its character is the result of a suggestion by its dedicatee, the distinguished gynaecologist Ian Craft, who proposed a symphony that might be compared to the growth of a living creature from a fertilised germ. Such an idea is so close to the essence of one kind of symphonic music that there is no need for programmatic description; the growth of the music should be enough. Since the creature that made the symphony passes for a member of the species we may as well suppose (and that was Professor Craft's optimistic notion) that its subject is human – but since it was composed without any very clear recollection of the earlier stages it is supposed to depict, it could presumably apply equally to almost any form of life. About halfway through the symphony there is a great upheaval we might liken to a kind of birth, contractions and all, repeated spasms of shortening frequency culminating in a sense of release. So perhaps we might say the creature is born alive and active after a period of gestation – vivaparous rather than oviparous! The laying (or the hatching) of an egg cannot be ruled out entirely, though an egg of such apparent proportions would probably have inconvenienced a brontosaurus." After a technical description, he continues: "After that (the central eruption), we could say, the conscious, mobile individual emerges. It is not as yet fully formed; as an infant it is at first dependent – so the next stage is gentle and exploratory. But there is an accelerating gain in freedom and energy, both physical and mental, and the symphony ends in full vigour – in the prime of life, so to speak, when at length a clear tonality is evolved (D). This pseudo-programme is no more than an account of the music itself. Nielsen acutely remarked that music is "the sound of life"; here is an attempt to take him at his word, without abandoning for illustration's sake the purely musical integrity he valued above all things."

The single-movement work plays for about thirty-one minutes. Simpson refused to accept a fee from Professor Craft, saying later that he didn't mind taking money from large and reprehensible institutions such as the

BBC or the Arts Council, but that a bloke with children to support and a mortgage to pay was another matter. He was, however, persuaded to accept the gift of an engraved silver tankard.

Three years elapsed before the première. Simpson became exasperated by the delay, as his letter of 31st August 1978 to Fiona Grant, Assistant General Manager of the Philharmonia, shows:

"I'm afraid it really won't do. That score has been with the Philharmonia (at its request, with the première in mind) almost a year and a half. I now understand from you that Andrew Davis is "trying to find out 'whether it is something that can be programmed". I assure you it is good enough, and that my reputation does not warrant such circumspection, and doubt if that is his attitude. If the Philharmonia were to fix a date and ask him to conduct it he would be unlikely to refuse. Should this be impossible, I'd be grateful if you'd kindly do more than endeavour to get the score back from him. I shall need it, and might well have been able to secure a performance elsewhere before now."

Davis never did conduct the Sixth, and the premiere was finally given at the Royal Festival Hall on 8th April 1980 by the London Philharmonic Orchestra conducted by Charles Groves. The remainder of the concert comprised three overtures by Dvořák – In Nature's Realm, Carnival and Othello – and Rachmaninov's Second Piano Concerto. Referring to the programme note, Edward Greenfield (Guardian, 9th April) wrote:

"Happily Dr Simpson's metaphors are incidental to his genuinely musical imagination. So after the fragmentary germinal motives at the start, he turns very quickly to a bold tonal melody such as Nielsen might have written. One might even say that another of Dr Simpson's great influences is represented too; he has often acknowledged his debt to Beethoven and here he has in effect written a Pastoral symphony for the 20th century, a view of nature observed not through the eye of the individual but through the microscope."

The performance did not satisfy the composer; in fact he is reputed to have replied, in response to a tape of it, with the single word "no". In the 1980 interview with Lewis Foreman he expands on the reasons:

"RS: Orchestral works hardly ever get enough rehearsal, certainly not the proper kind of rehearsal. The usual kind of thing that happens if you have a new symphony… the last one of mine that was performed for instance – the orchestra saw it for the first time the day before the concert. They read it marvellously well actually. It really was an astonishing achievement in the time, but it still wasn't my symphony. I don't really think how it can be – there's no time for anybody to get inside it, or get the feel of it. Just hanging on for grim death and reading and counting like mad and keeping in or avoiding getting out. And the conductor beating as clearly as he can and helping everybody.

LF: Does it affect the tempo? Especially in fast passages?

RS: Of course. It tends to get cautious. It either gets cautious or it goes too fast because they think they can get over it better that way. Sometimes it's easier to get over a passage by rushing it than by playing every note clearly."

Slightly later, he adds: "I make no criticism of the orchestra or the conductor. It's just that in the time it could not be done." The Sixth fared considerably better when it was recorded for Hyperion by the Royal Liverpool Philharmonic under Vernon Handley, coupled with the Seventh, and released in 1988. Reviews were most enthusiastic. David Fanning (Gramophone, June 1988) called the Sixth "A work of immense inner power", and in the December edition of the same journal it was selected as the Critics' Choice: David Fanning, again: "Boundlessly energetic", Stephen Johnson: "The momentum of a planet in its orbit", Robert Layton "A true symphonist with the breadth of vision and command of architecture so rare in our age."

Despite this, the Sixth has had only two further performances that I can trace. It was played by the Royal Holloway Orchestra conducted by Matthew Taylor at St Johns Smith Square on 22nd March 1996, in the company of Beethoven's Third Leonora Overture. Sadly, the audience was a small one, but included an Alsatian guide dog, who kept quiet during the music, but joined in the applause by barking enthusiastically. Up until then, I had not counted the symphony among my favourites, but this performance changed my mind; the final section, especially, went with terrific verve and precision, a true brother to the finale of Schubert's Ninth. Russell Keable and the Kensington Symphony Orchestra gave the symphony at the Queen Elizabeth Hall on 20th January 1977, along with the Sibelius tone-poem Night Ride and Sunrise, and the Brahms Double Concerto, with Alan Tuckwood (violin) and Joseph Spooner (cello).

"THE END IS C SHARP"
(1977 - 1980)

The origins of the Seventh Symphony from the same year, 1977, could scarcely have been imagined before the mid-twentieth century. The America RCA company were, at that time, issuing a series of recordings of British music, sponsored by Harveys of Bristol, the sherry merchants. Simpson's Second Symphony was selected for recording; these being the days of LPs, the company wanted another symphony of comparable length, and for a similar sized orchestra, to put on side two. The composer was to have conducted: Simpson duly wrote the work, "Then somebody came over from New York and wiped the whole slate clean and it never happened." *(from the 1980 interview with Lewis Foreman).*

For his potential audience, Robert Simpson envisaged "one man sitting in a chair, by himself" and the Seventh is dedicated to Hans and Milein Keller. It is in a single movement, lasting some twenty-eight minutes, and subdivided into four sections: Sostenuto, marcato – Fugato (intensivo) – Adagio – Allegro finale. Simpson's programme note states:

"The slow opening section begins with an assertive unison bass theme; there is sustained inner tension, with moments of stillness. This is not an introduction. After some time it moves into a fast tempo that eventually drives into a high-powered fugato, keeping up a fortissimo for several minutes. This reaches a tense climax that gives way to a new slow phase, marked Adagio, a period of much quiet, with two brief intensifications. At length a muttering rhythm brings about a new Allegro, in which the motives undergo more change; this is a finale, but its end is perhaps unexpected – a fierce storm abates abruptly at its height, scattered fragments vanish, and nothing but a bare mezzopiano C sharp stares us in the face."

As I mentioned in the introduction, the bleakness of this closing "stare-out" drew various comments likening it to a dead planet, or the aftermath of a nuclear holocaust. The composer at first stoutly maintained "The end is C sharp", but later admitted that it might reflect his experiences in the peace movement, coming up against people refusing to accept facts that stared them in the face. It is, I think, the most personal of all his symphonies, and has an intensity, power and scope that belie its modest orchestral strength and relatively brief duration. The composer admitted that the Adagio section touched him more than anything else in his own work.

Following RCA's decision not to go ahead with the recording, the Seventh had to wait even longer than the Sixth for a first performance – seven years, in fact. Stanley Pope wanted to conduct it with the English Chamber

Orchestra, but could not raise the funds. It was finally premièred at the Royal Philharmonic Hall, Liverpool, on 3rd October 1984, with the RLPO conducted by Brian Wright, a keen admirer of Simpson's work who gave a talk at the RSS's 1991 AGM. The concert also included Elgar's Introduction and Allegro, and the Beethoven Violin Concerto, played by Nigel Kennedy. On the whole, reviews were favourable. Neil Tierney (Daily Telegraph, 5/10/84) thought the music "brilliantly structured within its one continuous movement. The harmonic language is rich, the handling of the "classical" orchestra as grand and bold as anything Dr Simpson has ever done. It shows an indisputable mastery of large-scale transitions." Desmond Shawe-Taylor (Sunday Times, 7/10/84) felt that it had much in common with the Eighth, premièred two years earlier, and observed: "Although it has become a critical cliché to detect Northern, even specifically Scandinavian, features in the work of this well-known authority on the work of Carl Nielsen, we cannot help noticing again that the two men are indeed spiritually and technically on a near wavelength. They are both composers for whom the symphony is essentially a struggle, and often a battle of tonalities; and the persistence with which both pursue their schemes, even the wayward charm of their subsidiary passages, together with a liking for string and woodwind passages in rapid conjunct motion – all this declares a natural affinity."

Referring to the classical influence, Gerald Larner (Guardian, 5/10/84) remarked: "The difference is that Simpson, unlike his models, leaves the outcome of the conflict less than absolutely clear. This is probably just as well, since it is difficult to imagine how he would have won through to the conventional triumphant or radiant ending without approaching the clichés he has, miraculously, so far avoided." Paul Griffiths (Times, same date) observed: "Simpson's strictness with his listeners is tolerable only because it comes from a strictness with himself. Possibly he longs to make more of incidental moments, such as in this work a beautiful little chorale for trumpets and low strings, but there is room for expansion only in a brief adagio towards the end, and even this is succeeded by the penance of a ferociously renewed argument that leads to the work's most distressing moments of conflict. For there is that as well: if Simpson's music speaks of anything beyond its stark and dynamized architecture, it speaks of the severest tensions and the most alarming single-mindedness." "Bayan Northcott (Sunday Telegraph, 7/10/84), comparing the Seventh with the Tenth String Quartet, premièred during the same week, wondered if there were actually two composers called Robert Simpson. "I found it disorientating, indeed, to discern, behind the familiar fugal flights and hammerblow rhythms of this doughty defender of traditional techniques against avant-garderie, a vein of musical thinking within hailing distance of serialism and the athematic continuities of an Elliot Carter." I doubt whether

Simpson would have cared much for either comparison: he was, indeed, wont to jokingly threaten to inflict on visitors the complete works of Elliot Carter, which he claimed to have in his study; interesting, all the same, to note how the same work can strike different listeners in utterly different ways. In a letter dated 15th April 1985 to a Mrs Wall, who had requested an item to be raffled as part of a fund-raising effort for the Liverpool Orchestra, Simpson, who enclosed the original score, wrote with disarming modesty: "I don't suppose that it will fetch much money on its own value", adding that it was written with Nielsen's propelling pencil, and also that it would probably need interleaving: "The paper was rather old when I used it, and it's a bit frail."

The Hyperion recording, sponsored by the Arts Council (although their grant did not meet the full cost) followed in 1988 – RLPO conducted by Vernon Handley, coupled with the Sixth. David Fanning (Gramophone, June 1988), who evidently preferred the earlier work, remarked of the Seventh "if (it) is a more cryptic statement this recording brings it into clearer focus than before." Pleased though he was at the first recording of any of his symphonies for eighteen years, and fine though he thought the performances, he was even more affected by the London première at St James's Piccadilly on 24th April 1988, by the Thames Sinfonia conducted by Matthew Taylor, in a concert including Mendelssohn's Hebrides Overture and the Bach E major Violin Concerto, played by Hilary Sturt. Simpson admitted, in a brief introduction to the première of his Eleventh, at Malvern in 1992, that he had been "moved almost to tears" by the extraordinary insight into his deepest thoughts shown by this young conductor and players – the Eleventh was, in fact, written as a sort of "thank-you" present for Matthew Taylor (qv).

Two other performances of note should be mentioned: the United States première took place on 24th May 1999 at the Margaret A. Webb Theater, Los Alamos, California. The Arts Chamber Orchestra of Orange County High School were conducted by Christopher Russell, and the companion pieces were Mozart's Apollo and Hyacinth Overture, two arias from Don Giovanni, and Joseph Klein's Lament.

Equally encouragingly, the Seventh was performed in Russia on 13th March 2003, by the Classical Orchestra of St Petersburg, conducted by Kantorov, in the Shostakovich Palace. Simpson always preferred to use the name Leningrad for the city, and it is perhaps ironic that the Soviet Union's composer laureate should have a palace as a monument. I can well understand why the Russians took to the deeply introspective Seventh: the opening unison sounds momentarily like Shostakovich (the opening of his Eighth Symphony), although it soon pursues a very different path. The later

1970s saw two new quartets, another brass band study, and a four-hand piano sonata added to Simpson's oeuvre.

The Seventh String Quartet was written in 1977. It was requested by (Lady) Susi Jeans, organist, scholar and widow of the celebrated astronomer Sir James Jeans, who wanted a work to celebrate the centenary of her late husband's birth. Funds were supplied by the Arts Council. Simpson clearly relished the astronomical connection; in a letter to Lady Jeans on 28th January 1977 he wrote:

"This is just to say how honoured I am that you asked me to write something for the centenary; afterwards I felt that I had been so hesitant about it that I failed to convey this. It is only that I'm under such pressure most of the time that I have to think pretty hard before risking letting anyone down. Last night, as it happens, someone phoned me to ask for a cello concerto – I just had to turn it down. But I really am looking forward to writing a contemplative piece for string quartet and am certain it could be an impressive programme, with Sir Bernard Lovell and Beethoven to provide the real substance! Another speaker I thought of beside F. Graham Smith was Sir Fred Hoyle; I don't know if you saw the recent television programme about him, but he said that his interest in astronomy was first kindled when as a boy he read Sir James Jeans.

The programme I suggested would then be:

Herschel: Organ Concerto

Yours Truly: New Piece

First Performance

Speech by Lovell, Hoyle or Smith

INTERVAL

Beethoven: Quartet in C sharp minor, Op.131."

No, I had no idea that Herschel (Sir William Herschel, 1732-1822), was also a composer! Simpson's quartet is in a single movement, in three sections: Tranquillo – Vivace – Tempo primo. It plays for a little over nineteen minutes. The première took place at the Jeans's house, Cleveland Lodge, Dorking, in the music room designed by the late astronomer. The players were the Gabrieli Quartet (Simpson's suggestion – they were at the time getting to know his three "Rasumovskys"), and the programme followed the composer's plan, with the addition of Handel's F major Recorder Sonata. The composer wrote in his programme note:

"The quartet is in one movement and D is its tonal centre. Two elements are especially important: 1) the interval of the perfect fifth and 2) a rising (occasionally falling) line passing across and through a held note. This second idea can be heard right at the beginning, between the two violins, and when the other instruments enter they follow the same process a fifth lower. The music is quiet and mysterious, slow, and on a vast scale, as if contemplating the immensities of space, the macrocosmic aspects of the universe. Informing all this are incalculable energies, in the atoms and "fundamental" particles; this microcosmic aspect could be said to prompt the central part of the work, extremely active. This fast phase is greatly extended and eventually reaches a climax of a size and intensity rare in a string quartet. At its height the slowness and the vastness again become dominant; the music falls back to its original contemplations, though nothing can now be exactly repeated. The work ends as it began with a plain unharmonised D."

The first broadcast performance came on 6th May 1978, again by the Gabrieli Quartet. The quartet was also played at the Purcell Room on 4th October 1979 by the Edinburgh Quartet, in a concert which also included Lennox Berkeley's Third and Thomas Wilson's Fourth Quartets. Berkeley wrote on 7th October:

"Dear Bob,

I didn't see you after the concert the other night – we had been to talk to the Quartet in the interval – so this is just a note to tell you how much I liked your piece. Quite honestly I thought it the best of the three, and in particular I found the middle part, where everything starts to fizz, terrific and exciting.

Many congratulations.

Yrs ever Lennox

Don't answer this."

A further performance drew a very enthusiastic notice from Nicholas Kenyon (Times, 7/3/84): "To write a string quartet which aims to capture the immensity of a Bruckner symphony might seem like tilting at an extremely lofty windmill. But Robert Simpson's Seventh Quartet achieves just that, and as a result it bestrode last Wednesday's recital in the Park Lane Group's admirable British String Quartet series." Kenyon's enthusiasm seems to have abated later, of which more anon. The Seventh was recorded by the Delmé Quartet, coupled with the Eighth, and the recording was released by Hyperion in 1984, originally on LP, and later reissued on CD. Robert Simpson's quartets in general have been performed far more frequently than his symphonies, but one performance is particularly worth mentioning – the Seventh was given in St Petersburg in 2009 as part of a series devoted to British music. In 1978 Simpson wrote Volcano – Symphonic Study for

Brass Band. This work was commissioned as the test piece for the 1979 World Championships, and was premièred on 6th October that year, the champions being the Black Dyke Mills Band (another evocative name!) conducted by Major Peter Parkes. It is dedicated to Edmund Rubbra and lasts a little over twelve minutes. Volcano was also the test piece for the 1991 National Championships. It was recorded by the winners of the 1979 competition on a Chandos disc released the following year, along with music by Paul Huber, Gilbert Vinter, Morley Calvert and Edward Gregson, and re-recorded by the Desford Colliery Caterpillar Band in their disc of the complete brass band music issued by Hyperion in 1991. The tempo indications are 1) Calmissimo 2) Allegro 3) Meno mosso 4) Allegro 5) Meno mosso 6) Allegro 7) Lento.

Simpson said that Volcano could be heard as an evocation of a volcanic eruption, or the expression of a volcanic temperament. When sending the manuscript to his publishers, Simpson commented: "Enclosed please find one Volcano. There may be some danger to life and limb." I have not been able to locate a programme note by him, and will instead quote from Robert Matthew-Walker's sleeve-note for the Chandos record:

"Volcano is in one continuous movement, and draws most of its material from the interval of a perfect fifth, heard at the outset, quietly sustained. A cornet solo, over the fifth, maintains the mood, but gradually various stirrings begin, to rise eruptively and culminate in an immense explosion (marked fff). After this tremendous climax the music dies away mysteriously, with solos for cornet and soprano cornet, before ending quietly, in a sinister mood, with staccato notes on trombone and side-drum, as if to suggest that having happened once, the eruption could well happen again. The basic tonality is D, and the writing demands great skill and stamina."

There followed in 1979 the Sonata for Two Pianos, written for Bracha Eden and Alexander Tamir. It lasts about twenty-five minutes, a single movement fast-slow-fast, and was premièred in a radio broadcast on 18th May 1982. It has yet to be recorded.

The Eighth String Quartet was written the same year. It was commissioned by Brunel University, with funds made available by the Greater London Arts Association, and is dedicated to Professor David Gillette, first chairman of the Robert Simpson Society. The quartet is in four movements: 1) Grave, molto intensivo 2) Molto vivace (Eretmapodites gilletti) 3) Allegretto grazioso 4) Risoluto e concentrato. It lasts about 31½ minutes. Simpson's programme note says of Professor Gillette, that he "was for many years in charge of biological studies at Brunel University and is a world authority on the mosquito, a fact reflected in the second movement of this quartet. Like

No.7 before it, this work explores some of the possibilities of the perfect fifth. On the broadest plane, its four movements rise in tonality by fifths, ending in C sharp, G sharp, D sharp and A sharp. The themes themselves make clear use of fifths (mostly rising) and much of the harmony evolves from this common but inexhaustible interval.

The first movement is a large fugue in which high intensity alternates with quiet thought, finally giving way to it. The second movement is a little scherzo, suggesting the formidable delicacy of the mosquito named after its discoverer. The next movement is also on a small scale; the quartet is muted and the music slips past gently, with one brief flurry of activity. To balance the opening fugue, the finale is a large movement, of deliberate pace beneath an often ruffled surface, like a steady stream whipped by a strong wind. For much of its length it is in fact a variation of the first movement, without the fugal texture."

The quartet was premièred at Brunel by the Delmé Quartet on 21st June 1980, and four years later they recorded it for Hyperion, coupled with the Seventh.

Of the CD reissue, Simon Cargill (Hi-Fi news and Record Review, November 1989) described the quartets as "Some of the finest music by a composer whose neglect has been almost criminal."

"THAT LOT OUGHT TO BE TAUGHT A LESSON"
(1981 - 1985)

In 1980 Robert Simpson made the radical decision to resign from his employment with the BBC. One year more would have brought him to the mandatory retirement age of sixty, and a full pension, but principle overrode self-interest. He had for some years – in fact since the Third Programme was re-named Radio Three – become increasingly dissatisfied with the cultural policies which had replaced those of the old Third, for which he loved working. The direct trigger was the decision by BBC management to disband five of their regional orchestras, which caused the first ever strike by the Musicians Union, and the cancellation of half of that year's Prom concerts. To quote the composer in his interview of the same year with Lewis Foreman:

"The rot started I think when they started making the Music Programme last all day and it turned into a production belt and sort of high-class aural wallpaper (What he would of thought of the present policy of twenty four hour music broadcasting I shudder to think - Author's note). Then the Music Division had to be enlarged and the load was enormous, producing all those programmes… This really meant that things were being devalued. A music programme, although it may very much have interested some people, or the producer himself, may have been very good, a very important programme, still lost a lot of its effect as an event because it was only part of a great stream."

Asked by Foreman if he could "recap your feelings of personal dissatisfaction and how they grew up", Simpson replied: "Not in terms that could be published. The trouble is, what I regard as the degeneration of the BBC is on such a scale and so widely diffused that it would be very difficult to criticise it without writing or saying a great deal.

LF: Are you not in fact criticising the total scene, not just the BBC, but everything? As you've already said.

RS: This comes into it, yes. The BBC is reflecting lowering standards all round and by reflecting them is feeding them back to the people who are giving the BBC the lowering standards. So it's a horrible feedback which makes worse what is already getting bad."

Later, he added:\ "I also felt the BBC Management consisted of people I could no longer respect, who I could no longer acknowledge as bosses or superiors in the usual hierarchical sense of the word. I could no longer accept their authority… without shame. So I felt I had no alternative but to leave the place because I wanted to be free to say anything I wanted to anybody at any time."

Simpson not only rocked the boat with his resignation, but stated his reasons in a letter to The Times (printed 18th July 1980, under the heading: BBC values: 'a sense of betrayal'

"Sir,

On July 11th you reported an assertion by the Musicians' Union that I had resigned from the BBC. This report, presumably made on hearsay, and without consulting me, was at once correctly denied by the BBC, as it was not at the time true. I had in fact already privately indicated to the BBC my intention to resign, but when it was suggested that such action might attract publicity disturbing to the delicate negotiations then proceeding between the BBC and the MU through Acas (Advisory, Conciliation and Arbitration Service) I offered to delay it until after their completion, successful or otherwise. Flattered though I am by the assumption that my resignation might be of any significance, my sincere sympathy with the MU's cause was not warmed by this hasty attempt to use the hearsay of it as a weapon in the dispute. Now that the Acas discussions have broken down and no action of mine can disturb them further, I have resigned from the BBC, for reasons wider and deeper than the current argument over the orchestras, which is only a symptom of a larger problem. Not long ago I confirmed to a newspaper reporter what was widely known, that a letter asking the BBC to reconsider its position (in the matter of the orchestras) had been sent to the Director General by a number of senior members of the music staff, including myself. Although this was not really a "leak" it broke the rules, but the BBC did not request or suggest my resignation; on the contrary, efforts were made to persuade me otherwise. The determination to resign was the logical end of a long period of growing disquiet at the drift of the BBC under a management for which I could find only dwindling respect.

"When I first joined the Corporation nearly 30 years ago it was a wonderful and promising place to be at, the envy of the whole civilized world. Since the BBC's capitulation to the urge to compete on the lowest level with commercial broadcasting, values have degenerated; one can regard only with dismay the multiplying factors that impede the search for the best in the scramble for ratings. Mr Christopher Bishop, Managing Director of the Philharmonia Orchestra, has recently asked how long it will be before the inscription on Broadcasting House is changed from "this temple of the arts and muses" to "this temple of news and current affairs". I would further ask how long before "temple" becomes "market", finding it difficult to believe that this Government's refusal to increase the licence fee by a tiny 2p a day is without ulterior motive (an increase from 9p to IIp a day would solve a great many of the BBC's financial problems). It has still been possible for me as a producer to do many things I have wanted to do, sometimes on a large scale, and there is no narrow personal frustration involved. But I can no longer work for the BBC without a profound sense of betrayal of most of the values I and many others believe in, and its management includes elements whose authority I cannot accept without shame. It is now necessary for me to be able to say what I wish to whom I wish when I wish, without the shackles imposed by that all too sinister phrase "corporate loyalty". This is why I have resigned."

The BBC is akin to the civil service in that employees are not supposed to discuss internal matters with outsiders, curious when one considers that they are both publicly funded and (other than the MOD) do not deal with national security. To say that senior management were displeased with Simpson's behaviour would be a considerable understatement; he told me some years later that they had at first tried to sack him, then attempted to stop his pension: finding out that they could not legally do either, he was summoned to the beak's office to be told that this was all highly irregular, and that he could either work his notice (three months) on condition that he didn't speak to the press during that time, or go on to a pension from the next Monday. He chose the latter – as he said, he didn't particularly want to talk to the papers, but nor was he going to be told that he couldn't. He never regretted his decision; asked by Lewis Foreman if there were other BBC employees who felt the same way he said: "Oh yes. I had tremendous support from inside. When I finally did resign I had notes and letters of support from my colleagues from all over the country – from Glasgow, Manchester, Cardiff, Birmingham, London, everywhere. A lot of them obviously wished they could have done the same thing but it's harder for a lot of people because they've got mortgages, families and children. Not easy just to step out of a good job. In my case it was easier because I was due to retire next year and I was faced with a choice: either I leave quietly and in a rather sort of vapid way next year, or I throw a bomb now. So being a sort of natural bomb-thrower I threw one.

LF: Were you surprised at the reaction?

RS: No.

LF: I mean, l'affaire Simpson is something which is obviously long going to remain on the horizon.

RS: I was surprised at the intensity of the reaction certainly; internally and externally. I got lots of letters from outside, from the public too, from all over the place. And also, rather touchingly, from some old colleagues, old retired colleagues, who'd seen it from outside and been watching things happening – or worse still, not happening. So I was surprised at that; not at all surprised at the BBC Management's reaction."

One of the most moving letters of support came from fellow composer Elizabeth Maconchy, on 1st November 1980.

"Dear Bob Simpson

I want to thank you again for the 'Now and Then' programme (which you put on last year) with Jill Gomez & Roger Vignoles – it has just had a repeat performance and as I listened I felt very grateful to you for your insight & independent-mindedness as a producer.

But there is more than that to be grateful to you for – I have hesitated to write because you must have been inundated with letters of support for your most courageous letter about the 'degenerative policies' of the B.B.C. – and your resignation, & your refusal to accept a Proms. commission – I know of no-one else who would have acted so bravely and put principles before self-interest in the way you have: it is most important and inspiring to fellow-musicians.

So I want to send you my admiration and best wishes

Yours ever

Elizabeth Maconchy"

How far his decision, and the publication the following year of The Proms and Natural Justice, affected the Corporation's willingness or otherwise to publicise his music is a large question, which will be reserved for a later chapter. It is at any rate worth noting that some ten years later John Drummond still referred to him as "the enemy".

During the same year, Robert Simpson managed to offend another section of the establishment. Offered the C.B.E., he replied in a letter dated 2nd May 1980:

"Dear Sir

C.B.E.

Thank you for your letter of 30th April on behalf of the Prime Minister. While I am most appreciative of the intended honour, it could not properly be accepted by a determined republican in whom memory of the British Empire arouses no nostalgia.

Yours sincerely,"

He had, however, been happy to accept a rather more unusual award the previous year from Cyril Clemens, the editor of the Mark Twain Journal, and evidently a descendant of the celebrated writer. The letterhead bears endorsements from some famous names: "I never miss a copy of the M.T. Journal." – William Faulkner; "Put me down ditto to the above statement." – President Lyndon B. Johnson, and the citation dated 15th August 1979 reads:

"Dear Robert Simpson

In recognition of your outstanding contribution to Modern Music, you have been unanimously elected this day A KNIGHT OF MARK TWAIN."

Simpson replied on 22nd October:

"Dear Mr. Clemens

My thanks to you for your letter of 15th August, which took some time to reach me. I am greatly honoured.

Yours sincerely,"

1980 saw the foundation of the Robert Simpson Society, with the intention of bringing his music to the attention of a wider public. The Chairman was Professor David Gillette, while Edmund Rubbra agreed to be President, and Hans Keller, John McCabe, Ronald Smith and Ronald Stevenson, Vice-Presidents. Simpson was at first undecided as to the wisdom of this project; on 22nd January 1981 he wrote to James Douglas, of Scotus, the publishers: "I've got reservations about a society for my music, but they are very enthusiastic and determined!" In essence, he felt that such promotion might backfire, and that questions along the lines of "if his music is so good, why does it need a society to push it?" might be asked. However, he came round and, even after his move to Ireland, attended AGMs, even if he did refer to the RSS in a thank-you letter for his seventieth birthday present as "the glorious Nut Case society".

During 1981, Robert Simpson reached the age of sixty and produced not only his formidable Eighth Symphony and a highly unusual chamber work – the Quintet for Clarinet, Bass Clarinet and String Trio – but also lobbed another grenade in the BBC's direction: the booklet "The Proms and Natural Justice".

His sixtieth was marked, among other things, by a Birthday Hansel published in Tonic, the Robert Simpson Society journal. A hansel, or handsel is defined by Chambers (and where else would one look?) as "an inaugural gift …something thought of as an inauguration or beginning", along with other meanings. The beginning was presumably the start of Simpson's full-time composing career, after decades of having to fit it into his spare time. Appreciations were contributed by Sir Lennox Berkeley, Sir Adrian Boult, Derek Bourgeois, Peter Racine Fricker, Vagn Holmboe, John McCabe, Goffredo Petrassi, Edmund Rubbra, Humphrey Searle, Ronald

Stevenson, Sir Michael Tippett and, a little later, Anthony Milner and Mogens Wöldike. Tippett's contribution, coming as it did from a very different fellow composer, is particularly touching:

"Robert Simpson is one of the rare composers who care for their colleagues, past and present, with a true generosity of spirit. He also cares for enduring values and proper quality within the vast bureaucracies of all our musical institutions. "I shall not cease from mental fight" might well be his motto."

Time had certainly not mellowed Simpson's disposition. Until his last years he looked much younger than his age, and if he felt that something was wrong he would say so in uncompromising terms and with a youthful energy, the more so now that he was no longer constrained by his employment. His next target was the running of that most sacred of BBC institutions, the Henry Wood Promenade Concerts, in a short polemical book "The Proms and Natural Justice" published by Toccata Press in 1981. There is a foreword by Sir Adrian Boult: Boult was very bitter at being compulsorily retired at age sixty; he always referred to it as "sacking" and said privately to Simpson "That lot ought to be taught a lesson!" It does seem a myopic decision, bearing in mind the many fine recordings (and public performances) which were yet to come, and the general principle that conductors if anything improve with age, until physical frailty prevents them continuing. Simpson began his book with a brief history of the Proms: originally, Sir Henry Wood chose the repertoire and conducted every concert himself; thus "the case for or against personal monopoly was scarcely in dispute." The BBC assumed responsibility for the Proms from 1927, but Wood remained artistically in charge until 1941, when other conductors began to share the burden, and a committee came into existence. They took full control upon Wood's death in 1944. In 1960 William Glock, the new Controller, Music, abolished the committee and for the next fourteen years selected the repertoire himself; in 1973 Robert Ponsonby took over as Controller, and also inherited Glock's role as Prom planner – thus, what had been an aberration became institutionalised.

Robert Simpson made it clear in his book that it was not intended as a personal attack on Glock (or Ponsonby): his point was that one man's taste determining the entire repertoire for a period limited only by retirement or death would, and did, result in the exclusion (or virtual exclusion) of gifted composers whose music he disliked. To illustrate his point, he drew up a list of composers who got nothing played during the Glock years: Richard Arnell, Niels Viggo Bentzon, Derek Bourgeois, Stephen Dodgson, Benjamin Frankel, Berthold Goldschmidt, Vagn Holmboe, Herbert Howells, Kenneth Leighton, Francesco Malipiero, Frank Martin, John McCabe, Ildebrando Pizzetti, Max Reger, Franz Reizenstein, Hilding Rosenberg, Franz Schmidt, Gerard Schurmann, Matyas Seiber, Nikos Skalkottas and Bernard Stevens.

There follows a further list of composers who got less than an hour's music played during the same period:

Arnold Bax, Richard Rodney Bennett, Ernest Bloch, Havergal Brian, Alan Bush, Ferruccio Busoni, Arnold Cooke, Aaron Copland, Luigi Dallapiccola, Peter Racine Fricker, Alexander Goehr, Arthur Honegger, Elizabeth Maconchy, Bohuslav Martinů, Darius Milhaud, Anthony Milner, Albert Roussel, Edmund Rubbra, Humphrey Searle, Ronald Stevenson and Karol Szymanowski.

Simpson was not pleading for the return of the committee; he felt that the programming should be entrusted to a single pair of hands, but that this individual should be replaced regularly, after five years at the outside. The programmer need not be a salaried employee; he or she could be an outsider, paid a fixed fee for the job.

He also considered that large savings in costs could be made by full use of the BBC's own orchestras, which he thought as good as any given the right direction.

He summarised his arguments as follows:

"1) Very large financial savings can be made if the BBC deploys its own resources properly.

2) The funds saved will be usable for other music broadcasting; it would be logical to direct them to studio concerts for non-BBC orchestras.

3) Positive and effective marshalling of resources will result in nearly total command of repertoire for the Proms.

4) The responsibility placed on the BBC orchestras will produce a striking development in their standards of performance that will reflect much credit on the BBC.

5) The ability to plan and control repertoire well in advance will make it completely practicable to change the planner from time to time.

6) A committee, to judge from past experience and taking into account the scope of the artistic issues at stake, would be an unsatisfactory way of planning.

7) A conception of this kind must be distinctive and individual, though based on a wide view of music.

8) The principle itself. It is not morally justifiable that one person should dominate the planning of this vast publicly funded festival, its repertoire and its casting, for an unspecified period; the purposes of equity may be served only by changing at suitable intervals the set of prejudices in charge."

Perfectly sensible and reasonable criticisms, one might think – The Daily Telegraph certainly thought so, and commented in an editorial on 31st July (headed The Sound of Whose Music?): "Dr Simpson's combination of utilising in-house resources, putting a time limit on absolute power and trying to think ahead sounds very much like sense." Yet the BBC reacted as though someone had blown a raspberry during the Queen's Christmas speech. They went straight on the defensive, asserting that the present system was perfectly justifiable without explaining how, that it would never do to change the image of the Proms, and generally presenting Glock's coup d'état as having established a sacred and unquestionable tradition. All mention of, or discussion about, the book on the air was barred. The ban was confirmed by the Sunday Times on 19th July, who quoted a BBC source as saying "Nothing will be said on air about either book. It's a decision by management." The other volume referred to is The Proms and the Men who made them, by Barrie Hall. Two BBC "heavies" – Robert Ponsonby and George Howard (Chairman) – rubbished the proposals in "Kaleidoscope" (Radio 4, 19th August) without permitting any reply. The Listener showed itself more independently minded, and contributions were invited: Peter Heyworth defended the present system: "one of the very few departments of our musical life which it would be better to leave well alone.", while Alexander Goehr made fundamental criticisms of the BBC's general music policy, from which he felt the Proms could not be separated ("The debate about the future of the Proms", 10th September). Simpson himself contributed a full-page article to The Listener on 17th September headed "Personal power is always an ethical matter." He concluded:

"None of these matters removes our central ethic. The Controller protests too much in cumbrously saying "that I have been responsible for the Proms over eight seasons and so would have been replaced once, if not twice, under his proposals, is not the point." It is precisely the point, and he must not take it personally if it is insisted upon. What is done in the BBC is always an ethical matter, when it concerns directly the exercise of power. Predictability only sharpens dismay when the Corporation's figurehead tries to wave it away as "a load of nonsense."" Several years later, the debate was still raging. A comment by Robert Ponsonby provoked the following letter from Simpson, printed in The Listener on 19th September 1985:

"SIR: I'm a little puzzled that Robert Ponsonby says I continue to rumble like a 32-foot organ pipe, since I have not lately been active in publicly objecting to the persistent personal monopolies the BBC still allows to devastate the Proms. I can only suppose he must be referring to what was not publicly known – that for the second time I have had to refuse the première of a work at the Proms as a BBC commission. In making another attempt, Mr Ponsonby must surely have remembered that when the Proms and Natural Justice was published in 1981, I had already declined a Proms commission and declared publicly that I would take no such commission until the Proms system was made ethically acceptable; he must therefore, have known that I was bound to reject it. To some people plain statement of principle seems, on occasion, no more than the distant rumble of some old organ. I suspect your contributor is really hearing a cipher in his own low note."

This may in part, have contributed to the almost total neglect of Simpson's music during the years of Ponsonby's stewardship. However, as ARM Sedgewick pointed out, in a letter to Classical Music (17th January 1987), Ponsonby's position is not the only one he could have taken.

"Sir – In his letter on the Proms (29 November), Robert Ponsonby cryptically mentions his' regret' that during his period in charge there was 'for a particular reason – no Simpson'. Although we well know that Robert Simpson, because of his belief that the Proms were inequitably run, had publicly declared that he could not accept a BBC commission for the Proms until the system was changed to something he felt to be ethically more acceptable, there was, nonetheless, ample opportunity for Mr Ponsonby, in his 13 years of exclusively personal control, to have included any of Robert Simpson's published works, which were readily accessible, had he wished to do so.

"Neither the composer nor anyone else could have prevented him and had he done so the composer's declaration would not have been flouted. Indeed, the inclusion of Simpson's music at the Proms would have been a clear demonstration that RS was not being penalised for his published views.

"May we then be told the 'particular reason' why this was not done? It could have effectively assuaged Mr Ponsonby's 'regrets' while respecting the composer's scruples."

Hits the nail on the head, I think. As far as I know, Ponsonby never explained his position further.

On 17th December, Simpson had written to Ray Few: "Ideas for an Eighth Symphony are beginning to swirl around in my head, and the shape of the whole thing is getting clear. As you probably know, I turned down a commission for next season's Proms; it would have been totally inconsistent to accept it in view of my long-sustained criticisms of the way the Proms are being run. But the symphony persists, and will get itself written whatever does or does not happen. It looks like being a big one, and it suddenly occurred to me to wonder if the RPS (Royal Philharmonic Society) might be interested – you may have views about that." They were, and the symphony was commissioned, with funds provided by the Arts Council.

The general shape and character of the Eighth were suggested by Simpson's old friend, the painter Anthony Dorrell. One problem facing a composer in the present day – that of having no direct contact with his audience – is described in the last chapter of The Proms and Natural Justice. "One remedy I am at present trying is to get an articulate and intensely musical friend to describe the symphony he would wish to hear, and then try to oblige him. It is a little step towards Haydn's enviable condition, without the servitude." Dorrell initially had some difficulty putting his ideas into words, and sent Simpson a letter in which he included quotations from Edward Thomas, Brecht, Dylan Thomas, William Morris, Blake, Henry Reed, Jacob Bronowski, Yeats and Siegfried Sassoon.

Discussions followed, and the general idea began to emerge. From the programme note:

"He thought of a symphony in two halves, two movements in each, with the only break in the middle. The second movement was to be some kind of scherzo, and the third a strongly elegiac slow movement, reacting against a sense of menace in the first part of the symphony. About the finale he couldn't be too precise, though it was to be fast and energetic. I warned him not to be too microscopically expectant, because once you get involved in a big work, it takes you over. But the main lines were no problem. It seemed to me that the "menace" could gradually infiltrate the first two movements, at length dominating so much as to arouse an air of protest. Conversely, as the darker elements gradually took over in Part 1, brighter things could gradually infuse Part 2, making two opposite and complementary processes. In practice the "brighter" things proved not to be quite what I expected; they did not, for instance, reflect anything of the rather relaxed pastoral atmosphere in which the symphony begins, the result of Tony's reminder that his wife Daphne (the other dedicatee) hoped that gentler matter might take its place in the context." The movements are (Part 1) 1) Poco animato 2) Minaccioso (Part 2) 3) Adagio 4) Presto, and the symphony plays for forty-four minutes.

The work received its première at the Royal Festival Hall on 10th November 1982. The Royal Danish Orchestra was conducted by Jerzy Semkow, and the rest of the concert comprised Nielsen's overture to Masquerade, Schumann's Piano Concerto (soloist, Stephen Bishop Kovacevich) and Tchaikovsky's Francesca da Rimini. Reviews were mainly unenthusiastic; Dominic Gill (source and date unknown) thought that "Besides the Ninth String Quartet, Simpson's new Eighth Symphony seems no more than a genial sketch." "The quartet is an astonishing and unsettling work; the symphony seems merely unsettled." "It is expertly crafted, but the centre is soft." Andrew Clements (Observer, 14/11/82), in a piece entitled "Simpson's smooth machine", considered that "The music never satisfactorily justifies its own existence. There is no sense of a battle won or a quest ended, and because Simpson so obviously relates to these romantic archetypes, his music must be judged in those terms." Does he indeed? Must it indeed? Max Harrison (source and date again unknown) found that "The impression is of greyness." Another less than fervent review, by Frank (Granville) Barker in the Guardian, in which he pontificated "The hard tone of the Danish players and the stolid conducting of Jerzy Semkow were reasonably well suited to Simpson's gritty score" stung Simpson into a counterblast titled "Comment or perception? A Sentient Artist's Reply to Unjust Criticism" which I reproduce in its entirety:

COMMENT OR PERCEPTION?

A Sentient Artist's Reply to Unjust Criticism

The right to criticise can't be objected to. If criticism is based on mature reflection and solid knowledge it can become almost an art in itself, as many distinguished writers have proved. But there can't be much of a defence of the snap judgement experts, the professional opinionists of the newspapers. Their verdicts, on new works especially, are too often and inevitably based on insufficient knowledge. How can it be otherwise, when they so frequently have no chance to prepare themselves properly? Artists often and reasonably ask this question, notably those whose art depends on performance, whose work lies in other people's hands. Your work in their hands? Their hands in your work, mostly. We can't blame the unfortunate journalists (if they must do such work) when pressure compels them to make hasty judgements, when they are unable to tell what the composer really wants, or what the work really ought to sound like. The composer himself is usually the only person in the hall who knows that (which is why you can see him sweating). Both audience and critic may get an impression of efficiency and certainty in the performance, and that in itself might seem to the critic as good a reason as any to charge the composer for whatever he fails to receive from the music.

But we can blame the critic for not realising the obvious dangers in this stance, and we are entitled to regard his tactics as unfair and perhaps even disingenuous, if, like Mr. Frank Barker in *The Guardian* for instance, he goes so far as to dogmatise: 'The hard tone of the Danish players and the stolid conducting of Jerzy Semkow were reasonably well suited to Simpson's gritty score.' No music could be 'well suited' by a 'stolid' conductor; surely Mr. Barker must know that all music, of whatever quality, requires imagination from its performers. Is he really sure that the work, in a vivid performance, perceptive in every detail, absolutely free from stolidity, would not have struck him differently? Here is the perfect example of the apparently wishful snap judgement shattering all logic and good sense – to say nothing of charity.

It is always difficult for a composer to rebut criticism, however misdirected; in saying the performance was inadequate he can be suspected of trying to put the blame on somebody else. But orchestral premieres are nearly always bad. A string quartet will rehearse and rehearse, considering every note, every phrase, often with the composer's help. An orchestra has a set number of rehearsals (always too few) and depends utterly on the conductor; it contains a hundred people; such a crowd, however talented individually, can't hope to get to the heart of a difficult and unfamiliar new work – there simply isn't time. Remember the first performance of Tippett's Piano Concerto, when the orchestra produced a consistently inchoate swamp of sound; the soloist could do nothing to prevent the wholesale rejection of the piece by the critics, and it wasn't heard for another ten years or so. Then John Ogdon recorded it, and then conditions allowed a properly prepared orchestra; since then there has been no doubt about its appreciation.

So far only one of my symphonies (No. 5) has had a good first performance; significantly it's also the only one to have got a good press on its première. I don't think all the others are bad. No. 3 got an awful first performance and was immediately written off. Some ten years later Jascha Horenstein recorded a magnificent performance and the work was cordially received by nearly all the reviewers. This and other lessons have taught me that I would rather have no performance at all than a bad first one. So far as the most recent symphony (No. 8) is concerned, the very fine orchestra was not given the chance to penetrate the music; rehearsal time was inadequate and there was a number of works to prepare for the English tour. The result was a skilful tightrope act. Not much of the real music emerged, and how could it? We may scarcely expect the press to appreciate this. If the extravagantly praised Quartet No. 9 had been interpreted no better than the symphony, it would most likely have received similar treatment. This symphony is a difficult work, but far clearer and more direct than it seemed; when it was composed I thought it my best, and can still hear it in my head as it should sound.

Critics are sometimes apt to pick up things you say and make little theories from them, often with excellent intentions. But it is rather a mistake to propose that a deepening interest in intervals and their long-term resonances precludes the invention of actively expanding music. A more comprehensive performance of No. 8 will show that it subsists on large ideas, that it is full of stretching melody, and that not one note of it is automatic. The unromantic energy with which it concludes will no longer be 'puzzling', or naively thought some kind of failure to be 'a struggle won or a quest ended'. We have no such expectations of Bach, from whom this work derives more of its nature than from any later music. It is essentially a polyphony, growing accordingly, its inner forces and tensions (however extreme) becoming ever more closely balanced, canalised as energy. That has nothing to do with romanticism.

Two small factual matters need correction. One writer seemed to think it a pity the Danes hadn't brought with them a symphony by Vagn Holmboe. So do I; he is a magnificent composer. Mine was played at the request of the Royal Philharmonic Society, who thought it appropriate, given my associations with Nielsen. But next time they really must bring a Holmboe symphony – preferably one they have rehearsed to breaking point. Another critic supposed I might have been surprised by the length of my own work (42 minutes). Not so – the wrong space in Radio Times was no fault of mine; I had actually given a timing of 45 minutes, and this might in the end still prove to be the right one".

Traditionally, at least in this country, one is supposed to respond to hostile criticism by way of a dignified silence, which obviously suits the critics better than the artists; thank goodness the composer broke this senseless taboo on numerous occasions.

He certainly blamed the adverse reaction on the inadequacies of the performance, and went into some detail in a letter to Christine Hardwick (Head of Radio 3) dated 11th December 1982: "Thanks for yours of 6.XII. It prompts a few thoughts. The symphony didn't fail merely to go "as well as I would have liked"; it was totally inadequate, due to the conductor, who gave me a run-through, with no corrections, on Nov. 1st in Copenhagen, and another (also with no corrections) at the RFH on Nov. 10th (the day of the concert). He spent much time and detail on Tchaikovsky VI and Francesca da Rimini. Between those dates, as far as I know, there were no more full rehearsals of my work, though I'm told the players took their parts home, and had sectional rehearsals under another conductor before Semkow arrived. The orchestra's chairman told me Semkow had written to them earlier saying that the symphony was "impossible"; they had replied saying that it was not, and that they would play it. You remark that the orchestra "sounded pretty good". It is pretty good, perhaps the best in Scandinavia now, and I don't wish any of my strictures to be applied to it. The players did their very best, but what are a hundred people against one?"

In private he was less diplomatic, referring to the conductor as "that bastard". Simpson opposed a repeat broadcast of the "murder" of his symphony, asking instead that a further performance with an in-house orchestra be considered. This did happen – Edward Downes conducted the BBC Philharmonic in two studio performances on 1st and 2nd November 1983, the better of which was later broadcast. Not that the composer was enamoured of this rendition either, finding it "very stodgy".

The disastrous première did its worst; the Eighth has had no further live performances that I know of, although there is a very good recording by the Royal Philharmonic Orchestra under Vernon Handley, coupled with the First, which Hyperion released in 1996. On a personal note, I find the Eighth the most difficult of Simpson's symphonies, and feel that I have not yet quite grasped its essence, although I am sure I will in time.

In a letter to Tony Dorrell dated 6th December 1980, Simpson wrote: "At the moment I'm on the weirdest thing I've ever tried – a quintet for clarinet, bass clarinet, and 3 double basses! It's for a new ensemble giving a Wigmore concert in April. A bit of a challenge – but it's rather got hold of me, I must say." In the letter to James Douglas already cited he jokes that it will be "Incomparably the greatest work ever composed for this combination!" The musicians in question were the London Double-Bass Ensemble, leader Gerald Drucker. The work, finished in 1981, is in one movement, subdivided as follows: 1) Adagio tranquillo 2) Allegro 3) Adagio; it plays for some 16½ minutes. The composer's programme note is very short: "It is in one extended movement, beginning slowly and becoming very active in the middle, rising to a climax, at the height of which the original slow tempo is superimposed on the fast, bringing the work to a quiet close."

The quintet was premièred as intended at the Wigmore Hall on 27th April 1981, with Jack Brymer (clarinet), Stephen Tryer (bass clarinet) and members of the double-bass ensemble. The rest of the concert comprised Quartets for Four Double-Basses by Schuller, Hoddinott and Runswick, Mozart's Concert Aria K612 sung by John Shirley-Quirk, and Bottestini's Duo for Two Double Basses.

Simpson later arranged the work for the more conventional forces of clarinet, bass clarinet and string trio: it is this revision which was recorded by Hyperion and released in 1993, coupled with the Fourteenth and Fifteenth String Quartets. The Vanbrugh Quartet (Gregory Ellis (violin), Elizabeth Charleson

With the Delme Quartet, 1984

(violin) Simon Aspell (viola) and Christopher Marwood (cello)) were joined by Joy Farrall (clarinet) and Fiona Cross (bass clarinet).

A major personal event of 1981 was the death of Robert Simpson's first wife, Squibs, after thirty-five years of marriage. During later years she suffered from senile dementia, which was discovered when she wrote a cheque for an enormous sum of money, and included curry powder for the cat in a shopping list. She had a horror of hospitals dating from her experiences in Friern Barnet, and Bob had cared for her at home. He was the sole carer – Angela thinks it would probably not have occurred to him to ask for any help. He was, of course, based at home following his resignation from the BBC. He coped pretty well, though he was no chef – meals were mostly omelettes and fish fingers. The end came when Squibs spilled some boiling water on herself and was severely burned; she died in Stoke Mandeville Hospital on 11th November.

Simpson's next work was another epic journey; the huge Ninth String Quartet of 1982. The Delmé Quartet had asked Simpson and four other composers for pieces to mark the 250th anniversary of Haydn's birth. With his unbounded admiration for the Austrian master, Simpson would have needed little prompting, although whether the Delme expected anything on this scale is another matter – the quartet plays for almost fifty-eight minutes, and comprises thirty-two variations and a fugue. The composer wrote in his programme note:

"Dedicated in affection and admiration to the Delmé Quartet, this work is a second exploration of a palindromic minuet by Haydn, which he himself used twice, in Symphony No. 47 in G and in the Piano Sonata No. 26 in A. I first tried my hand at variations on it in 1948, for the piano, and it was looking at these that prompted enough shame to provoke the present attempt, alas on a much larger scale, with a fugue to boot. The variations are all palindromic (i.e. the same backwards as forwards) with occasional deliberate deviations… There are also various canonical devices of more or less complex kinds, none of which need detain the reader of a programme note, who (believe it or not) is expected to listen in the hope of enjoying the music … The last three variations form a large slow movement, which gives way without pause to the Fugue, beginning slowly and softly. It is a big fugue, and as it goes on it gains energy and speed. As a result of this the subject itself is constantly changing into something else; by the end it is completely different, though still evolved from Haydn's theme."

The première was given at the Wigmore Hall on 6th October 1982 by the dedicatees, along with Haydn's own Quartet Op.76 No.3 and Schubert's Quartettsatz. Reviews were hugely enthusiastic: David Cairns (Sunday Times, 10/10/82), in a piece headed "Robert Simpson – Composer for our time", wrote of Simpson's "heroic cussedness" and called the quartet "A superb feat of sustained and passionate musical argument and, with all its technical complexity, a delight to listen to."

Nicholas Kenyon (Times, no date), in a review headed "A powerful raising of ghosts" opined: "If there is one British composer who might be thought equal to the task of reflecting classical language without indulging in pale imitation, it is Robert Simpson, and his contribution to the series last night was an astonishing display of individuality and resourcefulness." The quartet was recorded by the Delmé for Hyperion, on an LP released in 1985. The recording was reissued later on CD; rather curiously, the original sleeve photographs showing the composer in discussion, utterly characteristic in stance, were replaced by an anonymous-looking row of classical columns. David J. Brown wrote of the recording (Tempo, date unknown): "Perhaps the most remarkable thing about this remarkable work is that Simpson's response to his self-imposed intellectual challenge is full of emotional power as well – mind serving heart and vice versa in a rare way." Simpson himself thought that the quartet had been "grotesquely overpraised" as compared to the Eighth Symphony; another example of the difference a first-rate performance can make.

On the 2nd of August 1982, Robert Simpson and Angela Musgrave were married at Aylesbury Registry Office. As he said later, having worked together for twenty-five years, they knew each other about as well as two people could.

Robert and Angela Simpson on their wedding day, 2nd August 1982

Angela describes it as "a most unromantic wedding day"; the house had been invaded by flying ants. Bob was listening to a Bruckner symphony at the time and refused to attend to the problem until the work had ended. A can of ant-killer was duly purchased on the way to the Registry Office. Asked for the wedding ring, Bob pulled out his car keys! I think anyone who knew both of them would agree that the sometimes caustic composer and the cheerful, intelligent woman whom he described as not just his wife but his best friend were ideally suited, complementing each other in the most natural way, and it is a personal as well as a musical tragedy that they had only nine unclouded years together before illness struck Robert Simpson down.

Simpson's next orchestral work was also in variation form: the Variations and Finale on a Theme of Carl Nielsen, from 1983. The circumstances surrounding its production were not the happiest; in a letter dated 6th November 1986 to David Richardson (Chief Executive, Bournemouth Symphony Orchestra) he wrote, in response to a letter asking if the Ninth Symphony could be shorter:

"May I tell you a little story. Some time ago the BBC commissioned from me a work for the BBCPO. I was asked to make it no longer than 25'00" and to stick to the orchestra's normal complement so that it could be taken on a European tour. I complied (the work was in the event 23'50") and they expressed themselves pleased with it. After quite a long gap I suddenly received from Manchester a letter informing me blandly that the work couldn't go on the tour as it was "too long" and that it would therefore be done in the studio instead. I couldn't understand why it was too long until I found out that the rest of the programme was Beethoven's C minor Piano Concerto and Bruckner's Fifth Symphony. This made me so mad that I withdrew the piece from the BBC and sent them their money back, something that had never happened to them before." I can amplify this; the fee was £7000, half up-front and half when the score was delivered. Returning a cheque for £3500 is an awesome demonstration of principle – I have seen the scathing letter which accompanied the returned cheque, but sadly it has not survived. The work comprises nine variations and a finale, and is dedicated to Ray and Rosemary Few. It was finally premièred at the Philharmonic Hall, Liverpool, on 27th November 1986 by the RLPO under the late Richard Hickox, with Nielsen's own Helios Overture and the Beethoven Violin Concerto, played by Kyung-Wha Chung. Simpson's programme note is a little technical, but also amusing, so I will quote it in full:

"The theme is from Nielsen's unpublished incidental music to Harald Bergstet's play on the Nordic saga Ebbe Skammelsen, and it is here scored for wind orchestra exactly as Nielsen wrote it. Its tonality is sardonically ambiguous – at first the tune could be in G (woodwind) but it is at once answered in F by the horns. The bassoons nevertheless belt obtusely away at

The first page of the Nielsen Variations, 1983

a pedal on C and G. They persist with this even through the middle part, which favours E flat. The first part then recurs at its original pitches (G and F), but now accompanied by a tuba who is under the delusion that the key is still E flat. During all this the bassoons continue mindlessly pumping out C and G. No agreement is reached between them and the tuba player, but their boot-faced obstinacy finally outstares him. All this seems apt to portray a fool, which it does in the play.

The nine variations do not try to enlarge on this curious mood; they are variously contrasted in character and tempo, all making different uses of the intervals displayed in the theme. The first two are lively and the third flows along gently; Variations 4, 5 and 6 are continuous and cumulative, and No.7 is vehement, with plenty of brass. The eighth is a prestissimo scherzo, and the last is slow, with divided cellos and trombones in soft counterpoint. This leads directly into a large finale, as long as all the variations together, starting like a contemplative fugue but slowly gathering energy until it becomes an exuberant symphonic movement. The growing activity compels the basic intervals always to behave afresh, causing continual transformation of the ideas, all of which evolve from the elements of Nielsen's theme."

Reviews were positive: Stephen Pettitt (Times, 28/11/86) described Simpson as "a composer of unquestionable integrity", adding: "however conservative the language and the essence of the structure it has something of compelling originality and drama to say, a something that can be said only in music." David Fallows (Independent, same date) criticised the neglect of Simpson's music, despite the support of some of the most thoughtful critics in the country, and said of the fugue: "every new gesture is beautifully presented and the whole leads up to an impressive climax." Both reviewers mentioned a man who shouted "pretentious rubbish!" at the end of the performance. A thing deviséd by the enemy? Maybe, but even allowing for this, and for the fact that some people seem to have tin ears, it was a baffling response: as Fallows rightly said, "If there is one thing for which Simpson stands, it is the need to avoid pretension of any kind."

Far from pretentious, the work is one of Simpson's warmest and most approachable, shot through with a broad, Haydnesque humour, and I would not hesitate to select it as the one with which to baptise the uninitiated, with the Fourth and Ninth Symphonies close behind. The Variations have the additional advantage of being fairly short; they could thus be included in the first half of a live concert, minimising the risk of the more conservative elements in the audience making their exit during the interval. Despite their appeal, the Nielsen Variations have yet to achieve a London première, or indeed a second performance. The City of London Sinfonia, conducted by Matthew Taylor, recorded them for Hyperion, coupled with the Eleventh

Symphony, the disc being released in 2004. Stephen Johnson, in his review for the BBC Music Magazine, aptly described the Variations as "Falstaffian", adding: "but there's magic here, too, especially in the dream-like serenity of the final variation."

A major work for brass band also appeared during 1983 - The Four Temperaments, although Simpson had already agreed to write it in 1981 – he mentions it in a letter to James Douglas, dated 22nd January. The movements are 1) Scherzo: Presto (Sanguine) 2) Intermezzo: Allegretto placido (Phlegmatic) 3) Elegy: Mesto, sempre non vibrato (Melancholic) 4) Fantasia: Allegro irato (Choleric). Simpson thus uses a different order to Nielsen, who in his Second Symphony of the same name placed them Choleric, Phlegmatic, Melancholic and Sanguine. The work plays for almost twenty-two minutes. Each temperament is dedicated to a personal friend whom he considered fitted the bill: Martin Anderson, Dick Edwards, Robert Barnes and John and Sylvia Brooks. Here are Simpson's own descriptions:

"The sanguine temperament crashes through life with irrepressible enthusiasm. Obstacles stop him only for a moment, and he goes roaring on as if nothing happened.

"The phlegmatic temperament is placid, not readily upset. It is not stupid or bovine (as is sometimes supposed) but it cannot be easily ruffled. Here it is seen to be unperturbed by a considerable disturbance from the timpani and snare drum.

"The melancholic temperament is not merely lugubrious. It is deep feeling, serious and dignified. There is something grand and courageous in its gloom and strength and its willingness to face grim facts.

"The choleric man is quick to anger, but is not simply vituperative – he has in him good and generous qualities, but even when he is calm something is smouldering inside him, ready to burst into flame."

The Four Temperaments was first performed on 15th October 1983 at Prince Henry's Grammar School, Otley, Yorks, by the Yorkshire Imperial Metals Band (another name which demands to be taken seriously!) conducted by John Pryce-Jones, for whom it was written. The concert also included music by Janáček, Giles Farnaby (arr. Howarth), Walton, Hindemith and (rather bizarrely) Glen Miller (arr. Stevens). The piece received another outing at the Duke's Hall, Royal Academy of Music, on 17th June 1997, as part of a Danish Music Festival, by the R.A.M. Brass under James Watson and Michael Hall. Other composers featured were Buxtehude, E.W. Ramsoe, Poul Ruders, Niels Marthinsen and Vagn Holmboe, Simpson presumably being considered an honorary Dane. It was recorded by the Desford Colliery

Band conducted by James Watson in their complete set of the brass band works issued by Hyperion in 1991.

A series of chamber works, and Robert Simpson's only piece for organ, ensued during the early 1980s, before the composer began work on the opus that he considered his best, the Ninth Symphony. His productivity during these years is remarkable; or rather it is until you consider the flood of music which came during the first six years of residence in Ireland. Evidently, both his resignation from the BBC and his relocation in County Kerry (1986) gave his creativity a powerful stimulus, as one might expect, and it is a tragedy that illness virtually ruled out composition during the last six years - despite his intensive productivity there is no loss of quality.

The Tenth String Quartet, entitled "For Peace", came in 1983. There are three movements: 1) Allegretto 2) Prestissimo 3) Molto adagio, and the work plays for slightly over twenty-seven minutes. Here is the programme note, which contains an important philosophical statement as well as a musical description: "This quartet was composed for the tenth anniversary of the Coull Quartet, to whom it is dedicated in friendship; it was commissioned with funds made available by West Midlands Arts. Its subtitle refers to its generally pacific character and to the firm conviction, based on plain logic, that unless the human species makes a conscious and decisive choice against violence, the technology it now has (which cannot be unlearned and against which mere fear is no permanent safeguard) will sooner or later destroy it. In the words of Martin Luther King "it is nonviolence or non-existence". Einstein's view that humanity must now change its way of thinking is at once compelling and pessimistic - he was not naive enough to suppose that this is likely to happen. Nor is this composer. The music, however, is not an outburst of tormented anxiety; instead it tries to define the condition of peace. This excludes aggression but not strong feeling.

"The first movement is gently paced, in an unassertive sonata form, making use of repeated notes against flowing lines. Its one climax comes when the second subject is given an intensified recapitulation. Then the music relaxes into a slower tempo and finds a quiet close. A playful little scherzo follows, with syncopations and quicksilver quavers; this also has one climax, which vanishes as fast as it comes. After this brief contrast the work ends with a long adagio, growing out of a simple up-and-down phrase that rises through a natural (or flat) note and descends through a sharp one. The whole movement explores the expressive possibilities of this quiet reversal of the usual expectations. As in the other movements there is only one climax, this time created by a sustained burst of passion. When this is at length supplanted by quiet, the first violin gives out a calm but graceful tune derived from everything else in the whole work. Then the music moves to a peaceful end."

The Coull Quartet (Roger Coull (violin), Philip Gallaway (violin), David Curtis (viola), and John Todd (cello)) gave the first performance at Warwick University in June 1984, and the London première at the Wigmore Hall on 26th September 1984, preceded by Haydn's Quartet in D Opus 20. Anthony Payne (27th September, source unknown) wrote: "The growing symphonic achievement of Dr Simpson as outlined by the symphonies themselves and by his impressive group of string quartets is something to cherish. Stylistically out of step with much that is going on in the contemporary musical world, yet truly of its time in spirit, non-conformist, life-enhancing, his vision finds a further moving outlook in the new 10th Quartet."

Dominic Gill (Financial Times, same date) considered "It is an impressive utterance, Beethovenian in its high moral seriousness and urgency; Brucknerian in its sound-world – darkly, calmly discursive, rising to a single sustained burst of passion before fading (neither optimistic nor pessimistic) to inconclusion." Simpson's programme note does not mention Bruckner, but he had often referred to the Austrian master's music in similar terms; Gill was quite right to pick up the connection, and in its rarely interrupted serenity I do not feel that the quartet has anything to fear from the comparison.

The Coull Quartet did the work proud, giving it nine performances in 1984-85, including one in Hong Kong. They recorded it for Hyperion, coupled with the Eleventh Quartet. The recording was issued in 1988, and the cover bears, very aptly, a photograph of a white dove in flight.

The Eleventh followed in 1984. Like its predecessor, it was commissioned by the Coull, with funds provided by West Midlands Arts. There are four movements, joined together: 1) Allegro molto 2) Adagio 3) Presto 4) Molto adagio pianissimo, and the quartet lasts for approximately twenty-five minutes. The composer's programme note is of a technical nature, and I will thus quote it sparingly, to give an idea of the work's character:

"Unlike No.10 ... this quartet is for most of its length intense and often turbulent, though it eventually becomes remote and ethereal ... The first movement is fast and full of fierce contrasts. Its concentrated opening clears space for quieter expansions (a lesson learned form Beethoven's Op.95) ... At length, with a tightening then a broadening of rhythm, the piece moves directly into an adagio, marked intensivo. Most of this movement consists of intense slow counterpoint ...A strong climax is raised; it subsides, leading softly into a very fast scherzo movement. From its hushed start the scherzo gradually grows in energy and volume ... All this boils up into ever more furious music, which suddenly vanishes into thin air.

"We are left with slow music that never rises above ppp. The basic elements are still all there, but everything is so remote that at length even these disappear into space." The quartet received its première on 30th March

1985 at Alfreton Hall, Derbyshire, played of course by the dedicatees, who surpassed their efforts on behalf of the Tenth by giving no fewer than eleven performances of the new work during 1985-86, four of them in the USA. After a performance at the Frick Collection, New York, Allan Kozinn wrote of the quartet in the New York Times (14/4/86): "The highlight of the afternoon.... "A spellbinding work... an acerbic edge, a propulsive rhythmic sense and, in the quick first and third movements, a brash and almost barbaric energy. The slow movements, alternatively introspective and eerie, are no less gripping."

Robert Simpson followed the quartets with a more unusual chamber piece, the Trio for Horn, Violin and Piano, also written in 1984. It was commissioned by the Festival Trio of London (Frank Lloyd, Carol Slater and Anthony Halstead) with funds provided by the Arts Council of Great Britain. The composer stressed that the work was conceived very much as a "genuine trio" – the characteristic qualities of all three instruments are always respected, but none dominates. There are three movements: 1) Allegro con brio 2) Tranquillo 3) Allegro, and the playing time is a little over eighteen minutes. It is a lively, straightforward piece, and the finale was described by Simpson as having "something of the character of a blunt scherzo."

The first performance was given at the Purcell Room on the South Bank on 10th April 1985 by the dedicatees. It was recorded for Hyperion by Richard Watkins (horn), Pauline Lowbury (violin) and Christopher Green-Armytage (piano), coupled with the Horn Quartet, and the disc appeared in 1994.

The Violin Sonata was written the same year. It was commissioned by Pauline Lowbury, with funds provided by the Arts Council and the Britten-Pears Foundation. It is dedicated to Pauline and her pianist partner, Christopher Green-Armytage. Upon enquiring about the violinist to Martin Anderson, Simpson discovered that she had been a pupil of his old friend Ernest Element, and averred: "If she was good enough for Ernie, she's good enough for me!" The sonata is in two movements: 1) Allegro 2) Variazioni e Ricercare: Andante-L'istesso Tempo-Doppo Movimento-Piu Animato, and lasts almost twenty-seven minutes. The allegro is vigorous, and the longer second movement combines the function of slow movement, scherzo and finale in a continuous increase of activity within the same basic pulse – roughly the same pattern as the Third Symphony and the Horn Quartet.

The première was given at the Wigmore Hall on 3rd February 1986 by the dedicatees, who also played violin sonatas by Beethoven (A minor, Op.23) and Brahms (A major, Op.100). Stephen Pettitt (Times, 5/2/86) opined: "If Robert Simpson's finished work on first acquaintance does seem to have its weak moments, it contains much that is as stimulating for the listener as it is challenging for the performers", while Alan Blyth (Telegraph, same date) wrote "One looks forward to another encounter with this work."

The sonata was recorded for Hyperion by the same players, coupled with the Piano Trio (sponsored by the Robert Simpson Society) and the disc appeared in 1995.

In 1985 Robert Simpson was appointed a consultant at Birmingham School of Music, which ended after two years – personal disagreements led to his not being invited back, although he would willingly have come, even after the move to Eire.

During the same year, Sir Michael Tippett celebrated his eightieth birthday, and the occasion was marked by the publication of a symposium, "Michael Tippett, O.M., a Celebration", edited by Geraint Lewis. While he had reservations about the veteran composer's later output, Simpson was a great admirer of Tippett's earlier music, and contributed a short (1½ minute) piano piece called "Michael Tippett, His Mystery", in much the same spirit as he had for William Walton's seventieth in 1972. The miniature received its first public performance at the Royal Northern College of Music on 23rd January 1993, played by Raymond Clarke. Clarke also recorded it for Hyperion as part of the disc of Simpson's complete solo piano output issued in 1996.

In 1985 Robert Simpson also completed his first (and only, although he intended to write another) organ work, Eppur Si Muove. I reproduce his programme note in full: "This large organ work is dedicated to the Danish organist Svend Aage Spange and his wife Annalise. It lasts about thirty minutes and its title is the words Galileo is said to have muttered as he turned away after having been forced by the Church to recant his view that the earth moved round the sun – "but it DOES move!" There is no programme, but the vast slow motion of the music has something to do with Galileo's words – the composer (a fellow of the Royal Astronomical Society) has long been fascinated by astronomy.

"The whole work is derived from a circling group of notes at the very beginning. There are two main sections – Ricercar and Passacaglia, both growing from the same germ. The Ricercar behaves at first like a chorale prelude, with the chorale lines in the pedals; these lines are also derived from the opening notes (this anticipates the first part of the Ninth Symphony of a year later). Gradually the Ricercar develops on a large scale, with varying contrapuntal textures and an unvarying pulse throughout. It reaches an animated climax before subsiding into the quiet beginning of the Passacaglia. The subject is also made from the opening notes, and in the course of the Passacaglia it is heard at all twelve pitches, starting with C sharp. When it reaches C natural, the original chorale appears in the pedals below it; soon afterwards a quicker coda finds the way back to C sharp, on which the final climax is founded."

Simpson referred to the work informally as "very angry!", adding "Herbert Lom!", referring to the latter's antics as Inspector Clouseau's deranged former boss and present arch-enemy in the classic Pink Panther film comedies.

The first performance was given by Christopher Bowers-Broadbent at Marylebone Parish Church of 25th May 1988. It was recorded for Hyperion by Ian Quinn, playing the organ of Winchester Cathedral, a disc which also included Simpson's slender vocal output and the Canzona for Brass, released in 1998. DJF, reviewing the disc in the Gramophone, found Media Morte "appropriately austere", and considered that the Eppur Si Muove "sets its jaw squarely against conventional organ-loft grandiosity, its intellectual monumentality is clearly in the Commotio mould, though I think it's only fair to say that it's considerably tougher going than Nielsen's late masterpiece."

On 18th February 1986 Robert and Angela Simpson moved to Siochain, Killelton, near Camp, County Kerry, in the Irish Republic. They had previously holidayed in the area, and fallen in love with it. Both felt very much at odds with the Thatcher government, with its union-bashing, culture of greed and unquestioning support for the USA – policies faithfully maintained, of course, by the succeeding Labour administration. Simpson had a great affection for the Irish people, their quirks included; he related an occasion many years previously, when he had been driving along a country road; as he turned the bend, an arm emerged from a ditch waving a bottle, and then sank back. "He's probably still there," mused the composer. Another time, he asked an Irishman if they made jokes about English people as the latter do about the Irish – "No! They're not funny!" the man replied, which he thought an excellent put-down.

Siochain means peace in Gaelic. Some time after moving in, Simpson was stopped by the police for speeding; upon giving his address, the officer asked what the name meant – he could not resist pointing out that it formed part of their own name (Garda Siochauna). The house is effectively a large bungalow (though with an extra bedroom and bathroom upstairs) built on the hillside, with a huge bay window looking down on Tralee Bay itself. It was architect-designed, originally for the designer's own occupation. Killelton could hardly even be called a hamlet, merely a small group of houses (although it does boast two pubs!) and it is sited by an old railway stop, the line itself being long closed. After a short walk down, one can walk for miles along the beach while hardly seeing another soul, seabirds excepted.

The Simpsons soon settled into their adopted homeland. In a letter to Harold Phillipson dated 1st April 1989, the composer wrote:

"Greetings from Ireland! We often think about you all in Aylesbury, but are glad to be out of ferocious, competitive England and in this beautiful country

At Killelton, late 1980's, writing with Carl Nielsen's silver propelling pencil

Robert Simpson outside 'Siochain', Killelton, County Kerry, Eire, his home from 1986 until his death.

with its warm and simple people. There are plenty of bad things in Ireland (including its politics and the stranglehold of the Catholic Church – connected to each other) but we haven't for a moment regretted our move. Angela is doing speech therapy for the local Cerebral Palsy and Down's Syndrome societies and I can work peacefully at my compositions, with a whole list of commissions to fulfil in the next couple of years and, certainly, more to come. So life is both tranquil and productive. Its tranquillity is sometimes modified by two obstreperous dogs, to say nothing of four cats and a tankful of tropical fish (these are the quietist and most soothing members of the household). No doubt you have heard from Peter what it's like here. We hope he and Sue are settled happily in the Peaks.

"I've felt obliged to leave AI (Amnesty International), as will be explained by the enclosed copy of my letter to them, which I thought you were entitled to see. I'm sad about it, but don't believe in doing things by half. Perhaps you'll disagree with my reaction, but I feel very strongly that AI must not compromise itself. If it does, I cannot associate myself with it.

"We have started a Kerry Peace Group here and our biggest achievement so far is to get Kerry officially declared a Nuclear-Free Zone. People here are naturally sympathetic to the peace movement, and Irish neutrality is an important issue that still has to be fought for. Some political elements here would like to steer Ireland into NATO, for ulterior motives and with obvious disastrous results, but they are given pause by the latest opinion polls, which show 88% in favour of complete neutrality. The peace movement is by its very nature political in that it wants to change the system, and I go wholeheartedly along with that aspect of it. The sight of Amnesty seeming to seek a kind of alliance with Thatcher against, of all people Gorbachov at the present time, gives me the creeps I'm afraid."

Later, the dogs increased to three and the cats to five – Angela could never resist taking in a stray. Both were contributors to charity, Bob tending to favour human charities and his wife animal welfare ones. Simpson didn't have a very high opinion of RTE, the Irish broadcasting corporation; in a letter to John Clarkson from 18/1/89 he describes it as "rather what Radio Bogota must be like", and felt that some of the brass players in the RTE Orchestra would have been rejected by most brass bands. For all that, he did introduce a series of the Bruckner symphonies played by the resident orchestra. He tried to improve standards at the station; in a letter to John Kinsella dated 15th June 1988 he gave a detailed critique:

"Having had to put up with "Morning Call" on Radio 1, where what can only be described as Drawing Room Disc Jockeys introduce often fragmented items with breathtaking displays of ignorance (the other morning we had "Gluck" pronounced as if it were to rhyme in an extremely rude limerick, and Burr-lee-Ozz, in the same programme), I was interested to see that FM3 is providing music in the early morning.

"I always switch the radio on at 6.30 am to get the news and weather, and often leave it on for a bit – though I must confess that I have been switching it off sooner and sooner. Venetia tells me that "Morning Call" comes under Light Entertainment and therefore has nothing to do with Music Department. Is the same true of FM3's opener? In the event it seems little better than "Morning Call", though we are spared the DRDJs. But we do get a similar stream of snippets, a proper dog's dinner without any discernible plan, and precious little information.

"The other morning we did get a complete Mozart piano concerto (K450), but not a word about who played it, and the reverb. at the end of it was brutally cut off, only to be followed by a long silence and then the irritating clatter of TWO pianos playing Bizet – irritating, that is, after the finest Mozart, without a word to cushion the effect. This morning we got the Andante from Eine Kleine Nachtmusik TWICE – it was then back-announced as "two movements from". Was anybody listening, and if they were, didn't they notice?

"In the BBC of unhallowed memory (so far as I'm concerned) we would at least have got one hell of a rocket for that! Again there was no mention of the performers of the items, except that Pavarotti was responsible for a particularly fearsome bit of can belto. Quite right - villains must be identified, but it seems to be forgotten that an announcer's job is to give the listener the information he needs, the more so if it's a complete masterpiece. This negligence exists in other more prestigious musical fields, too. Some time ago I heard the last movement of Haydn No.94; having been unable to switch on earlier I was anxious to hear who was conducting this very lively performance. It was obviously from the NCH and after the applause I was informed that the concert was introduced by so-and-so and produced by so-and-so. No more. To assume that the listener is more interested in the music than the introducer or producer is surely the least respect that can be offered, to say nothing of that due to the performers or, sometimes, even composers! Is it really necessary to have public concerts "introduced" by rather self-consciously ingratiating personalities, rather than by announcers pleasantly conveying quiet, unassertive authority, giving clear, correct information? This is all that's needed, and doesn't intrude extraneous elements into what, after all, is a concert.

"All this has been bothering me for the last couple of years or so, but I didn't want to trouble you with it, the less so since I'm an interloper in this country!"

He then goes on to make some planning suggestions, ending with: "Forgive me for all this. I love it here in Ireland and wouldn't go back to Britain for a million pounds. But Radio 3 has a point or two (degraded though it is now is compared with the old Third Programme, which is one of the reasons I resigned in 1980) and some hints could be picked up from it. More listeners would be gained than lost – of that I'm certain."

"A CATHEDRAL IN SOUND"

(1986 - 1988)

For the whole of 1986, Robert Simpson was preoccupied with the composition of his massive Ninth Symphony. This was commissioned by the Bournemouth Symphony Orchestra, with funds provided by the Arts Council. The fee was £4000 - not much for twelve months' work, but better than nothing. Simpson's practice, when asked as to how much a work would cost, was to forward a copy of a list of recommended charges drawn up by the Composers' Guild. On 3rd February 1986 David Richardson, the orchestra's Chief Executive, wrote to the composer:

"Thank you for news of the symphony. It's good to know that you are well into it but the length is a problem as far as programme is concerned. I am always hesitant about interfering in any way with the creative process but we were looking for a piece of around 30 or 40 minutes which could be combined with one or two other major repertoire pieces for reasons of rehearsal time and ensuring a large audience. At the risk of seeming philistine is there any possibility of coming in at a shorter length? I would not like to have to change the date of the first performance but I do have to look at the context."

Simpson's reply, on 6th February, referred to his unfortunate experiences with the Nielsen Variations, adding:

"I absolutely understand YOUR problem, which is far different from the BBC's arrogance. If the première of No.9 has to be postponed, that's my bad luck, and you may be well advised to substitute Tchaik 5 and make sure of a decent audience. And I don't believe you are a philistine – but I do believe that even risking philistinism IS philistinism! Once a creative process has begun, it must be honestly and ruthlessly pursued, and however sincerely I have to apologise to you for the problem this sets you, there's no escape from it for me. There's no chance of cutting the piece, or changing its internal demands.

"My intention was to produce an average-sized symphony; for immediate purposes it's unfortunate that this particular one happens to coincide with a "new road" in my work – not towards gigantism, but towards a calmer, broader outlook, perhaps influenced most by Bach, and to some extent by Bruckner, as opposed to the Beethoven-Nielsen terseness that has hitherto been my chief aim. The new direction has to be taken – it's part of a process, and in my sixties I'm too much of an old bird to attempt to compromise with it.

"I don't see why you shouldn't get a good audience if you were to get a really famous soloist to do the Emperor in Part 1 and the symphony in Part 2, rather than a relatively unknown soloist (however good) to do the Dvořák, together with which Tchaik 5 would be a safer bet. If we have to wait, so be it! I've always been prepared to take the rough with the smooth, and for a preponderance of the former."

At the Robert Simpson Society AGM (or piss-up, as Martin Anderson described the subsequent proceedings!) in the Institute of Economic Affairs, Smith Street, in the summer of 1986, Simpson showed the score of what was then the first movement (he had originally intended a multi-movement work) to his old friend Hans Keller. Sadly, Keller was by then dying of motor neurone disease and could barely speak, but wrote down his comments, calling it "a masterpiece" but adding "beware harmonics". The Ninth was finally completed on Christmas Day of that year. It is a single-movement work on a large scale (lasting almost fifty minutes) and the structure falls into three sections: Maestoso, tempo giusto – Molto vivace – Maestoso. Here is part of Simpson's programme note:

"Commissioned by the Bournemouth Symphony Orchestra with Funds provided by the Arts Council of Great Britain, this symphony is dedicated to my wife Angela.

"It is in one movement lasting some fifty minutes, and the whole is carried on a consistent pulse; although the scherzo-like molto vivace might be thought of as a "middle" section, it is really only the climax of two main parts, and its triple-time is the same as the soft triplets that open the symphony. In the deliberation of its movement the symphony may sometimes suggest Bruckner, and one passage is a conscious tribute to him; anyone knowing the Bruckner symphonies will not find it difficult to identify its origins. Even stronger is the influence of Bach; the whole of the first part is like a vast chorale prelude, in which periodic sustained entries, like the lines of a chorale, are heard in a polyphonic setting. It culminates in a release of energy, a scherzo-like climax in Beethoven's characteristic fast triple time, developing in new ways the same matter as before. It reaches a massive striding climax with the return of the Maestoso tempo, and the second part of the work is a long slow movement (also polyphonic, beginning like a fugue) nearly the same length as the first. At a fairly late stage, during the growth to the final climax, a series of variations is heard, increasing in activity as a great crescendo is built. After this, the music gradually comes to a peaceful end."

The tribute to Bruckner referred to comes towards the end of the "chorale prelude" and almost quotes a unison theme from the first movement of the Third Symphony. Some friends also asked the composer if the climax of the variations was a tribute to Bruckner's Sixth, to which he replied "perhaps it is, but not deliberate." It certainly seems to me to have a strong rhythmic kinship, fully absorbed into Simpson's own musical language. The composer continued his programme note with a detailed technical analysis which I will not quote. For those who like to know exactly what is going on, musically speaking, Simpson follows the Hyperion recording with an illustrated talk, delivered in his inimitable relaxed, reassuring manner. The Ninth certainly does seem to mark the beginning of a new phase in Simpson's musical development, and I am sure that his more congenial surroundings were a factor in the calmer and more spacious character of the later works; a majority of them end quietly, although he could still be ferociously dissonant when he felt it appropriate. The original plan for the première was adhered to, despite Simpson's misgivings, with Vernon Handley conducting the Bournemouth SO, and Felix Schmidt playing the Dvořák Cello Concerto. The first performance took place at the Wessex Hall, Poole on 8th April 1987, and the second at the Guildhall, Southampton, two days later. This latter, which I attended, was a near-disaster; the conductor failed to appear on time, and the audience was told that he had a nose-bleed, but should be fit to appear shortly. The bleed proved unstoppable, and the composer was called to the rear of the hall. There then came an announcement – the Dvořák was cancelled, and Simpson would be conducting his own symphony. After an interval, the composer appeared (wearing a borrowed tie) and the concert began. In a letter to the author dated 28th April he wrote: "… it all went too slow! Predictably it was over-cautious and I couldn't do more than try to beat time in such a long and difficult piece, without rehearsal and with jittery nerves. A pity you didn't hear the first performance – much the finest I've had of a new orchestral work. Tod Handley is really the best conductor in the country if only people would realise it, despite the understandable claims of the Birmingham fanatics!" (The reference is to Simon Rattle's popularity.)

Whatever the failings of the performance (Simpson only agreed to conduct if the intended live broadcast was cancelled) the work still made its impact, for all that most of the audience had probably come to hear the Dvořák. Sitting in front of me were two middle-class chatterers. The man in particular seemed determined to dislike the new work, and muttered at the opening double-bass pedal "that's enough." I was bracing myself to tell him to shut up when the music did it for me: as the triplet rhythm began he was drawn in, remained absorbed throughout the fifty minutes, and applauded enthusiastically at the end. Thus can Simpson's music communicate readily with the uninitiated, even the potentially hostile. The Ninth is an exceptionally compelling piece; the scope is vast, the climaxes staggeringly powerful, and one can readily understand why the composer thought it his best work. In a letter to Sally Willison of Faber (26/1/88) he wrote: "… the work got off to such an unfortunate start – no press at the première (except the local papers), only one at Southampton, since they were all expecting to hear it on the radio, and, so far as I know, only one notice of the broadcast. Amazing what a nosebleed can cause! Since everyone who has heard this symphony seems to think there is something exceptional about it (and I would defy any living symphonist to beat it)…"

The only national newsman to have attended the second performance was Paul Driver of The Independent, whose review appeared on 26th April 1987. "There are few musical minds in the musical world capable of completing such a large and complex symphonic structure (Maxwell Davies, for all his distance of style, is the only other one who comes to mind) and if one finds Simpson's idiom a little colourless or dry or anachronistic, it undoubtedly affords the manifold satisfaction of "pure" music." I doubt if Simpson appreciated this comparison; his opinion of the bard of Orkney's music was not a high one. I have been unable to trace the date of the broadcast, but on this occasion the Independent was far more enthusiastic: "Awesome." "Few symphonies have better deserved the description of a cathedral in sound since the first movement of Bruckner's Ninth itself." (Bayan Northcott, 16/1/88)

The work was played twice in Ireland during 1991; Handley conducted it again with the National Symphony Orchestra in Dublin on 9th February, and the RTE Orchestra played it under John Carewe, with Mozart's "Impresario" overture, and the Tchaikovsky Violin Concerto played by Young-Uk Kim.

The London première came on 12th February 1992 at the Royal Festival Hall, with Simon Rattle conducting the London Philharmonic Orchestra. The Ninth was preceded by Nielsen's tone poem Pan and Syrinx, and after the interval came Beethoven's Seventh Symphony, which I thought rather an odd piece of programming. The composer was present; though by then incapacitated following his stroke, he was able to stand with assistance and acknowledge the applause with a wave. Edward Greenfield (Guardian, 13th February) found the Ninth "one of the very finest of post-war symphonies." Anthony Payne (Independent, same date) felt that "it achieves heroic status", while Max Loppert (FT, 18th February) commented: "What makes this work so fiercely concentrated and exhilarating is the sweep, the plain-spoken majesty accrued as the structures build up: it may not be exactly a lovable work, but it is a hugely compelling one." The Ninth has not been played since, which seems curious when one considers the praise heaped upon the recording which Hyperion released in 1988, with Handley conducting the Bournemouth SO. The disc was sponsored to the very generous tune of 10000 dollars by the Rex Foundation of San Francisco, a charity set up by the rock band The Grateful Dead, and a further sum was raised by members of the Robert Simpson Society. The composer took the somewhat out-of-character step of suggesting a press conference to coincide with the release of the record, since there had been so little coverage of the earlier performances. In the letter to Sally Willison of Faber already mentioned, he said:

"I've never suggested anything like this before, but I'm sure it's now necessary to foster a bit of interest before the thing gets forgotten for the next twenty years, in which case all of us will be the losers. What about a press conference, not just for the press, but for conductors, orchestral managers, BBC, etc, at which I would be happy to give a short illustrated talk on the work before the CD recording is heard … as an interested party I would of course be willing to split the cost three ways with you and Ted, or two ways just with you, if the recording has cleaned Ted out. You know me well enough by now to know that I'm not a publicity-hound – but I would like to see a determined rescue act for my greatest work so far." This never happened.

The recording got rave reviews; the Penguin Guide to Compact Discs describes it as "A most powerful experience: Concentrated, awesome, and as mysterious as some astronomical phenomenon. Played superbly, and no less superbly recorded." The disc received the Gramophone Contemporary Music Award for 1989. A poll of readers of the BBC Music Magazine ten years later, asking them to nominate their favourite 20th century work and composer, gave Robert Simpson's Ninth Symphony joint third place alongside Britten's Peter Grimes and Shostakovich's Fifth Symphony, while among composers he ranked fifth, after Bartok, Elgar, Prokofiev and Richard Strauss. Some lesson here, surely? David Fanning commented: "In its own austere but equally inspiring way, Simpson had found what Sibelius in the end seemingly despaired of finding – a way of uniting the essentials of symphonic momentum with the essentials of modern consciousness."

Before embarking on his equally massive Tenth Symphony, Simpson turned his attention to chamber and brass band music.

The Twelfth String Quartet was written in 1987, completed on 22nd October. It was commissioned for the 1988 Nottingham Festival and first performed at Newstead Abbey, Lord Byron's former gaff, by the Coull Quartet, champions of the Tenth and Eleventh, on 6th June 1988. It is dedicated to the composer, conductor and musicologist Lionel Pike. There are two movements: 1) Adagio 2) Molto vivace, and the work plays for slightly over thirty-one minutes. I have not been able to find a programme note by the composer, and will quote instead from Matthew Taylor's sleeve-note:

"…the first (movement is) a deeply meditative, polyphonic slow movement and the second a colossal scherzo, in structure similar in some ways to the finale of the recent Eleventh Symphony (1990). The opening Adagio unfolds gently with a peaceful fugue subject announced by the first violin ... the second movement (Molta vivace) is perhaps the longest scherzo for string quartet in existence ... astonishingly maintaining the pace for nearly 1800 bars, though it is not, as the composer says, "all sound and fury". Large spans are in fact restrained and delicate, but even here the energy is latent. Throughout the piece there is also much humour, often of a rough, forceful kind, sometimes skittish and mischievous ... The Quartet ends abruptly in a blaze of immense energy." Peter Palmer, writing in the Nottingham Evening Post (7/6/88) found it "life-enhancing" and "vigorous proof that classical music is not altogether – or even primarily, a thing of the past.", adding a characteristic piece of Simpsonian humour: "As he himself puts it, he can't be classed with the spit-and cough brigade." The Quartet was recorded for Hyperion by the Coull, coupled with the First String Quintet, and the disc, sponsored by the Robert Simpson Society, appeared in 1992.

The String Trio was also written in 1987, and is in three movements (Prelude, Adagio and Fugue) lasting some 13½ minutes. The composer's programme note reads:

"This short work of 1987 is dedicated to Jillian White, who suggested it for one of the lunchtime concerts she organises in Bristol (for the BBC). Its subtitle is self-explanatory, and the piece is easy to follow. The short and vigorous Prelude is marked Presto, mainly light and transparent, with quick flickering figurations of thirds and fourths against which more sustained lines are thrown. The Adagio arises naturally from the Prelude, being also based on the same intervals (reversed – fourths and thirds); its mood is quietly thoughtful, not without intensity. The Fugue is marked Volante ("flying") and begins Pianissimo with muted strings. in fairy-like scherzando mood. Thirds and fourths are also its main sustenance, and after a while there is a contrasting, more singing subject. In time-honoured manner this is soon combined with the first, but as the excitement grows, the Prelude joins in, presumably out of resentment at having been cut short so early." The work was first performed in Bristol on 5th October 1989.

The Trio was recorded for Hyperion by the Delmé Quartet (or at least three-quarters of them) and the disc, which also contains the Third and Sixth Quartets, appeared in 1990, again recorded in association with the Robert Simpson Society.

Simpson's First String Quintet was written in the summer of 1987. As with Mozart's quintets it uses two violas rather than the two cellos favoured by Schubert. The work was commissioned by the BBC for one in the series of Monday lunchtime concerts in St John's Smith Square, and is dedicated to Frances Bain, a close friend of the composer and his wife. It is in a single movement, lasting a little over thirty-four minutes and contains two tempi, Andante and Vivace, which alternate; the opening is Andante, the Vivace then appears, growing longer every time it is heard, until it takes over completely, building a fierce central climax: the process is then gradually reversed, with the Andante gradually supplanting the Vivace, until the latter has gone, and in the composer's words "the end is peaceful and its sense of calm includes the intense energy at the heart of the work." It was first performed at the intended venue by the augmented Coull Quartet on 17th April 1989, and the programme also included Dvořák's String Quintet in E flat Op.97. The Quintet was, as previously noted, released on record by Hyperion in 1992.)

During 1987 Simpson also produced one of his rare essays in vocal music, Tempi (for full mixed voice chorus a capella). The work was commissioned for the 25th Seminar on Contemporary Choral Music, University College, Cork, and was supposed to be premièred during the event that year; however Colin Mawby initially rejected it as too difficult. It was first performed at the same event on 28th April 1988. The dedication is to Kenneth and Margaret Roberton. The composer was moved to write to Mawby afterwards, on 2nd May:

"I was sorry not to be able to talk with you after the Seminar at Cork – when I looked for you, you had disappeared, and it's a pity we didn't have the chance of an interesting discussion, in the course of which you might have found me a little less ignorant than perhaps you supposed. When you asked if I had ever sang in a choir I should, instead of displaying irritation at what seemed at the time a deliberately loaded question, have said No because my voice is so execrable that (to paraphrase Groucho Marx) I wouldn't join any choir that would have me as a member. This would have been the simple truth, as also was my only half-heard reply that I had never played in a string quartet, but nobody had ever complained about my quartet writing, least of all the players. I wonder if Berlioz or Wagner ever sang in choirs.

"Once I had a conversation with Dohnányi, who asked me if I was a composer. I said YES. He asked me if I was a pianist. I said NO. He said it was impossible to be a composer without being a pianist. I said "What about Berlioz?" He said, "Berlioz was not a composer!" End of conversation.

"While I'm not, like you, a choral specialist, thirty years of intensive experience in the BBC of listening to choirs in rehearsal and performance, talking to both singers and conductors, helping them get over problems, sometimes in very difficult music, has left me with more than a tyro's knowledge of the subject. All this plus more than fifty years' rigorous experience of composition has enabled me to get to know, pretty surely, what's difficult and what's not.

"I know very well that Tempi is not an easy piece. But the Allegri Singers at least showed that it was possible to get somewhere near it, and given a better conductor and perhaps more rehearsal they could certainly have made a better job of it. They are amateurs. When the piece was written it was on the understanding that it was going to be done by the RTE Choir, a professional body I had not in fact heard – but it was of course written for highly accomplished singers. This is something I couldn't possibly say at the Seminar.

"Given your view when you declined to perform it last year, your decision was honest and right. But it doesn't change my knowledge that the piece is perfectly negotiable by the right singers under the right conductor …"

Tempi did eventually get a worthy performance, by the Corydon Singers conducted by Matthew Best, on the Hyperion disc issued in 1998. It lasts for almost eighteen minutes. Here is Matthew Taylor's sleeve-note:

"The piece consists entirely of Italian terms whose meanings are reflected in the music.

"The work is in two parts. The first embraces a familiar Simpson fingerprint, first encountered in the Third Symphony: a gradual acceleration over a long span. Hence the music moves effortlessly from "Adagio mesto" to "Andante cantabile", from "Allegretto grazioso" to "Allegro con brio", eventually unleashing a sparkling "Prestissimo" which forms the culmination of the first part. There is an abundance of striking word-painting during this section; take the "Subito forte" eruptions, the stampeding "Impazientamente", the ominous sound of low basses singing "Susurrando minaccioso".

"Part 2 is shorter. It is heralded by a return of the slow tempo, "Lento molto intensivo", begun by tenors and basses and later taken up by female voices. Soon the intensity eases, and the music relaxes into one of Simpson's most magical stretches of reflective polyphony."

The full text is as follows:

Adagio mesto, Espressivo, Crescendo, Calmato, Adagio tranquillo, Andante cantabile, Dolce, Allegretto grazioso, Con grazia, Allegro con brio, Allegro brioso, Accelerando, Diminuendo, Prestissimo, Molto vivo, Subito piano, Subito forte, Prestissimo molto vivace, Subito forte, Subito pianissimo, Subito fortissimo, Prestissimo, Vivo, Volante, Vivace, Adirato, Impazientamente, Irato, Con furia, Susurrando minaccioso, Feroce, Furioso, Con rabbia, Lento molto intensivo, Calmato, Tranquillo, Calmo, Pochettino crescendo, Morendo al niente.

Finally, from 1987, comes what I think is Simpson's finest work for brass band, the Introduction and Allegro on a bass of Max Reger. It was commissioned by Howard Snell, director of the Desford Colliery Dowty Band, with funds supplied by East Midland Arts, and first performed by them at the Warwick Arts Centre on 27th February 1988. It is dedicated to Peter Wilson, and lasts almost sixteen minutes. The two movements are marked Adagio – pesante and Allegro vivace. Here is the composer's programme note:

"Reger's Fantasia and Fugue in D minor, Op.135b, is one of the greatest organ works since Bach: it was one of his last works, completed only a few months before his premature death at the age of 43 in 1916. The bass in this brass band work occurs towards the end of Reger's fugue (from halfway through bar 103 to the end of bar 105, in the original, complete version published in the collected edition of his music). Reger's notation is in 12/8 time: I have transcribed it in 3/4, and in this new notation it takes ten bars of quick time. In Reger's fugue it is part of a gigantic ritenuto – here it is treated throughout as an allegro, and one note of it has been flattened to make it combinable with a string of rising fourths.

"The line itself is not heard complete until the start of the Allegro. There are other themes, and the rising fourths that accompany the Reger theme (like the answer in a fugal exposition) are also important. During the final climax (bars 711-720) Reger's own magnificent treatment of this bass is used. The Introduction is mainly mysterious and deliberate; the Allegro is full of energy."

The first performance was given at Warwick on 27th February 1988.

I believe that the London première of the Introduction and Allegro was given during the City of London Festival on 14th July 1988, by the Brittania B.S. Band, again under Howard Snell. The work was recorded by the Desford Colliery Caterpillar Band conducted by James Watson in their disc of the complete brass band music. Simpson was delighted by these performances; in a letter to Hyperion boss Ted Perry dated 23rd May 1991 he wrote: "The playing is terrific – I don't think I've ever had my symphonies played with quite that astonishing brilliance." Miriam has given me a personal reminiscence of the recording sessions, which took place on the 3rd, 4th and 5th of August 1990. "Bob came and stayed here (Wigston Magna, near Leicester), when the Caterpillar Band recorded his brass band music at Lutterworth Grammar School. I drove him every day and stayed during the Hyperion recordings. I was surprised how many were very young artists. A very hot August week and they were all casting off their garments. They might have imagined playing on a seaside beach."

Robert Simpson embarked on what was to be his biggest symphony, the Tenth, on New Year's Day 1988, and completed it 10½ months later. Unlike the Ninth, this is a symphony in the classical four-movement form: 1)

Allegro 2) Allegro leggiere 3) Andante molto mosso 4) Largo – Allegro con brio. It is dedicated to Vernon Handley, and lasts almost fifty-five minutes. John Pickard wrote a lengthy analysis, to which the composer added the following:

"This might be thought of as a sinfonia espansiva, though not in the same sense as Nielsen's famous work, where the title comes from a particular feeling about human awareness. Here the words could be applied simply to the musical process itself, concerned with a special kind of expansion. The harsh first movement, being essentially preludial, rarely permits its ideas to be more than short and terse, accumulating brick by brick, so to speak, with a certain amount of deliberate reiteration and sequence, while the material is constantly transformed and any recapitulatory elements are disguised. This process is started by the two fragments thrown out forcibly at the opening; some might want to compare this with the beginning of Beethoven's Hammerklavier sonata, but Beethoven soon develops long lines in this movement, which is then offset by the brief and aphoristic scherzo (as was to happen later in the great B flat quartet, Op.130). In the first movement of this symphony the intention is completely different – long lines are purposely avoided in view of what is going to happen afterwards. There is a slight expansion at the end of the movement, to hint at things to come.

"In the rather ghostly scherzo the way of delivery is slightly broader, with many long descending scales of peculiar and unpredictable forms. But the melodic lines themselves are still fairly short, and they tend to gather steady momentum by piling quiet statements on top of each other, as in the final approach to the one restrained climax in the piece, where each level adds a note as a complex chord is formed. This is then dispersed. The Andante molto mosso and the finale now display long lines; both are markedly polyphonic. The central part of the slow movement in quicker (but related) tempo makes an allusion to the scherzo by recalling its method of piling up melodic elements to form a widespread chord. But this harmonic mass, instead of being mysteriously dispersed, now causes a large climax, from which the original material emerges with high intensity, then gradually winding itself down in peace.

"Harmonically open-edged, it makes way for the finale's exploratory slow introduction. This once more recalls earlier behaviour by issuing itself in quanta, or discrete bits. These gather themselves together, then dissolve. Out of the resulting hiatus springs the final fugue with its long energetic subject. Here is the completely expansive part of the symphony. Long lines proliferate, seeping from quiet to climax with contrasting subjects. Nearly everything grows from the minor third basic to the whole symphony, in which each movement starts with the same two notes. The symphony finishes with something like the blunt compression of its beginning, and with the same chord. The sense of contraction at the end matches the slight broadening at the close of its first movement, as if completing some kind of circle." In his essay on the Tenth (The Symphonies of Robert Simpson, edited by Robert Matthew-Walker), John Pickard recalled: "At the time of the première of Symphony No 9 in 1987 Simpson was quoted as saying: "I think I'm changing – getting calmer." Symphony No 10 does indeed contain much that is calm but, as the composer remarked in a letter to the present writer: "The poor old sod has a lot of ginger in him yet!"

The first performance took place in the Philharmonic Hall, Liverpool, on 16th January 1991, with the RLPO conducted by the dedicatee, the concert also including Sibelius's tone poem The Bard and Rachmaninov's Third Piano Concerto, played by Peter Donohoe. As with the Ninth, another near-disaster; Handley's car tyres were slashed while he took a break in a motorway service station, and Simpson had to do most of the rehearsing himself. I taped the performance from the radio broadcast and found it rather tentative. The London première followed on 31st January 1991, with the same forces, at the Royal Festival Hall, this time coupled with music by Beethoven: the Fidelio overture and the Triple Concerto played by the Israel Piano Trio, whom Simpson thought the best in the world. Any hesitancy vanished in this second rendition; the work made a tremendous impression. the sheer physical excitement of the finale, especially, with the two timpanists thundering away from opposite sides of the orchestra, can never be matched by a recording, however good. The composer was immensely pleased: "Yes, they've really got into it now!" A preview in the Daily Telegraph by Michael Kennedy on January 11th observed: "Simpson's music, strong, individual and shorn of gimmicks, owes its structural mastery to the composer's admiration for Beethoven, Bruckner and Sibelius." Neil Tierney's review in the same paper on January 21st was generally favourable, but added: "My only real grumble about this hour-long work is that it is in need of pruning." Where, pray? David Fanning (Independent, 18th January) headed his review: "Hard work and a hell of a fugue" and had some reservations about the length of the slow movement, but also said: "His stock has never stood higher."

Readers will not now be surprised to learn that, for all that, the Tenth has yet to receive a third performance. The recording was made by Hyperion a matter of days after the London première, by the same players in the Philharmonic Hall, and released during 1991. CD Review considered the piece "Of inestimable value. A major release." BBC Record Review considered the disc "Terrific. It's hard to imagine anything which could be improved about the presentation. A very rewarding experience."

So – where is it? Robert Simpson wrote a sincere tribute to the orchestra in 1990.

"To reach its 150th anniversary, the Royal Liverpool Philharmonic Society has had to surmount many adversities of all kinds. It has done so triumphantly, without ever compromising its artistic standards, maintained to this day at a very high level. Any composer is bound to regard its interest in his work as a compliment, and he can be sure that the greatest care will be taken in the performance of it. As I have always found, the splendid orchestra always works sincerely and hard if it is tackling a new and difficult score; without fail I have been impressed by the sheer concentration in rehearsal and by the kind of questions (and suggestions!) made to me by individual players, not only about their own parts, but about the music itself. The performance of a new work, especially a big thing like a symphony, is always a worry to a composer; if it is at all inadequate, he will be the only person in the audience who knows what it ought to sound like, and nobody can be blamed for assuming that what's unconvincing is his own fault. In Liverpool I have never had this grim experience! Heartiest congratulations to the Society, to the Orchestra, and to the admirable people who keep the whole thing in the air. I hope the City of Liverpool will continue to value and support this priceless asset. Here's to the next 150 years!"

A further chamber work followed this mighty symphonic effort: the Piano Trio, composed 1988-89 and dedicated to the late Pamela Bacon. The composer's programme note is short, and I will quote it in full:

"Trio for violin, cello and piano (1988-89).

Allegretto – Vivace – Adagio semplice – Allegro.

"This work was commissioned by the Da Vinci Ensemble with funds provided by the Southern Arts Association. It has four movements, played without a break, and lasts about 36 minutes. The opening phrase of the first movement generates the whole of the work, and the first movement itself is moderately paced, but displays a great deal of restrained but lively activity. The texture is mostly light and transparent, and often in four parts, like a quartet for the two stringed instruments and the two hands of the pianist. It leads to a fast scherzo in duple time, much of which is again delicate, but with formidable undertones (and sometimes outbursts). Then follows the slow movement, a set of increasingly elaborate variations on a very simple theme, given to the cello, with musing asides from the piano. The penultimate variation is very vigorous, but the last is deeply contemplative. The finale begins like a fiery fugue, but becomes less strictly contrapuntal as it goes on. After a climax it dies away into a mysterious ritardando coda."

The Trio was premièred by the Da Vinci Ensemble in the Turner Sims Hall of Southampton University on 13th February 1990, and the first London performance was arguably that by the Terroni Trio in Barnet College Hall on 30th June the same year, if Barnet be considered part of London. It was given again at the Wigmore Hall on 13th September by the Lowbury Piano Trio, who also played Haydn's Trio Hob.XV 28 in E and Ravel's E minor Trio. The Lowburys recorded the work for Hyperion, coupled with the Violin Sonata, a disc released in 1995. The recording of the Trio was sponsored by Pamela Bacon (the dedicatee,) in memory of her mother, a musician. Robert Simpson next turned his attention to the concerto form after a break of over twenty years. The Flute Concerto of 1989 was written at the request of Susan Milan. On the 25th of June he wrote to her:

"Dear Sue

Herewith please find one flute concerto, completed a couple of days ago. Enclosed is a reduction of the pencil score and a solo part, written out for you at least temporarily until the publishers produce a) a better one and b) a piano reduction, which I'm asking them to do as soon as they can. Can you tell me the date of the Cheltenham performance? Usually it's July, and I hope I can be free since I have to be at the Bornholm Festival then (date uncertain still) and my 9th symphony looks like having its first Irish performance in Dublin on the 20th. A pleasant but possibly inconvenient embarras de richesse!

I do hope that the piece will give you some pleasure, now that you have it at last. The end is a bit unusual, asking you to dismiss the conductor and sit down with the string quartet! The atmosphere at the finish is extremely intimate and goes into a world of its own. But the rest is pretty 'normal' – i.e. plenty of charging about in all directions. Smallish orchestra – one of each WW but including the 'extras', CA, bass clar., contrafag. No flute, but a piccolo, who once or twice steals a top note or two! And you have a duel with the timpanist. The piece as a whole is rather intense and concentrated and I got very absorbed in it – as you can see by the score from the dates of start and finish. If there are any problems, technical or otherwise, please let me know and between us we may be able to iron them out. I hope I haven't failed the instrument, to say nothing of your artistry. What happened in the end about the commission? Not that it matters too much – I'm glad to have done the work – though a little cash is always useful if it can be screwed out of the bureaucrats. Have you got any plans to record the Nielsen concerto? This one might go well with it on a CD."

The concerto is in a single movement, in three sections: Allegretto - Allegro non troppo – Adagio. The orchestra is a small one, and during the last pages, marked senza diretore, molto calmo, almost disappears, with only the soloist and a string quartet playing. The work lasts almost twenty-nine minutes. The projected Cheltenham première never took place, for reasons which I shall explain later, and the first performance was at the Elgar Hall, Malvern, on 24th May 1992. Susan Milan was accompanied by the City of London Sinfonia conducted by Richard Hickox, and the concert, in the composer's presence, also included Beethoven's Coriolan overture, the Nielsen Flute Concerto, and Beethoven's Seventh Symphony. The Flute Concerto has yet to be recorded. Stephen Johnson (Independent, 27th May) observed: "No other work of Simpson seems so carefully poised between orchestral and chamber worlds of sound and expression."

In July of 1989, Robert and Angela Simpson hosted a seminar at Killelton for some twenty members of the society, who were billeted in various holiday homes. Here is the programme:

Sunday, July 23rd

10.00 - 13.00
Symphony No.1 (1951) and Quartet No.1 (1951-2). Tonal polarities. The impact of Nielsen.
19.30 - 22.30
Control of tempo: Quartet No.2 (1953) and Symphony No.3 (1962)

Monday, July 24
10.00 - 13.00
Learning from Beethoven: Quartet No.6 (1975)
19.30 - 22.30
A 'psychological' symphony – No.5 (1972)

Tuesday, July 25
10.00 - 13.00
The relation between symphonic thought and living growth – Symphony No.6 (1977)
19.30 - 22.30
An 'astronomical' quartet - No.7 (1977)

Wednesday, July 26 FREE all day till 19.30
19.30 - 22.30
A 'private' symphony – No.7 (1977)

Thursday, July 27
10.00 - 13.00
How to save time and effort by writing things out backwards – Quartet No.9 (1982)
19.30 - 22.30
A slight touch of Bruckneritis - Symphony No.9 (1985-86)

Friday, July 28
10.00 - 13.00
A quartet for peace – No.10 (1983)
19.30 - 22.30
String Quintet (1987)

Saturday, July 29
10.00 - 13.00: SAFETY VALVE

Loaded questions, offensive personal remarks, advice to the composer, infrasocietal strife, additions to the English language, sardonic analytical theories, proposals for disposal of works discussed, suggestions for changing the eponymity of the Society, etc.

Angela repeats with some agitation that ALL rotten eggs MUST be FREE RANGE.

Needless to say, the event was a great success, with the talks delivered in Simpson's matchless relaxed, humorous but informative style, and the afternoons (and Wednesday morning) free for exploration of the locality and, for some irredeemable individuals, the consumption of copious quantities of Guinness and seafood.

Chamber and brass music make up the remainder of Simpson's output for 1989. The Thirteenth String Quartet was commissioned by the Cardiff Festival and completed in December. It is dedicated to Graham and Alex Melville-Mason. The 13th is the most compact of the later quartets, lasting some eighteen minutes. There are four movements, played without a break: Allegro molto – Andante – Vivace – Andante, and, like so much of Simpson's later music, it ends serenely with a "slow, chorale-like epilogue marked ppp, ma sempre espressivo, which swiftly eases all the former turbulence." (Matthew Taylor). The première was given by the Delmé Quartet in St David's Hall, Cardiff, on 2nd October 1990. The Delmé also recorded it for Hyperion (1997), coupled with the Clarinet Quintet and Second String Quintet, the recording made in association with the Robert Simpson Society.

The Brass Quintet is a fifteen-minute work consisting of a Prelude, Fugue and Scherzo. It was premièred at the Cheltenham Festival in the Pittville Pump Room on 19th July 1990 by Cambrian Brass. The companion pieces were Ricercare No. 5 by Stephen Oliver, John McCabe's Rounds, a Fanfare and March by Lord Berners, Chorale Variations by the Czech composer Petr Eben, an arrangement of some Early Spanish Music by John Miller, and Music from Chaucer by Michael Berkeley, for which the ensemble were joined by Kim Sargeant, Festival Organiser, as Percussionist. The Quintet was commissioned by Cambrian Brass with funds provided by the Holst Foundation, and is dedicated to Peter and Nancy Keane, local friends and neighbours of the Simpsons. It has yet to be recorded.

Vortex is Robert Simpson's last work for brass band. It is dedicated to the composer John Pickard as atonement for having stolen (inadvertently) a title that had already been used by him. It is the shortest of the brass band pieces (nine minutes) and, in Matthew Taylor's words "The music is truly vortex-like and is finally sucked down into one note, referred to by the composer as 'not really a tonic note, more a plughole note'

Vortex is in Robert Simpson's highly characteristic fast triple time pulse, which is maintained for the entire duration of the piece. Beginning quietly with a sinister muttering motive low on tubas and trombones, the music grows with considerable strength as powerful stretches of vigorous music contrast with quieter moments. These latter moments seem to reveal a new transparency of sound in the composer's band scoring. The work concludes with a formidable blaze of sound recalling the final pages of Simpson's Tenth Symphony (1988)."

Vortex received its première in Leeds Town Hall on 6th July 1990, by the Yorkshire Imperial Metals Band conducted by Geoffrey Brand. As with Simpson's other brass band works, it was recorded for Hyperion by the Desford Colliery Caterpillar Band under James Watson.

Robert Simpson's Eleventh (and last) Symphony, completed in 1990, is a world away from the huge scale of its two predecessors – then again, each of his symphonies is, like those of Beethoven, utterly distinct. In the Eleventh he returned to the modest orchestra used in the Second and Seventh; a classical orchestra with two extra horns, as in all four of the Brahms concertos. It seems to have been in the composer's mind for several years: in a letter to Simpson dated 7th January 1987, the late conductor Richard Hickox wrote:

"Dear Bob,

Thank you for your letter on Christmas Eve which I was delighted to have. It was a great pleasure to work on the Nielsen Variations and I am glad that you felt we did it as well as possible in the time available. I must tell you how many members of the orchestra enjoyed working on it and that is often the most testing criteria for any new piece!

I think the idea of commissioning a new symphony for classical orchestra is an intriguing one and I am going to take this up with the management of the Northern Sinfonia. I think it is just the sort of thing we should be doing.

I very much look forward to the pleasure of working with you again and thank you so much for your words of encouragement."

Evidently, nothing came of this, but Simpson carried on regardless, spurred by a performance of his Seventh Symphony conducted by Matthew Taylor during 1988 which greatly moved him (qv). In his own words:

"Matthew Taylor has clearly been too modest to mention the origins of this symphony. After hearing him conduct a superbly penetrating and sensitive performance of my No.7 with an orchestra mainly consisting of students, I felt an immediate compulsion to compose a symphony for him. It depends on his opinion of that performance whether he considers this new symphony a reward or an act of revenge! If the latter, I do not share his views."

The Eleventh is in two movements, Andante and Allegro vivace, playing for some twenty-nine minutes. To quote Matthew Taylor's programme note:

"Though No.II is significantly shorter than Simpson's three preceding symphonies, it is no divertimento. Far from representing a culmination in Simpson's symphonic thinking, it seems to hint at new directions and new manners of expression hitherto unprecedented in the history of modern symphonism. One of the most striking features of the Eleventh Symphony is the chamber-like quality of most of the Andante and of a large part of the finale. Simpson once said that he wanted to create a sort of luminosity of texture not unlike that of Sibelius's Sixth Symphony. Indeed, there is a sense of spaciousness and eloquence, reminiscent of much of the slow music from the ninth and tenth symphonies but never expressed with the economy of scoring enjoyed in No. 11.

"The first movement, Andante, is largely polyphonic in design; its pervasive feeling is one of tenderness and quiet serenity, despite continual shifts of orchestral colour. This is apparent from the work's opening paragraph, where a motif on the first violins, which provides the basis for much of the argument throughout the symphony, is answered by oboe and muted horns. The accompaniment is often very sparse, sometimes consisting of a single line. The music evolves slowly, seldom rising above piano, continually transforming the opening violin theme into new patterns. Soon the texture becomes more animated until the whole orchestra reaches a majestic unison C, before the music floats off into an ethereal coda.

"The Allegro vivace must surely be one of the longest symphonic finales since Mahler's Fifth Symphony. Simpson once suggested that the opening might have 'something of the character of a Mendelssohn scherzo, though I'm not trying to imitate Mendelssohn's language. Anyone who tries to do that is an idiot!' Certainly the woodwind flickers supported by delicate string pizzicati that launch this movement recall the style of Mendelssohn (the Scherzo of the Octet, or the music from a Midsummer Night's Dream), but as the piece gathers steam it is taken over by a more muscular vitality and Beethovenian

The last, to date, in the Hyperion series (2004)

energy. The final climax is combative, dominated by an insistent B flat, before disappearing on a defiant timpani note in a similar manner to the corresponding part of Simpson's Ninth Symphony. The coda is made up of strange rustling fragments, 'until the whole thing ends with a flick of the wrist, as if dismissed' in the words of the composer. So ends one of the greatest symphonic cycles of the twentieth century."

The Eleventh was due to be premièred at the Cheltenham Festival in 1991, but differences of opinion precluded this, and it received its first performance at the Elgar Hall in Malvern, with a short introduction by the composer, on 23rd May 1992: Simpson was one of the featured composers at that year's Festival. The City of London Sinfonia was, of course, conducted by Matthew Taylor, and the concert also included Mendelssohn's Hebrides Overture, and the Beethoven 'Emperor' Concerto with Anthony Goldstone as soloist.

The same forces recorded the work for Hyperion, coupled with the Nielsen Variations, and the disc was issued in 1994. Angela Simpson, the City of London Sinfonia, and various companies and individuals contributed to the recording costs, and the disc was produced by Simon Perry and dedicated to the memory of his father, Ted. Stephen Johnson, in the BBC Music Magazine, wrote after hearing the recording: "Having been initially disappointed by Robert Simpson's 11th, I'm beginning to think it might be one of the finest of his later symphonies – what a difference a performance makes!" Shamefully, the Eleventh has yet to receive a London première, although Matthew Taylor has made serious efforts to secure the necessary funding.

Works continued to flow thick and fast from Simpson's pencil during the ensuing months, until illness brutally cut short his composing life at the height of his powers. The Fourteenth String Quartet was written in 1990. This is a classical, four-movement quartet, the first since the Sixth of 1975: 1) Allegro non troppo 2) Presto 3) Andante 4) Allegro, with a duration of about thirty-four minutes. It was commissioned by the Vanbrugh Quartet, and is dedicated to the composer's friend John Young. Matthew Taylor describes the quartet thus:

"The opening Allegro is fluid, highly active and predominantly contrapuntal in texture. Though the movement avoids strict sonata form, a clear second subject appears; a nervous, double-dotted figure which generates further contrapuntal entries and immense rhythmic energy at a later stage. The ending dies away quietly in a mood of temporary stillness.

"Simpson has mastered the art of writing true Beethovenian, one-in-a-bar scherzi. The second movement of this Quartet is such an example: lithe, energetic and vital, with plenty of dynamism packed into a mere four minutes. Much relaxation is provided by the next movement, a noble, eloquent Andante which grows steadily from the cello's opening phrase. In much of Simpson's later slow movements a Bach-like serenity and deep contemplation can be sensed. Here is a fine example of such, as well as being one of the most beautifully transparent quartet slow movements this century.

"Rough humour dominates the Allegro finale, a piece of great force, deliberation, and physical strength. Much of the movement is subdued, however, and there is a long stretch in the middle that is mainly pianissimo, carried along by a gentle momentum. The final bars generate massive excitement as the music gathers steam, and explosive triplets are scattered amongst all four instruments."

The première was given by the Vanbrugh in the Bank of Ireland, Dublin, on 14th May 1991, and they followed this with the British première at Rangers House, Blackheath on the 25th May, and the Purcell Room on 20th November, along with John Kinsella's Third Quartet and the Dvořák 'American'. In all, during 1991, the Vanbrugh Quartet played the new work a dozen times at various locations in the UK and the Irish Republic. They recorded it for Hyperion, coupled with the Fifteenth Quartet and the Quintet for Clarinet, Bass Clarinet and String Trio – the disc appeared in 1993. David Fanning, reviewing the disc for the Gramophone (July 1993), commented: "A wiry fugue subject and off we go – yet another deeply impressive quartet from Robert Simpson, giving the impression that he only has to reach out and a vein of uniquely invigorating music is there for the taking."

Simpson returned to piano writing the same year, with the Variations and Fugue on a theme of Beethoven. He described the stimulus thus:

"This work was composed for Raymond Clarke after hearing an impressive performance by him of Beethoven's Opus 111. The theme is little known – a 13-bar bagatelle in G minor (Woo 61a) he wrote in 1825 for Sarah Burney Payne, the grand-daughter of the English writer on music, Charles Burney. He often scrawled midget pieces in people's autograph or visitors' books and "they are by no means negligible. This one concentrates remarkable organisation in so short a space – Beethoven, the great miniaturist!"

The work comprises the theme itself, marked Allegretto quasi Andante, Variations 1-23, and a Finale. Lionel Pike considers that the Variations form natural groups, roughly corresponding to the movements of a quartet or symphony: numbers 1-11 a sort of slow movement, 12-21 a scherzo, and 22-23 a slow movement. He adds "The finale starts with a grotesque fugue, the subject of which consists of little fragments leaping down the whole keyboard while its countersubject rockets upwards in an effort to "discommode the subject by crossing it" (as the composer puts it). This opening to the Finale, however, is a feint, for only three entries of the subject occur. After this fugato, the movement, to use Simpson's own words, 'turns into a sonata-like finale with many contrasts, at length disappearing suddenly down a hole after a resonant climax.'" For all its variety, the work is a short one, lasting only a little over seventeen minutes. Raymond Clarke gave the première in the Purcell Room on 11th April 1991. The remainder of the programme comprised Liszt's Funerailles, Rachmaninov's Etude-Tableaux Nos 4 and 9, Op.39, Nielsen's Second Piano Suite, Four Bagatelles by Matthew Taylor, and the work which had inspired Simpson, Beethoven's C minor Sonata, Op.111. The composer was delighted by the performance, and wrote the pianist a warmly appreciative letter on 15th April. "Just got home last night, so this is the first chance to write to you after that magnificent recital, at the end of which we were all pretty breathless. I was more than delighted by the performance of the variations, superbly vital and full of spontaneous insights that kept the thing in the air all the time – you may have worried about the odd mishit, but it never bothered me, and I doubt if anybody else noticed! I certainly couldn't have wished for a better send-off for the piece – I've always been nervous about writing for the piano, being about as good at playing it as a chimpanzee with boxing gloves on. Everything else seemed to go marvellously well, especially the Arietta in the Beethoven – beautiful. There's no more sublime piece of music in the world. Perhaps the whole programme was a shade long – I could have done without the Liszt, and maybe just one of the Rachmaninov pieces might have served well as a prelude. Funerailles starts off impressively but when he gets hold of that mawkish little phrase and drools over it interminably, I give up. A wizard with the piano but a BAD composer! I enjoyed Matthew's unpretentiously individual pieces, played with great sympathy. Nielsen – very fine – what a piece! The best performance I've heard from a British pianist, close at times to Rasmussen, sometimes of course different in emphasis. He was for me the greatest interpreter of Nielsen in any medium – CN's daughter Irmelin said to me after he had just played this same suite 'When he plays I seem to see my father standing by the piano'. Have you heard his recordings? If not I'll copy them for you.

"So – congratulations, and the next thing is that something has to be done (a) about your career and (b) about getting you a decent piano from somewhere or other. I shall do all I can to further the first aim, and if I had the money I'd buy you the best piano you could find!"

Raymond Clarke recorded the Variations as part of his disc comprising all Simpson's solo piano music (Hyperion, 1996). In February 1990 John Manduell, former colleague of Simpson's at the BBC, who was the co-dedicatee of the Canzona, and who had contributed to the Pelican symposium 'The Symphony', wrote to the Robert Simpson offering him Composer in Residence status at the Cheltenham Festival the following year – Manduell was the Programme Director. Simpson was initially delighted, but as the months rolled by the correspondence became increasingly acrimonious. Simpson objected to the fact that his programme suggestion had not been acted upon and that his favoured artists – the Delmé Quartet, the Israel Trio and Raymond Clarke – had not been asked to perform and (the last straw) that the concert which was to have introduced his Flute Concerto would be sponsored by Nuclear Electric. By January 1991 the composer had decided to dissociate himself from the Festival, and Matthew Taylor (who was to have conducted the first performance of the Eleventh Symphony) followed suit. At Angela Simpson's request, I have not quoted from any of the letters; suffice it to say that their sometimes vitriolic tone may well surprise those who remember the composer as a mild-mannered, gently humorous individual. They do, however, illustrate his fierce loyalty to musicians whom he admired, and his strongly-held belief that as the composer his views on the matter should carry some weight. The Beethoven Variations were in fact given their première in April 1991, before the Festival got going, but the Flute Concerto and the Eleventh Symphony had to wait until Malvern the following year.

The composer's seventieth birthday fell in 1991, and Dick Edwards wrote in December 1990 to Adrian Thomas, Head of Music Programmes, to see if the BBC were going to mark the occasion. He got no response, nor was the occasion celebrated. Was Simpson still regarded as 'the enemy'? Admittedly, the Corporation had also failed to mark his fiftieth and sixtieth, so we should not be surprised. In fairness, it should be noted that in 1971 he was still a senior employee, and that any such treatment could have been seen as nepotism, but no such caveat applied in 1981 or 1991.

"IT SCARES THE LIVING DAYLIGHTS OUT OF ME"
(1989 - 1990)

The conductor Brian Wright (who had conducted the first performance of the Seventh Symphony) not only wished to mark the occasion, but to commission a new choral work. Simpson replied to him on 12th August 1988:

"I'm very touched and honoured by your idea, and only wish that I could do us both justice. I said I needed time to think about it, but looking at the commissions and promises that stare me in the face, it seems obvious that I couldn't guarantee to produce anything in the time. There's a Tenth symphony (in progress now), a piano trio, a flute concerto, a piano work, a brass band work, another symphony (No.11), a string octet, and possibly a concerto for string quartet and orchestra – all either commissioned or promised, the last two agreed in principle without actual certainty but very probable. So you can see that a poor old sod like me is going to be hard put to it to knock off that lot in three years or so. Even if I risked saying yes, I couldn't be sure what the result would be like.

Looking at it from another point of view, I suppose a composer's 70th birthday ought to be the occasion for displaying his best work, rather than for squeezing just a bit more juice out of the poor old lemon. In this case you might get only a pip! So far choral music has brought me only trauma; the big thing I described to you might not even come off – it scares the living daylights out of me, though it's been one of my most cherished desires for years. By nature I'm really an instrumental composer. Since it's a Goldsmiths concert, your programme must be choral, and the more choral it is the better. If the second half is Beethoven IX, could I suggest the Haydn Te deum (1800 – magnificent, 10 mins) and Nielsen's Hymnus Amoris (25 mins) for the first part? This would make a glorious concert. You'd need a couple of extra soloists and a children's choir for the Nielsen, but it would be worth it – this masterpiece still doesn't get performed anything like as much as it should. Nor does the Haydn.

"The 'big thing' referred to was a projected choral symphony, or possibly oratorio, the conception of which I will deal with in more detail in the following chapter.

Fortunately, the Robert Simpson Society stood by their composer, and there were three chamber concerts at the Wigmore Hall: the Coull Quartet played the 1st Quintet on 2nd March, with Haydn's Op.33 No.5, and the Dvořák 'American', on 7th March the Eleventh Quartet with Schubert's D.87 and Beethoven's Op.135, and on 9th March the Twelfth Quartet, with

Mozart's K465 ('Dissonance') and Mendelssohn's Op.13. The composer was very pleased, as he was with the Society's gift of a fax machine, and wrote on 24th March: "Dear Friends, It's hard to know how to thank you all for giving me such a wonderful send-off into the seventies, especially at those marvellous concerts the Coull Quartet gave; being surrounded by such kindness and enthusiasm made me reject finally and utterly the hoary old idea of the Allotted Span. I never did go much for mysticism. On the contrary I'm at one fired with fierce intentions and also terrified that I have to satisfy YOU! In common with my old friend Havergal Brian (who said it at a much greater age) I can say 'I'm not going to die – I've just bought a new pair of trousers!'. In this case Angela actually bought them because she'd been bootlessly (or should it be trouserlessly?) bullying me for ages to get another pair.

All I can say is that I can't possibly say it – how much I appreciate the support and love you have made me aware of. As for that incredible Fax Machine – my first assault on the instruction book broke down at page 2. But I'll persevere, and when it's all connected up the glorious Nut Case Society which you all constitute had better get itself one double-quick.

Our love to you all. Save up for another celebration in thirty years time.

Your tame composer,

Bob."

Another birthday celebration came later in the year, at the Royal Academy of Music on the 9th of July – the RAM Brass and friends played the Reger Variations, the Four Temperaments, the Quintet for Clarinet, Bass Clarinet and String Trio, and Vortex.

A word on commissions may be appropriate here. Since coming to prominence as a composer in the mid-fifties he received more than he could actually accept – his letter to Susi Jeans from 1977 regarding the Seventh Quartet mentions having to turn down a cello concerto. After leaving the BBC he was able to take on more, though there were some he turned down, either because he felt unable to do the request justice, or because he simply had too much on his plate. In a letter to James Douglas (14/7/81) he observed "It looks as though I've got enough to keep me going for about three years to say nothing of the music I just want to write." On 1st February 1981, the distinguished soprano Jane Manning wrote to the composer:

"Dear Bob, Would you ever consider the idea of writing a work for me? I would be simply thrilled if so – wouldn't dream of imposing any kind of time limit, deadline or instrumentation – it would be entirely up to you if you liked the prospect." She ends: "Do hope things are well with you, and that we'll meet again before long. We're still lost in admiration at your courage and self-sacrifice at the time of BBC crisis, and hope very much that we'd be able to follow your example if ever put to the test – principles seem to count for so little in some quarters."

No such work ever emerged; Simpson's problem with words is summed up in an article by Robert Dearling in Records and Recording, October 1979: "They scare me. I don't want to spoil them. It's the same for opera and for songs. If I feel deeply enough about a text or a poem (and I would have to feel deeply in order to be moved to set it in the first place) I would be afraid anything I could do to words would spoil their effect. And if they are great words they don't need music anyway."

Ian Craft, who had requested the Sixth Symphony, wanted a string quartet to be dedicated to his wife Jackie. Simpson replied on 14th January 1990: "Many thanks for your letter with its heartfelt request. I wish it were possible in the foreseeable future … ," he goes on to suggest John Pickard instead, and adds: "My regard for Jackie makes the stronger my appreciation of your offer – but my music is getting tougher and more elliptic, so I doubt if it would give her a lot of pleasure!"

John Harrison, of the New Zealand Brass Bands Association Inc., wanted a test piece for the 1990 championships – Simpson had to turn this down as he had other commissions in hand. He certainly intended to write another organ work for Robert Crowther (it is mentioned several times in his letters) but this never came to fruition. An offer of a grant from the Welsh Arts Council for a 30-minute quartet for the 1990/91 Cardiff Festival (they had previously commissioned the 13th for the previous year's Festival) had also to be politely refused.

The string octet already mentioned in the letter to Brian Wright was intended to be played at the Warwick Festival in 1991 by the Coull and Delmé Quartets, but this is another tantalising unwritten piece. Matthew Best (February 1991) wanted a concerto for orchestra lasting 30 or 40 minutes.

Jonathan Small, of the ensemble Aldebaran, requested an oboe quintet. Simpson replied on 9th May 1991: "Many thank for your kind letter. How could I refuse a request from a fellow astronomical enthusiast? But it's all a question of timing. I'll try but can't guarantee success in time for one of next year's festivals, and obviously you'd have to have time to learn it as well." He ends, with characteristic humour (I should add that Aldebaran is the name of the brightest star in the constellation Taurus):

"Aldebaran – it will get comprehensively and no doubt ingeniously mispronounced – I'm not sure I know the correct way to say it myself.

But I suppose it's a bit more euphonious than Azelfafage, Dschubba, Sadalachbia, or Kaffaljidhma. Alphirk would get deliberately mispronounced. Arkab Posterior, Yed Posterior or Tejat Posterior would have inappropriate connotations. Nunki is a bit cosy I fear. And Unuk Elhaia sounds kind of insulting. As for Wasat, people would think the question mark had been left out. If you were buskers you could use Kerb. But any of these might be asking for trouble."

Another request which he felt obliged to turn down was from Julian Bream, the most famous classical guitarist since Segovia, for a guitar sonata. He pondered for a while, but finally wrote back on 11th May 1991:

"After an awful lot of cogitation, I'm afraid it has to be bad news! The big problem is that somehow I need to be sparked off by the instrument itself – on the face of it, it seems an unprofessional objection, yet I'd rather admit that than serve you up a piece that might embarrass us both…

I've always enjoyed and been impressed by the sheer musicality of your playing, second to none in the world. If Casals had asked me for a cello piece (and you are on that level, to my mind) I'd have been frightened out of my wits – but at least the cello is an instrument that's somehow in my blood, through quartets, orchestras, etc, as well as through having had a shot at it myself, unfortunately too late to become any sort of a player – it was just to get acquainted with the basics. The guitar is for me an attractive but intractable foreigner! So alas, with deep disappointment, I have to say it isn't on."

Even after his stroke requests continued, although of course the petitioners may either not have been aware of the severity of the illness, or were hoping for a recovery. In 1993 he was, rather touchingly, asked to write a short piece 'in memoriam' for members of the Hagley School orchestra killed in a motorway crash, and in 1994 Mark David requested a trumpet concerto. One work he was fortunately able to complete was the Cello Concerto for Raphael Wallfisch, written early in 1991. It is a single-movement work lasting around twenty-three minutes. Matthew Taylor's programme note follows:

"This work is in one continuous movement and is cast as a set of variations on an opening orchestral statement. The first orchestral paragraph (Allegro), or 'theme' presents a number of small motives that provide the basis for the ensuing variations. Variation 1 is marked by the entry of the soloist.

The first four variations form a section in themselves, the cello taking the lead throughout: Nos.1 and 2 maintain the original tempo, closely following the outlines of the theme. No.3, at a slightly slower speed, transforms the material into richly lyrical melodic lines from the cello, whereas No.4 moves into triple time, featuring frequent shifts of orchestral accompaniment.

The fifth variation is again entirely devoted to the orchestra, but here the mode of expression is more full-blooded than at the start.

Variations 6-9 form another section, of Scherzo-like character, revealing many aspects of virtuosic cello writing. Variation 10 is the climax of the work; a final blaze of orchestral music and the most sustained burst of energy in the Concerto. It generates a massive momentum that is abruptly halted by three isolated cello notes, that reveal the main slow movement of the work (Variation 11). Here, the strings are muted and the atmosphere calm and reflective.

The tempo quickens for the next variation (Allegretto) as the cello sings duets with piccolo and then oboe, before relaxing into an even slower tempo for variation 13 (Adagio molto). The final variation (No.14), which acts as a coda to the entire work, begins with a gentle fugato, again introduced by the cello and imitated in turn by violins and solo wind."

The Cello Concerto received its premiere on 17th May 1992, at the Elgar Hall, Malvern, with Raphael Wallfisch as soloist and the BBC Welsh Orchestra conducted by Vernon Handley. Elgar's overture 'In the South' and Sibelius's tone-poem The Swan of Tuonela and his Fifth Symphony completed the programme. The composer, though by then wheelchair-bound following his stroke, was able to attend this and the other first performances given during this Malvern Festival. The concerto has yet to be recorded.*

During 1991 Robert Simpson also produced a major addition to the string orchestra repertory, his Variations and Fugue on a theme of J.S. Bach for Strings. The work had its origins in a request by Denis Brookes, who had attended the 1989 Killelton seminar, and is dedicated to Denis and his son Simon. I recall Denis asking me how much I thought Simpson would charge for a commissioned work for strings; I had no idea, only finding out later that he would furnish a copy of the decidedly modest Composer's Guild rates following such enquiries. In a letter to Denis Brookes dated 30/10/89, Robert Simpson wrote:

"Nice to get your letter. I'm much flattered by your proposal. Before accepting, could I ask what sort of string orchestra – youngsters, amateurs, professionals? Obviously I wouldn't want to saddle relatively inexperienced players with stuff only stupendous players could tackle. The trouble is that when I get the bit between my teeth I bolt! Is the commission from a local education authority, or from an orchestra? I'd like to have a go at it, but need guidance, or there could be a fearsome massacre. I've never actually been drawn to the string orchestra as such, despite the fine works that

---

* *The Cello Concerto has now been recorded on the Lyrica label, coupled with works by Joubert and Wright. - Raphael Wallfisch with the BBC Welsh Orchestra, conductor, William Boughton*

exist for it – but that means nothing. I'd never have written a flute concerto without a commission, but once it got going I thoroughly enjoyed it, and now I can't wait to hear it.

The other question is a matter of time. At the moment I've three outstanding promises – a set of piano variations, another symphony, and another organ work – all big pieces. So it might be a couple of years before I could get down to it. Do you have a deadline?

Alas, I'll be in England when you're in Limerick, but do give Angela a ring. The most grotesque, the most bizarre of all honours has come my way – I've been asked to present the prizes at my old school! There's nobody left there who remembers me throwing a stink bomb into the Head's study while he was there! I never got a prize for anything, either, and was the bolshiest brat they ever had. Miracle I wasn't expelled. I just hope the present head doesn't do a bit of research."

The work was duly written, and Simpson typically refused a fee. Letter to Denis Brookes dated 9/5/91:

"Happy to get your nice letter. But I return the cheque incontinently, in accordance with my original proposal. If you do want to spend something on the work, there could be a way in which you might perhaps be able to help with it. My main publisher (Lengnick) is it seems about to go bust.* This is an appalling problem for all the composers whose music they hold, not least because we all no doubt have works due for publication which wont now get off the ground, unless somebody else rescues the company. NO – I'm not suggesting that!!!! But we're going to need parts for this work, which the publishers would normally supply. I don't know what it would cost – copyist, photocopying, etc. My MS score is reasonably clear to conduct from (what you have is a reduction, the full size is much more usable) and could be photographed and ring-bound without desperate cost. Would you be interested in finding out what it would entail? Proofreading would also be necessary, which you might care to undertake – a great easement for me. If it's too much I'll try to knock off some parts myself, but this year I have to write three, possibly four, more major works, no joke for a poor old sod like me. Matthew has a copy of it, and I think it would be better to wait until we can be sure of a really good, experienced professional performance. The kids at the Menuhin School are obviously talented, but it's pretty difficult, as you can see, and needs a lot of experience. I'd feel safer with crack players and it would be worth waiting for. Tod Handley was interested when I mentioned it to him, so let's keep our options open, as they say. The Vanbrugh Quartet has just done a 'preview' of the first

---

* *Simpson was being unduly pessimistic. The Lengnicks imprint still survives, although the company has changed hands twice.*

performance of Quartet 14 (next week in Dublin) for the students at the University College, Cork. Superb playing, and it should go marvellously well. One of my best pieces I think."

The theme is taken from the Sarabande of Bach's Fifth Cello Suite in C minor. In a letter to Matthew Taylor Simpson said of variation 6 (an elastic canon at the interval of the twelfth) "Bach would have died if he'd heard this!" The work, although continuous, falls into three main sections, Allegro energico, Andante and Finale, and lasts 16½ minutes. It did not receive its first performance until 3rd June 1995, at the Elgar Hall, Malvern, with the Goldberg Ensemble conducted by Matthew Taylor. The concert also included Bach's Third Brandenburg Concerto in G, his D minor Concerto for two violins, and Mozart's Serenade 'Eine Kleine Nachtmusik'. Sadly, the composer was by then too frail to attend. Matthew Taylor conducted the City of London Sinfonia at St Johns Smith Square in the London premiere on 29th January 2002. The other works were Elgar's E minor Serenade, Taylor's own Adagio: Tribute to RS, Arnold's Concerto No.1 for Flute and Strings, and Simpson's Allegro Deciso. Like the Flute and Cello Concertos, the Bach Variations still await a recording.

Robert Simpson's last completed String Quartet, the Fifteenth, was written quickly in the summer of 1991. It is in a single movement in three main sections: Adagio – Severo – Allegretto, and lasts about eighteen minutes. It is dedicated to the Vanbrugh Quartet, and funds of £2800 were supplied by the Arts Council. I quote from Matthew Taylor's sleeve-note:

"The overall mood is tough and turbulent, perhaps suggesting an affinity with the language of Quartet No 11 (1984). As with much of Simpson's more recent work, the chief roots are a collection of intervals – here a minor seventh (both ascending and descending) and a sequence of falling minor seconds, but as Robert Simpson once stated "the listener can safely forget about trying to identify them consciously; in any case, no amount of textual ingenuity can give the music a flow it does not naturally possess."

The opening Adagio assumes the character of a brief but stern introduction, contrasting moments of extreme nervous tension with more gently flowing counterpoint. Major sevenths are particularly prominent here. The most extended part of the work is the second section, 'Severo', a large paragraph in a broadly flowing triple time based on a variant of the Quartet's opening theme. The severity and intensity are maintained for a considerable period without relaxation, until eventually a new section emerges alternating hushed, ghostly, repeated-note figurations for all four players with softly sustained writing. Tension rises again, at first culminating in a harsh chordal passage made of sevenths piled on top of one another, finally reaching the climax of the Quartet which fades away leaving a high C suspended on the first violin.

The concluding Allegretto is in the nature of a calm Epilogue, as tenderness and delicacy pervade the work for the first time. The plaintive violin melody which begins this section is in fact yet another use of the work's original intervals. Even here there is a brief moment of intensity, perhaps reminding the listener of the 'Severo' for the last time before the work floats away into silence."

The Vanbrugh premiered the Fifteenth at Downs School, Colwall, on 22nd May 1992, also playing Janaček's First Quartet and the Beethoven A minor Op.132. They recorded it for Hyperion, coupled with the Fourteenth and the Two-Clarinet Quintet, with sponsorship from the Robert Simpson Society, and the record was released In 1993.

"I'D RATHER NOT BE AN INTERESTING CASE"
(1991 - 1997)

Robert Simpson was well advanced with the writing of his Second String Quintet when he broke off to fly to England on 27th September 1991. The purpose of the visit was to conduct a seminar on the music of Max Reger at Missenden Abbey, Great Missenden, Bucks. He had given many such since the 1960s covering a vast range of music, easier of course when he lived at Chearsley, some twelve miles away, than when resident in County Kerry. No doubt he wished to continue serving the cause of musical education regardless, even if only occasionally – not that he could have foreseen the outcome on this occasion. I was one of the pupils – my first and last seminar at Missenden, and I will never forget that weekend.

An evening meal was followed by an illustrated introductory talk; necessarily, since Reger was (and remains) a virtually unknown quantity in England, unjustly regarded as a late-teutonic nightmare, a composer of lumbering, gargantuan, over-elaborate monsterpieces. "Poor old Max!" mused Simpson apropos of this. The composer was on top form, and a string of anecdotes followed; Reger's appetite for food, beer and cigars as well as music was legendary, and no doubt contributed to his early death at the age of forty-three. We were told of Max arriving at his favourite restaurant and commanding "Bring me steaks for two hours!" On another occasion he was walking home from the tavern, half cut as usual, and stopped to relieve himself in the street. In imperial Germany you were (quite rightly) fined on the spot for such behaviour, and the local constable approached the great man with some diffidence. "Herr Reger, you know you must not do that. Ten marks, please." Reger handed him twenty and grunted "Have one yourself!" Then there was the ultimate put-down of a critic who had written a hostile review of his Sinfonietta. "I am sitting reading your review in the smallest room in my house. At the moment it is in front of me; soon, it will be behind me." We were left wondering how a man of such gross material appetites and often coarse humour could also have been the author of such grave, serene, delicate music as 'The Hermit on the Rock' (from Four Böcklin Pictures, and favourably compared to a Bruckner slow movement) or the exquisite G major Serenade, which were among the examples played. Later we repaired to the bar, where discussions continued.

At breakfast, I noticed nothing untoward – in fact Simpson went back for seconds – although he later told me that walking felt like wading through water. During the morning session it became clear that something was seriously amiss: he was fumbling and dropping things, dragging one leg, and there was the tell-tale droop at the side of the face. Evidently he had suffered a stroke, although how severe we had no idea. The composer's willpower was undiminished – he made his way to the afternoon session unaided, supporting himself against the wall, although I need hardly add that people rushed to help as soon as he appeared. During the tea-break we got into a huddle and agreed that he should not be allowed to carry on; the composer reluctantly agreed to abandon the remainder of the programme, leaving us to play the rest of the music, and to take the rest he so sorely needed. A doctor was called and the diagnosis of a stroke confirmed. The mood among those of us on the course was one of shock, along with hushed concern. On the Sunday, he was given a lift to Stansted Airport for the flight home: Miriam is firmly of the opinion that if her brother had stayed in England for a week or two of rest and recuperation his condition would not have become as serious as it did: in fact, he did have a relapse while on the plane, but as Simpson said "I just want to get home", the natural reaction of anyone in pain or distress. On return to Ireland, he was admitted to Tralee Hospital and discharged after a three-month stay ("I behaved so abominably!") with medication and a course of physiotherapy arranged. the following year at a rehabilitation centre in Dunlaoghaire, near Dublin (Spring 1992, after the Malvern Festival). This was supposed to be a two-month course, but he found the physiotherapy utterly gruelling, and went home after a month.

What none of us realised until later was that the stroke itself was the lesser of his problems. True, it was on the left side of the brain, and thus exceedingly irksome for one so positively left-handed, but at all events this is better (or at least less hazardous) than a stroke on the right side, which can seriously impair the sufferer's reasoning power and intellect. To be exact, the clot itself was on the right side of the brain, but the damage was to the left. Angela is sure that, without the complication of thalamic (or thalamoid) syndrome, he would have learned to walk with a stick, and continue his work.

The thalamus is situated just above the spinal column, and in normal times reduces the sensation of pain. Robert Simpson's thalamus was damaged by the stroke and effectively malfunctioned, sending messages along the central nervous system telling him that he was in pain when there was no physical cause; as he said, normally if you are paralysed you feel nothing. The condition is a rare one (as Simpson said, with masterly understatement, "I'd rather not be an interesting case") and as such has been not much studied, with the consequence that the medical profession has little idea of how to treat it. Since it is a neurological pain, analgesia is ineffective. In the past, an operation of brutal simplicity was sometimes employed, whereby a needle was plunged into the thalamus, which either stopped the pain or killed the patient – usually the latter, which is why it was discontinued. The pain was constant, from waking up until taking the knockout drops which put him to sleep at night. He described it as "A frozen pain, like an ice burn" and in a dictated letter to Matthew Best (24/3/92) said "The pain is now as persistent as that bloody C sharp", a reference to the end of 'his Seventh Symphony. While he was on medication which numbed the pain slightly, this was at the expense of making him drowsy; on a lower dosage he was much more alert, but the pain was excruciating, while a higher dose left him zombified. Various conventional and alternative treatments were tried without success; a nerve block (twice), hypnotherapy, acupuncture, shiatsu, even an amulet supplied by Axel Bruck of Berlin. Professor Ian Craft tirelessly fired off letters to various medical institutions and individuals whom he thought might be able to help suggest a treatment, but nothing emerged. Miriam and I thought that cannabis might be of use; initially suspicious, Angela did approach Bob's doctor but he was unwilling to prescribe the drug (he could have done so as a controlled experiment in pain relief) not only as illegal, but also on the curious grounds that it would stifle his creativity, when the pain was such that he felt unable to work anyway. Nor was Angela prepared to take a chance with an illegal supply when her husband was on so much other medication. Simpson bore the pain with great stoicism; initially impatient (the only time I ever saw him short-tempered) he calmed, and on my last visit he was, although weaker, much more at peace with himself. As he said "At first I thought it would go away in time, and I couldn't wait for it to go away; later I came to realise that it wasn't going to go away, and I accepted that I either had to learn to live with it or do something else."

Friends and musical colleagues rallied as soon as they were aware of the composer's plight, and among the many letters of sympathy I may mention those from Menachem Brever of the Israel Piano Trio and pianist Peter Wallfisch. David Matthews wrote him a convalescent canon; Both Matthew Taylor and Martin Smith offered to be his amanuensis, as Eric Fenby had been to the blind Delius. Matthew dedicated his Piano Trio of 1993-94 to Angela and Robert Simpson. Simpson's weakened condition made him prone to falls, and in August 1992 he broke his left leg. Angela gave up most of her work to become a full-time carer; neighbour and friend Peter Keane took over as minder one day a week to give her some respite. It is hardly surprising that the vile affliction of thalamic pain virtually ended Robert Simpson's life as a composer – constant pain is both debilitating and destructive of concentration. His native obstinacy may have contributed; after discharge from hospital he did attempt writing with his right hand, but after a few bars threw the pencil across the table, saying "It looks like a child's writing", and could not be persuaded to resume until, with the aid of another very generous cheque of 5000 dollars from the Rex Foundation, a suitable computer and the Sibelius musical notation system could be installed, and he was able to dictate to Angela the ending of his Second String Quintet. This was in 1994, and the Quintet was to be his last completed work. It was commissioned by the Maggini Quartet, who gave the premiere with Pal Banda, second cellist, in the Pittsville Pump Room, Cheltenham, in July 1996, funds for the commission having been supplied by the Cheltenham International Festival of Music and 'a loyal friend'. Companion works were Haydn's Op.27 No.2 and Arensky's Second Quartet Op.35. Simpson's last work is dedicated to his sister Miriam, who was delighted. The Maggini and Pal Banda also gave the London premiere at the Wigmore Hall on 30th April 1998, this time with Mozart's B flat Quartet 'The Hunt' and the Schubert String Quintet. The Delmé recorded the Second Quintet with Christopher Van Kempen (second cello) coupled with the Thirteenth Quartet and the Clarinet Quintet, and the disc, recorded in association with the Robert Simpson Society, was released in 1997. I quote from Matthew Taylor's programme note:

"Like the First Quintet, the new work is cast in one movement whose structure is determined by alternating two contrasting tempi. But whereas the speeds in the earlier work were closely related (one bar of Vivace matching a crotchet beat in Andante), the Moderato (Tempo 1) and Allegro (Tempo 2) of the Second Quintet behave more independently. In Quintet No 1 the Vivace gradually invades the Andante, generating the central climax, before the process is reversed and the faster tempo has been totally supplanted. In the Second Quintet the two speeds are felt to co-exist to a greater extent, so there is less concern with initiating conflict between them.

Unlike late scores such as the Flute Concerto (1989) and Symphony No 11 (1990) which seem to be evolving towards a calmer, more transparent expression, the Quintet is outwardly severe, alternating some of Simpson's toughest contrapuntal writing in the Allegro (a kind of gigantic Scherzo) with austere, sombre lyricism.

The entire argument of the Quintet revolves around the opening melody, shared between the cellos. Two sets of intervals are fundamental to the work's architecture – rising and falling perfect fifths, and tritones, both of which are prominent in the first phrase. The Moderato sections are stated four times in all, enclosing three Allegro episodes. The third Allegro is the most extended and tumultuous, acting as the Quintet's summit as it explodes into a shower of reiterated quavers. The opening intervals constitute the last appearance of the Moderato section, now arranged vertically. The final diminuendo is one of the darkest endings Simpson has ever conceived." Despite its scope, the Second Quintet is comparatively short, lasting 14½ minutes. Stephen Johnson, (Independent, 6/5/98), reviewing the London premiere, with the title 'A Sense of Completion' commented:

"The end is grim and deeply saddening. The driving forward movement suddenly ceases; muscular counterpoint is replaced by quiet, icy chords. The final sound is dissonance, left unresolved… still a very impressive piece of music."

A Sixteenth String Quartet had already been commissioned by the BBC for a fee of £7500 - Simpson's friend Jillian White wanted it for one of her Bristol lunchtime concerts. This would have been a very big work – the composer estimated fifty-eight minutes, while the producer begged him to reduce it to fifty-three, otherwise it would simply not fit into her scheduled time! Simpson made a start on the work, but managed to dictate no more than one page before the pain destroyed his ability to concentrate.

Another unwritten work was the projected Twelfth (choral) symphony. This had been in his mind for some time – he mentions it in his letter to Brian Wright of August 1988 from which I have already quoted ("it scares the living daylights out of me") and prior to that, in a letter to Edward (E.P.) Thompson from 24th October he tentatively suggested that Thompson (historian and fellow-pacifist) might consider writing the words:

"One of my chief reasons for approaching you was that I suspected we might think similarly, and I had in mind a severely nonreligious treatment of the subject, perhaps under such working headings as these, which might make separate sections of the 'oratorio' (what a word!):-

1. The formation of the sun and solar systems in a gas cloud.
11. The appearance of the most primitive form of life.
111. Division into plant and animal kingdoms.
1V. The active, aggressive animal – the growth of intelligence.
V. Violence. The aggressive stimulus to inventiveness.
V1. Wisdom. At all times it has existed, but has never been able to prevent the pervasive violence.
V11. The species has hitherto been able to survive its own violence, but no longer. Now it can destroy itself.
V111. Non-violence or non-existence (Martin Luther King). The laws of chance provide for no other solution.

I tabulate these ideas to give you a chance to turn them over, or out."

It seems that Thompson (whom Simpson described to his widow, Dorothy, on 6th September 1993 as "One of the greatest men in Europe") had reservations about the project; in another letter dated 22nd April 1989 the composer said:

"But don't worry – I absolutely understand your problem about writing and the amount of things you have to do. Perhaps one day I'll attempt some sort of text myself and submit it to you for comment. I'm no poet, except in tones, but poetry isn't what's needed in such a libretto – clear, precise terms that simply act as spur to the music."

The text never was written, and in later years the notion of an oratorio seems to have been dropped in favour of a choral symphony. He still had a problem with the choice of words, considering setting some of Milton's Latin verse or Shakespeare's sonnets. He was always very positive about the work when speaking to Matthew Best (who even had a date for a first performance, in 1994) but not a note was ever written.

In 1992 Robert Simpson appeared in three television programmes (recorded pre-stroke) centred around the six Nielsen symphonies. Excerpts were conducted by Simon Rattle, and the two musicians argued good-naturedly about Mahler. He also appeared in a programme filmed after the stroke, about the Grateful Dead and their Rex Foundation, screened in 1993. He continued to receive letters from old friends and new admirers from all over the world: Bogdan Gieraczynski wrote from Wroclav, Gabriel Serafina from Radio Municipal, Buenos Aires, and other fans from France, Japan, the USA, Argentina, Poland, Norway, Brazil, Estonia, Australia, India and the Netherlands. One of the most touching letters came from William D. Cline, Assistant Professor of English at a college in Osaka, Japan. Cline played a recording of the Sixth Symphony, and the students noted their reaction to the music (not unanimously favourable, it must be said!) and these were posted to the composer. Upon hearing of his illness, all the students contributed to a letter of best wishes for a speedy recovery, and Cline included one of his own: "Noting Mr Simpson's fascination with the way Western music has been accepted in Japan and Asia, my students' response to Vaughan Williams' "The Lark Ascending" may be of interest. Our class listened to "The Lark Ascending" a few weeks before Mr Simpson's Sixth Symphony. Almost all of the students responded by writing that they couldn't believe that the music was British. They wrote that it sounded either Chinese or Korean. A few thought that it sounded like some type of old Japanese music. That was very surprising to me as I was imagining scenes of the English countryside with a lark rising and flying over it. The background to the viola solo sounds so very British to me. After thinking about their comments, though, I did realize that many of the Chinese songs are imitative of birds and other elements of nature which the viola solo also imitates. Nevertheless, I was delighted by my students' insights that found such a link between the music of the two cultures."

More bizarrely, a Herr Bohlke wrote from Germany in 1994, saying that he wished to leave his fortune to the composer – it later transpired that he had made the same offer to Harold Truscott, who was by that time already dead!

In 1995 the conductor Stanley Pope, who had often worked with Robert Simpson during the BBC years, died. He had been ill for some years with bone cancer; as soon as one bone healed another fractured. Despite his own frailty, he frequently rang form his home in Switzerland to find out how Simpson was progressing after his stroke. Here is the composer's tribute to his old friend:

"We have lost in Stanley Pope a conductor of exceptional gifts which were never properly appreciated, except by musicians. I remember in the old Third Programme days my colleague, Leonard Isaacs, asked me to come with him to the Festival Hall to hear a concert conducted by this man of whom I had heard good reports from orchestral musicians. I remember very vividly what we both agreed was, one of the most beautiful imaginable performances of Beethoven's Pastoral Symphony. I went to see the conductor afterwards and found him a charming, modest fellow and afterwards we had some correspondence about Haydn, initiated by him. We gradually got to know each other very well and became close friends. One of his great enthusiasms was also one of mine – Bruckner. Klemperer said that Stanley Pope was the best British conductor of Bruckner and after a glorious performance of Bruckner's Fifth Symphony in the BBC studio, I spoke to one of the players and expressed my delight. His reply was "it's the chap out in front." Stanley was always polite to orchestras, perhaps sometimes a shade too polite. With a bit more fire in his belly he might have made a bigger name for himself. He always took great care to study Havergal Brian scores I asked him to conduct and these extremely difficult and often enigmatic works usually received somewhat tentative first performances, whoever was at the helm. It was always hard for orchestral players easily to make sense of music 'that was completely idiosyncratic without being avant garde, but Stanley did, I think, better than most. We shall miss him greatly not only as a musician but as a kind and sympathetic person, who showed remarkable courage during his last and often painful illness. My wife and I spoke to him regularly on the telephone between the west of Ireland and Geneva and he always sounded as if there was nothing much wrong with him, although he well knew that he hadn't much longer to live. That kind of cheerful fortitude is an example to us all.

Robert Simpson

24.4.95

Following the stroke, Robert Simpson developed cataracts in both eyes, to the extent that he could only see as far as the other side of the room. Surgery was decided upon, and an attempt to remove the cataract on the left eye under local anaesthetic failed when he went into spasm. A general anaesthetic was administered which almost proved fatal, but the job was done. The right eye was successfully treated under a local.

Simpson's seventy-fifth birthday fell in 1996, and I (and no doubt many others) eagerly seized the Proms prospectus as soon as it appeared to see which of his works would be played. There was nothing. I and other RSS stalwarts wrote to Nicholas Kenyon, then the programmer, for an explanation, but no satisfactory one was forthcoming. In a reply to Jim Pattison (12/8/96) Kenyon made the curious observation (as he did also to me) that "we are, of course, dependent on the wishes of conductors and soloists in this matter." Really? In a follow-up letter to Mr (now Sir Nicholas) Kenyon I said I thought that it was his job to select the repertoire, and did not realise that the players had a veto. This point was never answered. Sir Nicholas had in the past written hugely enthusiastic reviews of the Seventh and Ninth Quartets, and he did admit in a letter to Dick Edwards, then RSS chairman, that he found the symphonies "significantly less successful" than the quartets, which is certainly one point of view, but which fails to explain why not a single quartet by Simpson was included in the parallel Proms chamber concerts.

The writer Edward Pearce also did his bit for the cause. I recalled a thoughtful Guardian article by him (31st July 1991) entitled Proms and Prejudice, in which he stated in typically uncompromising fashion: "… a Proms programmer should keep Robert Simpson's heroic pamphlet, The Proms and Natural Justice, at his bedside and make it his business to work through its two lists of neglected composers (see page 101)… he would then work through them until that wrong had been righted." I thus wrote to advise him of the slight, intended or otherwise. He replied on 18th September:

"Thank you very much indeed for your note about Bob Simpson whom indeed I do greatly respect. It came very late because of the postal strike and I wouldn't have expected to be able to command space to comment on that disgraceful behaviour, but we got lucky. I had written for the Independent a review of the Humphrey Carpenter book on the history of the Third, and I have rung the literary editor, John Walsh, to insert for next Saturday's book page, a line to the effect that after Simpson's recorded cycle of symphonies had been acclaimed, Radio Three characteristically marked his 75th birthday with silence.

That's enough. It nails up the affront and I am very grateful to you for alerting me."

It is difficult to believe that this omission could have been an oversight; Malcolm Arnold, also seventy-five that year was (quite properly) honoured, and one has to conclude, reluctantly, that the ignoring of Robert Simpson was a consequence of partiality rather than ineptitude. Perhaps John Drummond's view of Simpson as "the enemy" had by then become fossilised in the ranks of the senior BBC musical hierarchy, not that one is ever likely to get an admission of this.

If the BBC failed to pay due respect to their former employee, the Vanbrugh Quartet did him proud, travelling by road to Killelton to play him Beethoven's Quartets Op.135 and Op.127, his personal favourite. The Robert Simpson Society sent a case of various quality whiskies, which no doubt went down well. Matthew Best had intended to give a 75th birthday concert at the Queen Elizabeth Hall on 2nd March with the Corydon Singers and Orchestra, playing the Haydn Te Deum, Simpson's Seventh Symphony and Media Morte in Vita Sumus, and the Beethoven Seventh Symphony, but this never came off.

John Manduell, despite past differences, organised a concert at the Royal Northern College of Music on 19th March, including Simpson's Canzona and Reger Introduction and Allegro, as well as music by Bliss, Brian, Ewazen and George Benjamin, with ensembles conducted by Sir Peter Parkes, Christopher Houlding and Michael Fowler. At the Guildhall School of Music and Drama on 25th September, the Guildhall Brass Band conducted by Paul Cash played Simpson's Vortex, Volcano and Four Temperaments along with Malcolm Arnold's Padstow Lifeboat, Little Suite for Band No.2 and Four Scottish Dances (arr. Farr). Finally, on 20th October at the Barbican Hall, the LSO Brass and the Desford Colliery Band again saluted both composers, playing Simpson's Canzona and Four Temperaments, three movements from Nielsen's Aladdin Suite, Berlioz's Roman Carnival Overture, and Arnold's Symphony for Brass and Fantasy for Brass Band.

During the same year, the painter Ken Jones visited Bob and Angela in the course of a walking holiday. He took some photographs and later painted a portrait of the composer which he presented to them. Miriam greatly admired the picture, and wrote to the artist to tell him so. I quote from his reply of 26th April:

"The sound of Bob's voice coming from an ancient radio (wireless!!!) tuned to the 'Third Programme' was encouraging and revelatory to the adolescent Ken Jones of the late '50s and early '60s. The sound of his voice was comforting, the quality intimate not aloof, and his content engaging and enormously rewarding. So different from the majority of broadcasters then and since! Can you imagine how it felt to meet him?" And later:

"Responses like music and painting seem so improbable, their doing is a constant source of amazement to me as to the 'WHY?' There is endless speculation. That they are such a potent influence for humanity and understanding is clearly evident from Bob's work."

During his last years, Robert Simpson became increasingly prone to urinary and other infections, was in and out of hospital, and became resistant to the antibiotics which he needed, but which had ceased to have the desired effect. The end came on 21st November 1997 at Tralee General Hospital.

In a reply to my sympathy card, one of so many she must have acknowledged, Angela wrote: "I wouldn't have wanted Bob to have gone on living any longer the way he was. The music will live, and I have many happy memories."

There was, needless to say, no memorial service. The composer had willed his body to Cork University for the purpose of medical science. After research was complete, Angela arranged for a gravestone to be erected in the cemetery attached to Cork University Hospital. In side the Hospital stands a sculpture called 'Flame' by the Krakow-born artist Alexandra Wejchert, who became an Irish citizen in 1979 and died in 1995. The inscription reads: "To signify the altruism of all those who donate their bodies for medical science and education – the flame of knowledge which leads to the light of education."

The broadsheet newspapers all published lengthy obituaries, and a particularly moving tribute came from the composer Frédérick Martin (his note is undated):

"It is in Denmark, during a rehearsal, that a trombone player, who is a good friend of James Loughran, told me about Robert Simpson's death. I had to receive the news from the society to really believe it.

So, I wanted to compose something to the memory of our dear man. If you agree with that, I'd like to give the manuscript of this small quartet to the RSS. There is not much I can do, but this is a prayer in music for the peace of his soul through the eternal journey.

In "Stargazer" (what RS actually was), there is a couple of references to the 13th quartet; it's been written pretty quickly under the pressure of the emotion.

I am to send Douglas Gordon a few lines for "Leading Notes", I haven't yet exactly worked out what, but anyway, Robert Simpson will never be remembered of in balance with what he gave us all. Tell me about the manuscript. I wish there were many composers to testify to what they owe to our master.

Friendly yours

Frédérick MARTIN"

Graham Melville-Mason acted as Simpson's musical executor, and discovered among the papers a four-hand piano arrangement of Nielsen's Commotio for organ, made in 1950, and an incomplete double concerto for cello and piano.

Following the marriage of Zara Nelsova and Grant Johannison in the late 1970s, Simpson decided to write a piece for them both, but the marriage was short-lived and the concerto abandoned.

After eighteen months, Angela sold Siochain and returned to England, where she now lives in Chipping Norton, and pursues voluntary work with vigour. She has also joined the Religious Society of Friends, more commonly known as the Quakers.

A memorial concert was held at St Johns Smith Square on 19th September 1998. The address was given by John Pickard, and the Delme Quartet played Simpson's Seventh Quartet and Matthew Taylor's Adagio - Tribute to RS. This was followed by the Violin Sonata, played by Pauline Lowbury and Christopher Green-Armytage, the Beethoven Variations played by Raymond Clarke and, to round the evening off, Beethoven's E flat Quartet Op.74 'The Harp'. Performances have been sporadic since the composer's death; the most notable was a series of concerts at the Wigmore Hall in 2000, collectively called A Tribute to Robert Simpson. This was sponsored by the Bluff Field Charitable Trust, named in memory of Susan Bluff, an economist and Simpson aficianado, who died of Marfan's Syndrome, a condition also suffered by the composers Sergei Rachmaninov and John Tavener. On 11th March the Lindsays played Simpson's Second Quartet with the Haydn G major Op.76 and the Beethoven A minor Op.132. This was followed by the Vanbrugh on 15th March with Simpson's Fifteenth, the Beethoven Second Razumovsky and Smetana's 'From My Life'. On 29th March the Chilingirian Quartet played Simpson's Second Quintet (with Stephen Orton, second cello) with Haydn's last (unfinished) Op.103 and Beethoven's First Razumovsky. Next came the Vertavo Quartet on 1st April, playing Simpson's Seventh, Bartok's Fourth and the Brahms Piano Quintet, with Pascal Devoyon, piano. The Vellinger Quartet rounded off the series on 12th April, playing Simpson's Sixth, Haydn's Op.55 No.2 in F minor 'The Razor', and Beethoven's Third Razumovsky. A splendid effort, although it is a great shame that the original intention to play all of Robert Simpson's

Quartets was not realised. Laurence Hughes (Independent, 20th March) commented on the series:

"While the likes of Boulez and Stockhausen are currently the object of lavish celebrations while still living, it is somehow typical of the way we treat our own composers that we should have to wait for three years after Simpson's death for this modest, but welcome five-concert tribute." The 90th anniversary of the composer's birth was marked by a splendid performance of the Fifth Symphony by the RCM Sinfonietta at the Amaryllis Fleming Concert Hall, Royal College of Music, conducted by Peter Stark on February 12th 2011. The work was preceded by Bax's Tintagel and the concert was dedicated to the memory of Vernon Handley, that stalwart champion of British music. It was good to see the composers David Matthews and Anthony Payne among the audience. On 17th June of the same year his home town of Leamington Spa honoured the composer's memory with a blue plaque on his birthplace, 21 Rosefield Street, unveiled by Miriam, his sister. Angela Simpson was also present, and a sizeable crowd attended the ceremony, by no means confined to RSS members; Robin Taylor, organiser of the Leamingto Blue Plaque Society, observed "we've never had anything like so many at previous ceremonies." The present owner of the house, a professor at Warwick University, had been unaware of the building's history, but by a happy coincidence possessed a recording of the Ninth Symphony, and broadcast this through the window while we awaited the mayor's arrival. There followed a reception at the Town Hall, where Roger Coull gave an entertaining account of he and his quartet's memories of working with the composer. The day was rounded off with a performance of Simpson's Seventh Quartet, preceded by Haydn's Op. 33 No. 3 "The Bird", and followed by Beethoven's Op. 59 No. 2, in the Studio Theatre.

The 90th birthday of Bob's sister Miriam on Friday 14th February 2014 was celebrated in an unusual but highly enjoyable fashion; Mim's great-niece Naomi Reynolds performed a dance "The Sob in the Spine" set to the music of the 7th Quartet, finely played by the Dante Quartet, at a modern dance centre, The Place, just off Euston Road.

Portrait of the composer by Ken Jones

Robert Simpson's grave in Cork University Hospital Cemetery

Unveiling the blue plaque at Robert Simpson's birthplace, 21 Rosefield Street, Leamington Spa, on 17th June 2011. Left to right: John McCabe (President, Robert Simpson Society), Miriam MacEwan, Jürgen Schaarwächter (Chairman, R.S.S.), Angela Simpson and the Mayor and Mayoress of Leamington.

A PRACTICAL IDEALIST

The life in music outlined, what of the man? Here is a pen portrait from the Robert Dearling interview:

"He speaks softly, precisely, choosing his words with care and yet maintaining fluency, surely a mark of deeply-considered, clear-cut philosophical conclusions. His dark, rather intense eyes can be a little unnerving as they gaze penetratingly at his listener, yet there is a reserved warmth and humanity in them that is reflected in his philosophy, his beliefs and his hopes. "Yes, I suppose I am in accord with Scandinavian culture. I am attracted to the humane attitude of the Scandinavians. After all, they were the first to abolish capital punishment. They have a severe climate to conquer, yet they have conquered it and gone on to become the most humane and nearly civilised people in the world. Humaneness is of prime importance.""

He was short in stature (5'6"), stocky and decidedly hunched from a lifetime spent poring over music paper and scores. His hair was originally dark; though he latterly went grey, he never suffered the widespread curse of male pattern baldness. He was a fast walker until the crippling stroke – before this, he looked considerably younger than his years, nearer fifty than seventy. The voice was low-pitched and husky, a kind of cockney growl, very reassuring when heard over the radio or in conversation. He was highly articulate and would speak for hours on subjects which interested him: "I'm no good at small talk." His knowledge of music was phenomenal. He had a seemingly inexhaustible supply of anecdotes and jokes, the latter ranging from the genuinely witty to ones which I could not possibly reprint here. He was never politically correct – one story will suffice. He was driving to Aldeburgh with Basil Lam. The car stopped at a set of traffic lights; to the left was a shop whose window display included boxes of Omo soap powder. "The aitch is silent, as in Aldeburgh," quipped Lam. As an example of the broader side of his humour, I will relate the story about a very promising pianist. He wins an international competition, plays at leading venues, and signs a recording contract. Then it goes wrong: he takes to drink, turns up to recitals half-cut or not at all, and the contract is cancelled. His wife leaves him, his house is repossessed, and he is reduced to wandering the streets trying to find a job as a pub pianist. The trouble is that his appearance tells against him; long, matted hair and beard, and clothing in rags, sometimes revealing what should not be. One publican after another takes a look and says "Sorry, mate". Eventually he comes across a landlord who is a kindly soul, and thinks "He doesn't look much, but I'll see what he can do." Sitting at his instrument, the tunes flow from the pianist's fingers; all his old skill has returned.

"Gosh!", thinks the publican "He's a natural – he'll go down a bomb on Saturday nights. But his appearance – how can I put this tactfully?" Putting his arm round the pianist's shoulder, he says "That was brilliant! There's a job for you here any time. But there's one thing I have to say to you. (Sotto voce) Do you know your arse is hanging out of your trousers?" "No" replies the pianist, "But if you hum it I can probably pick it up." Now one from the more abstruse end of the spectrum. On 5th August 1989, the Rev. Brian Duke wrote to the composer, drawing parallels between musical examples from symphonies by Sibelius and Simpson. Duke's letters were always rather like cryptic crossword puzzles; one had to decipher rather than just read them, so I will merely give a flavour by quoting his last paragraph:

"About bringing J W Dunne into things I'm far less happy. The experience is very familiar here. I suspect an easier way of thinking about it is to suggest that each cerebral hemisphere has a certain autonomy, an integrity that includes the ability to see into the other. All this demands is good lines through the corpus callosum and possibly an unusual view of cerebral dominance. The infinite regress that philosophers rightly flee is physically saved; it's like placing two mirrors facing each other, parallel. But the cerebral hemispheres aren't IDENTICAL twins, of course, and a good survival strategy is to be "My brother's keeper." One trick if woken sleepily at dead of night is to switch on only just those functions needful at the time. And it's just the same at the opposite extreme; even at the point of breakdown one may notice the local generation of a little heat – as a dispassionate observation!"

Simpson's reply, sent on the 14th, is a tour de force:

"Many thanks for your perspicaciously plausible plethora of purposeless Procrustean pluralistic palindromic polyphony, plainly a play on pilfered or purloined propositions.

"Perhaps we could get the Royal Philharmonic Society to perform it, and present you with the Gold Medal the same evening. Like Satie's piece it could be repeated 836 times, with a notional variety provided by having it both ways. Or maybe we should get Brian Ferneyhough to compose 836 variations on it; it would have to be for VERY large orchestra, so that it could, as it stands, act as an unusually complicated if somewhat involuted subject for a final fugue, the countersubject being itself its own inversion, shifted by whatever amount of time decided upon to create maximum cacophony, answered at the tritone, ending of course with an 836-bar pedal on C sharp. It would undoubtedly be a bastardpiece, inscribed to the Dogs Of Lilith."

A word here on the composer's tastes and interests other than music. He had a healthy appetite. His first wife cooked him enormous meals and, since she came from the kind of background where meat-free fare was not considered real food, he was not originally a vegetarian. Angela converted first; she was originally intending to continue eating fish but Bob, with his characteristically black-and-white view of things, assured her that if she did she could not be a true vegetarian. After Squibs's death, and their own marriage, he was happy to follow suit, and even came to the view that people were unlikely to stop killing each other while they continued to kill their fellow creatures.

In his earlier years he drank beer; always lager rather than bitter, unusual for the 1950s, and perhaps a legacy from his visits to Denmark. Later, other than the occasional half, his preferred tipple was whisky, which he drank moderately but with gusto. He was not a wine drinker. He also eschewed tea and coffee – "I never developed a taste for them" – preferring a glass of water with meals.

He was a smoker, originally of cigarettes, later a pipe, and then an occasional pipe of herbal mixture – "It's better than herbal cigarettes, they're like smoking air", finally giving up during his time in hospital post-stroke, where of course he had no choice.

He was casual in dress: in fact, on the occasion when he deputised for Vernon Handley and conducted the Ninth Symphony, he had to borrow a tie. He was very positively left-handed, and wore his watch on the left wrist; unusual, but for me the sensible thing to do, since the habit of wearing watches on the opposite wrist only came about in the first place because the early models were not shock-proof. His serious health problems have been covered in the main narrative, but the British Bandsman interview with Ron Massey (1979) also mentions insomnia: "He doesn't sleep very well, he says, so his hobby (astronomy) fits in nicely with his insomnia, though he did put the point that we don't get too many clear nights for peering through telescopes."

As regards the other arts, Simpson professed himself "very inarticulate" about painting, although he certainly responded to it, finding in Rembrandt especially a depth and humanity comparable to that of Beethoven. He had a restless, enquiring mind and was widely read; he was also a writer of distinction himself, as I hope the numerous extracts from his books and articles have shown.

His Oxford Dictionary of National Biography entry describes the composer as "pugnacious in manner" – I cannot say that I found him so, except in the immediate aftermath of the stroke. He certainly held strong views and never hesitated to express them. He has been accused of being as intolerant of serialism and the avant-garde as proponents of the latter are towards more traditional forms of expression: here, however, I think one is entitled to ask: who started it? In my experience, the promoters of modernism were always far more proscriptive, and prescriptive, than those who took another road. It has been said of the 1960s that if you can remember them you weren't there. I will re-phrase this, and say that unless you were around at the time you would find it difficult to credit the ferocity with which the avantgardists tried to make their own prejudices into universal tenets. An example from the visual arts here: in 1968 I began a four-year course in the Art Department of the University of Reading. I (and two other innocents) assumed that we would be allowed, nay encouraged, to pursue what we had already decided we wanted to do, painting from life. Not a bit of it – painting was dead, we were told, and we were plunged into an imbecilic first-year course comprising various Blue Peter-like projects lacking the slightest practical value. No energy was spared rubbishing our work or principles; two lecturers who tried to encourage fellow painters were sacked. Among their replacements was a man whose final show had consisted of a room with tables and chairs set for dinner, and printed invitations – nothing more. What we were supposed to learn from him, other than how to be a successful con-man, I have no idea; but then we were, as he rightly said, fixated on being "tied to the end of a pencil" or "masturbating on canvas". Charming.

As in painting, so in music, although here the process seems to have begun somewhat earlier. I quote from "Colin Wilson on Music" (originally published in 1964 as "Brandy of the Damned"):

"There was recently published a volume of interviews with British composers ranging from John Ireland to Peter Racine Fricker and Alexander Goehr, which reveals the kind of total split that exists in the musical world. Thus the interviewer (Murray Schafer) can open his interview with Goehr (born 1932) with the staggering remark: 'In comparison with your European contemporaries you might be called a "reactionary". Your music owes more to Schoenberg than to Webern... [Goehr sensibly replies that the merit of a composition does not depend on whether it is experimental or not, and that experimentalism has been greatly overstressed.] The result is that the symposium has the curious effect of a volume on philosophy written by a mixture of militant atheists and bigoted Roman Catholics."

Wilson (who wrote with enthusiasm about Simpson's First Symphony, then the only one available on record) also notes that in "Twentieth-Century Music", edited by Rollo Myers (Calder, 1960), the name of Sibelius is not mentioned even in the index. Such worthy attempts to deter the bigots by ridicule as "Punkt Contrapunkt", an item from the Hoffnung Interplanetary Music Festival in 1958, in which two German professors earnestly discuss a work supposedly by Bruno Heinz Jaja (actually an avant garde parody by Humphrey Searle, himself a serialist), or "Mobile", supposedly by Piotr Zak, but actually Hans Keller (a Schoenberg enthusiast) and an assistant improvising on percussion against an electronic background (Third

Programme, 1969) failed to dent the blazing zealotry of the modernists. In the days when I took Gramophone magazine (late 1960s) there appeared a letter wherein the writer snarled that if a previous correspondent wished to wallow in the "sentimental decadence" of Rubbra and Vaughan Williams that was up to him. Well, yes. This was nothing to do with art, it was politics verging on open warfare, akin to the Great Proletarian Cultural Revolution in China, though fortunately without the accompanying physical brutality. In such an atmosphere, it is hardly surprising if those charged with being conservatives or reactionaries should occasionally hit back – and Simpson was, as John Amis has said, the master of the gentle put-down. I refer you to the final chapter, "Simpson Antagonistes". Maybe it was the effectiveness of his ripostes that so enraged the opposition. I will round off this subject with a couple of quotes from the 1981 Julian Budden interview, with Budden playing devil's advocate:

"JB: People used to say – I don't agree with them - that the Third Programme was something of a cultural ghetto…

RS: …I have never heard anyone say that the National Gallery is a cultural ghetto."

"JB: Bob, quite a lot of people nowadays say the symphony is dead. What do you think of that proposition?

RS: Well, for a start, I don't really know of anybody who is able to write symphonies who says that the symphony is dead, which does seem to me rather significant. I think that most of the people who say that it is dead are those who don't want to write symphonies – either that or they can't."

Robert Simpson's interest in astronomy has already been mentioned, although he was modest about it. "I have a little observatory of my own with an 8½-inch telescope. I'm not an expert." His expertise was nonetheless sufficient for him to "be made an Honorary Fellow of the Royal Astronomical Society. In 1973 he took a sea cruise with Squibs to West Africa to see a total eclipse of the sun. Among others attending was Patrick Moore – Sir Patrick is well known for his robustly right-wing views, and it is fascinating to speculate on what course the conversation took, if indeed the two did speak.

Another activity was prison visiting, which Simpson undertook for many years at Grendon High Security prison – not in the usual sense of befriending a particular inmate, but as a lay member of the parole board who would interview the prisoner in order to identify any specific needs following release.

Robert Simpson's personal kindness is shown by his readiness to write testimonials on behalf of musicians he knew and admired; one for Dr.

Lionel Pike when he applied to be Professor of Music at Leeds University in 1981, another supporting John Pickard's application for the Headmaster's post at the Purcell School (1988), one for Matthew Taylor from the same year (headed TO WHOM IT MAY CONCERN), another supporting Mark Doran's application to take an M. Mus degree (1991), and a tribute to the Bournemouth Symphony Orchestra for a 1993 programme.

Simpson agreed to be a judge for the Amadeus Prize for young composers (Dublin 1991) and many good causes of various kinds were supported; I will mention a few from his later years. Robert Ponsonby (his former boss at the BBC) wrote in his capacity as Administrator of the Musician's Benevolent Fund requesting a signed manuscript; nothing of Simpson's own was available, but he sent a signed score of Sorabji's Third Piano Sonata. He supported the campaign against a plan to enlarge the Elgar Centre at Broadheath – with the extension, it would have been six times the size of Elgar's cottage. A contribution was made towards a statue of Sir John Barbirolli, to be placed outside the Hallé's new concert hall. He dictated a letter in support of the Lowbury Trio's application to the Heinrichson Foundation for a grant for the first performance of Matthew Taylor's Piano Trio in 1995, and the following year contributed toward a named seat in the Adrian Boult Hall as part of the Birmingham School of Music's centenary appeal. Most touchingly, again in 1996, a man serving a life sentence in Gartree prison wrote asking for funds for a new mouthpiece for his saxophone (or, if that was not possible, towards a new saxophone; he was very specific about what was required) and a sum was duly donated.

Robert Simpson's personal philosophy and his political beliefs were closely linked, and both were strongly influenced by his pacifism and atheism. Precisely when he lost his faith is not known: he was certainly an atheist by the time he met Angela, in 1956. I would guess that he was already a non-believer by the end of the war; Elisabeth says that "During the early years at the A.R.P. Depot he was still an orthodox Christian", but it seems that by 1942 he was already beginning to have doubts, as expressed in a letter to his fiancée:

"May 1942.

If I am asked about my beliefs about the hereafter, I merely say "What does it matter? Why try to make statements about such hypothetical things?"

I don't know a single thing which can baldly be called a fact. I'm not pontificating, all my thoughts have been engendered by a thoroughly interrogative frame of mind. I have come to no conclusions whatsoever about the nature of the Divinity. I simply think that it isn't what most people seem to think. God, as I see it, must have been a very illogical and unjust being to have created man as he is with the definite purpose of giving free will. For an omnipotent creator who could presumably see the results of his creations and their characteristics must have foreseen what would happen. If God is completely and perfectly good (in the accepted sense of the word) then everything he created must be essentially "good". And if God created something which had more of something "bad" than "good" why didn't he destroy it and create something better? Could he not have given a form of free-will which acted without the knowledge of evil. Adam and Eve had free-will but Satan didn't put the tree there. God did, why? A useless tree for they weren't allowed to touch it and it was the only thing to tempt them from their perfection. According to the legend if it hadn't been for God's initial action Satan wouldn't have had a way of getting at Adam and Eve and man would have been perfect to this day. Of course neither you nor I believe literally in this legend but it serves to illustrate my point.

"Now we come to the real crux of the matter. Since I can't believe in the logic of a compassionate God I'm inclined to think that man's evil must necessarily be connected with the animal part of his psychology. It wasn't the Creator who put it there. The Creator, as I understand, is a stupendous dispassionate being who created the universe producing conditions which somehow produced life and developed in myriad ways becoming most complex physically and mentally in man. The nervous system of animal life so developed that it became capable of what we now know as reason. Conscience is only the distilled essence of the reasoning powers and the greater the powers of reasoning the more intense and subtle the conscience. If apes have consciousness their actions indicate that they are undeveloped, as is observable amongst the lowest classes of humanity. I've mixed with them so I know. If you find one who has a bit more conscience than his baser fellows he's greatly superior in intelligence. Criminals who have brilliant intellects are not normal and the abnormality lies in the lack of subtlety and intensity of conscience. I'm crystal clear on some points. My conscience is the perfect instrument of guidance for my life, it has never failed to tell me the truth. Dogmatics have not taught me anything. Why should they be in possession of more spiritual facts than I. I believe that the spiritual world is the subconscious realization of beauty in all its forms. No one can give a satisfying description of a spiritual state.

"I observe my reactions to other people. I am driven to do my utmost to consider the emotional and physical reactions of my fellow creatures. I would rather suffer than see anyone else suffer. Many things produce in me strange emotional states, ecstasies and raptures, satisfaction and inexplicable happiness. These things I come to know as beautiful. Other things produce feelings of distaste, disgust, annoyance and unnecessary wrath. Others produce queer physical reactions, taste, smell and sight. I have also discovered that to exist one must work and fight the corruption and bestiality of others.

"Another thing I know above all others is that which affords me most aesthetic satisfaction is that strange entity called music. I am dominated by the urge to create it. These express my creed in terms of the only thing I understand: beauty. And here we reach the ultimate object of my creed (for no real creed is worthy of consideration if it is useless) to create beauty, beauty in my way of life, beauty in the lives of others, beauty in my thoughts and actions, beauty in my art, beauty in my very reasoning."

It is also worth noting that Simpson's first marriage in 1946 took place in a registry office: since neither he nor Squibs had married before there would have been no impediment to a church wedding, had they wished it, and this is perhaps secondary evidence that he was already an atheist. His sister believes that his wartime experiences led him to lose his faith, and this is entirely credible. Not that differences in outlook prevented friendships with believers – that with David MacEwan has already been mentioned. John Young, dedicatee of the Fourteenth Quartet, is a devout Christian; on one occasion he was staying with Bob and Angela at Killelton and the composer was anxious that he should not miss church on Sunday, driving him to the Anglican Cathedral at Killarney (designed by Pugin, but not built until long after the architect's death) – making sure, however, that he parked round the corner, lest anyone who knew him recognised the car, and thought that he was attending church himself!

Robert Simpson's general philosophy of life was jokingly summed up in a letter to Ian Hughes from 27th April 1991:

"I have two mottos that have served me well all my life –

1) Expect nothing and you will not be disappointed (ambiguous but safe either way).

2) Enjoy your expectations in retrospect."

There was, of course, more to it than that! His long-held pacifist views have already been discussed, but are summed up in a letter to Professor Gordon Wood (Chairman, Cricklade Music Festival) from 22nd October 1990:

"Pacifism – in logic the only possibility for human survival now that we have the means, not merely to continue the tooth-and-claw method, but to destroy utterly ourselves and all other forms of life on this planet. Einstein was right – we must change or perish. Martin Luther King was right - it's either non-violence or non-existence. Gandhi was right - an eye for an eye will make the whole world blind – perhaps it already is! Of course you're right about the nature of the tooth-and-claw evolution. But this could itself be an aberration on this particular planet – there may be others in the immensity of the universe where different systems, not based on self-devouring competition, have evolved.

Who can tell that?

"But our only chance is to take another step, and not merely a technological one like the one on the moon! It must be decisively away from violence, the root cause of all our problems. Not being a romantic fool I have no illusions about the chances of this happening – they are astronomically against. But that doesn't alter the need if we are to survive.

"War was devised by mankind as a means of settling disputes between large communities, and to accept it as the natural result of tooth-and-claw seems to me only cynical, which I'm sure you're not. It is after all the ultimate denial of the rule of law. At least in the last few minutes of my life I want to be able to say I tried - I didn't simply 'accept' the tooth-and-claw philosophy or the so-called 'rule of law' as decreed by those in whose short-term interests it is to preserve the status quo. The rule of real law has to be the result of a profound change. Little hope of that - but if enough of us try, there might just be a faint chance. Otherwise – curtains for sure. Who said 'It only needs a good man to do nothing for evil to prevail' – or something like that? Burke?

No apologies – you invited it!"

His beliefs certainly had a pessimistic edge to them. In the Simon Cargill interview he said: "I don't believe in free-will even." So you are a good old-fashioned Humanist-Determinist? "I'm not either. I'm not a humanist, because look at what a mess the human race has made of the world. I'm not an optimist but I am anti-pessimist. I try to behave in a sane manner, as if there were some hope of changing things.

"We have to accept what Einstein said that the human race has to change its way of thinking, or perish. And I agree with that. I also agree with him that we are <u>not going to do that</u>. So we will all perish. In that sense I am pessimistic, but am not going to behave like that, or lie down and do nothing."

In a further letter to Gordon Wood (12th November 1990) he expanded on this bleak world-picture:

"Then there's pollution, on a scale never before even hinted at; possibly irreversible and if so terminal, as a good many reputable scientists tell us. That's also a form of violence, against our own planet in the belief that we own the thing, that it's all there for the taking. So we wipe out vast areas of rainforest, driving out and/or slaughtering the inhabitants, we create new deserts, we make a world for a few faceless boardroom rulers – the Trilateral Commission, and the new Europe is simply one of their instruments. The UN is not 'there'; it's as much a mockery as the old League of Nations I remember well; it's a forum for gangsters to snarl in. Fake moralities and the 'rule of law' are the order of the day, a means (when the hypocrisy wears out) for Bush, Thatcher and their ilk to use violence to protect their oil interests (and how badly Thatcher needs another war now!). That scoundrel Saddam just happens to be the odd man out - a ruthless idiot to be sure. For all this, thousands, maybe even millions will pour out oceans of blood, if none of these sharks give way."

Simpson's views sometimes led him into heated disputes. On 26th January 1980, he wrote to the conductor David Willcocks after a brief discussion following a concert at the Royal College of Music: "I came away pondering your remark that you'd rather die fighting than live under an oppressive regime. The crosstalk between four people prevented me from proposing that since world war means the probable destruction of humanity and perhaps even all life on this beautiful planet, any thought of "defending" one's kith and kin must be unrealistic", going on to say that total passive resistance would be a surer and less costly way of defeating tyranny. Willcocks strongly disagreed, as his counterblast from 6th February makes clear:

"To say that "if the Nazis had met TOTAL passive resistance everywhere instead of arms they would have been powerless far sooner than they eventually were, and the world would have been a better place" reveals either an ignorance of, or a cynical disregard for, the brutality of the Nazi regime. Do you really believe that, if Allied forces had not stood fast against Nazi aggression, the millions of Jews in France, England and America would have escaped the gas-chamber? Are you really suggesting that the men and women who died in two World Wars died in vain?" The composer replied on 22nd February:

"Thanks for your letter. It answers only one sentence in mine, one that should have been clearer. "TOTAL passive resistance" 'of course includes the Germans. No despot could even begin in a civilized world; he would be a joke. You ask if all those people died "in vain". I think yes, and ask if the war saved the six million Jews who died, most of them during it. It added to them another 100,000,000 mostly inoffensive lives (20,000,000 of them Russian, I might add) and preserved the conditions for another war. If we had not crushed Germany in 1914-18 the conditions would not have been there to produce the Nazis. I also saw the last war, and spent it trying to save lives instead of adding to the slaughter – but that's irrelevant to the present argument."

A 1991 BBC interview led to a revelation which greatly surprised me when I read the related correspondence. In a letter to Gordon Harkness dated 29th April the composer said:

"The fact is that I was told by the producer (who is an old friend and colleague of mine, for whom I have considerable respect) that if my pacifism or my conscientious objection during World War 11 were mentioned in the interview, the matter would have to be 'cleared'. I didn't embarrass him by making a fuss, and the interviewer (presumably briefed) didn't mention the subject – so it didn't arise." In an earlier letter to the producer concerned, Arthur Johnson (15th January) he reveals more:

"I must say I'm still scandalized by that piece of paranoid totalitarianism and would be intrigued to know who was responsible for it. If it was Drummond (you said it would have to be cleared by 'your boss') there could be other, ulterior motives, but on the other hand there is an MI5 office in BH (Broadcasting House) – in all my years at the BBC I was aware of this, and of some of its perpetrations, even back in the 1950s. I remember when Frankie Leonard applied for a music producer's job and got a letter confirming his appointment, it was suddenly reversed without explanation – which turned out to be that he had been 'screened' and it was discovered that he had given some talks on music to the WMA! (Workers Music Association) Maurice Johnstone was told to tell him he hadn't after all got the job but was not allowed to tell him the real reason. Leonard Isaacs was so furious that he immediately rang Frankie and told him the truth. This wasn't the only incident."

So, even our own dear BBC was involved in cold war shenanigans – which brings me rather neatly to the next subject, politics. Robert Simpson was decidedly on the left; in the Lewis Foreman interview he declared: "I am a democrat; I am a Socialist. I'm not at all a sort of far right-winger who bleats about decadence." The term Socialist can cover many shades of red – I would say that Simpson was at heart 'Old Labour' or Bennite, though he was never a member of the Labour or any other political party. He was, however a CND member, and a member of MANA (Musicians Against Nuclear Arms). While he agreed with the far-left view that present society was unreformable, he rejected the revolutionary road, fearing the implied violence. His opposition to capitalism was quite clear; in a letter to Martin Anderson from 30th July – Anderson had previously sent him a copy of his dissertation on chaos – he wrote:

"You jolly old 'right-wingers' always say we have what you call the 'best' of a bad job, but this actually means we have to accept the 'chaotic' status quo, when the more energetic shysters can get the best deal for themselves. It's not the best deal for everybody else, i.e. the vast majority. You mention

Marx, but that's not what he was after. He was making what now seems a pathetic assumption – that the species was ultimately capable of co-operation. It is not. Marx wasn't an anarchist. The 'new right' isn't new; the jungle is very old, and our failure is not having climbed out of it."

As his letter rejecting the CBE makes clear, Simpson was a convinced republican, and was puzzled that the Scandinavian countries he otherwise much admired had kept their monarchies.

He took a keen interest in political events, and often wrote to the newspapers or to individual politicians. The earliest surviving is a letter to the then Foreign Secretary, Michael Stewart, dated 7th May 1970. Though rather long, it sets out his political position very clearly, and I will thus quote it in full:

"Forgive me for troubling you with this letter; there are times when one absolutely must! It seems to me a tragedy for all of us that a gentle, honest, entirely admirable man such as you are should allow anti-communism to drive him to a defence of the American position. I also am against the communists, who do not, in my view, practise communism anywhere in the world, and who have committed many enormities. But I would say this much – if the British Labour Party had to cope with either the Republicans or the Democrats in an election campaign, it would be unable to find words bad enough for them, and would soon be longing for its dear old enemies, the Tories. If in this country we had the CIA and the Pentagon instead of the equivalent bodies we do have, I for one would emigrate. If our police were like the American police, civilised people like you and Mary would be falling foul of them, as do a great many humane citizens in the United States. Therefore I was saddened by your refusal to protest, not just at the way America behaves in Indo-China, but at all blatant power machinations wherever they occur, whether they are Russian, Chinese, or American. The present government has been a deep disappointment in this respect; had it been a Tory administration its stance would not have been surprising. We need a government with the courage to condemn moral horrors wherever they occur. The alacrity with which Russia was (rightly) condemned in Czechoslovakia is not matched in the other direction, where far greater horrors are being perpetrated in the name of a freedom which does not exist in the country that boasts it, that makes of freedom a titanic confidence trick, that is busily engaged in debasing values everywhere, that is already debasing ours, and will succeed finally unless the diminishing civilized world not only protests against it, but refuses it also.

"I know that you are convinced otherwise, and I'm familiar with all your arguments (as you are no doubt with mine); I'd beg you not to trouble to reply, knowing how busy you are. But though you <u>are</u> sure of your ground I submit the fact that even when Fascism in Germany was openly showing its teeth, there were a great many who refused to see it. In America it is already sharpening its claws though it tries to hide them; I predict that it will be in control there within thirty years. Unlike Hitler's, however, it will be cleverly disguised by the mass media. Unless we resist it, we shall be swallowed up, and all human decency, too. If we are, most culpable will be the very government that ought to have foreseen it."

He was particularly incensed by the Falklands War, and on 9th May 1982 wrote a short letter which was sent to all the quality newspapers:

"Mrs. Thatcher and General Galtieri, who are so willing to sacrifice lives in order to save face, should be put together in a small open boat in the South Atlantic and left to settle matters."

He followed this up with a letter to the Prime Minister on 20th May:

"Dear Mrs. Thatcher,

In April 1980 you proposed to suggest me to the Queen as a suitable recipient of the CBE. I am now more than ever glad to have declined this proposition from a government that is increasingly and more blatantly revealing its true nature. Would you kindly inform me a) of the full functions and international connections of the Falkland Islands Company, and b) of the full extent and nature of Mr. Denis Thatcher's interests in this Company?"

Not surprisingly, he got no answer.

He wrote to the Guardian on 31st May, taking exception to "… comments that do no more than suggest that Mrs. T suffers from delusions of grandeur amounting to some kind of personality problem. This may be so, but it would surely have been pertinent to point out that now the facts of the Belgrano incident are becoming known, there can be no case for voting back into power a person possibly capable of ordering a massacre to prevent a peace settlement."

In a letter to the Guardian and Evening Standard from 24th June (not printed) he went a stage further:

"It appears that last February Mrs. Thatcher wrote to a lady in Beaconsfield, reassuring her that the garrison in Port Stanley (normally some twenty-odd Marines) was adequate to deter an invasion of the Falkland Islands. This was represented in the Evening Standard headline (June 23) as a 'blunder'. Does anyone really believe that the Prime Minister is so unintelligent? If so, this opinion must also include the faculties of her cabinet, her military advisers, and the Foreign Office, all of whom must be quite unfit to hold responsible positions. Such a view is presumably untenable.

"What motive, then, might have been behind this stance? Hindsight shows that Mrs. Thatcher's alarmingly low ratings in the opinion polls have recently been greatly boosted by the flurry of war hysteria accompanying the dispatch and success of the task force. We know that the present US administration wishes to preserve this British government rather than contemplate another that might give up nuclear weapons and dismiss US bases from this country. It has also been reported that the Americans hinted to the Argentines that if they took over the Falklands the British would do nothing. The British, by giving the impression of being content with a tiny garrison in Port Stanley, must certainly have encouraged the invasion. A blunder? The invasion took place, was duly defeated (with various forms of US assistance), and the opinion polls were rectified."

This seems to me to be going a little too far – my guess is that incompetence rather than contrivance led to the invasion. Not that we are ever likely to know the full facts – the Falklands War was heavily censored.

Simpson's suspicion of NATO as essentially a tool for the advancement of American interests is exemplified by a letter of 9th July 1983, again to the Guardian:

"Chancellor Kohl's complaint about the division of Germany should have been directed at NATO, not at President Andropov. In March 1954 the USSR applied to join NATO on the grounds that if it was, as claimed, a defensive pact, everyone should join it. In May this was refused. In October West Germany was invited to join NATO, with the object that it should be enabled to re-arm. In January 1955 the USSR ended the state of war with West Germany, claiming that there would be no need for this rearmament. In March 1955 the USSR agreed to the Austrian Peace Treaty, which left that country politically but not militarily aligned with the West. At the same time the USSR offered a similar treaty for the whole of Germany, with a democratically elected government. This was rejected by the West, which secured, in May, the membership of a re-arming West Germany in NATO. It was not until then that the Warsaw Pact was signed – six years after the formation of NATO."

In 1993 – Sheila Gordon sent Robert Simpson Hugo Young's book "One of Us". Simpson admitted that he found Young "rather irritating, if not exasperating because of his obsession with "objectivity"", but added some highly disturbing information:

"Young does not mention either the notorious secret agreement with Reagan in 1983 which was first uncovered by the New Statesman then got into all the main newspapers and even into the BBC news. This was that if the Americans, for any reason of their own, declared a state of emergency, they would have the power:

1) To take over all British seaports and airports, all railways and main road systems.

2) To take over 30 of the largest hospitals for their own use.

3) To impress British civilians into forced labour.

4) To arrest, imprison or even execute any persons deemed to be subversive.

I think there's more but my memory isn't as good as it was. No British government or Prime Minister has ever sold their own people down the river to this extent."

He stood up for the Greenham women, whose camp was pitched beside the missile base, in a letter to Brian May dated 14th March 1984: "You were very hard on the Greenham women; the 'litter' accusation is a myth – my wife has been there a couple of times and talked to them and seen how sane, calm, dedicated they are, and how they have to endure appalling threats, excrement thrown on their flimsy little tents, litter distributed about by illwishers, and even fire-attacks. Through it all they are without bitterness or vindictiveness. Now they are being evicted after a series of legal subterfuges too petty and complicated to be described in a letter, and the government has admitted that it's now about to spend hundreds of thousands on a new road system at the base which can certainly be no use - except to provide the excuse to remove the camps."

On 8th January 1985 – Simpson commented wryly in a letter, again to Brian May, that "So far as David Owen is concerned, his views on nuclear weapons seem to me to constitute a breach of his Hippocratic Oath." Simpson's contribution to the 1983 symposium UNHOLY WARFARE – the Church and the Bomb – "Our Shy Masters" – is his only published political essay, and is reprinted as Appendix 12.

The political, and the general atmosphere of his adopted homeland suited Simpson far better than had Thatcherite England. In a letter to Andor Gomme (20th January 1989) he wrote:

"We have sympathy for those less fortunate than we are – i.e, those who see how awful it is and haven't been able to clear out. Decent people are becoming more and more ashamed of being British. We're conscious of that here with our English accents – but we get nothing but kindness and warmth. Amazing when you think what the English did to the Irish over centuries." And, from a letter to Matthew Best (25th February 1991):

"My shame at being British, constantly fed by the steady deterioration of human rights in the wretched country and its abject hypocrisy and pandering to USA oil imperialism over the Gulf War, together with the gradual erosion of the much-vaunted 'British Justice', has finally overwhelmed me and I'm going to apply for Irish naturalization. In the European Court of Human Rights Britain has the worst record next to – who? – TURKEY! I've no brief for the little tyrant Saddam, but he's small beer compared to Bush, with his history of drug-trafficking and crooked dealing on a vast scale, with such power as Saddam never dreamed of."

In fact, Simpson remained a 'Brit', his illness meaning, of course, that there were other priorities. It is perhaps as well that he never lived to see the Second Gulf War, the invasion of Afghanistan and the bombing of Serbia, all enthusiastically supported by the nominally Labour government of Tony Blair. While he sympathised with Mikhail Gorbachev's attempts to liberalise the Soviet system, and thought the Baltic states unreasonable in demanding immediate independence, he had no illusions about Stalinism. In the 1980 letter to David Willcocks already cited he said:

"Don't imagine I have any brief for the stupid and brutal invasions of Hungary, Czechoslovakia and Afghanistan, which even the British Communist Party has rightly condemned." On 29th December 1989, he wrote to the Guardian: "Your front-page headline, 28 XII 1989 – 'Romania ditches Communism' assumes that country to have had communism. True communism has never been practised in any country in the world. If it had, it would have been impregnable. No one need be surprised if a people eventually rejects bureaucratic or personal totalitarianism. The tragedy is that these evils have been masquerading, from Stalin onwards, under the name of communism. In misplaced triumphalism, we Westerners cannot speak of the 'ditching' or 'demise' of communism. There can be no demise of what has never lived."

As with religion, political differences did not preclude amiable personal relations; his lifetime friendship with David MacEwan has already been mentioned, and he said of his old colleague, ally and intellectual sparring partner Hans Keller: "For a German Jew who fled the Nazis, he had the most appalling right-wing views". The late Pamela Bacon, to whom he dedicated the Piano Trio, he once playfully described as "a fascist", while upon our arrival for the Killelton seminar he drew our attention to a drawing of Beethoven's life mask, which some visitors had mistaken for a portrait of Mussolini: "I have got some right-wing friends, but he isn't one of them!"

The most rumbustious statement of his political beliefs came in a letter to Lionel Pike from 25th October 1987:

"For years I've been trying to think of something noisome enough to dedicate to Mrs. Thatcher, so that I can send her a really evil-smelling MS that also makes deafening noisome noises by itself, and is non-inflammable, being written on a combination of asbestos and an indestructible plastic.

Needless to say it wouldn't be a string quartet – rather one for road-drill, sewage pump, metal crusher and intercontinental ballistic missile, to which last the offending harpy would be firmly strapped on its climactic discharge into outer space, from where it would land accurately on Ronald Reagan and all his accomplices, with salutary effect on the health of the world – but NO! – it would produce terminal pollution in the upper atmosphere from those ineradicably noxious vaporised bodies, from which a fallout undreamt of by the most nightmarish prophecies of nuclear holocaust would descend on the fools that put them into power in the first place. Alas, I have not yet found the inspiration for such a magnificent work, so the Goddess of Coprophagy is for the time being saved. But be assured I am bending all efforts towards the infernal Gutterdamnerung apt to her immolation, protracted by a tempo of such slowness as Wagner never conceived, an eternally excruciating coda that never reaches the limits of affrighting dissonance at which it aims, yet always finds worse."

It seems appropriate to end this chapter with a Simpson squib. A Mr. A.J. Lewis, Chairman and Chief Executive of the Hartwood Investment Trust, wrote to the composer in 1987, soliciting funds for the Tories. Why on earth this gentleman ever thought Robert Simpson a likely supporter is a mystery; here, at any rate, is his reply.

"Your appeal to support the Conservative Party has reached me here, having been sent to my old British address. I note your fears about the breakdown of our 'traditional values' if Labour win the next election. You seem unaware that it is the present government that has systematically undermined all the caring values and sense of corporate responsibility that had become traditional (and envied all over the world) since 1945. On the other hand, you seem only too aware of the real function of the Conservative Party, intensified by the present administration – to protect the rich, of whom you appear to be one; your assumption that I too belong to this elite and will therefore support your contentions is, if I may say so, offensive."

He ends the letter: "I hope the results of your appeal will fail to cover the cost of postage."

Touché

CODETTA

Here, as a kind of appendix, is something of a curiosity. Graphology has not received any scientific recognition but, like astrology, holds some interest in considering how closely the analysis fits the person one knows. Manfred Lowengard, a practitioner in this field, wrote to Simpson on 1st November 1974, following the London première of the Fourth Symphony: "My intentions were to return a gift for the great musical pleasure you gave me when your symphony was performed last week. It was an experience of rare beauty, and I am sorry that my report lacks the intensity only music can convey. All the same, I do hope that you will accept the enclosed in the spirit in which it was written, and even find some pleasure in looking into this strange mirror?

"Thanking you once more for an unforgettable evening."

The analysis follows:

"This fluent, speedy and pleasantly simplified writing comes from an intelligent man who shows a rapid perception, combined with a fine power of observation and a fabulously retentive memory.

"His is a mind which likes to penetrate to the very heart of the matter, and since this man is curious by nature, his mind will find it not so easy to decide on which facet of life it should concentrate.

"It is the mind of a man who can and will acquire any knowledge, and one feels that at one time in his life he may well have been undecided as to where his real talents lay. There is present that intuitive penetration, which works so well in conjunction with his capacity for objective observation, allowing him to have a wide range of interests, and since he is concerned to bring harmony where he finds disharmony, one would almost suggest that psychology, healing, perhaps medicine of sorts, may fascinate him. On the other hand, one does find that in spite of his genuine idealism and almost romantic desire to give some beauty and pleasure to a world where unrest and disharmony prevail, his basic realism and ability to be practical and indeed methodical in everything he does will win the upper hand in the end.

"He is very methodical indeed, and in spite of being anything but pedantic, he insists on orderliness. He can plan his movements carefully, and he will insist in a friendly but persuasive manner that the people working for and with him will fall in with his way of doing things. He can be quite determined, perhaps even obstinate, here, and people who do not take him seriously will have a difficult time with him. He simply lives the example, and anybody who does not follow his lead is merely dropped by the wayside. Since he is kind and has a neat sense of humour, he will laugh such incidents off, but this does not mean to say that he forgets, and one will find that he rarely makes the same mistake twice, but elegantly and intelligently arranges matters in such a way that any repetition is impossible.

"His quick grasp of essentials is so well developed that he will always be a few steps ahead of those around him, and in particular of his superiors. It is not so much that he is ambitious per se, as that he aims to be as near perfection as possible, and, what is more, he has the gift of always finding the simplest and most direct route available. This is the reason why he gets irritated by slow and pedantic people who pay attention to details rather than to the wider and more important issues involved. This man is a hard worker, and, what is more, he enjoys working hard, for the simple reason that he finds pleasure in seeing bits and pieces forming themselves into a whole, and here once again the desire for harmony and order expresses itself. It is here too that his musicality comes to the fore, because he finds that music is the easiest, most outspoken and satisfactory way of expressing his almost religious desire to make his wish for harmony heard.

"Strangely enough, one finds that this writer is rather shy at heart, and that in the emotional sphere of his life harmony is not as well established as one would wish. Even though he enjoys comfort and warmth, it is difficult for him to relax, due to a strange mixture of shyness, a sensitivity that prevents his being demonstrative, even on an emotional impulse, some impatience, and an inability to adjust himself easily to any routine other than the one that he himself has designed. He may find it a little difficult to express himself in words; it is his shyness again that causes him to poke fun at situations or people, the more sincere or serious his feelings and understanding of them are.

One can also detect a kind of religious feeling, not necessarily an adherence to any dogma, which finds expression in his yearnings for harmony. He is generous to the point of extravagance, and giving will come easier to him than taking; but on the other hand one will find that he can organise and handle monetary matters very efficiently where other people's interests are concerned. He could be described as being a practical idealist."

Some of this seems well wide of the mark - the composer never had difficulty in expressing himself verbally! – but in other respects it is pretty accurate. I cannot help wondering what Robert Simpson himself made of it. At any rate, he didn't throw it away.

MUSIC AND MUSICIANS

I begin with an extract from the 1980 interview with Lewis Foreman:

"LF: Well, Bob Simpson, why do you compose?

RS: Impossible question. (laughs) I've always wanted to compose. In fact the only reason I can offer, if it is a reason, is that it strikes me there must be a kind of music which doesn't exist and so I want to fill the gap. I want to supply what doesn't exist. You know what it is like when you discover a composer you have never come across before – you suddenly find out it's marvellous. Like when I found Nielsen for instance, it seemed to me that I always knew that music existed. It ought to exist somewhere, and there it was. There is also a kind of music which ought to exist which you haven't really any hope of finding unless you write it yourself, or try to. That, basically, is it, I suppose.

LF: Is it a compulsion?

RS: Absolutely.

LF: What is the nature of the compulsion? What triggers the compulsion?

RS: What triggered it in the first place, what triggers any creative urge? Well, as a kid I suppose it must have been musical. The only thing that makes you want to compose is having heard music. If you've never heard any music in your life, if you were brought up deaf or completely isolated from any possibility of music, it is extremely unlikely that you would want to be a composer. It's very unlikely, for instance, that you would invent the idea of music. It seems to me that you become a composer because you hear music and you want to make some of that. And if you naturally have the talent you're drawn to it."

In a 1981 interview with Julian Budden he said:

"I remember Edmund Rubbra being asked this question (about his working methods) and he said 'I start at the beginning and go through to the end', which is very logical and sensible, and in fact that is what I do most of the time…" In another interview with Robert Massey, for the British Bandsman (6/10/79) he added: "I always remember the words of Berlioz: 'Get the beginning right and the rest will follow'", also commenting wryly: "There is no more horrible sight than a blank sheet of paper."

Asked by Gordon Roland-Adams if he ever sketched (Tonic, Spring 1984) he replied:

"Not much sketching – only if I want a very long melodic line: sketching it out helps to 'see' it from start to finish and to get details in the middle right. Shorter ideas get shaped firmly in the head and don't get written till they're fixed. Composing a large work is usually started from a small idea, which is then allowed to proliferate under sharp discipline; as it proliferates it undergoes metamorphosis, so that the continuity is (one hopes) organic. The whole thing is really a process of controlled improvisation on paper. You have to get rid of what doesn't feel right and find out what does. You worry at it until the current starts to flow. If an idea feels wrong, chuck it out; if it feels right, keep it. It's purely a matter of intuition – it's not analytical, consciously, and it's not theoretical. That's work for other people, afterwards. If the intuition is working, and the composer intelligent and honest with himself, the result should bear any kind of analysis. Nothing should be 'imposed'.

"All very difficult, or easy, according to how you feel. Everyone has different methods – Haydn was helpless without a piano. Some composers write orchestral works in reduced score – I have to do it in full score, right from the start, partly because I tend to keep off the piano. (Everyone knows what would happen if I wrote only what my fingers would play.)"

His daily routine is described by Angela Simpson in a letter to Professor Edward Green of New York dated 24th January 2006: "After breakfast he would go into his study and work until lunchtime. He would then spend the rest of the day doing other things such as walking the dogs and me on the beach, listening to a lot of music, particularly Beethoven quartets (his favourite was Op.127). He rarely sketched and would write directly into full score, including writing the correct keys for the transposing instruments. He would occasionally use the piano to try out chords, but did not compose at the piano. Ideas would 'gel' in his head and so, if I apologised for making a noise when he was working, he'd say "it doesn't matter, I'm only writing it down"! Sometimes if he felt things weren't going well he'd say "it's just not right yet" and would take a day or so until he'd got the particular problem sorted."

"Bob usually worked on one piece at a time and would take a commission only if he felt it was the right medium for him. Julian Bream once asked him to write a work for him – Bob gave it a lot of thought but turned it down as he felt that writing for the guitar just wouldn't be right for him. He did reject his Violin Concerto – he had plans for revising it but, sadly, this never happened." "Normally Bob worked very quickly and once he left the BBC he became very prolific as he at last had the time to compose." Simpson said himself, in the interview with Julian Budden (1981): "Somebody once asked me what it was like, composing. "Well," I said, "it's quite easy, you know. If you do something bad you get rid of it, and put something good in its place. No problem!" This is a horrible joke really, because it is a diabolical problem. When you sit down and work at it, it's murder, it's terrible! I sometimes finish up with my whole back aching, my neck aching, my legs aching, my arms aching, my eyes aching, my head aching, and I just want to go to bed, or collapse, or something, or even watch the television!" In an interview with Simon Cargill (Hi-Fi News, 14/10/91), Cargill said to him, after some pessimistic comments about the future of humanity:

"But surely art can never be truly pessimistic, because it is an assertion of the artist's desire to transcend his fate…

"Yes, it's an optimistic gesture. One puts down notes on paper and expects them to be played. Naturally I hope somebody will respond to them in the same way I responded myself when I wrote them. But I don't assume this is going to happen."

Christopher Ford observed, in his Guardian interview from 23rd October 1974:

"He can be modest about his own work because he, at least, feels no need to be defensive about it. He is sure of the position he has taken up, as critic and artist. His talk is persuasive and stimulating. Yet it's fighting talk, too: and his utterances, put into print, give the impression of a very spiky and dogmatic character." I would say that, while he never bragged, he had a due sense of his own music's worth, as witness his efforts to publicise the recording of the Ninth Symphony, and he was never shy of firing a broadside when he felt that his work had been misunderstood – for example, his comments on the hostile criticism directed at his Eighth Symphony. He was philosophical about the neglect of his music. Robert Dearling, in an interview for Records and Recording (October 1979) asked him "in all innocence" how many times the LSO (who commissioned the piece) had played the 5th Symphony since the tumultuous reception given to the first performance in 1973. "Not once since then. The Symphony has not been performed again at all in this country although it has been given, once, by the Moravian Philharmonic Orchestra under a conductor called Nohejl. Somebody in Czechoslovakia seems to like what I write. But the LSO have not played it since.

"No, it doesn't depress me. Of course, I would like to hear it performed occasionally, but think of Beethoven – how little acknowledgement he got. His Fourth Piano Concerto was performed only once in his lifetime and that's when he performed it himself. No-one else played it, but now it is one of the most popular works in the whole repertoire. If that could happen to Beethoven, who am I to complain?"

He felt strongly that classical music was sidelined in the British Isles, as a sort of optional extra. I quote from the interview with C.B. Rees London Musical Events, July 1959: "He thinks that the paucity of municipal support for music outside London is scandalous and that it is artistically monstrous that Newcastle Upon Tyne (for example) should not have their own permanent regularly functioning orchestra. On subsidies for music and the arts generally he thinks our situation is "appalling" compared with provincial centres in Germany where opera and symphony are as indigenous and available as lager. "No nation can claim to be civilised where this does not happen." Lack of governmental and municipal support is inhibitory to potential conductors, soloists, composers. You cannot bombinate in a void. Creative and executant talent in this country is at least equal to that elsewhere, but lack of opportunity is crushing here."

He would rather not have his music performed at all than badly. He took exception to a decision by Gareth Hudson, of RTE, to, programme the Seventh Symphony under an unknown conductor rather than Brian Wright, whom he knew and trusted, and wrote to him in a letter dated 30th October 1989:

"If you wish to perform any of my symphonies I would ask that they be treated with proper respect; when introducing them to a new public it should be ensured that their performance is in the hands of someone known to understand them. I have suffered so much from inadequate performances that I now feel impelled to defend my works against what seem to me to be hazards. The Seventh Symphony, moreover, is a powerfully introspective work, and quite unsuitable to start a concert, the more so for being followed by the bland Saint-Saëns concerto. To begin such a programme you need a Rossini overture or perhaps a jolly little suite by somebody or other, not a tough half-hour symphony. The current fashion is to put the contemporary work at the beginning of a concert, presumably to get it out of the way so that everybody can settle down to enjoy some nice music. I object to this practice. No doubt these are not your intentions, but the effect is the same.

"May I propose you take No.7 out of that concert? This would seem to me the sensible course, and I'm sure the conductor would agree to something more enjoyable. If you wish to insist on the present plan, I shall have to ask the publisher not to supply the material. It would pain me to have to do this, but the proper representation of my music to a new audience is in my mind the real priority; if I'm not happy with the arrangement it's my duty to say so, and to take what steps I can to remedy the matter."

As will be perfectly clear by now, he was essentially an orchestral and chamber composer. His problem with words precluded much vocal music; to Julian Budden he said:

"I would love to write a big oratorio. I don't think I would ever write an opera, because I don't think I've got that kind of kink. I wish I had, but I don't think

I have." Not that he was indifferent to opera; Dearling observes: "…he is by no means opposed to the form. His god is Beethoven, and of course Fidelio is his favourite, others he admires being those of Mozart and Berlioz, and Verdi's Falstaff; but it is The Mastersingers that he singled out for special comment. "Wagner was in the middle of The Ring when he stopped to write The Mastersingers, and all his egotism seemed to disappear. It is an incredible masterpiece." Rather surprisingly, he observed during the Foreman interview: "… I've never thought of myself as – and I don't expect anybody else has thought of me – as a ballet composer. But if I was offered the chance to write a ballet, say to Heine's scenario for a ballet for 'Faust', which is really very marvellous and not very well known, I would have a go at that with tremendous excitement." I dare say he had in mind something along the lines of Vaughan Williams' 'Job' rather than 'The Nutcracker' – VW of course stoutly refused to call 'Job' a ballet, describing it as a Masque for Dancing. It is equally difficult to imagine Max Reger writing a ballet, but the formidable German master did produce a Ballet Suite, somewhat heavy though it is in places. At the end of the interview with Dearling, he said simply: "If I were to be condemned to compose only one kind of music it would be string quartets."

Robert Simpson always considered himself a composer first and last, and on 20th March 1978 wrote a distinctly frosty letter to Arthur Jacobs, Editor of the British Music Yearbook:

"Dear Mr. Jacobs,

I know no dictionary that says a musicologist is a composer who writes down and occasionally publishes his impressions of other composers he admires. Quoting dictionary definitions (which often differ) is a popular but futile evasive tactic. You know perfectly well what I meant. It is generally understood that a musicologist is a special kind of researcher – as is any kind of "ologist". My solitary excursion into this field was to go to the Beethoven archives in Bonn in 1970 with Jimmy Loughran to make sure we didn't play any wrong notes in the symphonies. He is a conductor and I am a composer and this little expedition didn't turn us into anything else. We remain plain musicians. By no stretch of the imagination can you describe me as first a musicologist, second an employee of the BBC, and third a composer. Berlioz was not a musicologist and nor am I. Please get the priorities right next time; that's not much to ask. If you don't, you might one day be an amusing quote for somebody. Kindest regards."

He considered Bach and Beethoven to be "the two giants of music." About earlier music than J.S. Bach he wrote little. I quote an exchange from the Budden interview: "JB: I suppose one can say that it is to British insularity that we owe such things as the Perpendicular style of Gothic architecture, which has got absolutely no equivalent abroad, and the late polyphony of early-seventeenth-century English composers like Thomas Tomkins.

RS: Yes, and going even further back, to the sixteenth century, there are Tallis and Byrd – marvellous individuality, totally English music. If you compare it with Palestrina you can't mistake it for anything but English music. And that's also a very interesting aspect of the conservatism (or conservationism, if you like) of English music at that time. In Byrd's and Tallis's music you find roughnesses in the counterpoint, dissonances, false relations, and things like that, which Palestrina was in the process of getting rid of. They were the up-to-date composers, they were smoothing everything over. The English weren't interested in that, they were interested in expression, and they used whatever came to hand."

Simpson thought Giovanni Gabrieli a master, and also found Gesualdo's madrigals powerful, finding in them a sense of evil unique in music – Gesualdo, of course, murdered his wife and her lover. With Purcell he could not get on, reacting against "that particular kind of English melancholy."

Bach's B minor Mass and St Matthew Passion were to him among the towering masterpieces of music, and he took strong exception to the belief in some quarters that the former work was not written to be performed; "If such people exist, they may be safely ignored." (EMG record review). He also referred to the "profound science" of Bach's art, and in the Cargill interview he said "... in his preludes and fugues and the organ works everything is there in the notes and not beyond them. I feel this about all great music – should it illustrate words or ideas or whatever – that it still has to stand up on its own two feet, independent of any associations."

Robert Simpson made an arrangement of Bach's The Art of Fugue for string quartet, with the completion of the unfinished Contrapunctus 14 by Donald Francis Tovey which he thought entirely appropriate.

The exact date of composition is not known, but it can be dated to the 1960s, since the first performance, of four of the arrangements, was given at the Victoria and Albert Museum by the Hirsch Chamber Players on 26th January 1964. The first complete performance was given by the Delmé Quartet at Brunel University in eight concerts between 3rd May and 21st June 1980, also including quartets by Simpson and Beethoven. The Delmé did another complete rendition at Conway Hall, Red Lion Square on 26th November 2000, at which Simpson's Thirteenth Quartet was also played, and they recorded the arrangement for Hyperion the same year.

Simpson could not resist observing, in the Ford interview: "Fashions are of no importance whatsoever. There's no such thing as an 'advanced school of composition', there's only advanced music - in other words great art.

Beethoven is far more advanced than anyone writing today. Bach was 'behind the times.' His sons thought he was a stuffy old bird. But look where he is now, and where they are."

Of Bach's great contemporary, Handel, he once remarked "He was the Richard Strauss of his day." Noting my pained reaction, he added: "Yes, you're right to wince at that. But he was an opportunist – he only turned to oratorio because his operas failed." Nevertheless, he admired the German-Englishman's prodigious creativity, and considered him to be, along with Mozart, Schubert, Bruckner and Dvořák, one of music's great melodists.

His love for Haydn should be abundantly clear by now, if only because he quoted themes from the master in three of his own works. In an EMG review of a set of the six 'Paris' symphonies by the Little Orchestra of London under Leslie Jones, he forthrightly condemned the use of a harpsichord continuo in these "magnificently and completely orchestrated works", adding: "if a continuo instrument is to be used, it should be a fortepiano, not a harpsichord", and that the latter's faint tinkle was "as irritating as a spider's web in the face."

About Mozart he was decidedly cooler; while recognizing his incomparable contribution to the symphony, concerto and opera forms, and that his was a "musical genius on the highest level", he felt all the same that Mozart was "too knowing", a "magician" rather than a supreme craftsman, and that the quality of his music might well have declined in later life. I think part of his problem here may have been those soi-disant music lovers who rhapsodise about Mozart while being sniggeringly condescending about Beethoven.

The latter was, of course, the greatest composer as far as Robert Simpson was concerned. His essay on late Beethoven is reprinted as Appendix 7. He also wrote a monograph on the symphonies published as a BBC Music Guide in 1970, and other essays, lectures and talks were edited by Lionel Pike and published under his own imprint in 1996. Two items are, I think, of particular interest; one concerns the Fifth Symphony, and his view that the work should be performed as Beethoven originally conceived it, with double repeat of scherzo and trio and the repeat in the finale, rather than the published version which he thought a 'mutilated makeshift'. The original score was recorded by the Berlin Staatskapelle under Otmar Suitner in his superb series, and I must say that, having heard this, I would never again want to listen to the usual truncated version.

Regarding this most famous of symphonies he was, in the same book, characteristically scathing about bad performing habits: "The dramatic nature of No.5 has ensured its frequent maltreatment by the type of romantic conductor who is the equivalent of the ham actor. Beware of the fool who knocks out the opening bars in a slow tempo, then tears off like a maniac from bar 6; we may be sure that he will perform the same maddening trick at every similar point, in order to demonstrate two things (a) his lion-tamer-like control of the orchestra, and (b) (unconscious) that he has no idea of the tempo. There is, in fact, a magnificently cogent tempo in which every quaver is like a hammer – the pace must be of incorruptible steadiness, halted only by those mighty pauses that mean nothing without a proper pulse to measure them by. Mahler once gave some sound advice to a young conductor: 'If you think you are boring your audience, go slower, not faster. '"

The other concerns the vexed question of "authenticity", about which he was a decided agnostic. Orchestras in the late eighteenth or early nineteenth centuries were smaller because the works were mainly performed in small halls or large rooms, while an "authentic" body of strings sounds starved in a modern concert hall, hence the resort to doubling. He also said, in the Julian Budden interview:

"This is a very difficult question. People get very hot under the collar talking about it. I would say that if a work has real enduring qualities, if it has real substance and is going to last beyond its own time, then it possesses certain qualities which can adapt to new times. If we hear a Beethoven symphony now, played by instruments which Beethoven did not have – the kind of modern clarinets, horns and trumpets with valves, strings with metal strings, and so on – we are used to this sound. You might as well say that if you are going to listen to music as Mozart or Beethoven or Bach listened to it, you not only have to change the instruments, you've got to change your ears too. You've got to have an authentic period pair of ears in order to hear it. We haven't got that. So, in effect, the music means something to us in terms which we understand, which we are conditioned to appreciate. So the interpretation of a work by Beethoven or Brahms or Bach or whoever from the past must stand or fall by its integrity internally, by its vitality, and not by its "authenticity" – which I don't think is altogether possible in our time."

Of the quartets, he loved best the E flat Opus 127, of the piano sonatas the "Hammerklavier" in B flat, Opus 106, and he owned that there were things in the Missa Solemnis that moved him as much as anything in music, instancing particularly Et Incarnatus Est from the Credo – "No ordinary man wrote that".

Simpson did, of course, write a late set of piano Variations and Finale on a theme of Beethoven and, well before that, his Fourth, Fifth and Sixth String Quartets used Beethoven's Razumovskys as models, something unparalleled in music as far as I know. I will end with an extract from his 1970 essay on the Ninth Symphony, which is musical writing of a rare order:

"Beethoven's trio, for the first time in the symphony, seems to be ordinary human music; but its sense of delight does not comprehend the enormous forces pent in the scherzo – to a child a pantomime fairy is as magical as a real one, and the gaiety of the trio is as real as a child would think it. And a man is a child in the face of things that are either too vast or too minute for him to grasp – or so it is at this stage in the Ninth Symphony. This trio, moreover, is in D major; in the first movement the sound of the major mode was as a flaming cosmic catastrophe, terrible and almost unimaginable; here it is entrancing and delightful – a child might not see much difference between photographs of the Crab Nebula and an exploding rocket."

Simpson loved Schubert's music, especially the later chamber and keyboard works, and sometimes speculated as to what the Austrian master might have achieved had he lived beyond the dreadfully early age of thirty-one, once observing: "Nothing would have stopped Schubert, except possibly a bullet." He was highly critical both of attempts to "complete" the B minor Symphony and of the widespread conductor's habit of slowing for the second theme in the first movement of the Ninth, and in the coda of the finale.

He greatly admired Mendelssohn's scherzos, especially, and in a letter to Philip Martin dated 22nd March 1993 observed: "I would say that Mendelssohn was one of the few composers in the nineteenth century who understood the quartet medium – much more, for instance, than Brahms, Dvořák or Schumann, who wrote, of course, fine music for the quartet but never with ease."

Nevertheless, he adds: "P.S. It seems to me fairly obvious that from Beethoven we receive profound musical visions, whereas from Mendelssohn we mostly get staggering facility. There is, therefore, a great danger in playing a Mendelssohn quartet after one by Beethoven."

Schumann he admired as both a composer and a critic. In the Budden interview he said: "Schumann was perhaps the best critic-composer there ever was, because he spent most of his time telling people what they should try to understand, what they should try to get to know. He spent a lot of time advocating things rather than pulling them down, and, as a creative artist himself, he was a generous man. He could read a score. Not many critics can do that – especially nowadays."

Another early enthusiasm was (and remained) for the highly imaginative, if not quirky symphonies of the Swede Franz Berwald, hardly known in this country in the 1940s, not that he is exactly a household name today.

Of the two great operatic masters of the mid-nineteenth century, Berlioz and Wagner, his preference was definitely for the former (note, however, his admiration for The Mastersingers expressed earlier in this chapter.) On 4th December 1952 The Listener published an article by him entitled The Restraint of Berlioz, to accompany, very appropriately a broadcast of 'L'Enfance du Christ', the most delicate of his large-scale pieces. He begins by saying "One of the most common fallacies of twentieth-century criticism assumes that 'understatement' is a virtue", going on later to say: "In any art, there must be neither understatement nor overstatement: only adequacy is tolerable.

"Berlioz has often been accused of 'overstatement', of 'megalomania', of the habit of exaggerating all the extremes of his music. He has been widely regarded as the archetype of the 'romantic' composer, the mentality to which no excess of apparatus or expression is too absurd or pretentious. Now Berlioz, it is universally admitted, is a profoundly original composer; there are many things in his work that may, in one performance, sound crude and even amateurish, and, in another, brilliant and powerful strokes of genius." Later he adds: "In some ways it might be true to say that Berlioz and Mozart are the two most difficult composers to perform, the one because his apparent eccentricities are balanced on a razor's edge, and the other for the exactly opposite reason that he is so infallible that only the finest art can penetrate into the incandescent core contained by his smooth and easy mastery."

His admiration for Wagner's mastery of development was somewhat tempered by feeling that he, like Mozart, was a little too knowing – however, as well as his love for Die Meistersinger, he felt Götterdämmerung to be his favourite of the Ring cycle, and said of Tristan und Isolde: "if we listen to Tristan we get a feeling that this is something beyond sex because it is so magnificently composed…" (from an undated radio broadcast).

Bruckner has already been adequately covered, but Simpson also had a great admiration for Brahms, whom he considered the greatest symphonist directly in the Beethoven tradition, and also the only man to have consistently maintained the classical (and, he thought, best) practice of beginning a concerto with a ritornello, with the soloist only entering later. He contributed a number of thoughtful programme notes on some of the German master's major works, and thought it a great shame that Bruckner and Brahms should have been pitted against each other by the Viennese musical elite, when they had more in common with each other than Bruckner with Wagner.

Of the earlier Russians, he most favoured Borodin and Mussorgsky, considering the former to have been an admirable man as well as musician, with a house full of children, animals and friends, but for him Boris Godunov was "the greatest Russian work". Of Tchaikovsky he was less fond, considering him firmly in the German tradition; however, in The Symphony he did instance the first movement of the Fourth as a locus classicus of true symphonic construction.

On November 25th 1965, the Listener printed an article by Simpson entitled "The Essential Dvořák", which began thus:

"Dvořák is at once one of the greatest and most neglected of nineteenth-century masters. There is no difficulty in enjoying his music, but there is real difficulty in writing or talking about it, and that is a factor that has contributed to his neglect. He is known to the large public by a mere handful of works; the most popular of his symphonies and quartets are by no means the strongest, and in the case of the most often played quartet (the F major, Op.96, now called the American), not even the most obviously beautiful. One scarcely ever hears his name mentioned in those places where the élite are wont to discuss the more rarefied values; there is little to argue about and, as we all know, talking about music is a greater comfort than concentration on the thing itself." After praising the earlier symphonies, especially the great Seventh in D minor, Simpson observed: "No one would wish that Dvořák had torn up the 'New World 'symphony, but if he had done so it is likely that his stature as a great symphonist in the line of Beethoven, Schubert and Brahms would have been clearer." He ends the article: "When art is once more aiming to improve life, Dvořák will come more fully into his own, for his finest music is love made audible."

With Janáček, he felt less affinity: "He's too short-winded for me", and he found the return of the opening fanfare at the end of the Sinfonietta irritating (I find it thrilling!) – but he did like particularly among the operas 'The Cunning Little Vixen', which does perhaps have more in the way of sustained lines than the others.

We must next consider two formidable pairs of composers, Mahler and Strauss, and Sibelius and Nielsen. Simpson was considerably more enthusiastic about Mahler in the 1950s and 1960s than he was later to become. In a letter to Peter Field, from 2nd January 1993, and dictated, he said:

"Many thanks for your letter. Simon (Rattle) did rather exaggerate my attitude to Mahler. I've learned a lot from his music, especially his treatment of the orchestra and I admire very much those pieces in which there is real concentration of musical thought, like most of the scherzos for instance. The side of Mahler I don't like is the enormous amount of self-regard his music contains. Often he stands himself on a great stage and bewails his fate and that of humanity in general. I soon get tired of that kind of personal exhibitionism and there is some of Mahler (but only some) I dislike very much."

In a letter to the author dated 16th November 1976 he said in reply to a question of mine:

"It's true I don't really like Elgar very much (I always get the feeling I won't be spoken to like that!!!) but I'd rather have him than Strauss, who seems to me completely hollow." For all his antipathy, he considered Elgar's Introduction and Allegro a good piece, and in his centenary booklet Sibelius and Nielsen he observed, while comparing Sibelius's Fourth Symphony and Elgar's Second (composed about the same time) "where Elgar's balance is achieved by a process of accumulation, Sibelius's comes out of one of elimination." He also conceded that Strauss's Elektra was "an amazing score." Much has already been said here about his long association with Nielsen, but I will quote from one section of the centenary booklet, concerning Sibelius's Seventh (with apologies for the occasional technicality):

"Sibelius's Seventh is rarely comprehensively performed, not because of any exceptional technical difficulty, but because of the almost superhuman concentration it demands from its interpreters. Too literal a treatment of dynamics, for example, without grasp of the sheer size of some of the paragraphs, can be fatal. Consider the immense opening of the symphony; the wonderful trombone theme that begins on page 9 (second bar) is marked only sonore, and the rest of the orchestra (all of which is playing) is variously marked mf and f. This passage is the climax of a massive growth, and it must sound like it; the trombone must dominate, even if (as Sibelius obviously intends) it is sounding through rather than over the orchestra. Yet the player must save something for the apex of the phrase, especially for the noble crescendo on a rising arpeggio in his sixth bar. And the orchestra must not be too considerate of him. The natural evolution of this theme from previous material must be made clear by an absolute steadiness of tempo in all that goes before, and dynamics are also vitally important in the vast, serene C major string passage earlier. Sibelius does not give much help here; over a huge stretch he indicates only poco a poco meno p – without intermediately graded dynamics (which the conductor must supply) there can be no coherent growth in tension amongst sixty string players." After some further analysis, he goes on to say: "If all these matters are faithfully attended to, with full exercise of the imagination and abounding vitality of execution, with Herculean sustaining power in the long slow periods, there is no more thrilling and awe-inspiring work after Beethoven. Music as great as this makes commensurate demands on the performers, and we must not blame the composer if they fail him. The last quartets of Beethoven have always had to overcome a reputation for obscurity and difficulty (and even a kind of hesitancy) for this very reason."

A more light-hearted approach may be seen in his short article about the Violin Concerto (Radio Times, 10th September 1963): "One of the rather amusing things about the musical fashion-monger is the way in which often, quite suddenly, he gets cold feet about some composer he has been trying to push into limbo; all at once a fearful misgiving flobbers in his belly: 'Am I making an ass of myself?' he grates. Alas, it's too late. (When you begin to wonder if you have made yourself a right nit, you already have, nine times out of ten). But our vogue merchant is cunning – 'Better praise something,' he snarls. 'What do the Sibelius-ites tend to deprecate? – Ah yes, the Violin Concerto; praise that and make 'em even wronger. Then we can suggest that Sibelius is a talented popular composer, but a bad serious one.' Now it's true that some Sibelius enthusiasts have tended to write off his Violin Concerto as being less weighty matter than the symphonies. So it is, but it is a masterpiece all the same, utterly characteristic of its composer. If Sibelius had published nothing else, it would still have marked him as one of the most original minds of his time."

Robert Simpson rarely referred to Debussy or Ravel, although he did take exception to the lazy habit of bracketing two very different composers together as 'impressionists', and he thought Ravel's Daphnis and Chloe one of the most perfect scores, "not a wrong note in it." Patric Standford once observed that Poulenc's music came as useful light relief after more substantial fare, to which Simpson replied "Oh, you can't – not that buffoon!" (Letter to the author, 16th June 2011.)

His reputation as a serialist-basher is a little wide of the mark – while it is true that he said, in his 1979 interview with Robert Dearling: "Twelve-notery has had its day. It is barren. Moribund. Tonality is one of the great natural resources and a composer abandons it at his peril because he deprives himself of a powerful means of expression.", later adding of Schoenberg: "I should like to maroon my worst enemy on that over-populated desert island with the music of Schoenberg, but I suspect he might enjoy the experience." He nevertheless owned in an earlier article (Against Lipsius, 1971, Appendix 8):

"Schoenberg is far from being my favourite composer, but it so happened that the idea for a new treatment of tonality came to me from listening, not to Nielsen or any other composer I love, but to Schoenberg's Piano Concerto, many years ago. It struck me that, in spite of the serial technique, the work was fixed to a tonal centre which loomed periodically beyond the murk, and was deliberately avoided at the end – as if Schoenberg had finally made a fearsome effort to exorcise a ghost. I thought then, though I didn't know how, that it might be possible to make a positive use of this phenomenon. I didn't want, as Schoenberg did, to deny tonality, I wanted to find a way to make tonal centres react against each other, not make non-tonality react against tonality." In addition, in a letter to The Listener (23rd November 1967) he wrote a strongly-worded defence of Schoenberg, following what he thought was unjustified criticism. Later in the same essay he says:

"… Webern has certainly had no influence on me at all, except the negative one of indicating to me in wonderfully precise terms exactly what I don't want to do. Bartók and Stravinsky have interested me in certain aspects of sonority, but I have reacted strongly against the inorganic nature especially of Stravinsky. I'm convinced that if there's ever a better age, he won't be its favourite composer."

In the letter to Philip Martin already cited in respect of Mendelssohn, he added:

"I would be careful if I were you of quoting Hans Keller. Did he really write about the Bartók quartets being the next important series? He once said to me that Bartók was the most overrated composer of quartets ever (I actually agreed with him)." He expanded on his reaction to Bartók in the Simon Cargill interview: "I always feel that a slow movement by Bartók… was like a witches cauldron with steam coming off, but where nothing actually happened. It was fascinating and marvellously managed, but that was not what I wanted to do."

Alban Berg he disliked, finding the Violin Concerto "a slimy work". About Hindemith, the other 'big name' among earlier twentieth-century composers he was far more positive. In the Julian Budden interview, he observed:

"Perhaps Hindemith has been treated just a bit unjustly, because people tend to think of Gebrauchmusik as a cold-blooded utility music; but what Hindemith was really trying to do was to get back to the time when artists wrote music for other people, for whatever the purpose happened to be. Hindemith, I think, sometimes writes dry music, but at other times he writes really quite marvellous music. I wouldn't call Mathis der Maler, for instance, Gebrauchmusik in that sense."

Simpson was very much in tune with certain composers of great individuality who have been inaccurately described as 'conservatives', as indeed he was. In a piece written for the Havergal Brian Society newsletter in 1984, he said:

"There are some formidable composers who rarely stand in the limelight but who will always be returned to – Busoni, Reger, Pfitzner, Alkan and some more – Brian I think will belong to this perennial band." I would myself have included Franz Schmidt among this band of brothers, but

Simpson admitted that he had a blind spot for the Austro-Hungarian master: "I can see that it's good, but for whatever reason it doesn't get through to me." He also thought highly of Georges Enesco, and wrote a short (undated) piece for the Radio Times to accompany a broadcast of his First Symphony:

"There can have been few more naturally gifted musicians since Mendelssohn – Enesco was a great violinist, a fine pianist, a perceptive conductor, and a wonderful teacher (as Menuhin will testify), as well as being a considerable composer with a truly vast knowledge of music.

"Those of us who had the honour of his friendship were certain, not only of his genius, but also of his towering greatness as a man whose profound authority was never undermined by his childlike humility. His musical ear was miraculous – I well remember how, when I showed him a new quartet of mine, he settled in an armchair and read through the horrible pencilled manuscript, muttering and humming to himself. The idiom was quite unfamiliar to him, but he was still able to find wrong notes with unerring instinct ('Don't you mean B flat?') and he was always right; he knew what I meant, even though he was seeing the piece for the first time and hearing it mentally only."

Of the later Russians, he admired Prokofiev's musicianship rather more than that of Shostakovich. In response to a copy of David Fanning's book about the composer, he sent the author a closely considered critique, of which I quote part (letter dated 9/6/88): "So far my feeling about him is that there's somehow a great hole in the middle, something desperately important that's missing. His chronic inability to write a real allegro, as opposed to a frenzied battering or a dancing up and down on the same spot, may have something to do with it. The only real momentum I can find in him is usually slow – and then he often seems to fall into a kind of paralysis, from which he breaks out into obsessive and often deafening repetition. He seems unable to achieve the kind of momentum to be found in Bruckner's or Mahler's scherzos (to think of two composers in similar scales) – why not? I may be at fault, though I've listened a long time. Perhaps I ought to be looking another way. In Shostakovich I've always found something psychologically 'frozen' - a case of all passion stifled rather than spent – there's plenty of sound, fury, at times even concentration, but inside – what? I always find deeply impressive the inexorable gloom of the opening and closing paragraphs of the first movement of No. 10, a very Russian kind of gloom, but utterly without the passion of a Mussorgsky, in whom I sense always profound pity for human suffering, awakened by his own. Shostakovich's suffering, which we all know of, seems to have aroused in him either darkly passive or vituperative responses. These are expressed with undeniable genius, but at the end I've always been left with a sense of empty desolation. Never have I felt better for Shostakovich!"

Nor was he a great admirer of the Russian's quartets. In the Simon Cargill interview he observed: "I've never really been happy with Shostakovich's quartets. I have always found them unidiomatic and not really quartets, in the sense that, in many cases, you could orchestrate them and they would sound like his symphonies. The one that is played the most – the Eighth – I confess that I think it is a dreadful piece. It nags away at the same DSCH figure, but it never grows into anything, or <u>becomes</u> anything. I feel exasperated by the time I get to the end of it." He was contemptuous of the then fashionable Russian avant-gardist Alfred Schnittke, removing the 'n' from his name when referring to him, and feeling that the post-Soviet musical scene resembled that of the West in the 1960s, with all manner of rubbish being let out of the woodwork.

A word here on English composers, past and present. As previously noted, he was less than ecstatic about most of Elgar's output, but revered Vaughan Williams. When he wrote, in the Nielsen study that VW "makes no further explorations after his Fourth Symphony: the rest of his work (even the celebrated Sixth) penetrate no new territory. His 'unknown region' (the last movement of No.6) is a dead planet", he nevertheless felt obliged to qualify this with a footnote: "These remarks should not be misunderstood as an 'attack' on Vaughan Williams; he is great enough to reward attempts to understand him."

Holst he considered a profoundly original minor master, saddened by his own realisation that he was incapable of large-scale symphonic construction. Delius he thought spineless, although unmistakable for anybody else. He admired Parry's Symphonic Variations and found the symphonies "pleasant, but not earthshaking", sharing the general feeling that Parry was not a good orchestrator. An early enthusiasm for Bax later waned: "He's one of these people I always wish I could like more than I actually do", though, as with Stravinsky, he admired the perfection of Bax's ear: "He always gets exactly the sound he wants". Walton he thought a very gifted young man who had become soft-centred in later life. His tribute to Edmund Rubbra (Friends) needs no amplification here, and he also greatly admired Michael Tippett, at least his earlier work. In the Lewis Foreman interview he said: "I think Michael Tippett has his roots in the classics in a similar way. One of his first great enthusiasms was Beethoven; a lot grew out of that, and I feel that in his music. I'm not sure that I go along fully with the way some of his later music is composed, in a kind of mosaic fashion it seems to me." Benjamin Britten's music appealed less to him: "He always seems to me to take the easy way out." He felt Billy Budd to be the best of the operas, but also to be "about half an hour too long." In his letter to the Arts Council already quoted in the main narrative (1977) he cites, along with Rubbra, Kenneth Leighton, Arnold Cooke, Franz Reizenstein and Ronald Stevenson as composers with "only quiet independence and integrity in common." In a letter to Raymond Clarke, who had sent him a copy of his recording of Stevenson's monumental Passacaglia on DSCH (27th February 1995) he said:

"When I first heard what he had done, I was a bit sceptical about concentrating on four notes for such a long time. Now I must confess to some feeling that the motto does rather outstay its welcome, especially when it's so often the same notes. But it's an amazing piece, nevertheless, one of those things that intrepid pianists will tackle from time to time, simply because, like 'Mount Everest, "it is there"."

About the two latter-day knights of British music he was less enthusiastic – Harrison Birtwistle he thought "just plain nasty", while for him Peter Maxwell Davies often simply did not hear what he was writing down. He admired Nicholas Maw, saying in a letter to Bob Hill (29th August 1991): "Nick Maw – I have a great respect for him, a solid chap and genuine composer. Odyssey strikes me as a kind of neo-Straussian effort, perhaps a bit too much so, almost self-indulgent at times, done with great skill." He was always willing to do what he could to help less established composers if he thought the music worthwhile. Hugh Wood wrote to him on 13th April 1978:

"Dear Dr. Simpson, I've been meaning to write this letter to you for an extremely long time. I'm very grateful to you for programming the Chilingirian's excellent performance of my Second Quartet – not just once, but a number of times: and now latterly on The Innocent Ear – and this in particular I really do account an honour. I find this all the more generous and magnanimous of you because I cannot help feeling that the piece can hardly be entirely in accordance with your own strongly held musical ideals.

"So thank you very much. It seems silly that we've never met. Would you think of coming out for a short drink sometime when I'm in London and in the Yalding House area?"

In the June 1968 edition of Music and Musicians, Noel Goodwin wrote a scathing attack on the young composer Oliver Knussen. Goodwin's diatribe is a long one, but I will print it in full:

"Symphonic variation

And where, you may ask, does that leave 15-year-old Oliver Knussen and his First Symphony, the première of which he so gallantly conducted when István Kertész fell ill? I hope that the composer is asking himself the same question - or, perhaps, his father, who is the LSO's principal double-bass and a member of its board of directors, and presumably therefore assumes a share of the responsibility for the symphony's performance in the orchestra's so-called 'International Series' at the Festival Hall.

"The next morning The Times captioned William Mann's generally favourable, but also considered, review: 'Daring first symphony by teenager'. To my mind, the only daring aspect of the whole affair was the action of the LSO management in asking the public to pay up to 35s (£1.75) for the opportunity to hear a student work, performed under an inexperienced and juvenile conductor whose main concern was probably to avoid the experience of seeming ridiculous (and if it wasn't his main concern, it should have been). As it happened, he succeeded – but I question whether such a responsibility should ever have been put on him. The symphony itself, as I have written elsewhere, was the kind of prentice work that I hope the composer will be glad to disown when he grows up. In suggesting that, I am not in the least denying his evident, even precocious, talent. He was able to demonstrate that, so far, he knows the capacities of orchestral instruments, has a fondness for bold blocks of colour, a sense of planned contrast, the ability to use a note-row as an anchor and to write a fugue, and the saving grace of a good feeling for rhythm.

"Had the introduction of new music been a significant element in the LSO's artistic policy, there might have been some reason for including a work of this kind as representing the embryonic talents of a coming generation. In fact, Knussen's symphony was the only new work in a season's repertoire that otherwise relied entirely on known (if not always familiar) works of substance, and consequently acquired a freakish status that was unjustified and ill-deserved. Moreover, since the commission was paid for by an independent television company, the LSO did not have to dig far into its sizable share of public funds to bring about its presentation.

The proper and welcome place for such a symphony should have been in a programme by the National Youth Orchestra, or some comparable school or student organisation, of which there are now several doing admirable work in focusing attention on young musical talent. As it is, the composer gained a certain notoriety which is out of all proportion to the actual merits of his achievement. Since the London performance, I see that he has conducted two movements of the Symphony in New York (what happened to the remaining movement has never been mentioned), and is also this year's 'composer-in-residence' at the Florida Festival.

"Not even the US Embassy in London seems at all sure what the duties, privileges or expectations of a 15-year-old 'composer in-residence' at Daytona Beach are likely to be, but we may hope that Oliver Knussen enjoys the swimming (if they still do any in Florida). We may also hope that his musical individuality may be given more chance to develop before it is again exposed in public, and that next time it will be more carefully directed instead of being pitched straight into the deep end of musical life. We may further hope that the LSO, without going to the other extreme of embracing Great-uncle Havergal for its next venture into contemporary music, will not overlook those mature talents who could justify more representation in their programmes."

No doubt mindful of the psychological damage done to, among others, Bruckner, Hugo Wolf and Rachmaninov by such relentless hostility, Simpson counter-attacked in a letter to the Editor:

"Dear Sir,

Mr Noel Goodwin's remarks about Oliver Knussen constitute the sourest and most unpleasant revelation of character that I have encountered in years. But perhaps it is as well that a talented young musician should at an early stage be under no illusions about the way the jackals will bark."

Simpson's letter is dated 20th May, but this has to be an error since neither Goodwin's comments, nor an equally dismissive concert review by Ates Orga appeared until the June issue. Evidently, Knussen never forgot this support, and wrote to Simpson almost a quarter-century later (11th September 1992):

Dear Robert Simpson

– A small blast from the past – I think it was Dartington about 8 or 9 years ago that we last met (tempus fugit). I have thought about you & your music frequently, especially since my father died 2½ years ago; he admired you very much & used frequently to say "Instead of that *** Mr. X, why don't you listen to Bob Simpson's work – that's real modern music!" Anyway, sentimentalities aside, I've been planning a new orch. thing, & having heard the broadcast of your 'cello concerto from Malvern (unfortunately on the radio of a car which itself sounds like a' lawn mower so I probably only got about 50% of what was actually played) & been very struck by what I actually could hear, I decided to do a little homework while moving into this house the last few weeks, & listened to the CD's of Symphonies 3 7 & 9 with score in hand. Also looked at nos. 1 & 2 (I got scores of 2 & 3 via Chester's warehouse, by the way, and tried to get 10, which Lengnick advertise as being on sale but doesn't appear to be – I have the CD).

"This is rather hard to express on paper, but I'm absolutely staggered by the stature of your achievement. I'd been knocked out by the 1st broadcast of Sym. 5 a long time ago, and always been interested, but somehow – whether I've changed or whether seeing it as well helps me – I was this time absolutely aware, I think, of what you are about & just how strong this music is & its importance to a composer from another planet (namely me.) It's very difficult not to gush & talk nonsense when one has been hit in the solar plexus like this (incidentally especially by 1st "movt" & scherzo of no.9 & slow "movt" of 7) but I wanted somehow to let you know that I felt very humbled indeed, & stimulated to do better.

"I've been going through a phase of ridding my own music, as far as I can, of both non-sense (in terms of how it's made) & decoration-as-disguise; while I suspect that you would probably find some of my means nonsensical, I cannot express strongly enough how important for me it was to come across some music on my own door-step, as it were, which is absolutely devoid of baloney & yet still big & generous.

"Enough said – I'll start writing rubbish if I keep going much longer. I know you've been ill & are in a lot of discomfort, & hope this letter might cheer you a bit. Also hope we'll be able to meet again sometime – all best, Olly."

Of all his contemporaries, Simpson most admired the immensely prolific and powerful Dane, Vagn Holmboe. On 24th March 1955, The Listener published an article by Simpson, from which I will quote some extracts.

"In Holmboe's mature style there is a remarkable fusion of apparently disparate elements. The tang of Rumanian folk music is sometimes there, as well as the strong Hungarian influence of Bartók, whom Holmboe greatly admires. Occasionally one scents a whiff of Nielsen in some of his more diatonic and characteristically Danish themes, though their treatment rarely recalls Nielsen's methods, except perhaps in the symphonies, where he gives freedom to a fine talent for spacious, clear-cut architecture."

"This Danish composer seems to have been determined (consciously or otherwise) to have the best of both worlds. Although his musical personality is not as powerful as either Bartók's or Nielsen's, he has undoubtedly succeeded in achieving a homogenous individual synthesis; he seems free to move suddenly from a Nielsen-like continuity of contrapuntal texture to a Bartók-like abrupt percussive astringency without damaging the cogency of his thought. A description such as this, of course, is an oversimplification; Holmboe's music has many other facets, many of them entirely peculiar to himself."

Simpson was reluctant to give direct advice or criticism to any other composer. A Swedish musician, Torbjorn Iwan Lundquist, submitted a work of his for comment. Simpson replied as follows, on 25th April 1979: "Many thanks for your letter, the score and the record. I am most reluctant to try to advise other composers – in a sense we are each more lonely than a boxer in a ring – he at least has an opponent! I would say that we need to find our own way regardless of what anyone else says. No critic, nor even any other musician, has seriously influenced my attempts at composition – I find I have to discover the current of my own spirit, and do it alone.

"To do this it is necessary to be sharply objective and to distinguish between emotional impulses of the moment and ideas which are genuinely relevant to the artistic whole. Different individuals are bound to have different ideas about this and we have to trust only our own judgement. I suspect that in your very skilfully written symphony, with its sometimes original orchestration, you have not always made the distinction between what is simply emotional gesture and what is vital to the development of an organic piece of work. But it is reluctance to make assertions on these lines which leads me always to refuse regretfully to attempt to give anyone lessons in composition. With kindest regards to you and best of luck."

He had no time for popular music of any kind. From the Julian Budden interview: "… crude and simple. The pop enthusiasts are pathetic victims of commercial exploitation."

"It is perhaps significant that most pop pieces are in the same tempo. The beat, so I've heard it said, is about that of the average human heart, which is the sound that the baby first experiences in the womb. It has been suggested that presumably pop music reflects the instinct to want to crawl back into the womb, to go back to the original primitive sound.

JB: So it doesn't offer you anything?

RS: It doesn't appeal to me."

This chapter would be incomplete without reference to the avant-garde (or derriere-garde, as Simpson liked to refer to them) and especially their exemplar, Karlheinz Stockhausen. The German's arrogance annoyed him; he related an occasion when an exasperated BBC employee asked: "Does he think he's God?" to which Jascha Horenstein replied simply "Minimum!" As for the work, his view is clearly expressed in a letter to Nicholas Kenyon (15th January 1985):

"… I think Stockhausen is a romantic! – giving him of course the credit for sincerity, which doesn't pay much respect to his intelligence, or to those of his paralytic victims. If he is simply sustaining a cleverly engineered bandwagon, his adherents don't come out of it very well. You have to admire Stimmung as an outstanding example of what you can get away with – you keep it going for an enormous length of time, with nothing but a few textural variations in a (VERY!) tonal monotony; you then make a mysterious fade-out, seemingly mysterious enough to convince all the charlies that it must after all have been marvellous. This works like a dream, which of course it is. If you get into the state Stockhausen recommends, the dream is all too pleasant – no nightmare, this stasis! But you could easily get yourself into the same condition by means of any unassertively soothing form of monotony, or with drugs, and it has nothing to do with things growing. The opposite.

"Either Stockhausen is a romantic – or his gullible audience. I find it deeply depressing that the BBC is now purveying such mishmash as if we were all in the presence of another Wagner. At least Wagner's five-minute chord of E flat proved to be merely the prelude to a great work. Stockhausen's ninety-minute dominant ninth (with a few inoffensive embellishments here and there) isn't meant to be preludial, and in that it must be adjudged successful, for any expectations it at first arouses are left far behind in a boundless sea of nothing."

Not that Stockhausen represented the very looniest of fringes. From the Julian Budden interview:

"Someone like John Cage will say to the audience: "Right, here are some traffic noises. You are expected to react to them." Sometimes he will sit at the piano and not play at all. He puts a stop-watch on the piano (he's got a piece called 4'33") and he sits at the piano with his arms folded. On one occasion when this happened, in New York, half-way through this period someone called out, "Too slow!" That is the sort of reaction which John Cage would say that he wanted to evoke. He positively wants the audience to react in some way, no matter what it is, to what he is doing or not doing. This is a deliberately anti-artistic attitude which is being pursued not only in music but in all the other arts as well – the pile of bricks in the Tate Gallery in London, and so on.

"I remember another story I can tell you, about an avant-garde concert in New York in which the composers appeared on the platform after each piece to answer questions from the audience. One composer appeared, and a man in the audience said to him, "Tell me, if you heard that piece without being told what it was, would you recognise it as your own?" The composer was absolutely furious: "How dare you suggest that? How dare you suggest that I would recognize it? Of course I would not recognise it! How dare you suggest that?!" And he carried on quite alarmingly for some time. Then the man in the audience said to him, "In that case, why is it you standing there answering questions and not somebody else?"

Simpson had a few ideas of his own for "happenings". From Appendix 8: "Not long ago a man came and showed me a score (or rather a diagram) and I jokingly said I didn't understand why no-one had thought of the idea of inviting the audience to go up and poke the musicians with umbrellas, to see what effect this would have on the sound produced. To my horror he said with incorruptible sincerity and seriousness, "Well, ye-es… maybe…

interesting idea… perhaps… why not?" And, believe me, there are not a few critics who would write solemnly about it."

And from Appendix 9:

"I once offered the organiser of a series of fashionable concerts a work in which the performers ate each other; his refusal no doubt sprang from a suspicion that he might not, yet, be able to get away with it. When he feels the climate of opinion has advanced enough, the offer is still open, though I shall stipulate that he is one of the performers and the other a certain well-known critic. To prolong the performance as long as possible they must start with each other's feet."

As Simpson wryly observed: "…this is the first period in history when in order to be a composer it is not necessary to be a musician. This is true of any of the Arts… You don't have to master your materials. You don't have to understand much about them. All you do is something at random and you hope – you don't even hope, actually – you just see what happens."

Let us hope that this is merely a passing phase, which we will eventually grow out of, although I am not too hopeful, considering that the avant-garde can be assumed to have begun with Marcel Duchamp's signed urinal and obscenely inscribed Mona Lisa copy almost a century ago, and that the most recent Turner Prize shortlist was the first to include anyone producing actual paintings. Ho hum.

POSTLUDE

During his years with the BBC, Robert Simpson worked with most of the major conductors of the time (that 'dangerous breed', as he described them in his tribute to Sir Adrian Boult), the exception being Herbert von Karajan, whom he thought "the last great conductor." He did once watch Karajan rehearsing and found his methods different to anyone else's. "He would say 'chord of E major', then sing it, and expected the orchestra to play the chord as he had sung it." His admiration for the Austrian's musicianship did not preclude reservations about his character: "He was a good Bruckner conductor… unfortunately." Horenstein and Boult have already been covered in the 'Friends' chapter, but I cannot resist including an anecdote about the former from the interview with Julian Budden: "He told me once that he was conducting or rehearsing a concert consisting entirely of new works, and one of the composers came to him and said 'Excuse me, Sir Adrian, but I wonder if you would mind taking this a little slower.' Adrian turned round to him and said to him, 'I'm sorry, but this isn't your piece."

Sir Thomas Beecham was another matter; I quote from 'The Proms and Natural Justice: "We learnt the hard way; not knowing that Sir Thomas disliked being addressed through the studio loudspeaker, I ventured to observe through this medium that the second bassoon was not audible in one passage. In a voice that mere print cannot possibly suggest, he remarked to the orchestra: 'The British Broadcasting Corporation says it can't hear the second bassoon!'" Another story concerns Beecham's reaction to the young producer's enthusiastic proposal of the Symphonie Funèbre et Triomphale by Berlioz; I quote it as Simpson told it to me, which differs slightly from his account in the above volume. "No, no, my boy, it would be the most god-awful noise you ever heard – you'd never get all those clarionets to play in tune!" Simpson was mystified as to how Beecham got his results - "His beat was all over the place" – and could only assume that the great man was able to shake semiquavers out of his shirt cuffs. Beecham's own explanation was simpler: "You just get the best players and let them get on with it!"

For Sir Malcolm Sargent he had less time; he describes in his Sibelius and Nielsen booklet how Sargent refused to allow the side-drummer to improvise in the climactic passage of Nielsen's Fifth Symphony, and wrote him out a part – "He couldn't bear anything not to be under his complete control."

Another story, which isn't true but which ought to be, gives a good idea of a musician's view of two eminent conductors. Beecham and Sargent were sharing a railway carriage (inconceivable in itself to anyone who knew them). Just as the train is pulling out of Euston station, the door is flung open and in stumbles a builder's labourer. Dusting himself down, the man takes out a clay pipe, and then says "'Ere – is this first class?" "That's right" replies Beecham. "I'd better get out, then," says the churl, "I've only got a third-class ticket". "Not at all, my dear fellow," replies Beecham. "Please join us!" and within minutes the two are chatting away like old friends. After a while, Beecham heads for the buffet car to get some drinks. Sargent, who until this point has not said a word, turns to the labourer and says: "Do you know who that is?" "No. 'Oo?" replies the man. "That's Sir Thomas Beecham." "Blimey!" replies the other. "Him what conducts them symphonies on the wireless?" "Quite so." "Cor! Sir Thomas Beecham! But tell me, what's a toff like him doing talking to a couple of ignorant bastards like us?"

The other knighted conductor of the day, Sir John Barbirolli, did of course conduct the first performance of Simpson's Second Symphony. On 22nd June 1963 he wrote to the composer:

"My Dear Bob

Thank you for your letter of the 19th, with the news of the ideas for a new Symphony. I am very touched that you should want to compose somewith (sic) with me especially in mind. I am happy to accept the dedication, especially as you so generously suggest I could accept this if the symphony turns out so that I do like it, nothing would give me greater pleasure than to perform it. On the other hand, you know that I am musically sincere enough not to pretend to do this if it is not genuine.

Would it be an idea for us to meet occasionally while you are at work on it and discuss it as it goes along? If you are averse to this idea, please say so.

I am glad you like the recording of Nielsen 4. It has been held by Danish critics as the finest recording of any Nielsen work to date.

The Orchestra has just returned from the Scandinavian tour which was a real triumph from beginning to end. In Helsinki there were 15 minute ovations for performances of Sibelius 2 and 5, and of these Jussi Jalas, Sibelius' son-in-law and chief conductor of the Opera said publicly "we feel humbled that it should have taken Sir John and the Hallé to make us realise the true greatness of Sibelius". I know this will give you pleasure. With warmest regards to you and your wife.

Ever yours

John B."

This is something of a mystery; the symphony in question cannot have been the Third, which was completed the previous year, and is dedicated to Havergal Brian. The Fourth was not even begun until 1970, a year after Barbirolli's death.

He shared my puzzlement about the mystique surrounding Wilhelm Fürtwängler, whose main characteristic was to pull the tempo around in a way that conveyed more about the conductor than it did about the music, but relented when it came to Tristan und Isolde, which he felt was one work that did suit Fürtwängler's flexibility.

His admiration for, and gratitude towards, the late Vernon Handley did not preclude occasional exasperation at the conductor's habit of cancelling an appearance if he felt below par – "He'll ruin his career if he goes on like this" – and making comparison with Sir Charles Groves, who conducted a lengthy and demanding concert at the Albert Hall while suffering considerable pain from a thrombosis in his leg.

He came to feel that Colin Davis was the best British conductor, and wrote to him following his first Bruckner concert; Simpson's letter has not survived, but I quote Sir Colin's reply (the letter is dated 19th January, but no indication as to year):

"Dear Bob,

I was vastly encouraged by your note. After all one's first Bruckner symphony is a solemn occasion that may so well be one's last! But with your blessing I shall tackle another; but not in the R.F.H. I think. Bruckner may be a far cry from Berlioz but they are both supreme melodists – the opening of the VIIth is like the dome of the sky – & I'm so glad you agree about "a tempo". Poor B. seemed only too ready to agree with every conductor who wanted to interfere. I'll think about the scherzo. Colin"

Robert Simpson considered Otto Klemperer to be "a major artist", and especially admired his earlier Beethoven recordings for Columbia, and his often wonderful later Haydn and Mozart interpretations, although he did feel that there were other occasions on which the great conductor had fallen asleep. Two anecdotes are worth re-telling. On one occasion, Simpson was the producer while Klemperer rehearsed the Philharmonia at the Maida Vale Studios. Come break time, the orchestra headed off to the canteen, leaving the maestro in splendid isolation "with a face like a hanging judge". Bob wondered if he should offer the conductor a drink, but before he could do so he was pre-empted by Ernie, the studio's general factotum, who trotted up to the rostrum, put his arm round the great man's shoulder, and handed him a cup of coffee with the words: "There you are, old chap, you drink that up – it'll make you feel a lot better." Klemperer's reply, if any, is not recorded.

On another occasion, Klemperer noticed an absentee from the orchestra. "Where is the second trumpet? We cannot start without him." "He's gone to the dentist," came the reply. "Very well, we will wait for him. No smoking!" Eventually, the man appeared. Klemperer was most solicitous, was reassured that he felt well, and waited for the player to take his seat. "Good! Now we can begin. Eine Kleine Nachtmusik!"

To round off this section, another story which Bob did not relate to me, although he may well have known it.

Klemperer expected the highest standards from an orchestra, and was notoriously stinting of praise. Once, however, the Philharmonia played with such outstanding fire and precision that he was moved to say "Good!" The orchestra broke into an ironic cheer: "Not that good!" grumbled the great conductor.

FRIENDS

I have necessarily had to be highly selective here; a full survey, of Robert Simpson's many friendships, musical and otherwise, would require a volume to itself. Among his most regular correspondents were John Pickard (fellow composer), Professor Sir David Gillett (biologist and first chairman of the Robert Simpson Society), (Professor Sir) Ian Craft (gynaecologist and commissioner of the Sixth Symphony) Ronald Smith, Pianist and Alkan specialist), Andor Gomme – Professor of English Literature and author of a book on Charles Dickens, Dr Lionel Pike (composer, conductor and musicologist), Bob Hill (psychologist and RSS stalwart), John Marshall (flautist), Ray Few (orchestral manager and dedicatee of the Nielsen Variations) Mina Miller (USA), Peter Emmett, composers Philip Martin and James Stephens (who also had unhappy memories of the Glock era).

Fellow composer Derek Bourgeouis, who much admired the Seventh Quartet, persuaded Simpson to rejoin the Composers Guild of Great Britain in 1979 He was also a member of the Society of Professional Composers. Other correspondents included conductor Myer Fredman (from Australia), Peter Garvie (USA), and fellow composers Halvor Haug (Norway), Patrick Piggott, William Mathias, 'and Paul Pellay. Pianist Moura Lympany was an admirer, and wrote to Simpson in the late 1980s, as did fellow players Nina Milkina and Artur Balsam (from the USA). Old friends from the BBC; Leonard Isaacs (former music department head) wrote from his retirement home in Canada, where he died in 1997, and former Radio Three announcer Cormack Rigby, who after leaving the BBC took orders as a Roman Catholic priest. Other correspondents included Australian composer Brenton Broadstock, Edward Lowbury (violinist Pauline's father, and a poet), Wilfred Chadwick, Douglas Gordon, composers Philip Goddard, Torbjorn Iwan Lundquist, David Johnson, and Nicholas Simpson, wanting to know how to get his music performed; Simpson referred him to William Robson, whom he thought would be the most sympathetic music Producer at the BBC. Alison Huntley and Frederick Vansen (both poets), Brian May, Ian Milnes, Alan Belkin (Canadian composer), Simon Phillippo, composer and conductor, (who in 1994 invited Simpson to be Patron of the Thames Sinfonia), poet William Bebbington, Robert Baker (another Canadian composer), cellist Zara Nelsova, John Vetterlein (another poet, resident in the Orkneys). Poets seem to be particularly drawn to Simpson's work; Brian Cunningham sent him a poem about Nielsen's Sixth Symphony in 1997, presumably sparked by Simpson's musical analysis. As well as Ronald Smith, composers Thomas Wilson and Bernard Stevens wrote with great enthusiasm after hearing the 7th Quartet; Stevens called it "bloody marvellous – wonderful". Another composer, Arthur Butterworth, wrote after hearing the Second Symphony in 1979, recalling that he had played in the 1957 première.

Many of these names will mean little to the reader by themselves; I mention them in order to illustrate the wide range of response to Simpson's music, not only across national (indeed, continental boundaries) but among men of science as well as men of letters and fellow musicians. Now to consider some friends in further detail. As far as possible, I have used either Simpson's words (he wrote appreciations of a number of people close to him) or theirs if he pre-deceased them, and they contributed to the memorial issue of 'Tonic'.

SIR ADIAN BOULT C.H. (1889-1983)

"Friendship with Adrian Boult came later (than that with Herbert Howells, q.v.), at the BBC. I worked with him many times. He was always ready to conduct anything you put in front of him, and you got no clue as to what he thought of it, though he always did everything he could for it, and the result was nearly always a proper performance. In music he loved he could be, in his gentlemanly way, inspiring. Long before I met him I went to a concert in which he did Debussy's La Mer not long after Toscanini had given an absolutely electrifying performance of it in the same (Queens) hall. Adrian was never a competitive man, but something must have got into him that night: the top of his bald head went a fierce red, his whiskers bristled, his eyes flashed, and his nose seemed about to impale the nearest members of the orchestra. The performance was hair-raising, and Toscanini must have heard the climax of it in New York. Years later I reminded Boult of this and he said, 'Yes, it did go rather well'. When he conducted my own music I found him always anxious to find out exactly what was wanted, to the smallest detail, and the dedication of my First Symphony to him followed the first performance in Britain. (It had been first done in Denmark, but not nearly so well). He then recorded it, and the performance is still satisfying after a quarter of a century.

He had a goodness, a kindness, rare among the dangerous breed of conductors; he had so gentle and unassuming a nature that it was hard to believe that he could ever have had the urge to be a conductor. Yet he could bark if he liked – though it never lasted long, and there was no malice in him. Orchestras and composers alike loved and respected him. In his last years, when he had stopped work, I would sometimes go and see him for an hour or two, and he still loved to talk about music, its interpretation and its structure. He read carefully and critically every word I wrote in 'The

Proms and Natural Justice', and added a preface, saying 'That lot ought to be taught a lesson'. They weren't, of course. Adrian never really got over the cold routine of his compulsory retirement by the BBC at the age of sixty, and always insisted on referring to it as 'the sack'. The BBC lost, and could not replace, the ideal radio conductor; this was mercilessly made plain to them, not only by his successors, but by the magnificent Indian summer of his association with the LPO. There have been more spectacular and more compulsive conductors, but before Boult only Henry Wood was able to do equal service to the music of his contemporaries. You might say, what about…, and name some avant-garde specialist – but all the new music Boult brought out was placed against the background of the masterpieces of history; this gave it a truer perspective than one could perceive in any esoteric ghetto. This great and modest man has gone – but has he? Everything he was lives on in those who were lucky enough to know him."

Robert Simpson

In a separate tribute, written for the Havergal Brian Society, Simpson adds:

"If I asked him what he would like to do, he would say, "That's your job. You put it down and I'll conduct it".

….(even after his 'sacking' by the BBC) it was still one of his greatest pleasures to come back to his old orchestra as a guest. His character was such that he was able to retain the loyalty of that great leader, Paul Beard, even when Toscanini tried to take him to America. No-one ever lived who was kinder or more honest, more generous, less pretentious, freer of the egotism that plagues the breed of conductors. He was a noble and gentle spirit. It is not true to say, as someone did, 'We are all diminished by his loss'. We are all enriched by his having been in the world. The tiniest things we do live on in our fellows who witness them; they may be good things, they may be bad, they may seem trivial. But they do not vanish – they become absorbed into following humanity and achieve in this way spiritual immortality. Adrian Boult's life was a demonstration of how important it is that what we do should be necessary to the improvement and survival of the race as a civilized species."

To end, here is a touching letter from Gwen Beckett (Boult's private secretary – always known as Mrs Beckett) dated 28th September 1978.

"Dear Doctor Simpson

Thank you for your kind letter to Sir Adrian. I only returned from leave yesterday, but he shall have it to-morrow. I know he will be very pleased to see you, and I will write again soon to suggest a date. He likes to see his friends at 11a.m. or 5p.m., and it would be at his London flat in Hampstead.

Are these times convenient for you? It is such a tonic to him to have a talk. He is perfectly well musically and mentally, but his spine will no longer hold up that long back, and so it has become too pathetic to get him on and off platforms and rostrums in front of an audience, but he is recording, and enjoying that, and also seeing a number of younger Conductors to help them with their scores.

Thank you for all your kindness to me. I miss you all very much, but live quietly here in this tiny cottage, working for Sir Adrian every morning." In his second 'appearance' on Desert Island Discs, Boult included a work by Simpson – with typical selflessness. Horenstein's recording of the Third Symphony rather than his own of the first – quite a contrast to the soprano Elisabeth Schwartzkopf, whose every selection was one of her own recordings!

HAVERGAL BRIAN (1876-1972)

Brian could hardly be omitted from a list of friends, but his long musical association with Simpson is documented in the main text, and his musical assessment in the previous chapter. Here, therefore, are some extracts from a Radio Three talk broadcast on 23rd September 1976.

"Havergal Brian would have been 100 this year, and he only just missed his own centenary celebrations. He died four years ago, when he was 96, and I for one was quite convinced that we'd get him on the platform at a public centenary concert. Anyway, he was still lively enough at 95 to tackle Gibbon's Decline and Fall of the Roman Empire. But he had a slight accident, and although he didn't break any bones, it shook him up very badly and a sudden general collapse of his system set in, resulting in what I still regard as his premature death.

If Brian were only a contender for the Guinness Book of Records I wouldn't be suggesting that you bother with his music. But it so happens that he's a composer of remarkable originality, often of compelling force. One of his biographers, Kenneth Eastaugh, has just written a play about Brian's life, called "Awkward Cuss" – and this unamiable term (which I must confess I suggested) does sum him up, not only in his awkward, difficult, bloody-minded life, but in much of his music too – unpredictable and dogged, without transitions, direct, yet disconcerting in the directness 'of its apparent perversity.

You couldn't tell what he was thinking or feeling."

Elsewhere, in his notes for the pioneering Unicorn disc of Brian's 10th and 21st Symphonies, Simpson observes:

"...he was a man of immovable obstinacy ... As a man you could take him or leave him – it was all the same to him..."

Brian and Simpson corresponded extensively, but only the former's letters survive, and they are decidedly laconic. Here, then, is a sketch of the Brians' relationship as seen by their frequent visitor, a tribute which Robert Simpson wrote for the HBS Newsletter after Hilda Brian's death in 1980.

"To be the wife of Havergal Brian required fortitude of an order normally associated with medals; even in his later and mellower years he was not an easy man to live with – before that most of his companions and even his best friends found him at times impossible. Through a great many of those difficult years, Hilda remained a steadfast and deeply loved mother to his family. To them, even at her advanced age, she must have been a severe loss. Anyone who has been a family friend for 25 years or so cannot have failed to discover a deep affection for this remarkable and humane woman, so free of respect for personages, so gifted with sardonic humour, so full of instant sympathy when it was deserved, so quick to see justice or injustice, yet never dogmatic or self-righteous. She was a person of natural simplicity, not unreasonably chary of intellectuals but often quick to see the point of an argument; she never pretended to understand what passed over her head, and looked at things in the most direct human way. Her sense of humour and her uncomplicated ability to see through pretensions often saved her the necessity of using sophisticated means of expressing her opinion. She never affected to understand her husband's purpose in life, or his work as such; circumstances often rendered her scepticism not at all surprising; she was not reared in artistic circles and at the beginning cannot have had more than the usual romantic ideas about what life with an artist must be like. "I must have been mad", she said. Mad or not, she set about giving her children the securest possible emotional base in the face of their father's unpredictabilities, coping with daunting financial as well as psychological difficulties. That is why the family never ceased to adore her, and why she was always regarded as a haven of sanity in a sometimes crazily incomprehensible world. If anyone was mad, it was never Hilda!

It was sometimes wryly amusing to hear the two old companions and adversaries being short with each other – a long-established habit, no doubt – yet Havergal was never at rest when Hilda was away or even out of the house. When I first visited them in the 1950s she was in Zambia visiting her daughter Freda, and he greeted me at the front door with a brightly coloured pinafore across his middle, full of apologies that I would have to put up with a meal cooked by him. It turned out a very good meal, but he kept returning to the absence of his wife – I wondered what she must be like, and innocently imagined that this must be one of those long, mythically perfect relationships one reads about in Victorian biographies. Yet even after the facts were all clear to me I could still be struck by the way he would sometimes stand at the gate waiting for her to come back from shopping, impatiently and as if half afraid some life-line was under threat. He was a self-centred man, and we could suppose that his own security lay behind his concern; but who can say what goes on in a man's mind – in so strange a mind? We must account for those unexpected touches of human tenderness in his music, often occurring at the very moment when we have begun to get used to the bull in the china shop. He was used to Hilda, and she was inured to him. Of the two, he seemed the harder, but only because he was the less considerate, the less imaginative when it came to other people's feelings; yet if Hilda had died first he would have been the less able to survive calmly, the less able to remain a stable part of his own family. Hilda's natural independence and her quick awareness of others' needs made her reluctant to become dependent on the children, but she was quietly part of the family in a way the old man would have found impossible. Towards the end she seems to have suffered some depression, but this can only have been due to ill-health; to the last she was surrounded by love, which was no more than she richly deserved. She was one in a million; there would be no threat to human existence if her honesty, courage and gentleness were its normal condition."

DERYCK COOKE 1919 – 1976

Cooke was a long-term friend and colleague of Simpson's at the BBC, and contributed an article on Bruckner to the first volume of 'The Symphony'. He was also, like Simpson, a keen cricket fan. This appreciation was printed in 'The Listener' on the occasion of his death.

"It is a safe assumption that Deryck Cooke will be remembered as the man who completed Mahler's Tenth Symphony. He would not have had it so. Modesty certainly played a part in his refusal to allow any description of his achievement to go further than "a performing version of the draft for the Tenth Symphony" – but he was also, as in all matters, greatly concerned about being honest. He was acutely conscious of the fact that Mahler, even if he had lived to complete the score, might very well have revised the whole in ways that no one could have predicted. In this sense it was unthinkable to him that anyone could claim to complete the work. He also repudiated hotly my sincere assertion to him that nobody could have done it better, or come nearer to the possibility of a completion. I still think this is true, and that the imaginative insight that lay behind all the painstaking faithfulness with which he sought the composer's intentions was something of an order beyond the reach of the mere musicologist or critic – his sympathy with Mahler was so profound and his musicianship so masterly that I (and I don't think I'm alone in this) get the impression that the composer would have been amazed that another mind could have come so close to his own. At any rate, there is now some satisfaction in having said this to him while he was still with us, even though it only made him laugh. I think in at least one respect he was a better man than the composer he loved so much; his sense of humour was something Mahler would totally have failed to grasp.

In the early days of the Third Programme it was something of an event to hear a Bruckner or Mahler symphony; the younger listeners of today hear them so often as to take them for granted. In 1947 when Deryck Cooke joined the BBC Music Department he was (even there!) a voice in the wilderness, and his enthusiasm for both composers was treated by his colleagues as an amiable eccentricity. In 1950 I found myself there and was at once helped through the maze by a large, 'genial, generous fellow who quickly proved to be a musician of considerable brilliance. This brilliance was never consciously displayed. Its root was enthusiasm, and if a piano was handy his thoughts about music would seem to flow spontaneously through his fingers. What he knew he had got to know through wanting to, not through learning by routine or rule of thumb)Mention some detail in some work (and it could be anything from Pérotin to Tippett) and it would set him off. I have known few people enjoy a conversation about music with so much alacrity and so little egotism. It was the same with cricket.

In more than twenty-five years I learned much from him, human and musical. His death was a painful and enexpected blow, and there are many things we shall have to do without, notably some volumes that might have constituted one of the most significant of all books on Wagner. But all that is really lost is what might have been. What was cannot utterly vanish. Whatever we do as individuals, good or bad, clever or stupid, must remain if we do it among our fellows; we cannot eradicate it; its effect is unknowingly felt by all the unremembering generations that follow, and the quality of the human race ultimately depends on the quality of its individuals. For this purpose Deryck Cooke was and will remain a necessary man.

TONY DORRELL (1923 - 1987)

Tony Dorrell was a painter and graphic artist of great versatility and sensitivity. Although he never received any public recognition, some of his fen landscapes (the 'Black Earth' series) are on view in the dining hall at Fitzwilliam College, Cambridge, and his portrait of Simpson, painted during the 1970s, hangs in the Philharmonic Hall, Liverpool. The two met during the late 1940s in the course of the Exploratory Concert Society recitals. Tony attended one concert, then another, after which he stayed behind and the pair chatted at length. Simpson described Dorrell as "my best friend for over thirty years" (letter to the author). In 1958 or 1959 Tony left England for Prague to do radio work for the British Council; there he met Daphne) who was divorced and working as an international conference organiser. In 1960 they left Czechoslovakia for China, having been offered teaching work by the Chinese Embassy. They married, and returned to England in 1963. Here is Daphne's own account from her contribution to the memorial edition of 'Tonic'. (Sadly, Daphne Dorrell died in 2010)

"I met Bob in the late 1960s when Tony and I and our two children were living in Berkshire, but I already knew a great deal about him from Tony, from recordings of his music, and from his book on Nielsen. They had in common music and an intense interest in people, and consequently in what was happening in the world. Though my work took me away from home for long periods during the sixties and seventies, I have many memories of his vivid presence: Bob seated quietly in a chair while Tony painted his portrait, Bob walking at an incredible pace along the then peaceful Berkshire lanes where you could still spot deer grazing and occasionally, in a copse not far from the house, hear a nightingale. Sometimes, as dusk fell, he would stop in his tracks and point out the various constellations in the evening sky. Then there were evenings when music was played at a volume only 'Bob or Tony could easily tolerate, followed, by long discussions over the odd bottle of whisky – usually into the small hours – during which the talk ranged from music to nuclear energy and vivisection, and the two would swap reminiscences and frequently hilarious stories. Bob often told me, then and later, that Tony was the most intelligent non-musician he had ever met. In the 1970s, no doubt on Bob's recommendation, the music department of the BBC commissioned a series of talks from Tony that were repeated later.

Our daughters loved Bob's visits and he enjoyed their company. At our elder daughter's 21st birthday party he firmly ensconced himself behind the makeshift bar, saying he had always wanted to know what it felt like to be a barman… But it was our animals that fascinated him, and once, when during an evening meal I was scolding our Labrador mongrel for anxiously watching each morsel as it disappeared from our plates, he remarked: "If concentration could do it, Sooty could have written all Beethoven's symphonies".

Small, wiry, energetic and uncompromising in every way, with a wonderful sense of humour and an infectious laugh, he was exciting and stimulating company and I shall always be grateful for his extraordinary ability to explain, or should I say open my mind to music that I found difficult or inaccessible, including some of his own.

When later we moved to London and then to Cambridge, and Tony's health continued to deteriorate, we did not see so much of Bob. But we still met at concerts, at Bob's remarkable Fiftieth Birthday party to which so many of his fellow musicians and friends came to show their admiration and regard, and at first performances of his work, notably the Eighth Symphony dedicated to Tony and me, and the wonderful one-movement Ninth dedicated to his wife Angela.

We only really got to know Angela after our move to Cambridge in the eighties, and to know her was to love her. She and Bob complemented each other so well that after their marriage Bob seemed to take on a new lease of life. Nearly every time we met it seemed he had either completed or was in process of writing a new work. When they told us they were planning to move to Ireland, we were both devastated. The physical distance this would put between us was daunting, particularly for Tony who was beginning to lose the battle against emphysema." I will conclude this section with extracts from some of Tony's letters to the composer.

13/11/1970

"Which brings me to one small addition or emendation that I must make to some remarks of mine after the last recording session. In the pub we were discussing this difficult question of the unevenness in quality of Shost. in the light of certain other music – and when you mentioned the Eroica symphony I said something to the effect that it is a 'ragged' work – whereupon you gave me a sample of that peculiarly unsettling glance that I have had from you perhaps twice before! Well, I know what I meant – but in case I failed to make it clear, I certainly did not mean that I considered the symphony itself to be ragged in composition! Had I thought this, I would have said so, and tried to argue it out with you. What I meant was that, that particular work gives me a sense of things in a state of developing – of emerging out of youthful incoherence. I do not mean on the part of the composer, but on the part of human beings generally. Which is the same as saying that the Eroica is a fairly youthful outpouring by a composer of such mastery that he can convey the idea of immaturity while himself evincing none of its shortcomings. Does this make sense? I think it does – simply by calling to mind some of the later symphonies.

Being such a Protean genius, Beethoven provides for everything that happens in human development - not in an ascending or descending scale, but interwoven at the very core of the music. Thus, I recall two personal incidents connected with him, many years back. I was one day working on a mural painting (which in itself was a very immature, almost clumsy piece of work), with the Eroica playing on the radio or gramophone. My work happened to be going well – and all of a sudden Sheila said that it was like the music – like that particular Beethoven. And I knew she definitely did not mean that the music shared the weaknesses of my work – but that my work had taken on something of the vigour of the music. Then, on another occasion, she came into the room when I was sitting listening to the 9th symph. and she said she felt sad on my behalf because of the music. For the 9th symph. is sad – despite its immense and comprehensive hope!"

29th June 1971

"As you are well aware, I agree with your views in the main – while reserving the right to call myself a pessimist without the risk of your ferocious opposition! As you yourself indicate, the question whether you are an optimist or an anti-pessimist is an academic one – for the very use of the word implies a choice of attitude that has little to do with creative art: the man may choose a viewpoint and then contradict it in his work. So I may not, after all, be a pessimist – merely rather a misery!

…If the inertia – the old Caliban – in man is to be put down to a genetic flaw, it doesn't seem to me to quite explain the coexistence of Beethoven with the rest of us. Nor does the concept seem in key with your words about 'things going seriously wrong'. The slave mentality is there alright – but it has been constantly belied by the actual work that people have done, from the dawn of history. The work they have done has been from necessity – and its content of necessity is epitomised and spiritualised in works of art. This is why it is possible to speak of art as holding up a mirror to mankind – and the 'optimism' of this act is in the fact that man can do it. The poet reaches the summit of the mountain and finds himself face to face with – himself. In his last self-portrait, Rembrandt leers at himself from the canvas, with the toothless grin of an old, tired man. <u>But he is not afraid to look</u>. At such a point of self-insight, the human being is at last free of his inherent inertia… It is not simply that a 'power-hungry minority' has always dominated the inert mass; it is that the relations into which men are obliged to enter, in order to survive, confer power on one over another – and that in the modern state this power exists at every level. To be sure, there have always been power-hungry individuals or groups; but they would be powerless were it not for the existence of those institutions that are necessary for the ordering of human affairs. The very thing that makes us human is what destroys us. And the most destructive of our institutions – as you suggest – is ideology. Ideas are the creative output of humanity – but the moment they become institutions (which they do with tedious inevitability), they lose their life as ideas and become the means of oppression. This is the condition of our relationships as beings with a consciousness; in a sense it is the price we have paid for being human. Or rather, for having set out on the road in that direction."

9th January 1978

"I don't agree about the need-to 'cut ourselves off from the jungle', as you put it. It is in the fact of having done so that the human race has come into existence. This has meant both gain and loss: the gain of a rational consciousness and individuality, the loss of immortality. The gain of love, at the price of death. I didn't say this, but this was the consideration behind my thesis of 'solidarity': I made no value judgements about "nature". The 'wastefulness' of nature is in its superabundance, in the relentless movement of its processes of evolution. Human waste, on the other hand, is a squalid and contemptible affair. There is no evidence, as fat as I know, that the human species at this present stage are any gentler or more decent than their earliest ancestors. The whole point about 'solidarity' is the need for a larger and more inclusive feeling for our fellow creatures, if we are to become more 'human'."

Portrait of Robert Simpson by Anthony Dorrell (1923-1987), which hangs in the Philharmonic Hall, Liverpool

RICHARD LOVETT ('DICK') EDWARDS (1922 - 2003)

Dick Edwards was another early and lifelong friend, born in Worthing, West Sussex. Following army service in World War 2, he worked as an insurance broker until retirement, with a sideline dealing in gramophone records, especially 78s. He was a founding member of the Robert Simpson Society, of which he was for many years a conscientious and meticulous chairman. His death was unexpected; although eighty-one he seemed much younger, with a vigour that belied his years. An early letter from the composer (20th August 1947) still has a certain formality to it:

"Dear Mr. Edwards,

It was very kind of you to take so much trouble in sending me your most interesting list of records. I have no doubt that occasions will arise when we shall be only too grateful to make use of them. As you probably know, we hope to have periodic lectures as well as concerts, although 'live' performances will naturally predominate, since we are really a Concert Society. Most of these lectures will, at present, be probably given by me, since our funds don't permit us to pay professional musicians fees. You will readily understand that a lecture of the type that we require needs far more lengthy preparation than most actual musical performances and that it is therefore easier to ask a professional to play without fee than to ask him to prepare an analytical lecture. Consequentially, I shall be keeping most of the lectures going until we can afford to relieve the monotony. I hope it won't be long.

Meanwhile, I'll keep your list handy. Please accept my thanks for your thoughtfulness. I'm only sorry I can't come to your concert of Telefunken records. I shall be very glad of an opportunity of hearing the Telefunken Bruckner 4th and 7th. Could you perhaps ring me (HIT 1504) and arrange when you might come here with them(I have a PAM reproducer)? Perhaps one week-end you could come in the early afternoon, so that we could hear one symphony then and the other in the evening? I have also Horenstein's Bruckner 7th (Polydor), the String Quintet, the G minor Overture, and the Scherzi from Symphonies 1,11,111, and the posthumous D minor symphony.

yours sincerely

Robert Simpson

P.S. I hear that Bruckner's 6th has been recorded in America. Do you know anything of this?

Dick's own account of the friendship follows, from his contribution to the memorial 'Tonic':

"My first encounter with Bob was in 1947. I saw an announcement by the Exploratory Concert Society of a lecture on Bruckner's Seventh Symphony to be followed by a gramophone performance of the complete work. I was immediately struck by the personality of the lecturer, one Robert Simpson. He knew so much about the music, and was able to communicate his enthusiasm so well. I therefore hung behind, and after most of the audience had dispersed I ventured to introduce myself. I told him that I had been recently discharged from the Army and had brought back a quantity of records, many of these being of Bruckner's music. He was very interested, and from that time on, until I had to leave London, we spent many happy hours of listening together. Much happened to prevent our meeting very often over the following years, but I did visit him from time to time when he was living in Muswell Hill.

It was there that I heard my very first LP, of Toscanini conducting Brahms. On one such occasion when I knocked on his door, he let me in and introduced me to General Eisenhower. For a few seconds I was completely taken in, only to be told that his visitor was a distinguished Danish novelist who bore an uncanny resemblance.

When he moved to Chearsley, and I to Colchester, I still continued to visit him. Colchester and Chearsley are exactly 100 miles apart, and whenever I had more than just a weekend I used to ride there on my bicycle. Eight hours to get there and ten back, the wind being against me for the return journey. I learned so much there, as he tried me out on many 'Innocent Ear' projects (often 'Ignorant Ear' as far as I was concerned). Also I heard much of his own music. One unforgettable memory is of Bob, behind closed doors, working on the Clarinet Quintet. I, stripped to the waist on a hot summer day, raking the grass from his newly-mown lawn, listening to him trying out chords on the piano. Yes, in those days he did use the piano a bit.

So many meetings, so many memories. Through him I met many distinguished musicians, and I remember with gratitude the day I spent at the Albert Hall on the occasion of the first professional performance of the 'Gothic' Symphony of Havergal Brian. Bob gave me the job of looking after the aged composer telling me to make sure he didn't get too tired. Some hope! He was in great form, telling me of his encounters with Elgar and Richard Strauss. At the same time he was busy signing autographs for all the children of the Orpington Junior Choir!

I lost immediate contact with Bob for ten years or so, though we did keep in touch by telephone. This was due to Squibs (the affectionate nickname for his first wife) having become rather frail and unable to cope with many visitors. It was during one of these calls that I suggested to him the idea of a Robert Simpson Society.

Much happened to alter the course of Bob's life from 1980 onwards – his resignation from the BBC, the death of Squibs and later on his marriage to Angela. We all thought that they would remain at Chearsley where he would continue to compose and be close enough to London for other musical activities. This was not to be. Bob was always full of surprises and not all of them musical ones. A holiday visit to Ireland became a turning-point in their lives. They fell in love with the country and the people of Kerry and made immediate plans to move there.

All their many friends who had expressed dismay at this sudden move were most pleasantly surprised. 'Siochain', their spacious house commanding a spectacular view over the Bay of Tralee, became a place of pilgrimage, where we could listen to great music and partake of much spirited conversation, not to mention the good whisky and the superb vegetarian cuisine. Holidays, year after year in those days, were planned around Bob. He has gone now, and we are left with our memories. Memories of a man of the utmost integrity, spiced with wicked but never cruel wit and humour. A man with a passionate concern for the fate of the world, and an equal concern for its less fortunate inhabitants. This is exemplified by his many years of service as a prison visitor, and his active participation in humanitarian causes such as Amnesty International and CND. Farewell, old friend."

JASCHA HORENSTEIN (1898-1973)

Horenstein was one of the great master conductors, of equal stature to Klemperer or Karajan, but who through ill-luck never achieved their fame. Born in Kiev, his family moved to Vienna during his teenage years: thus, although he could speak Russian, German was his first language. He studied violin with Adolf Busch, theory with Joseph Marx, and composition with Franz Schreker in Berlin. His conducting debut came in 1923, with the encouragement of Wilhelm Fürtwängler. He worked with the Berlin Symphony and the Dusseldorf Opera, and making the first ever complete recording of a Bruckner symphony – number Seven, with the Berlin Philharmonic.

In 1933 he fled Nazi Germany, as did so many other distinguished Jewish musicians. He was unable to secure a position with an orchestra of international standing – the New York Philharmonic could not live with his meticulous (though never egocentric) methods, and conducted orchestras in the Soviet Union, Palestine, Australia, New Zealand, South Africa, South America and Mexico. During the 1950s he made an extensive series of recordings for the Vox label; sadly, both the orchestras and the recording quality are often second-rate. In 1967 he was briefly taken on, and then dropped, by EMI; two years later, he had better fortune. The Unicorn label was founded, among other things, to get Jascha Horenstein on disc. Here, at last, were first-rate orchestras and sound quality to match the interpretations. Tragically, he only lived long enough to complete some half-dozen discs. He was engaged by Covent Garden to conduct a season of Wagner's 'Parsifal'; Simpson was adamant that the additional strain put on an already weakened heart by this long and demanding work killed him. At the end of the season, he went to see his consultant, who said he was willing to operate, but warned the conductor that there was only a fifty per cent chance of success. Horenstein opted for surgery, and died on the table.

In some ways, Horenstein resented his image as a Bruckner and Mahler specialist – he even referred to them sardonically as 'Marks and Spencer' - since his repertoire was a wide one, ranging from Bach to Schoenberg. Fortunately, the BBC have to some extent remedied the dearth of recordings by issuing a number of his performances in their 'Legends' series, including a definitive Bruckner Eighth. Fascinating too are the reminiscences included on some of the discs, in heavily accented but very fluent English.

Horenstein's epistolary style was as sparky as his verbal: Undated, but from 1966:

"I am enjoying enormously studying your symphony. I also have listened to the tape several times. I hate to criticize the interpretation of my colleagues and I do apologise for doing so. However I beg you to <u>confirm</u> that as far as the tape is concerned the tempo on page 43 at figure 36 is WRONG. You indicate "pochissimo" while they are playing MOLTISSIMO MENO... making it impossible to do "poco accel" on page 44 third bar after fig 38 when the "Tempo 1" should be reached what Mahler would call "unmerklich", I feel that the tempo at fig 36 should be ALMOST the same but "etwas rühiger", not even "etwas langsamer" as there is a very subtle difference between "slow" and "calm", "composed", "quiet. The whole movement is <u>too slow</u>!!" Later, he adds "The second movement is beastly difficult for the players!!"

19th December 1969

"My dear Bob,

AGES that I have not heard from you. I hope that you are both in good health and flourishing. What about the SCORE, THE score?" (Presumably that of the Third Symphony)

By 14th June 1971, his illness is evident:

"We have been here back home for a while and are still waiting for you to "drop in one afternoon" as you had promised in your first letter. There is not the slightest chance for you to miss us as we have decided to remain here at least till September 7th, not leaving Pully (Lausanne-Pully, Switzerland) even for one day. The doctors are satisfied with my progress, I am on a fair way to recovery and the doctors in America as well as those here though not committing themselves are pretty sure that I will be able to resume my activities in September, it means the "PROM" on September 14th. I certainly am NOT going to force this matter and the doctors will be able to give me their OK at the beginning of August and all of them are a very conservative sort of people! I am walking now almost one hour a day and the doctors insist that in two months from now I shall walk not less than 3 miles a day, and daily! It will be hard to comply!

Regarding my conversation with Deryck you MUST have noticed that both of us were half-asleep!! I consider everything I said as pure nonsense and I was asking the lady in charge (Miss Cooke) to destroy the tape and to arrange another discussion scheduled at a NORMAL hour!! As to sentimentality, I meant sentimentality and not "sentimentality". There is plenty of sentimentality, almost nothing but in op. III and a lot of "sentimentality" in Cavelleria Rusticana and both brands of sentimentality in Sibelius."

In a PS he adds: "You happen to mention Bruckner 5th in your letter. Just for your information that I will not be available for the Bruckner Fifth or the whole Bruckner cycle and God-knows-What unless it is NOT with the RPO."

During Robert Simpson's own illness, Horenstein called him almost daily, enjoining him to "Obey the doctors!"

Simpson broadcast this tribute to his own friend on 4th April 1973:

We have just lost one of the great conductors of our time and I have lost, in him, one of my dearest friends. This makes it doubly difficult for me to find the right words for the occasion, if indeed they exist. He would not have enjoyed a eulogy, for he was, despite the unmistakable impressiveness of his personality, the least pretentious of men. I well remember his quick reply to an enthusiastic young man who gushingly told him that he was the greatest conductor he'd ever come across – "Are you sure you don't mean the second greatest?". At such times he didn't take care to be tactful, though he could at the same time be both tactful and tactless, and with humour, as he was when someone tried to draw from him opinions about other conductors – "I think all my colleagues are wonderful". Remembering these things helps to alleviate while it intensifies the sense of loss – we think of the man and what an irreplaceable experience it was knowing him, so that in this sense he is not gone. His deep interest in human beings made him totally memorable to even those who encountered him slightly, and he had an extraordinary memory for, not merely faces and names, but people. It always astonished me what he would take in during a casual conversation; once when he was about to go to Australia I happened to remark, in passing, that I'd like to go there some time, as my father lived in Sydney. At the time I didn't think he'd even heard what I said. A couple of weeks later I got a telegram from Sydney – "Please send your father's address". Somewhat taken aback, I did so at once; after a while I got a letter from my father describing how the conductor Horenstein had suddenly telephoned him, taken him twice out to lunch, given him tickets for his concerts, and talked to him for hours about everything under the sun. A simple thing, perhaps, but how many such preoccupied people with such intense work to do would have bothered? The fact is that persons and their situations interested him as much as music, and this is why he kept his friends. It's also one key to the great range of his musical sympathies.

This direct and honest humanity came out in the way he made music. There was never any attempt to put a glossy surface on it, or to ingratiate himself with either the orchestra or the audience. Sometimes in rehearsal he would work with a kind of stoic persistence that could put the orchestra's good will at risk – but always in the end the nobility and faithfulness of his vision would emerge at the important time – the performance itself, when he would radiate concentration, will-power, and intense purity of feeling. The purity of his feeling was one of the chief things that distinguished him – I've many times heard him conduct works that were usually not congenial to me because they seemed to me always cloying, sentimental, or bombastic. Every time, he seemed some-how to purify, to strengthen them in some way, and this was because he always sensed and grasped the essential structure behind everything else. Yet the intensity was such that very rarely was there a hint of coldness or pedantry. When the music was really great he could reach its essence on both the emotional and the intellectual levels. An ineradicable memory for me was the finest performance of Brahms's Requiem I ever heard.

The music we're about to hear is by composers close to his heart. One of them, Nielsen, he knew personally and could describe evocatively. As a young conductor he rehearsed Nielsen's Fifth Symphony for Fürtwängler with constant help from the composer, which makes his recording of that work of special interest. The Dream of Gunnar [Saga Drøm], which is on the same disc as the symphony gives Horenstein the means of revealing his insight into the subtle contemplative depths of which this composer is capable. The other composer, Bruckner, appealed to his sense of space and true grandeur, and the performance of the first movement of the Eighth Symphony is one of the most splendid examples of Horenstein's grasp of architecture, and his powerful sense of the dramatic that never allowed a moment's exaggeration. The tragic character of this movement is perhaps apt to what many of us feel now that he isn't with us any more. But the intense dignity and irresistible force with which he interprets it is a salutary reminder of the piercing instinct for truth which, in him, we were privileged to encounter."

The composer related a further reminiscence in a tribute to the Royal Liverpool Philharmonic Orchestra for their 150th Birthday in 1990:

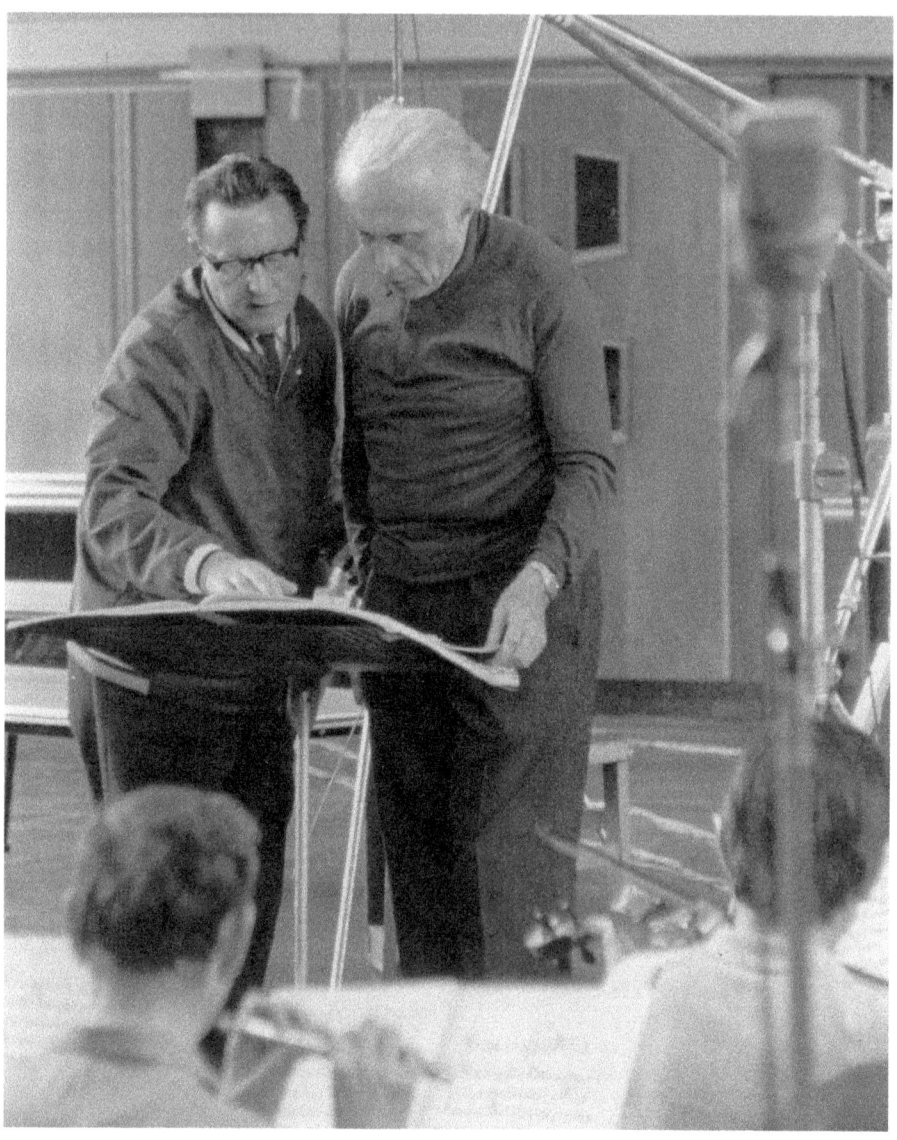

With Jascha Horenstein, 1970 (Third Symphony recording

CONFESSION

The RLPO has always been kind to me, which is perhaps surprising, if it's true that I did them an appalling bad turn back in April 1970. Jascha Horenstein was conducting my Third Symphony at the Philharmonic Hall and the programme also included Beethoven No 7. Our discussions were never confined merely to my own music, and in this case we talked a lot about the rest of the programme during a drive around the city so that he could see things he normally wouldn't be able to. I remember how impressed he was with the Anglican Cathedral, though we both agreed that the Scherzo of Beethoven 7 would be a problem in it While we were on the subject of Beethoven I mentioned the age old question of repeats in the symphonies. He agreed that Beethoven didn't put them there either for fun or for mere convention's sake, and I said somewhat passionately that to leave them out was to cut these masterpieces.

One of the marvellous things about Jascha was his complete freedom from fixed ideas – many conductors (I'd say most) 'I've tackled on this matter have been gloriously convinced that their bad habits arise from a judgement superior to Beethoven's. This attitude is fading now, especially with the fashionable devotion to 'authenticity', from which perhaps we might suppose no good reasons for anything whatever. Among the older generation of conductors Horenstein was the least dogmatic, or bound by habit; but he was a very strong character, and once he had made up his mind there was no stopping him. Nevertheless, he was the most reasonable of dictators.

So we talked about Beethoven's repeats, sitting in the car, and in the Adelphi Hotel, and I begged him to do ALL of them in No.7, just for me. The Seventh has huge repeats in the first and last movements, and the scherzo positively bristles with them, the trio as well; since the scherzo comes three times and the trio twice the piece is already lengthy without them (I remember Stokowski used to cut out the second appearance of the trio and the middle one of the scherzo, and I never managed to convince him that it was vandalism). I maintained (and still do) that the remarkable momentum of the movement depends not only on the circular motion of scherzo and trio but also on the internal repeats, too. Jascha hadn't been in the habit of making all these repeats, but he saw the point, and said 'We will do it, but not just for you! We'll do it for Beethoven!' And so it was, with the result (I'm told) that THE ORCHESTRA HAD TO BE PAID OVERTIME! All these years I've had it on my conscience - costing the poor old RLPO a lot of extra money they needed to save! But perhaps its NOT true – if so, I can breathe once more. Maybe somebody could look it up. But be warned – if it is, I'd do the same again. Beethoven comes first."

Jascha Horenstein wrote the forward to the 1971 fiftieth birthday booklet:

"When I agreed to write an introduction to this symposium it was, not because I had any thought that I could add anything of value to its publication. I consented because I felt that this was an opportunity for me to express my appreciation for an important figure in the large edifice of contemporary music. With this object in view, and also with the idea of acknowledging my own indebtedness to the composer and scholar, I have ventured to say a few words.

I must admit to the reader that whatever I have learned of Robert Simpson's beginnings as a musician is made up of scraps of information that the composer inadvertently revealed, be it in small talk or in more serious conversations. Although the details of his boyhood and early musical development are not available to me, it is my strong feeling that his was obviously of an austere character; his parentage, childhood and temperament all seem to have combined in the unfolding of the creative personality that soon made itself apparent.

When Simpson was born, Schoenberg and Stravinsky had set their stamp on the mainstream of European music-making as well as on the expressive media and methods at the composer's disposal. When Josef Mathias Hauer and Webern, in addition to Schoenberg, introduced serial composition, they transformed the language of music. It is indicative of both Simpson's character and his powerful talent that he was able to resist these influences to a very high degree. He has not only refrained from turning down the traditional language, but he also emphasized his link, and the similarity of his language, with old conceptions, at the same time combining familiar materials in a novel form. However instantly Simpson's music may be welcomed, it is because this music has been mastered organically and fashioned with self-contained craftmanship.

In recognition of his achievement, and celebrating Robert Simpson's fiftieth birthday, I am taking the liberty of giving the "up-beat" to a chorus of tributes from some of his friends and admirers, far and near."

HERBERT HOWELLS (1892-1983)

English composer, best known for his choral music, especially 'Hymnus Paradisi'.

Robert Simpson studied with Howells from 1942 to 1944. His tribute to the senior composer appeared in 'Tonic' under the title 'Friends and Mentors'.

"Herbert Howells, composer and teacher; Adrian Boult, interpreter and encourager – both gone within a couple of days. They enjoyed long and valuable lives, and it was a privilege to count them as dear friends. Howells I knew longer – from the time when I gave up medical studies and it was necessary to prove to my parents that I was not a drop-out. I didn't know how to get the kind of lessons I needed to have a go at the B. Mus. and I couldn't afford to go to a music college full-time. In any case, the war was on, and, as a pacifist, I was working in civil defence on a mobile surgical unit, as driver and orderly. So I wrote to the registrar of the RCM, asking if he could tell me who might give me private lessons (not too expensive). He suggested either Herbert Howells or Gordon Jacob. I had heard more of Howells' music, and so I approached him. He took me on – and what a teacher he was. He was one of the most naturally gifted musicians I have ever met. I remember taking him a fugue once, on a subject of my own – just an exercise. He read it through and found a few bugs here and there, which he showed me how to get rid of. Nothing remarkable about that, you might say. But then he got a few sheets of MS paper and said, 'Let's see what else could be done with that subject'. I watched while he wrote, about as quickly as you'd write a letter, a fugue of maybe a hundred bars on my subject, which he hadn't seen before that day. Then he took it to a piano (it was in open string quartet score) and played it through, most beautifully. It was a lovely little fugue, and I felt crushed and encouraged at the same time – which is the only spirit in which you really can learn anything. He was always forthright, but always kind. If he was five minutes late for a lesson he would refuse to take any money for it; even so he would often add the time to the other end. It's probable that if he hadn't spent so much time teaching and adjudicating he would have produced a lot more music. I remember him with love and gratitude, both as teacher and kind friend. He inspired the confidence that meant you could put yourself unreservedly in his hands, as you might with a trusted doctor. After all, a student is a kind of patient, isn't he? – though it was Herbert who showed most of the patience."

Elisabeth Benians (nee Matthews) describes (in a letter to the author, 18th March 2009 "...an occasion during an Easter holiday which Robert and I were spending together visiting a large conservatory where the relationship between keys and colour was to be explained to me. But first there was a Composition lesson with Herbert Howells at St. Paul's Girls School. So I was taken along too and sat at one end of a large room reading my Chaucer (or maybe it was Shakespeare) whilst the lesson proceeded at the other end. I was somewhat embarrassed – although I had become used to Robert doing the unusual and unexpected. But I needn't have worried; Herbert Howells came over at the end of the lesson, and talked to me in a most friendly and gracious way." Howells kept in touch with his former pupil; several letters to Simpson survive, beautifully written in a stylish longhand.

8th December 1972

"My dear Robert,

It's marvellous to hear of your recovery and resumption of composing and getting back to your day-by- day place of work. And may you continue fit and busy – but not <u>too</u> busy as yet! I really am glad of your feeling so much better.

<u>And</u>: I can't tell you how I have blessed you for the four concerts, and the great kindness in getting them put into production to mark my 80th year. I've been so deeply touched by your trying to give me some sort of hearing over the air: and it has been a specially <u>effective</u> hearing, too.

And then there's gracious and unique Angela! No other could have been so patient or so resourceful. So I'm in debt to her, too! – and in <u>yours</u> more than I can say.

My love to you both,

yrs ever

Herbert"

30th January 1973

"My dear Robert, Only <u>yesterday</u> did the record reach me! Not GPO's fault. Simply that the "woman help" received it from the postman, and put it safely away until I got back home. By chance I found it.

But you must have wondered if it had reached me – I'm so sorry for the delayed thanks for the record.

You've been so good to me, about everything to do with this grim business of my reaching the 80th birthday – I can't begin to thank you – and our dear Angela – for all you both did for me – You won't need me stressing how touched I've been. The more so that you yourself fell into trouble at the time, in matters of health – We were all very vexed about <u>that</u>. And then one heard of your getting back to the Symphony, and-going on as if there had been no hiatus!

I want to hear its performance, if possible, when it comes to a hearing. So – in the most persuasive, dulcet tones you can command – get Angela to let me know when and where it's to be given its first hearing, will you? BUT – for heaven's sake don't <u>overwork</u> these days!

There must be a lunch – mine for, you – as soon as the right day crops up.

Meanwhile my love to you – and to Angela, if she can bear it!

Yours ever, Herbert"

6th May 1973

"My dear Bob,

Nothing in recent years has warmed my heart more than the obvious success of the five symphonies and all it means for you yourself and all of us. It has been an exciting and real recognition of your sheer powers – the more so since it has been looked-for long since by anybody whose sense of values has not been ruled by mere fashion. So much in the works moved me, their cumulative powers especially. When it came, the 5th was like a summing-up. But that's just what it <u>mustn't</u> be!

True, astonishing as it is, it's still an up-to-the-moment sign. It had me pondering three other men who knew the magic of "No.5" in their day. But neither Beethoven nor Sibelius nor R.V.W. in the glorious trio did <u>his</u> No.5 in the aftermath of a dangerous illness!

Bob my dear, what you've done and accomplished has so moved me: and the wide recognition that has come your way is so right and so comforting. Bless you!

Yours affectionately

Herbert

HANS KELLER (1919 - 1985)

German Jewish musician who fled Vienna from the Nazis in 1938 and became a BBC Music Producer working alongside Robert Simpson. His long-term partner was the distinguished graphic artist Milein Cosman. He contributed chapters on Mozart and Tchaikovsky to the symposium 'The Symphony': in the latter chapter, Simpson could not help taking issue with him on a couple of points:

(Page 34; H.K. "As for the folk material itself, Tchaikovsky and Shostakovich are perhaps the only composers who invalidate Schoenberg's contention that folkloristic symphonies are a structural impossibility;" R.S. "Schoenberg's irrational obsession with structural 'possibilities' and 'impossibilities' is an inevitable late stage in the Germanic nightmare. Anything is possible in art, given the necessary imaginative genius." (Page 345) H.K. "But history's decisive step in the symphonic assimilation of the waltz was made by Tchaikovsky;" R.S "What about Berlioz?"

In his last years Keller suffered from motor neurone disease, but his intellect remained undimmed. Here follows Simpson's appreciation of his friend, from a joint tribute to Hans Keller and Edmund Rubbra printed in 'Tonic', and characteristically entitled "Two Friends 'Gone'":

"Who could forget that sharp ear and brain, the eye that sparkles at the chance of an argument, the dark, thin, bewhiskered smile? They are still there for anyone who knew them. We all change one another's lives, and all of us mark the world we leave. Some mark it ill, others for good – no-one dies without a trace. Therefore the future of the species depends on the quality of its individuals. If the human race were Keller-like life would be pretty hectic but there would be no wars – only arguments; there would be no stupidity; there would be no sentimentality; there would be no dishonesty; there would be no vindictiveness, no hate. And a lot of the so-called music we have to endure would never have been written. Hans left a mark and no mistake. Anyone who knew him even for a moment was changed, and permanently; his very nature challenged all your thought. Even when you thought (or even knew!) he was wrong, he had shoved your mind onto a new road; you found yourself looking at fresh territory. Above all, Hans was determined to find the shortest way to the truth; it is what he saw in the great composers. Sometimes his love of paradox obstructed the unsuspecting reader, and he could cheerfully talk at considerable length (without illustration) about music completely unfamiliar to his audience, with somewhat dizzying results. But even while his hearers groped they sensed an altogether exceptional mind and personality. The better you knew him, the kinder he was. He was a good listener; if he was on the lookout for an argument, he was also anxious to help. No – he hasn't 'gone'. He has left tingling vibrations all over the place."

Hans Keller greatly admired Simpson's music; in a radio review for 'The Listener' dated 21st May 1981, he wrote: "Whoever heard Sunday's Seventh Quartet surely won't miss next Sunday's Eighth (and last), which I know from a close study of the score. Like the Seventh, it is a sovereign quartet texture – created, exceptionally, by a composer who is not a string player himself: his eavesdropping, concrete imagination has assimilated those ultimate secrets of quartet sonority which escaped a Schumann, Brahms or Stravinsky. Doctor Simpson celebrated his 60th birthday this year, and it is gratifying to note that the World Service, too, is marking the occasion by throwing this shamefully neglected mastermind into full relief. (Yes, let me say 'mastermind': why should we yield to the cheapening of the concept and avoid it?"

A letter to Simpson dated 20th September 1977 refers to the dedication to Keller and Milein Cosman of the 7th Symphony:

"Dear Bob,

When I said that I felt honoured I meant just that: that the word has been used up isn't my fault, for I have hardly ever used it. Nor was the reference to the Britten dedication merely leg pulling: when his letter arrived asking the question you asked, well, I had very similar feelings to this morning's. In fact, when I survey three dedications – those of Frankel's Fifth 4tet & Britten's Third as well as your natal rather than pre-natal symphony – I realize, happily, that amongst real friends, one knows what is at the centre of the other person's preoccupations: what these three works have in common (if I may include a safe prediction about yours) is a deep concern for the nobility and dignity of symphonic thought.

Yours ever,

Hans"

Another letter, from 9th December 1980, illustrates Keller's wide-ranging and restless intellect:

"Dear Bob,

Many thanks for yours of December 4th; Anderson has been on to me, and all is well. I am very happy to hear, incidentally, that despite one or two criticisms, Bayan Northcott's article about your music is of genuine musical interest: as I told you before, he is the only musician amongst contemporary critics. (So is Anthony Payne – who, however, would not allow one to describe him as a critic).

Most interested to hear about the unprecedented quintet; I think I know exactly what you feel like, and the required intensity of anything else, can easily result in thoughtful elevation – I mean, elevated thoughtfulness. ORIGINAL SIN: the division between thought and feeling, and the resulting feelingless thoughts & thoughtless feelings (if thoughts and feelings you can still call them).

Yours ever,

Hans

P.S Did you read the Reith Lectures? Straight theft from Thomas Szasz ('The Myth of Mental Illness'), whom they duly attack after misrepresenting him (Dec. 4). Far from being confined to the criminal classes, crime celebrates many of its ultimate achievements elsewhere, & not only in Aubrey Singer's office either.

As a matter of fact, both of them are distinctly talented composers – inventive in the first place, & by no means incompetent in the second. Tony Payne's str 4tet (commissioned by Stephen) you may have heard when it was broadcast; as for Northcott, he still keeps his work rather secret (tho' he has shown me some of it) – which, in the circumstances, one can understand. But tho' he can't have heard any of it yet, it certainly is his ear that composes."

Regarding Stravinsky, letter dated 14th April 1982:

"Dear Bob,

The miracle is that you know exactly what I mean, & I know exactly what you mean, & yet our respective impressions of the music 'stay uncorrupted': I'm glad I'm not called upon to explain that one' ... when I shook hands with him – one of the less exhilarating moments in my life' c'd have been my statement too* – but then, the relation you see between 'the man' & 'the music' is, or can be, far more straightforward than the relation I see, or (say, in the case of Mozart) don't. In short, I certainly loathed him personally.

The serial example from the, Symphony of Psalms I picked because it struck me when I first heard the work, before I'd seen a score, & indeed before I knew what 'serial technique' meant: I remain perpetually amused at what people don't hear, especially those who know all about what they don't hear. Very many thanks, anyhow.

Love,

Hans"

*Simpson said that it was as if Stravinsky couldn't snatch his hand away quickly enough.(D.M.)

Finally, a letter from 13th November 1982, following the disastrous premiere of Simpson's Eighth Symphony:

"Bob: when I get a latter from you? I always immediately feel like talking to you, so why shouldn't I behave accordingly? I'm reacting, that is to say, after having read no more than… your 1st 2 sentences:

Yes, I almost immediately noticed the conductor's utter unmusicality: the symphony's shapes & textures often make it easy for one to infer, from the distorted aural evidence, how it actually goes, in that one sees, as it were, the score before one's mind's eye, notwithstanding what he did to it.

Next reaction: yes, the wrong tempi & tempi characters were quite particularly striking, Milein is my witness. There were 5 stages at which I said, 'Wrong tempo'.

Next reaction: yes, again Milein must be my witness, the difficulties of the piece – many of them, anyway – struck one forcibly & incisively, all the more so in view of his idiotic behaviour.

Next: yes, yes, indeed, that was my loudest exclamation – the polar difference between the perf of the 4tet & the perf of the sym: 'To that extent', I said to Milein, 'my spontaneous comparison is illegitimate – except that I wasn't even born the day before yesterday'.

But your comparison with Milein sticking her pictures on the wall is overoptimistic, as you well know: what gets in the way are the viewer's learned, historical, inartistic, utterly irrelevant spectacles. Nowadays, a natural approach to her art (and to ours!!) is found so rarely that one can safely describe it as abnormal. Love from both to both.

Hans"

I often find Hans Keller's writing impenetrable, but the last paragraph of his contribution to the 1971 birthday symposium puts it in a nutshell:

"Extended, intense, hopeful integrity: this is the essence of Robert Simpson's art, in which we cannot discover a phoney bar. About a smaller mind and heart one could have wrItten a conventional essay on 'The Man and his Art'. With

Simpson, only 'The Art and its Man' will do: you understand him through his art, not his art through him. In view of his art, the fearless, artless integrity of the man becomes a matter of course, hardly worth mentioning: there is no more substantial compliment in art or life."

HARRY NEWSTONE (1921 - 2006)

Born in Winnipeg, Newstone and Simpson (who both studied under Herbert Howells) met in the 1940s. As well as his own Haydn Orchestra, he was in demand as a guest conductor, edited scores and made a number of recordings. Here is his own account from the memorial Tonic:

"My first meeting with Bob Simpson over a half-century ago might be called serendipitous. We were both browsing in a record shop in Shaftesbury Avenue and got talking. He told me that he was studying composition with Herbert Howells and having myself just left Dr. Howells half-an-hour earlier, a bond was immediately established and I was there and then invited to Bob's home to listen to records. On arrival, I was played the 4th Symphony of Bruckner of whose music I was then totally ignorant. He told me later that he always did this to new acquaintances – 'testing for Bruckner' he called it. My own reaction must have been satisfactory because I was invited back for another listening session a few days later – and so began a long and cherished friendship.

It was the middle of World War 11 and Bob was on the staff of a Civil Defence First Aid Post near his home in South London. The Post needed a driver and I needed a job; I applied and was hired. I was allocated a room in Bob's house and we were able to spend our days off duty listening to and talking about music and going together to Dr Howells for our lessons. We also kept a portable gramophone at the First Aid Post and when there were no air raids we played records of a great variety of music in one of the air raid shelters. We each put two shillings a week into a kitty and would take turns in choosing our next purchases, and these records (78s in those days) were our most prized possessions. In the back garden of the house there was an Anderson air-raid shelter; there the record collection was kept for safety while we slept in the house. One day, Bob suggested that I might like to listen to a rarely played Haydn symphony to be broadcast the next day. It was No.49 (La Passionel and it was unlike any other Haydn symphony I'd ever heard; in those days only a few of his most popular symphonies were regularly played, and so began my lifelong interest in this great but, at that time, shamefully neglected composer. It must have been around 1946 that Bob had the idea of forming a society to explore the considerable repertoire of music that was hardly if ever heard but deserved to be. With Bob as Artistic Director and myself as Secretary, the Exploratory Concert Society put on performances of music by a large variety of composers (Busoni, Reger, Medtner, Nielsen, Brian among them) supported by a subscribing membership and a minuscule grant from the Arts Council of Great Britain. By the spring of 1949 we had gone as far as our limited financial resources could take us and it was decided to wrap up the society with a bang by putting on our first (and last) orchestral concert of rare Haydn symphonies; and so the Haydn Orchestra was born, giving its first concert on May 19, 1949 in Conway Hall of the Symphonies No.28, No.46 (played before and after the interval because of its remarkable nature) and No.73.

Bob's advocacy of unjustly neglected music is now well known, and during his years at the BBC he produced and often personally presented works that we might otherwise never have heard, not least in the imaginative series 'The Innocent Ear' which he devised. His writings on Beethoven, Bruckner, Nielsen and Havergal Brian have become standard references and are models of perceptive and (just as important) human commentaries on great music and the great men who created it, worthy to stand by the illuminative writings of Donald Tovey. For Beethoven, above all others, Bob had the greatest reverence and it is no surprise that his own twin series of fine symphonies and string quartets should form the core of his output. His firm belief that tonality and movement are basic and inexhaustible resources in musical structure gives his music a tensile and creative strength that will surely guarantee its longevity.

It is inevitable that all music, even by celebrated composers, did not please him. Delius he found 'spineless', the romanticism of Rachmaninov hardly moved him, technical facility made him suspicious and tended to minimize his appreciation of a composer's other qualities. Atonal and wholly aleatoric music he thought 'blind alleys' and an 'abandonment' of a composer's creative abilities. These strictly held views, which some might see as blind spots, were not the result of prejudice or ignorance but the conclusions of a studied assessment of qualities in others that did not coincide with his own self-disciplined ethos. Never the one to take an easy path if his conscience dictated otherwise, Bob will remain in our memories as a man in whom impeccable integrity, great humour and inspired creativity, to say nothing of the fortitude of the last few years, came together in a person of a wholeness all too rare in our time."

Harry Newstone moved to Canada after the Haydn Orchestra was disbanded, and often wrote to Robert Simpson; he conducted Simpson's incidental music to Ibsen's 'The Pretenders' for the CBC radio broadcast from Vancouver in 1969.

TED PERRY 1931 - 2003.

Ted was the founder of the Hyperion record label, a firm which soon made its name as one unafraid to tackle obscure music largely untouched by the larger and more timid labels. Hyperion do mainstream repertoire, too, usually with gifted artists new to the recording studio. An early, and surprise, best seller was a disc of music by the mediaeval composeress and polymath Hildegard of Bingen; Perry was wont to comment ruefully "She pays for my mistakes!" The earlier recordings of Simpson's music, issued by Hyperion during the 1980s, were in part subsidized, but it soon became apparent that Ted intended to record everything, with or without financial assistance; a flood of releases followed during the 1990s, and under Perry's stewardship the results were remarkable – all of the string quartets, all but the latest of the symphonies, Simpson's other chamber music barring only the clarinet trio, all the brass band and piano music, and an 'odds and sods' disc comprising the two choral pieces, the sole opus for organ, and the Canzona (orchestral brass). This was certainly a labour of love, not a money-spinning enterprise; not even the highly praised recording of the Ninth Symphony has made a profit. After Ted's death, his son Simon paid tribute to his father by completing the symphonic cycle with No.11, coupled with the Nielsen Variations. Ted's own piece on Robert Simpson is typically down-to-earth:

"I knew Bob Simpson (though I used to call him 'Dr Simpson' in those days) before I'd heard any of his music. He used to come into EMG, the classy little West End record shop behind whose counter I worked in the early 50s. He used to make me laugh with his droll and, I thought, piercingly truthful (and not always complimentary) bons mots on the subject of music and composers and critics. Consequently I was curious to hear the sort of music which he wrote himself. The opportunity came with the first performance of the First Symphony.

Now the odd thing is that I remember hearing the first performance of Bob's First but I don't remember the occasion. So maybe it was a broadcast. What mattered, though, was the music, and as I might have surmised from the man himself, it struck me as what I then called, and still call, 'real' music. I sensed structure and shape, momentum, seriousness of purpose and – well, integrity, with no 'effects' or empty gestures or sonic doodling. (It didn't seem to have many tunes either.) I didn't 'understand' a note of it! Nevertheless, I had the same feeling that I've had every time since when I've heard a major Simpson piece for the first time: that it was bigger than I was, by which I mean that there was more to it than first met the ear, that subsequent performances would reveal ever more subtleties. And, of course, isn't that true of all of Bob's and all great music! I happen to exemplify the listener mentioned somewhere in Bob's writings (I think it is his Nielsen book) who 'can't tell a B flat from a rissole', so I'm the last person able to present a structural analysis of one of Bob's scores. But that was Bob's whole point when he used the phrase. The technical structure of a piece is merely the invisible skeleton upon which a symphonic work is built, and one doesn't need a degree in musical anatomy to recognise and appreciate the texture, shape, movement, momentum and direction of a piece of 'real' music – that is, music which isn't just a mathematical exercise. Bob' music has that mystical additional ingredient which makes it music and not just an assemblage of notes. (This is a subject that's fascinated me for a long time. In just which dimension does this 'meaning' exist over and above the order of the notes? Or even the performance of the notes. That is, why does Schubert's B flat Sonata sear one in X's performance whilst it doesn't in Y's, although he plays the same notes? However, I digress.) I believe in Bob's music. It satisfies me. It's quality. It is, as I say, 'real' music. And it will last. I'm proud to be responsible for helping to make it known to the world."

The two men evidently got on well; Ted's letters are mostly businesslike, but he often sparked a humorous response in the composer, even post-stroke. There was, however, disagreement concerning the choice of conductor for the Eleventh Symphony; Perry wanted Vernon (Tod) Handley to complete the cycle (as did the conductor himself) while Simpson preferred the dedicatee, Matthew Taylor, which eventually happened. In a letter dated 6th June 199!, Simpson wrote:

"Symphony No.11 – a tricky one, as you rightly surmise. But Matthew is a fine conductor and I wrote No.11 for him spontaneously, inspired by a remarkable performance of No.7 with a bunch of students. He's highly gifted (also as a composer) and I have great regard for him. If you should decide to let him record No.11 he will do a first-rate job, especially with as good an orchestra as the City of London Sinfonia. Do my symphonies depend entirely on Tod's reputation, or is there now enough interest in them to make it worthwhile to introduce a highly talented newcomer? I know Tod is keen to do the whole cycle, but I can do nothing about the fact that circumstances produce works for other people – No.12, for instance, is going to be for Matthew Best and his new Corydon Orchestra – he's another fellow I much admire. You know him well of course."

At the end of the letter, Simpson refers to the forthcoming Malvern Festival:

"We must in any case spend some time together, plus booze! I hope you can be at as much of the festival as possible, sober or not. A glorious tale I heard about Arthur Hutchings, onetime Professor of Music at Durham. He drank enthusiastically and one day was staggering up the steps by the Cathedral, down which the Bishop's wife was coming. 'Drunk again, Professor!' she exclaimed. 'So am I, madam, so am I!' riposted the redoubtable Hutchings. How's that for a counter-attack?"

A further letter dated 6th August 1991, refers to the invitation concert at Bournemouth, at which the Second and Fourth Symphonies were to be played prior to recording:

"Dear Ted,

You've probably heard what happened in Bournemouth. Matthew Taylor stepped in at a few hours notice and though he couldn't take on No.4 (never having seen the score) he did a really fine job on No.2 and a beautiful Beethoven 4, with the Coriolan overture. The orchestra responded to him very positively, and the Bournemouth Evening Echo had the headline (not flattering to me!) ILL WIND BLOWS BETTER FARE! Well… there isn't another 4th symphony as good as Beethoven's, so fair enough."

Later on:

"There's no need to tell you of my great regard for Tod, who has done so much and so well for my music – why else would I have written No. 10 for him without commission? But this is the fourth time in a row (Southampton, Liverpool, Dublin Bournemouth) involving my work, to speak of nobody else's. Always the explanation is different. But even if things were always normal he could hardly claim the whole series to the exclusion of everyone else, now that the last two symphonies are for other conductors - assuming of course (as I do not!) that I will proceed to the end, I can't guarantee to write symphonies only for Tod, much as I love him!"

Finally, a letter dated 15th February 1993:

"Dear Ted,

Many thanks for your letter and the proofs. Here they are with various little amendments. I thought I'd better remove the reference to snakes in Quartet 14 – I only said it as a joke and there are plenty of fools about who would take it seriously and I'd hate that quartet to end up with the nickname "The Snakes"! …I'm still very puzzled about the MCPS. Recordings of my works have been in existence since 1957 and I've never had a penny from them in all that time except when they have been broadcast when I get it through the PRS. In fact I didn't think a composer ever got anything from the sales of a record unless he had marketed it himself. Anyhow, a few extra pence would do me no harm. Who do we scream at? Or could Hyperion do some screaming for us?

I'm absolutely thrilled about the success of the Ninth. Astonishing to think that I've made nearly 10,000 enemies already from that piece."

It is a measure of the love, as well as respect, in which Ted Perry was held, that his packed memorial concert at the Wigmore Hall (17/7/2003) was performed by musicians whom he had introduced to the recording studio, and who gave their services free of charge.

EDMUND RUBBRA (1901-1986)

English composer of eleven symphonies, concertos, choral and chamber music. Simpson's admiration for Rubbra's predominantly quiet, contemplative music was fully reciprocated; Rubbra wrote a hugely enthusiastic review of the First Symphony when it appeared on record in 1957. In 1976 Simpson produced the senior composer's 75th birthday concert, in which the LSO under Vernon Handley played the Fourth Symphony, the Piano Concerto and the Soliloquy for Cello and Orchestra, with Malcolm Binns and Raphael Sommer as soloists. Ten years later, on Rubbra's death, Robert Simpson wrote an emotional tribute to his fellow composer, printed in 'Tonic'.

With Edmund Rubbra, 1976 (Rubbra's 75th birthday concert)

"TWO FRIENDS 'GONE'

But have they gone? Two opposites, the gentle, unaggressive Edmund Rubbra, one of the greatest English composers, and the provocative, argumentative, unforgettable Hans Keller, one of the clearest thinkers about music in our time.

Edmund has left behind him a rich and profound legacy that will never be exhausted. So far only a few have understood the scope of his achievement, but in time it will be unmistakable. Art is the study of relationships - between things, between feelings, between human creatures – the myriad experiences of which we are capable, concentrated into sensed form. Edmund's music is a distinguished and necessary contribution to this study, and so of essential value to all who wish to enhance human consciousness. Anyone neglecting it must be the loser. As a friend he was sympathetic, humorous, unassertive, and the neglect he suffered in later years did not embitter him. He had a serene sense that what he had done was as good as he could make it; he somehow knew that it would (in Beethoven's word) 'wash'. It was a considerable output, works of all kinds except opera, with a strong current of vocal music, for which he had a fine genius, reflected even in his instrumental work. Indeed, his symphonies have sometimes been called madrigals for orchestra, but we must be careful not to be misled by such easy words; deep within these genuinely symphonic works is powerful, steady impulse propelling subtle and resourceful development, in which the very nature of the matter itself is explored and transformed as it grows. Such an accomplishment is not possible without the human stuff of a man in it. In Rubbra's work the intellectual achievement is in the mastery of musical manipulation for the purpose of human expression. I miss him as a living, breathing friend - yet he is still with us in every note that he wrote, his nature, his very mind and heart. So he has not 'gone'."

On May 6th 1973, Rubbra wrote to Simpson as follows: "My dear Bob, No.5 is <u>magnificent</u>. I wish I had written it myself. It just shows what life there is in the old dog yet! (By 'old dog' I don't mean <u>you</u> but tonality!)

I may be in Yalding on Wednesday this week, and if so I will try to see you for a few minutes about the Trio recording on May 14.

All the best,

As ever,

Edmund"

Another letter of appreciation dates from 19th May 1979:

"Dear Bob,

I have now been able to hear Quartets 4,5 and 6, and together I find them an astonishing achievement & surely a landmark in 20th. century quartets. They all have an extraordinary intellectual energy (almost demonic!), but the point is it never gets out of hand & one is always conscious of a clear-sighted goal. Congratulations, & many thanks for your kindness in letting me have the cassettes, what performances, too! quite phenomenal. Angela must be proud of the dedication on No. 5: I'm sure she deserves it. Tell her I'll try to keep up with the changes in recording times of my quartets! – I want to hear the Coull do No.1 & I hope to come to the recording of that.

All the best

As ever

Edmund

P.S. I want to revise fairly drastically my Violin Concerto (commissioned by the B.B.C. about 20 years ago) for (perhaps) performance in the year of my 80th. birthday (1981). Any suggestions? But obviously no hurry."

RONALD STEVENSON (Born 1928)

British composer, particularly noted for his two Piano Concertos, Violin Concerto and the mammoth (eighty minutes) Passacaglia on DSCH, for solo piano.

Stevenson wrote this perceptive tribute for the memorial 'Tonic':

"Robert Simpson's sense of rhythm is organic, not motoric.

Rhythm for him is not an infantile drumming, but the proportion of paragraphs of large harmonic thinking. This he shares with Sibelius. Simpson's melody is not ingratiating. He is no miniature lyricist; this is why he is a true symphonist. But he has the ability to write a simple tune, and said 'When I write a tune, I bloody well mean it' – a gutsy conviction lacking in most contemporary composers. His harmonic vocabulary includes the most prosaic chords, sometimes in unrelated and unexpected progressions; like a plain man uttering his own philosophy in common parlance. His harmony also contains uncompromising dissonance of a stark, rather than sumptuous nature.

He worked at counterpoint at a time when fewer and fewer composers were doing so (to music's detriment, for polyphony has been till now the continuing language of great music). It is his contrapuntal prowess that gives his music its symphonic current. His orchestration is that of a constructor, not that of a colourist. His brass writing is written 'from the inside', as he was formerly a trumpeter. Before that, as a boy, he participated in Salvation Army band music; a first bond between himself and the boy Carl Nielsen, who played bugle and trombone in the Odense military band in Denmark.

Simpson never conceived of his music as 'programmatic', though he did compose with analogies in mind: often analogies drawn from biological or astronomic processes (he was a keen amateur astronomer). The intonations of his music are certainly Nordic. Anyone who knows the common language of very different Scandinavian composers will recognise their kinship to the sound of Simpson's music.

His maternal Dutch and paternal Scottish background converged in his solidity of character and independence of spirit. If I were to characterise Simpson's work in one epithet it would be 'integrity'. In a fragmented age, those who still value the humanistic tradition will prize this quality and the music which expresses it. Our knowledge of the nature of genius is limited, but I am convinced that one of its essentials is energy. Simpson had this (one of his works for brass band is entitled 'Energy'.) The energy basic to his industriousness plus the craftsmanship needed to embody them in musical forms, his aggressive anti-pessimism – all these things indicate his genius. He was congenitally incapable of experiencing or transmitting boredom. Whereas the argument of the earlier works concerns polarities of tonality, the later works explore tensions of pitch intervals. His concern with proportion in sonic structures is paramount; latterly he was concerned with the "minute particulars" which William Blake believed to be the hallmark of genius.

Simpson's music will live and its significance will be increasingly perceived, if only mankind does not destroy itself.

If the graph of modern history, from its trough of despond, can take an upward turn, his music will come into its own."

Following Simpson's TV talk on Beethoven's Third Rasumovsky Quartet, Stevenson wrote to him on 2nd March 1974:

"Dear Bob,

Happy birthday!

I was so impressed by the aptness and power of your quotation from Conrad in your Beethoven film that I thought the enclosed book on him may be acceptable as a birthday present. I haven't inscribed it, because you might already have it. In that case, you could give it to a friend – perhaps Angela (who is so like her name).

It occurs to me, Bob, that you might find in Conrad a text for your commissioned choral work. Just a thought.

I want to thank you from my heart for the encouragement you have given me over the past year (a period of re-assessment for me). We all need, <u>need</u> encouragement.

My wish is that this year, and many more, will yield more works from your pen. May I say simply and straightforwardly – without embarrassing you – that, while there is a Bob Simpson, the surrounding penumbra of puerility is blotted out for me.

In fond friendship and warm greetings to Squibs,

Ronald."

Another present, this time from Simpson to Stevenson, provoked a further letter on 13th April the same year, which illustrates Ronald Stevenson's wide-ranging erudition:

"Dear Bob, Your letter to me is dated 5th March: I reply after more than a month's <u>ritardando</u>. As the new classicist you are (better Busonian than I, in this respect) I know you are no friend of the <u>molto rallentando</u>; but as <u>my</u> friend, I'm sure you'll understand that such things are in my nature as a neo-romantic! And there's no harm done.

What a beautiful gift, this volume of Dutch art! The order, light, perspective and tranquillity of these pictures are indeed a palliative to perturbation. In this last month I've turned to these pages with need and closed them with the need satisfied. And I've thanked you many times in my thoughts, Bob.

During the last month, my brother has suffered a second stroke. For the present, he seems to be holding his own.

I've been glad of work at this time. Just finished the Busoni TV documentary. It went splendidly. Another indebtedness of mine to you (in a Leporellian list) is your introducing me to Barrie.

He's one of the best.

To return to Vermeer: his <u>sanity</u> reminds me of his elder compatriot, Sweelinck, whose deployment of chromaticism (in his <u>Fantasia cromatica</u>) has something of the serenity without etiolation (rare!) that I find in the chromatic palette of the Master of Delft. <u>Ganz</u> unlike that species of music mentioned in a note of Voltaire to his "La Pucelle" (1762):

"Le chromatique procede par plusiers semi-tons consecutif, ce qui produit un Musique effeminee, tres convenable a l'amour." (!)

To switch key (a la Richard Strauss): I'm practising your Haydn Variations with relish. I hear Nielsen's bassoons in Var.1; an unique gargoylesque grotesquerie in Var.111; IV is a pure joy to play, like a quaff of spring water – much of your two-part writing has this power to refresh; V is like

Busoni – or the end of my Passacaglia; VI – I play the "Lombard" (or Scots snap) rhythm <u>con affetto</u>; lovely how the next two variations flow on from it; 1X at first seems perfunctory but, on further acquaintance, reveals a Beethovenian gesture; X is my favourite – masterly! – I always want to encore it before going on; XI and XII I enjoy HUGELY; but – but – but the finale is a hard nut to crack. I shall crack it, though!

Will you please send me a brief programme-note on the work, for my Wigmore? Maximum: 100 words.

It would be wonderful if the dedicatee, Harold Truscott, could be there on 5th May. I've never met him but admired him <u>lontanamente</u>, in his talks and articles and Schubert Sonata completion.

I'd like to broadcast this recital, Bob, but feel a bit embarrassed about putting it to you, because it includes a work of yours.

Warm greetings to you and Squibs.

Your firm friend,

Ronald"

A later letter to Dick Edwards (13th March 1999) follows:

"Dear Dick Edwards,

Delighted to have your letter of 12.4.99, and the memorial booklet on dear Bob Simpson.

He was one of my most esteemed colleagues, and a dear friend. You will be interested to know that his letters to me are now lodged in the National Library of Scotland in Edinburgh, where they are building an archive of my MSS and papers/letters/photos of a lifetime.

Yes, you may well find the R. Stevenson Society interesting, with your long association with the first R.S. Society. I have had nothing to do with its formation, but it seems to be doing well, printing and publishing my music and issuing newsletters. Maybe you heard about it on the Internet?

All for now. Always <u>many</u> letters to write! Good to be in touch again.

Always <u>delighted</u> to hear of the Society's activities. Thanks for keeping in touch.

Warm regards,

Ronald Stevenson."

MATTHEW TAYLOR (Born 1964)

English composer and conductor, dedicatee of Simpson's Eleventh Symphony which he recorded along with the Nielsen Variations. His Adagio – Tribute to R.S. was played at the memorial concert, and two discs of his own music have been released. Matthew Taylor's first letter to Simpson is dated 13/11/82, following the Eighth Symphony's premiere. After Taylor's performance of the 7th Symphony, which much moved the composer, he sent him a tape of the concert. Here is Simpson's response (17th May 1988):

"Dear Matthew,

Many thanks indeed for the tape – you may not believe me, but listening to it has proved a kind of revelation to me. I know I wrote the piece, but I didn't suspect the depths of it until I heard this. You got something out of it that nobody has ever got out of any of my symphonies – an instinctive discovery of the essence of the music such as I haven't experienced before from an orchestral performance. The orchestra all relatively inexperienced youngsters, limited rehearsal – everything should have militated against this result. At the concert I was aware that it was going well, but on such an occasion (as you'll know yourself, as a composer) you tend to be anticipating problems to the extent that you fail to get fully caught up, inside. The tape suddenly made me realise what an astonishing and true interpretation it was, how finely it caught the dark thoughts, the reaching out in the slow movements for unattainably good, quiet things in a bad world, and the mysterious (and sometimes not so mysterious!) menaces that surround us all. All this – came through a performance less than technically perfect, recorded sometimes with very bad distortion (was this on the original tape or did it happen in the copying?). Amazing. It wasn't just me – Angela felt the same, and we felt it also in the Mendelssohn, which had so many lovely imaginative touches such as only a true artist could achieve. You have a rare gift, and I can't explain to you how deeply moved I am. I wish you could record ALL my symphonies!

Is there any possibility of a better tape? This one may have something wrong with it; in places the sound comes and goes in a peculiar gusty way, with intermittent distortion, as if the tape itself were faulty and not recording properly. If the original is like that, of course, there's nothing to be done about it. If not, you could try sending it to me, so that I can make you as many good copies as you like on my equipment. It would then be so much easier to play it to other people. But even with the defects, this is an interpretation I'll treasure and use as an artistic criterion, even in the face of the excellent new Hyperion recording with its magnificent sound. I don't think any of it's too slow - the slight deliberation enhances the atmosphere, the sense of searching amid surrounding menace, even in the allegros. I wrote this symphony for myself, more than the others, it having been intended at first for a recording rather than for public performance - so it's somehow more personal than the others, and that's something your performance revealed in a way that hasn't happened up to now. If only you could have stepped in and done No.9 at Southampton instead of me!!! So – congratulations is a stupid, feeble word! Love from us both, as ever,

Bob"

Matthew Taylor's own tribute, from the memorial 'Tonic' follows: "With the death of Robert Simpson on 21 November 1997, Britain has lost one of its leading composers and most forceful personalities. Central to his output are the cycle of eleven symphonies and fifteen string quartets whose mastery of organic growth and grandeur of design are easily worthy of comparison with Shostakovich. Simpson was blessed with the rare ability to redefine symphonic thinking from a completely modern perspective, proving that the form is just as durable, vital and crucial to our culture as it was in the era of Haydn or Beethoven. His piano music reveals a craggy, uncompromisingly individual keyboard style stemming ultimately from the great contrapuntalists: Bach, Bach-Busoni even, the Beethoven of the Hammerklavier, later Nielsen and Reger. The works for brass band comprise such an impressive corpus that Simpson easily surpasses all his contemporaries in this field. His three concerti, for piano (1966), flute (1989) and cello (1991) reveal a vivid identification with the human qualities of the instruments concerned, combined with an advanced degree of structural innovation.

Simpson's finest works have a timeless quality and monumental stature placing him in a unique, unchallenged position in terms of late 20th century music. The Ninth Symphony, for instance, radically reassesses the concept of modern symphonism. It is cast in one continuous movement, lasting nearly 50 minutes, and contains one basic pulse which remains consistent throughout. Within this vast span, Simpson demonstrates the colossal power and versatility of his mature language, opening with an austere Brucknerian nobility in the first movement, through to a central climactic scherzo of titanic energy, to a final set of variations of epic dimensions. The calm coda which constitutes the last four minutes of the symphony achieves an ethereal beauty surpassed only, perhaps, by the closing bars of Sibelius' Sixth Symphony. When listening to a work as impressive as Simpson's Ninth, the tired theory that "the symphony is dead" seems an utter absurdity. Equally absurd is the view (less frequently encountered now) that Simpson was a 'conservative tonalist'. Simpson's natural mastery of his particularly individual moulding of tonality in the earlier works showed that it really had the power to be as passionate, communicative and compelling as in the works of Beethoven, Brahms or Bruckner. It was certainly no 'easy' option. Anyone who knew Bob was quick to realise that there was nothing remotely 'conservative' about him. In 1986 he and his wife Angela moved to the South West coast of Ireland, thereby escaping the moral, spiritual and cultural decline all too evident during the Thatcher era.

Robert Simpson was a profoundly original thinker and a vigorous opponent of 'received opinion', especially in relation to postwar music. "Scepticism is important," he once told me "it should be taught in schools." Scepticism, not cynicism. His music never indulged in pseudo-intellectual imagery, quirky gimmicks or colouristic doodling; rather he infused a fierce vitality into the traditional and well-loved forms such as the string quartet, the concerto and the symphony. He was dismissive of temporary fashion. Fearless integrity and honesty infused everything he did."

HAROLD TRUSCOTT (1914-1989)

English composer, born Seven Kings, Ilford, Essex, pianist and writer on music, co-founder of the Experimental Concert Society, dedicatee of the Variations and Finale on a Theme of Haydn (1948), and contributor of chapters on Haydn, Schubert, Mahler, Sibelius, Franz Schmidt, Havergal Brian, and Rubbra and Tippett to the symposium 'The Symphony'. Robert Simpson' tribute to his old friend follows:

"Harold Truscott may justly be praised for his fortitude in continuing to compose for a lifetime regardless of whether or no the opinionists were interested in what he was doing. In this he has a natural affinity with Havergal Brian, of whose music he has a deep knowledge, and which he introduced to me many years ago. But even more justly the nature of his work itself deserves admiration, its determined concentration, its strength of form, the originality with which it extends the possibilities of traditional tonality, and its essential humanity. The spine of his life's work is his fine series of piano sonatas; these display not only a master's intimate familiarity with the instrument (which he has always played well, and on which he is one of the most astonishing sight-readers I have ever encountered) but a rare range of feeling and idea. Their time has still to come, and the fact that they are being gradually recorded will hasten an inevitable process that should long have been completed.

It is as a composer that he should most be saluted, though his vast knowledge of music, especially its great neglected areas, also makes his a distinguished presence in the musical world, for which many of us have good cause to be grateful. He has put us in touch with many works which otherwise we might not have found, so enriching our experience. The forty-odd years I have known Harold Truscott would have been far the poorer without the musical illuminations I have had from him." (August 1989)

Guy Rickards, who in 1993 advised Simpson that he was researching Truscott's music, secured the composer's agreement that there should be recordings, adding that he had a "very high regard for him both as writer and composer." Five discs of Truscott's music have since been released.

While he had many friends among his colleagues at the BBC, the senior men were, especially in his later years of service, another matter. Not so much William Glock ("We had our disagreements, but there was a certain mutual respect) but with his successors, Robert Ponsonby ("We used to call him the Ponce") and John Drummond ("that conceited ass" – letter to Colin Seamarks, 13/9/94). As public-school, Oxbridge men they would no doubt have been instinctively antipathetic to the grammar-school boy of humble origins, and largely responsible for what he saw as a continuing decline in BBC standards in the scramble for audience ratings. A sparky correspondence began with a letter from Simpson dated 12th September 1989:

Dear Mr Drummond, When I was in the BBC we took great care to ensure that an important first broadcast got a good placing in the evening. I understand that my 12th quartet has been placed early on a weekday afternoon, and perhaps I may not be the only person to whom such a placing of the first broadcast of a major work seems inadequate, even a little derisive. Here in the west of Ireland we can't hear Radio 3, so the matter is no problem so far as I'm concerned. But I would be interested in your comments.

Yours sincerely,"

Drummond replied on 8th November: "The only comment I would make on your letter is that the audience on Radio 3 remains constantly higher during the day than in the evening. The idea of the prestige attached particularly to an evening transmission is I suspect the legacy of the days when the Third Programme was broadcast only in the evenings. Today we achieve our highest audiences in the early mornings and around the lunch hour. We are making big efforts to carry that audience through into the afternoons. Placing your new quartet early on a week day was part of that intention."

Simpson riposted, on 14th November: "Head-counting is hardly the point. Most of the people who have the radio on in the morning are doing something else – housework, cooking, car driving, etc. In the afternoon, mothers are often fetching their children from school, and many older folk tend to take a rest, which is why the 'listening' figures fall off then. Why are public concerts normally given in the evenings? It is because most people are working during the day. Your statistical argument could be used in favour of recording the Proms for deferred relay in the mornings.

It is the quality of listening that matters. I would rather have a work of mine better attended to by fewer people than half heard by a multitude. Those who listen in the evenings are usually prepared to concentrate on nothing else; during the day few are able to use more than half an ear. It is, I'm afraid, a bad habit of even many intelligent people to have Radio 3 on all day, regardless of what's on, and these 'listeners' swell the figures. This has always been a strong argument against using the finest music as background, or part of a musical production belt. Because it was not exposed to this trap, the Third Programme was the envy of the whole world, and our attitude in running it was that the first-rate should be made available when even a small number of people could, or would, concentrate on it. Incomprehension branded this as elitism, but we believed that no country without such a service could call itself civilised. Your argument for numbers resembles a politician's."

Evidently stung into taking a defensive stance, Drummond replied on 29th January:

"I do not think I actually need anyone to point out the difference to me between listening and hearing. We do not know each other and you impute to me things that if you <u>did</u> know me you might re-consider.

There is a central fact which cannot in the current circumstances be ignored, even if you were able to ignore it twenty years ago. Radio 3 currently costs over £40 million a year. The BBC's income is declining, and everybody else wants to get their hands on my budget. It is absolutely essential that people listen to Radio 3. I mean listen, not just hear. It is no longer possible to ignore the presence or absence of an audience, and in our scheduling and presentation, and in the publicising of the network, we care about that. I believe rightly, as I do not know the virtue of the unheard programme, and my own philosophy has always been that, if I care about something, I want to make it available to as many people as possible. It is up to them to decide whether they listen to it or just hear it."

In a further letter dated 1st February 1990, Simpson observed: "From 6 to 12 only, broadcasting a serious network would cost very much less and would be a more distinguished contribution to the quality of life of those who would value it. If there aren't enough of these to 'justify' the expenditure, so much the worst for our throwaway so-called civilisation."

In time, both men acknowledged that they were never going to agree on the matter, and the correspondence ended. The forthcoming Prom performance of the Fifth Symphony provoked a further spat. Simpson (1st February):

"To enhance the humour of the situation, the publisher of No. 5 rang me to say that he had had a call from the BBC to ask if the Prom performance of it in August was to be the premiere! The BBC has broadcast this work four or five times I think, a shameful enough record in 18 years but perhaps not quite negligible." Drummond retorted furiously (6th March):

"I note with interest that you think four or five broadcasts of your Fifth Symphony is shameful. A lot of other composers would be grateful for as much.

Simpson's coup de grace (12th March):

"When I was at the BBC we never expected gratitude from performers or composers – we were grateful to them for being the reason for our employment."

Well said.

AFTERWORD

My own views on the value of Simpson's music are, I hope, clear enough; here is a selection of assessments by writers on music of various tastes:

Nicholas Williams, Sunday Times, 5th June 1994:

"...he has unrivalled command of musical movement (few living composers can write genuinely fast music as convincingly as Simpson) and an exceptional understanding of how music works. He remains the most challenging figure to emerge from the generation between Tippett and Britten and the Manchester school of Goehr, Birtwistle and Maxwell Davies."

Anthony Payne, Independent, 20th December 1996:

"How will future generations compare and contrast Simpson, Tippett, and their younger contemporaries? There may be a few surprises."

"It is quite simply easier now to see that Simpson's tumultuous Fourth Symphony is a great work, as indeed is his String Quartet No. 7."

Bayan Northcott, Independent, 2nd March 1991:

"There is nothing quite like the Simpsonian meditation, or the sound of Simpson in full cry, to be found anywhere else in music."

Of Robert Simpson's 'stature' I shall say little here; my own high regard is evident, and 'league tables' are always invidious, coming down as they do to personal taste. As I have already said, his music has no specifically 'English' character, which makes any comparison with Vaughan Williams or Rubbra largely pointless – the often gentle, reflective character of their music is a world away from Simpson's dynamism, and one should appreciate and love the differences. Shostakovich produced comparable numbers of symphonies and quartets but, here again, the Russian's quasi-official position inevitably rendered his output very uneven, while Simpson's remained consistent. Perhaps his nearest kindred spirit is the Dane, Vagn Holmboe, also grievously neglected, and it is to be hoped that in time both masters will emerge as the leading exponents of modern classicism in the latter twentieth century.

To tackle a question which has been implicit throughout this book – why is music of such power and intellectual scope, admired by so many distinguished musicians, not more widely played? I touched during my introduction on the 'modernist' problem, the almost automatic suspicion of anything new or unfamiliar. Commercial concert promoters are thus understandably chary of programming such music for fear of a half-empty hall. Simpson discusses this problem himself in "The Composer and his

Audience", the last chapter of "The Proms and Natural Justice", which I have reprinted as an appendix, in greater depth and with the inside knowledge which only the composer could bring to the subject.

This leaves us with the BBC as the only national state-subsidised promoters of both live and broadcast concerts and, one would have thought, the natural home of the unfamiliar and neglected, not having to worry about box-office takings. And yet the BBC, in common with all public services, has become seriously infected by inappropriate commercial considerations, the befuddled notion that public service broadcasting is, and should be, a profit-making activity, with 'customers' rather than listeners. We see this all too clearly in the Proms programmes, which have become depressingly mainstream for the last ten years or so. The list of composers who were either unplayed or received less than an hour's time during Glock's fourteen-year tenure could be repeated almost verbatim today, and would still apply. It would seem that the spirit of Glock survives as much in the choice of repertoire as in the Controller's unlimited tenure! On the few occasions when a rarity is played, the audience response is usually enthusiastic – I recall memorable performances of Busoni's Piano Concerto, Reger's Hiller Variations, and Franz Schmidt's Fourth Symphony and his oratorio 'The Book with Seven Seals', all well received but not followed through.

Let us examine the problem in relation to British music. Only two English composers have all their major works regularly performed – Elgar (rather overplayed, in my opinion: his small output has had to be augmented by 'completions' of works he left unfinished) and Walton, although with the latter one has to qualify with the word early, correct though this evaluation of his post-war work may be. Vaughan Williams seems at last to have re-established himself in the repertory after a forty-year period of neglect, at least as far as the symphonies are concerned. It may be worth noting that Tony Palmer's excellent film about the composer, 'O Thou Transcendent', was rejected by BBC television and eventually shown by Channel Five, which tells you quite a lot.

In my original draft I opined that Gustav Holst had been unfairly typecast as a one-work composer (The Planets, needless to say), but I have to modify this stricture because the 2009 Proms series also included the Choral Symphony and Hymns from the Rig Veda. There is still much more to explore, though.

Parry, also long misrepresented only as the writer of Jerusalem, was better served in the 2010 Proms, with the Fifth Symphony, Elegy for Brahms and the Symphonic Variations all being performed.

Havergal Brian may finally be coming into his own – see "I'm not going to die – I've just bought a new pair of trousers!" Rubbra's Fourth symphony was played on the occasion of his centenary (2001), but very little else before or since. Moeran, Finzi, Bax and Delius are also rarely heard. Both Tippett and Britten's stars seemed to have faded rather, particularly the former (perhaps an understandable reaction after the over-praising of his, to my mind, inferior later music).

Even established masters have not been immune from partial representation. How often does one hear Bruckner's first two symphonies (four, if you count the Study symphony and No. 0!), or Dvořák's four earlier essays, or any of Haydn's middle-period masterpieces, roughly speaking from number fifty to number eighty?

The duplication of repertoire – one can hear much the same works at the Barbican or Cadogan Halls (and soon, perhaps, at the Festival Hall too) as one can at the Albert, may well be a factor in declining classical audiences. People simply do not wish to hear the same works time after time, however well performed. This lack of adventurousness is in striking contrast to many of the smaller CD companies, who seem willing to record just about anything, however obscure – not that I am suggesting that all such material is worth the exhumation! Trusting live audiences to use their ears rather than their prejudices might well produce some surprising results, as witness the reaction of two initially unsympathetic concert-goers to Simpson's Ninth (qv).

It could be said, unkindly but not unfairly, that the British are not a particularly musically-minded, or even culturally-minded group of peoples. George Orwell said that the word 'poetry' would disperse an English crowd quicker than a fire-hose, and I have witnessed numerous times a similar cringing revulsion towards any kind of classical music. The Celtic fringes have, at any rate, held on to their folk-music tradition, while English folk music was on its last legs when Vaughan Williams and Cecil Sharp were collecting songs in the early 1900s. Popular music-making survived in the form of brass bands and choral societies, but both were dealt a serious blow by the Great War and the depression of the 1930s, while the programme of pit closures in the last two decades of the 20th century put paid to most of the colliery bands, excepting those lucky enough to get commercial sponsorship.

Along with the virtually untrammelled sway of the various forms of pop music (mostly moribund, when not downright anti-musical) has come the curious national obsession with sport – curious in the sense that a high percentage of the population are clinically obese, and quite incapable of playing these games themselves. This is not a new phenomenon; I cannot resist quoting Orwell again: "At the international level sport is frankly mimic warfare. But the significant thing is not the behaviour of the players but the attitude of the spectators: and, behind the spectators, of the nations who work themselves into furies over these absurd contests, and seriously believe – at any rate for short periods – that running, jumping and kicking a ball are tests of national virtue." (written 1945)

So far from discouraging this unhealthy obsession, and cultural philistinism, successive governments have done their best to encourage it. Harold Wilson was the first prime minister to invite pop musicians and TV soap stars as well as sporting heroes, to 10 Downing Street. Margaret Thatcher was determinedly middle – if not low-brow, in her tastes, while Tony Blair was even more shamelessly populist than Wilson, grinning with inane approval over the activities of various unsavoury Britpop performers and Young British Artists, not because they produced anything worthwhile, but because they made money! Cool Britannia, indeed.

The only prime minister within living memory who had a liking for classical music was Edward Heath, and since the Grocer's most noticeable characteristic was his total inability to communicate with other people, it seems unlikely that many would have been tempted towards classical concerts by Heath's example. Neither of the present leaders of the Labour or Conservative parties inspires the slightest hope of a change for the better, nor have the royal family been exemplars in this respect; I suspect that the last monarch to take a serious interest in the arts was Victoria, and this was probably Albert's doing. Meanwhile, there appear to be billions of pounds available to pour into the refurbishment of Wembley Stadium, or the building of the Olympic Games venue, while provincial orchestras and museums have their subsidies cut and face closure, when they could be saved for a tiny fraction of the cost.

Where does this leave us? It must be accepted that the fine arts are, and probably always will be, a minority interest. They cannot thrive without public subsidy, any more than can public transport. Their worth should either be publicly recognised and paid for, or the responsible authorities should be honest, admit their total indifference, and let them go to the wall. What we have at the moment is an unholy compromise which satisfies nobody. Until we have a government which accepts that proper support for the arts is an essential ingredient of any civilised society, and a clear indicator of the country's spiritual health, it seems likely that the neglect of Robert Simpson's, and of much other worthwhile music, seems set to continue.

SIMPSON ANTAGONISTES

My rather gloomy prognosis at the end of the last chapter should not be the final word; as John Amis has said, Simpson was the master of the gently effective put-down, and I have reprinted a selection of his bon mots under the title with which they originally appeared in 'Tonic'. I should note that the recipe for Barbequed Critic was mainly Angela Simpson's work, with some additions by Bob; while she was happy for the composer to have the credit, I feel that it should go to her.

Its four movements rise in tonality by successive fifths; the themes themselves make clear use of fifths, mostly rising; and much of the harmony evolves from this common but inexhaustible interval. But it doesn't matter if you can't tell a fifth from a rissole.

(Introducing Eighth String Quartet at Birthday Celebration, 25/4/1981.)

Most of his life he was consciously striving to be in front, and his very last period shows him striving not to be behind. (On Stravinsky, from talk on late Beethoven, Radio 3, 8/3/1979)

Evidently he has his own ideas about the value of perceptive criticism; these prevent him from blundering into it himself. ('Composer and Critic', The Musical Times, June 1955).

The European Broadcasting Union should now attend to the possibility of simultaneously improvised works by deaf mutes, afflicted of course from birth to ensure that the purity of their impulses should not be corrupted by the slightest experience of music.

('Why Compose?' Twenty British Composers, Chester, 1975)

I've sometimes been tempted to suggest to the BBC a series called the 'Ignorant Ear', with specially commissioned works from the most qualified practitioners. (Radio 3, 30/10/1977)

Nielsen's First Symphony, composed in 1892 (seven years before that of Sibelius) shows that, like all genuinely original minds, he flouts tradition only by reacting naturally to all the fundamental facts on which it is based. Tonality is a natural, inescapable phenomenon; his mastery of it saves him the embarrassment of trying petulantly to kick it to pieces. ('Carl Nielsen: A Great Symphonist', The Listener, 14/6/1951).

In any art, there must be neither understatement nor overstatement; only adequacy is tolerable. ('The Restraint of Berlioz', The Listener, 4/12/1952)

No one has ever written more individual or beautiful themes than Beethoven; where necessary he displays a power of self-denial that should not mislead anyone, and Stravinsky's claim that he lacked the gift of melody was surely a missile thrown from inside a glass house.

(Beethoven Symphonies, BBC, London 1976)

Beethoven was not the man to spend too long performing balancing tricks with a string trio; as soon as he had learned to enjoy handling a three-wheeler his interest in making more purposeful journeys took over, and for this four wheels were more comfortable than three, enabling the driver to concentrate on the road rather than sometimes wondering if he is going to overturn on sharp corners.

('The Chamber Music for Strings', in The Beethoven Companion, edited by Denis Arnold and Nigel Fortune, Faber, London, 1971)

Robert Simpson, on phone to Editor of Tonic (Martin Anderson): 'Now, what was it I was going to say to you?' MA: 'I don't know. "Bugger off"?'

RS: 'I don't think I've ever said that to you. (Long pause) But it's always ready!'

Webern has certainly had no influence on me at all, except the negative one of indicating to me in wonderfully precise terms exactly what I don't want to do.

('Against Lipsius', The Listener, 24/3/1971)

A composer must always create expectations and then defeat them with something better.

Missenden Abbey Lecture, March 1988

Your correspondent suggests that the Tate's pile of bricks might serve a good purpose in angering people into articulating their real feelings about proper art. By the same token we would be more conscious of the real value of public lavatories if more people used public transport for basic purposes.

(Letter to The Listener, 28/10/1977 – not printed)

Those responsible for degenerative processes are inevitably the last to recognise them.

(Letter to the Chairman of the BBC, 23/8/80)

Nielsen may well prove to be not on the sidelines (as some would have it) but on a clear by-pass that will get him past the confused tangle of industry that is at present causing the worst artistic traffic jam in history.

(Postscript on Nielsen, Radio 3, 1969)

You can easily baffle other people by first baffling yourself The professional opinionist will describe a specially alienated new work as being 'in an advanced idiom'. Surely you've heard that ringing phrase? But what the hell is an advanced idiom? Only an advanced idiot could tell you that.

(Any Advance? Radio 3, 1975)

Though there are Hanslicks still with us, they can no longer trouble him.

(The Essence of Bruckner, Gollancz, 1967)

Schoenberg did not ruin the art of music. There is no such thing in the abstract – there are only composers. His influence may have ruined some of these, but so did that of every strikingly powerful artistic personality. Those who were so ruined would in any case have been unable to do anything of great consequence.

Every artist's language is 'private' until it is understood by somebody else …Schoenberg's music happens to express (with great precision) a certain state of consciousness. Many hate it (as I do) but we must not assume that he has thereby ruined the possibility for someone else to express something else. Some states of mind are more comprehensive than others, and that is the criterion by which I would evaluate the relative achievements of artists of comparable talent. Most of the 'great' twentieth century artists (not only musicians) suffer, in one form or another, from the limitations imposed by the over-cultivation of personal distinguishing marks. This means, basically, that they are intimidated into produce defence mechanisms. By what? By certain very strong trends of thought and feeling that seem to them characteristic of their time; Schoenberg was himself too much a victim to have 'ruined' anything. We must try to evaluate talent by what statements it makes about life as well as by its own skills, and not get lost in wasteful discussions about raw materials – chromaticism, diatonicism, atonality, and the rest. These should be the private elements in the composer's thinking. He can use what means he likes, and should not like most of his contemporary colleagues, merely 'reflect' life; he should change it for the better if he can. There is no life in a mirror.

(Letter to The Listener, 23/11/67, answer to an attack on Schoenberg)

We must be very cautious about worshipping the gods that such an age as ours throws up.

The abrogation of the artist's authority is the snuffing out of his life. He becomes a symptom of a sickness, the smell of the corpse. I don't want to be either of these things, even if I end up as useful compost.

No-one born deaf could ever be a composer, though if it could happen, now is the time.

Scepticism's very important – it should be taught in schools. ('The ferociously anti-pessimist composer', Radio 3, 12/5/71, published in The Listener under the title 'Against Lipsius')

In No. 3 Sibelius has already slimmed away superfluous fat; here (in Symphony No. 4) the economy is so drastic as to create almost an impression of emaciation. Yet nothing could be less true; this music is not starved; nor does the notable tendency to elision result in any loss of substance. Sibelius does not, like some of his own contemporaries and plenty of present-day composers, imagine evisceration to be a proper cure for obesity. ('Sibelius, Nielsen and the Symphonic Problem' in Carl Nielsen – Symphonist, Kahn and Averill, 1979)

There is some excuse for the idea that the late romantic composer, bent on the colossal, extruded his vast and sometimes prolix masterpieces with protracted grunts and snorts; high aspirations could prove no more than ambitions, and if imagined inspiration brought quick results, they were apt to want substance. Mahler wrote his enormous Eighth Symphony in a very short time; its first part is solidly composed, but its second, from the first solo baritone entry, is thrown overboard into an ocean of shameless kitsch from which it is never rescued, least of all in the inflated ending, and it must be regarded as one of his weakest compositions.

('Afterthought: The Composer and the Audience' in The Proms and Natural Justice, Toccata Press, 1981)

…it is to be hoped that no one again asks the BBC Symphony Orchestra to play Le Sacre du Printemps and Bruckner's Seventh Symphony in one programme; the brass section is unlikely to forget this concert.

('The Planner' in ibid)

It's no use self-consciously avoiding this, eschewing that, abolishing this, excluding that.

Whereas in past periods the creative geniuses, the great exceptions, have by the subtlety and originality of their minds often set problems for their audiences, we are nowadays (if this is the criterion) all geniuses, crawling on our hands and knees, groping after four-leafed clovers, and banging our heads together.

Art is doing something imaginative, not imagining you have done something. (Composing, Third Programme, 22/11/59)

The human sense of tonality has many times been modified, but cannot be abolished. To attempt to abolish it is to cease to be comprehensive, to be narrowly exclusive. If I appreciate the kind of expression that Schoenberg achieved (I happen to dislike it, but that is irrelevant to my appreciation of its accomplishment), my sense of tonality, though it may be deliberately anaesthetised for the time being, is by no means abolished. Since all my musical faculties are not being engaged, I cannot feel that such music is comprehensive. It is certainly concentrated, but that alone will not make it 'symphonic'; if you lose a leg you have to concentrate in order to move about without it, but however hard you concentrate, you cannot escape the conclusion that it is better to have two legs. With these, you can forget problems of locomotion and concentrate on objects. With one leg you can hop about, but will find it difficult to invent new dance steps that have more than the temporary appeal of oddity.

(Introduction to The Symphony, Volume 2, Penguin, 1967)

In BBC auditions – about the fairest system I know – we don't even see the artist, so we don't even know what sex it is, unless its a singer and even then you can't always be sure. (Radio 3, 24/12/79)

Sir Neville's View

Sir – I would dearly like the opportunity to house-train a few music critics.

(Letter to The Guardian, 7/2/67)

After hearing an admiring comment on Pierre Boulez's faultless sense of pitch, Simpson is reported to have said "With ears like that, he should have been a piano-tuner."

BARBEQUED CRITIC

Note:

Critics only just qualify as cannibal fare. Like lobsters, they have a very tough shell, difficult to penetrate. Good heavy hammer (Mahler 6 type) required.

1 critic
Large pan boiling oil

Marinade:
1 bottle Nuit St. Gorge (sick) (Unwell Purges Night)
25 chopped o(pi)nions
Done t(hy)me and seizoning
Add emetic to taste

Method:
Catch critic; best time at concert interval, on way to telephone review of second half.
After thoroughly hammering (not painful as this species has few nerve-endings) lay critic on foolproof newspaper, preferably his own.
Roll up, tie firmly, plunge into boiling oil. If squelchy sounds resembling George Lloyd Webber come from saucepan, allow to boil dry.
Combine marinade ingredients, and marinade critic in this for at least two weeks to tenderize.
Cut critic into 12-note rows, hang on double bars, and then cook over hot barbeque.
Serve with cauliflower and nightshade polonaise and garnish with finely chopped o(pi)nions.

USES FOR OFFAL

GALL BLADDER; Can be used for Journalist Sauce.

HEART AND BRAIN; Rarely found.
SPHERICAL OBJECTS; An acquired taste. Give to cat.
LIVER; Potty de Foul Gas.
SPLEEN; Not palatable; over-used. Give to Caged Stockhausen.
LIGHTS; The critic cannot be de-lighted.
APPENDIX; Sub-edit and boil down.

Pencil drawing of Robert Simpson by the author, 1995. The composer's comment was characteristic:
"Who's that miserable-looking sod? I wish I could do this – get some of my own back!" To which I
could only reply that in depicting people I was harder on myself than anybody else.

AUTHOR'S NOTE

The Oxford Names Companion is characteristically, though infuriatingly, ambivalent as to the origins of both surnames. Simpson – English patronymic from the medieval given name Sim (short for Simon), or Ashkenazic Jewish deriving from Samson. Levick – three definitions. English nickname from Anglo-Norman French l'eveske, 'the Bishop', or English, from the middle English given name Lefeke, Old English Leofaca, a derivative of Leofa (dear, or beloved), or Jewish (Eastern Ashkenazic) from the Yiddish Leyvik, diminutive of the male given name Leyvi (Levi – 'Joining')

Any the wiser? No, nor I.

APPENDICES

1. SIMPSON FAMILY TREE
2. LEVICK FAMILY TREE
3. COMPOSING (1959)
4. INTRODUCTION TO THE SYMPHONY (HAYDN TO DVOŘÁK)
5. INTRODUCTION TO THE SYMPHONY (ELGAR TO THE PRESENT DAY)
6. ON CONDUCTING ONESELF IN PUBLIC (1968)
7. LATE BEETHOVEN (UNDATED)
8. AGAINST LIPSIUS (1971)
9. SYMPHONIES (1973)
10. WHY COMPOSE? (1975)
11. AFTERTHOUGHT – THE COMPOSER AND HIS AUDIENCE (1981)
12. OUR SHY MASTERS (1983)
13. ON COMPOSING CHAMBER MUSIC (1989)
14. LIST OF WORKS AND PUBLISHERS
15. DISCOGRAPHY
16. BIBLIOGRAPHY

Appendix 1 – Simpson Family Tree

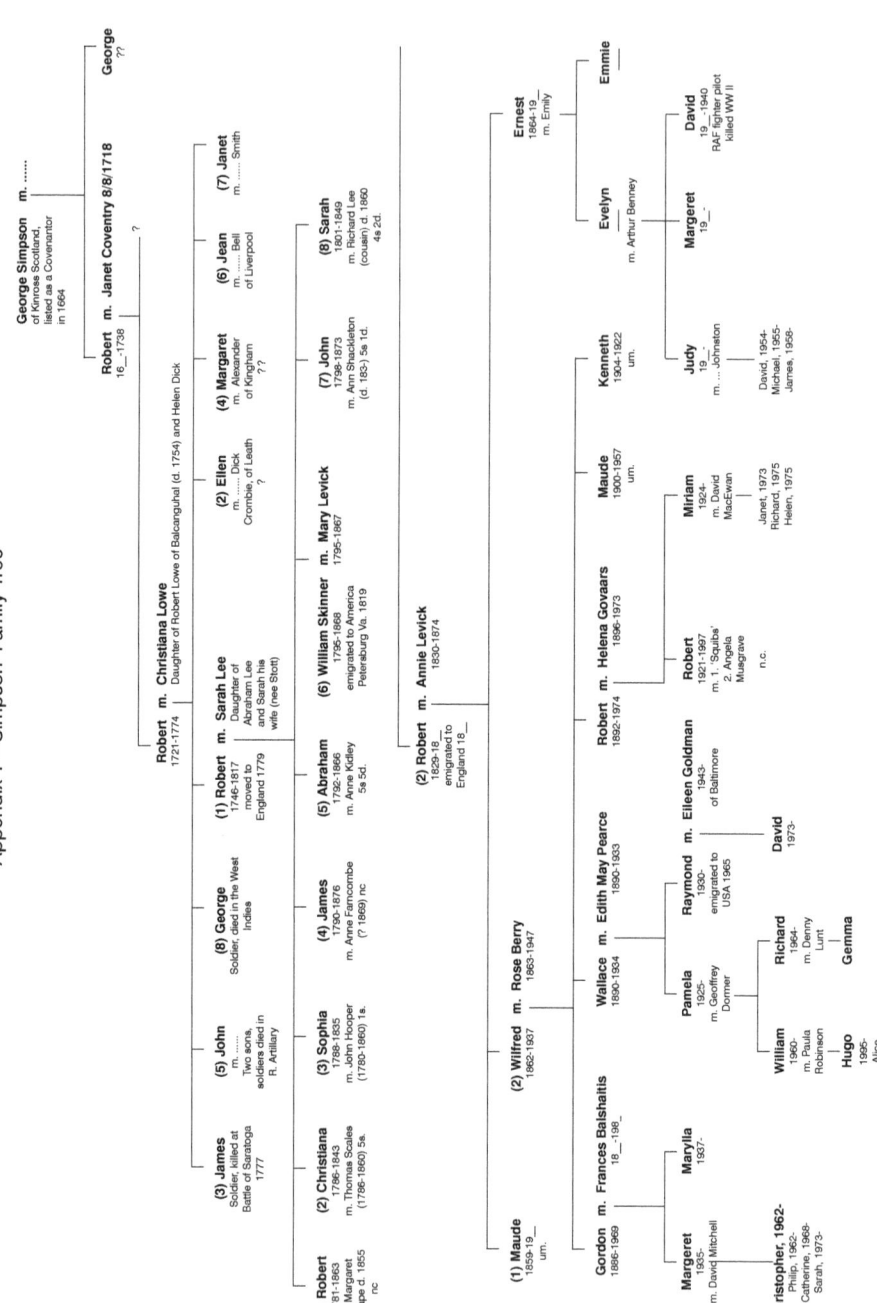

Appendix 1 – Simpson Family Tree

American Branch

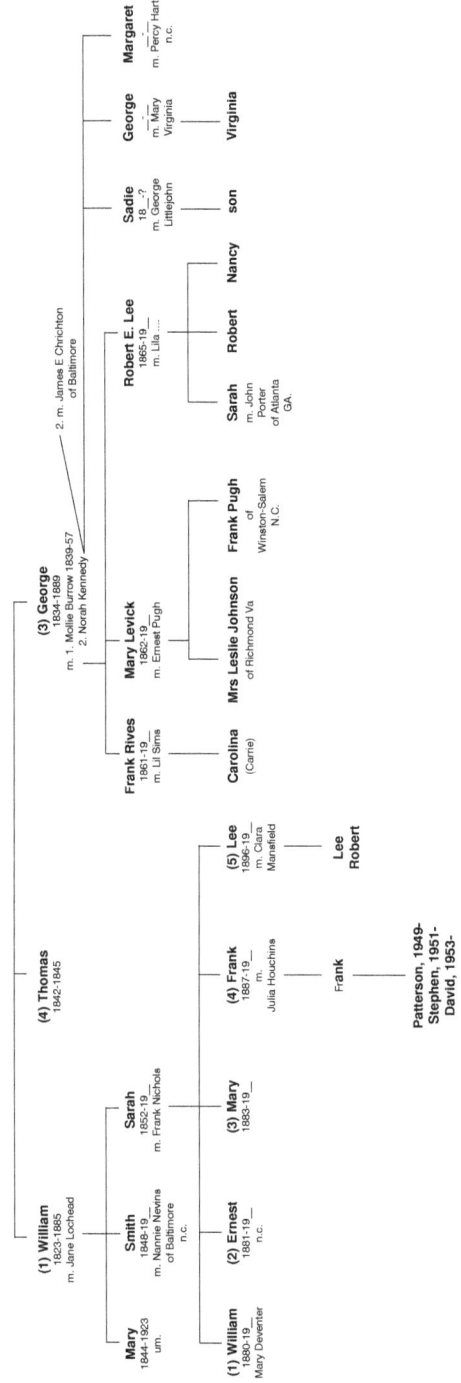

Appendix 2

Levick (From Notts)

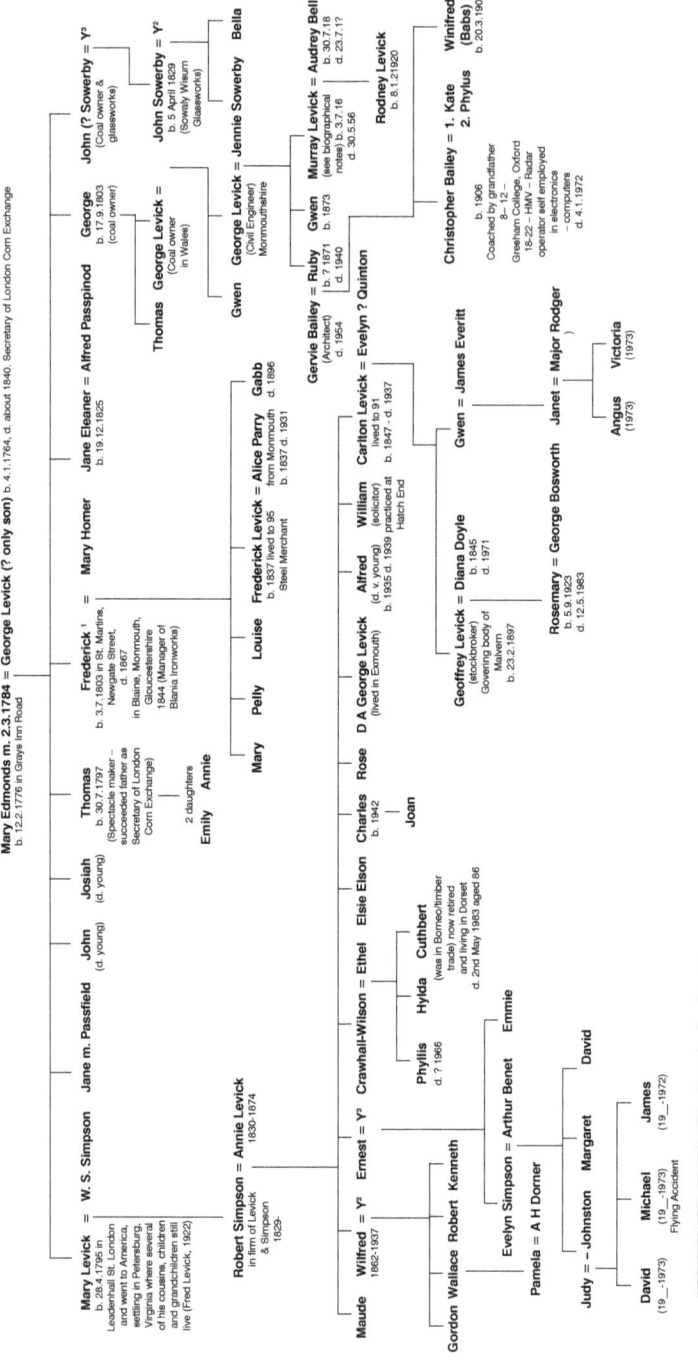

Page 318

APPENDIX 3

ROBERT SIMPSON

COMPOSING (1959)

They say it's lucky to find a four-leafed clover, but I've rarely heard of anybody finding one by actually looking for it. Your chances of coming across one are slightly improved if you happen to be an observant person, and you can become observant by training your own faculties. But however observant you may become, your hopes of finding a four-leafed clover are still pretty slim. It's an odd fact that many of the greatest discoveries have been virtually stumbled upon - but usually by people whose minds were in a condition to perceive them, who by training and inclination were looking in the right direction. However, the moment of revelation has seldom been coldly calculated – in art, never. But we can at least try to look in the right direction, and this is what I want to talk about.

First of all, let's get one thing straight. To vituperate against other intelligent people who don't share your views is no way of presenting a positive outlook – to say that certain kinds of music are 'impossible to listen to' is merely to expose your own weaknesses. Plenty of music is difficult to listen to, plenty of it far too easy, but none of it (however bad or apparently contemptible) is impossible. Something can be learnt by the most intelligent and musical among us from listening really hard, even to *Baa-baa black sheep*. So it seems to me that we are more likely to get somewhere by thinking in positive terms, rather than in those negative ones that seem to be causing so much argument at the moment. Composing is, after all, a form of positive creative action in which one doesn't have to run away from anything. So it's no use self-consciously avoiding this, eschewing that, abolishing this, excluding that. If humanity had never anything to say, we should all still be dumb – language would never have been invented. It follows that only the positive fact of having something urgent to say can produce genuinely vital expression, whatever form it takes. To many of you, this may seem a truism, but there are those to whom it is not, who would rather think it a kind of heresy. To them it is, to put it bluntly, an unfashionable point of view. Let's take a look at the present situation of the arts.

We're living in an age increasingly dominated by science. It's commonplace to remark that science is affecting almost every aspect of human thought, that it's caused a profound change in every single person it's touched, the simplest of labourers as much as the most complicated intellectual. At the same time, a ruthless commercialism is deliberately fostering public philistinism. The artist falls to a confused defensive position, and a great schism is created. What is especially significant is the bewildering speed at which these changes are happening. The unintelligent fellow scarcely notices this and settles down comfortably in front of his 'telly'. Intelligent and sensitive people, less content, less stable, tend to become either distraught and angry or so bedevilled by conformist sophistication that they can be easily betrayed into mistaking the wildest nonsense for serious fact. It wouldn't be difficult for a scientific specialist to gull an audience of intelligent laymen into the momentary acceptance of fantastic rubbish. In art, where matters of opinion are so much more treacherous, we are all in a sense laymen, and can, if we wish, gull each other to our hearts' content. One scientific miracle follows another, anything seems possible. Therefore anything is plausible, and a frequent reaction to the most uproariously obvious drivel is 'there might be something in it'. It's curiously revealing to notice that whereas in past periods the creative geniuses, the great exceptions, have, by the subtlety and originality of their minds, often set problems for their audiences, we are nowadays (if this is the criterion) all geniuses, crawling on our hands and knees, groping after four-leafed clovers and banging our heads together. What's more, some of us do it with our eyes shut and with thick gloves on The latest artistic sophistries would exclude the imagination (which is the eyes and sense of touch by which we *might* be looking for the clover), except as an afterthought – the haphazard is the thing – chuck the paint at the canvas, devise an arithmetical scheme for your composition, and then see what it looks and sounds like. To my mind, the one great difference between art and anti-art is whether the imagination is exercised before or after the act. Turning specifically to music, it is just as haphazard to devise an arithmetical scheme before considering the sounds it will produce as it is to sling half-a-dozen cans of paint at a canvas or to ride over a mess of pottage on a bike. If you want to do this, fair enough; but even if you solemnly contemplate the result and let it wreak its utmost on your imagination, you mustn't call it *art*. Art is doing something imaginative, not passively imagining you have done something.

This brings me to another point – that really great art will be something beyond its immediate intention. You take one of the greatest symphonies or quartets by Haydn – what were his intentions in writing them? Presumably to satisfy himself in the first place and satisfy his audience – which he knew – and he was very keen on being a good workman you know. What comes of it, the mind behind it is so remarkable, so fine that we get a sense of something quite beyond that when we listen to it, just as we do if we listen to *Tristan* we get a feeling that this is something beyond, sex because it is so magnificently composed, and on the other hand you can get a composer whose intentions are so sublime, who wants to knock you flat with some gigantic section and who simply fails because he isn't a good enough composer. He may imagine it's inside him, or he may feel it very intensely, but he may still not have the capacity to express it.

Deryck, you talk about awe and mystery, and you use the word religious. I don't think that the two things are necessarily the same. I feel awe and mystery, I'm often awestruck and overcome with this sense, but I don't interpret it in a religious sense. If I look at a mountain I'm awestruck, if I look at any great manifestation of nature, the stars, I contemplate everything, I'm awestruck. I think it's fantastic, it's mysterious, it's colossal, and when I hear some of Bruckner's music, when I hear Beethoven's music and Bach's music I get the same feeling. Now obviously this has not necessarily anything to do with the composer's particular beliefs – it's to do with something in the nature of his music itself. If I look at a mountain it strikes awe into me; now a mountain has no feelings, a mountain is just something, and it has this effect on me, it evokes in me the feeling. Now a great work of Bruckner, a great work of Beethoven's is in a similar sense a manifestation of nature and it affects me in this way, and so I don't necessarily need to say that it speaks to me of things that are outside, beyond these senses, it's something that strikes me as tremendous and magnificent. Also I think this sense of mystery and sublimity, that's another, and that's frightfully difficult to define, sublimity is created when an artist tries to impose some sort of order on his sense of mystery. The reason why the opening of Beethoven's Ninth Symphony is so mysterious and so tremendous is that the sense of order to create together with the mystery is so powerful, so wonderfully creative the way in which the rhythm accelerates, builds up to absolute precision the main theme. Now, we get this same thing with Bruckner, not with such greatness but the same basic principle behind him, we get the harmonies evolving a steady slow grand way from this movement, we get something akin to the sense when we think of the movement of the earth, we think of the movement of the planets and this vastness, we also get from it perhaps something like the grandeur of the mountain scenery, in Austria, I mean these things can all come to mind and I don't see why it's necessary to postulate some enormous figment of the imagination to justify it.

There are two other ways in which science has influenced music. The first of them concerns music perhaps rather more damagingly than the other arts. Science has provided us with an immense variety of new materials – take, for instance, the field of 'plastics', which has supplied a range of useful items from stockings to buildings. Every week some new 'plastic' material is put in front of our bedazzled eyes. We become fascinated. Technologists devise new formulae out of which exciting new substances spring like corks out of bottles. These materials are meant to be used for specific purposes, and their properties are calculated in advance to suit whatever object is at hand. A new 'plastic' substance – designed, say, for an especially formidable set of false teeth – must have certain characteristics. It must be tough enough to crack nuts, yet not so rigid that it will hurt the mouth in the process. The technologist will work it all out beforehand and if his prognostications are based on sound chemistry the right stuff will emerge. Its 'texture' as well as its other properties must be right – that's to say it must feel right. But the 'feel' of it cannot be calculated in chemical terms. Now the mere production of new textures in this way is a fascinating game in itself, and we are all interested in it. But it has led to some strange situations in the arts, especially in music. For a long time now it's been fashionable to cry after new 'textures' in sound. What these new 'textures' are for, no one seems to know – they are just 'textures'. But they aren't even that, since if music is a process in time (which I for one think it is) it can't very well process, in the strictest sense of the term, so static a thing as a 'texture'. We use these terms loosely until they cease to mean much, yet we still go on repeating them as slogans. Perhaps that's why they *are* slogans. Alastair Sim had the last word on the subject, when he described words as 'the anodyne for the pain of thinking'. But to stick to the point; assuming that the musician's use of the word isn't entirely meaningless, it's no use looking for new 'textures' unless you know what you want to say with them. If you know this, you needn't worry about texture because – whatever it is – it will emerge naturally as but one of many properties of the music, always, of course, provided that you are a talented composer. If you are not, you still don't need to worry about it, since nothing you can do will help matters anyway. Texture is only one aspect of form, and since in all art, good and bad, form and content are the same thing, you can't achieve one without the other. I find that if I sometimes carelessly use the word 'texture' about music, what I really mean by it is the surface 'feel' of the music. If you are genuinely imagining music and trying to get it down on paper in symbols that are for no other purpose than to represent the *sounds* in your imagination, you are expressing human feelings in music. If, like the technologists, without sensuous preconceptions, you are chasing new materials, new textures, new sounds, just for their own sakes, you're in serious trouble, for you'll fail utterly to find a new means of expression without something vital to express. If you're content with the attitude that says 'music expresses nothing, only itself', you are voluntarily eliminating yourself, a human being, from the argument, cutting the ground from under your own feet. You may, in a feeble way, dig up some intriguing noise that might, in its turn, release some great artist's humane imagination into vast new fields where you could never hope to follow him. If so, you'll have served your purpose. But I doubt if very many artists consciously think of themselves in so humble a light. If you insist on relegating yourself in this way, at least, *at least*, try to hear, imagine, and feel (not calculate by pseudo-scientific means) what you are going to do. I'm certain that many would-be composers fail to fulfil even this most elementary obligation. When, as recently, a young composer conducting a rehearsal of his own work can remain blissfully unaware of the fact that one of the players is maliciously transposing the whole of his part, something is wrong somewhere, and not only in the orchestra. Nowadays a lot of people are pretending to compose who, in Bach's or Haydn's time, would have been watch-makers, gunsmiths, or, on Sundays, finding an outlet for their musical talents, organ-blowers.

The other point concerning science is this; during the past forty years the branch of scientific research that has most influenced other fields of sensitive thought is the ever deeper penetration into the microcosmic. The secrets of atomic physics have been revealed beyond the capacity of the senses to appreciate them – hence the average intelligent man's somewhat woolly idea of the 'insubstantiality' of matter – 'insubstantial' meaning simply 'unfeelable', 'unseeable', 'inaudible' – beyond the reach of the crude senses. All this has, I believe, had an effect on artistic minds (which are quick to react to or even anticipate climates of thought and to create analogies to them). While science has so enlarged its frontiers, the scope of art has dwindled, and many artists have sifted themselves by a process of fragmentation that is superficially analogous but hopelessly unrealistic. Some pessimists might think that with 'the discovery of the single note' we have reached the point of no return from the padded cell of incomprehensible insubstantiality, creeping hypersensitivity, and phoney subtlety. My view, however, is that there is no need for pessimism. We may have reached the nadir but it is not a point of no return (except for those who have actually got stuck there). Science is at present opening out a new prospect – the exploration of space. This could bring with it a new climate of thought, more expansive and adventurous, perhaps more heroic, arising out of human action as well as mere introspection. At the same time anything artistic that's been discovered in the last few decades will remain, available at the service of a larger, more genuinely human purpose. Really objective art is an analytical criticism of life, not a mere reflection of science. If, as most of us hope, war recedes into the past and a long period of comparatively peaceful stability lies ahead, it could well be that artists will be more outward-looking, less circumspect, more willing to accept the *macrocosmic* implications of their work than to cringe and avoid, to exclude, to abolish. Hans Keller observed to me the other day that the human mind is always quicker to recognise pleasant facts about itself than unpleasant ones. This is probably true, and is borne out by at least some aspects of musical history. Beethoven, for the first time in music, laid bare facts about human nature that had been seemingly too unpalatable to be ingredients in a pleasing entertainment. All great composers, in all periods, have hinted at them, but Beethoven was perhaps the first to insist upon them. But he did so only as an aspect of a larger, more universaL objective vision, fundamentally hopeful. After him lesser mortals confused the issue - pessimistic egotism concentrated avidly upon the seamier side of things, and in the first twenty or thirty years of this century the arts began to incur the almost unwitting loathing even of many of their own practitioners. This process has gone on, but instead of putting the hateful despair and triviality into the perspective of a larger vision that would give them meaning, many would-be artists are deliberately and fatally ignoring the miserable nature of what their work actually says and gibbering over its mere lifeless materials. This is one of the processes that has led us to 'the discovery of the single note'. I expect certain people will call me naïve because I'm oversimplifying all this – but since it is my view that the paralysis of many artists arises simply from a fear of being called naive by their intellectual cronies and critics, I shan't mind that too much. It would seem to me naive to be pre-occupied by limiting one's awareness to a mere fraction of what one is capable of seeing – like a beautiful woman going cross-eyed because of a pimple on her nose. I believe it was Carlyle who said that after many years of wondering whether or not to accept the Universe, he finally decided he'd better. At that moment he was a real artist.

As you'll have divined from all that I've so far said, music is for me a matter of acceptance – acceptance of all the resources that are available, consonance, dissonance, melody, rhythm, harmony, tonality, atonality, instruments, voices, – all these things and more. But they have to be imagined vividly and with strength of mind. They are there to flow through the imagination, and none of them have anything to do with arbitrary systems of composition or empty theories of construction. I don't care a damn whether a composer is a serialist, an atonalist, or whatever fancy name he cares to call himself (or gets called, more often, by other people), any more than I care whether a composer uses the piano to help his ear (I don't use it, often, but Haydn did, and who am I to say he was cheating?). I am interested in the validity of what a composer is actually saying and the skill and judgment with which he controls what arises spontaneously from his mind's ear. Most of all, I'm profoundly concerned about the human attitude his music reveals to me – it's important to me that he should say 'yes' to life, not 'no'. Don't ask me how I can tell which he is saying, because I'm not always sure myself and the issue isn't always obvious – but when in doubt I'm inclined to assume it's 'no'. 'Yes' is more often unmistakable, whether the expression is tragic or comic. The right sort of tragedy can say 'Yes' and the wrong sort of comedy can say 'no'. If its creator is undazzled and farsighted, it will, whatever its subject, fulfil what seems to me a fundamental purpose of great art, to create confidence in the fact of living, growing, developing. Only such art is, to me, truly exciting; other kinds may provide momentary sensuous stimulation, passing morbid fascination, or real pleasure, but confidence in our own human potentialities is what really keeps us going, and it's always regenerated by great music. These values have nothing to do with being 'up-to-date', or trailing after the latest Dior of music, foisting trumped-up individuality on your audience. There has never been a more dangerous fallacy than that uttered by Sir Winston Churchill in his advice to Lady Violet Bonham Carter on public speaking: 'The most important thing is who you are, next, how you say it, and last and least, what you say.' The deeper values are true for all times and all arts and anyone with real gifts who cherishes them will never be merely contemporary – which is, to quote Hans Keller again, to be temporary. The real values are what a true artist should aim at; to fail to do so, if you have a talent, is a betrayal, at worst cynical and at best just messing about. But far worse than even this failure is to hold forth without any intention of saying anything whatever, whether the so-called style you are pottering and tinkering with is Continental, English, Ruritanian or Lilliputian.

APPENDIX 4

THE SYMPHONY (1) HAYDN TO DVOŘÁK (PENGUIN BOOKS 1966)

INTRODUCTION

Robert Simpson

One often hears musicians praising some work as 'genuinely symphonic'; if, however, they are asked what they mean by this, most are hard put to it to give a very precise reply. The subject needs definition. We must know what we are going to include in a book of this kind, and why. It would be simple enough to take all composers on trust, without looking further than the titles of their works, to include a work just because it is called a symphony, and so to avoid trouble. But the fact that musicians do speak of 'genuinely' symphonic music, in terms however nebulous, and criticize some symphonies as being such in name only, is solid evidence that there is some essence recognized by those who discuss it at all. There are, of course, many present-day critics and composers who do not discuss it, who say that the whole idea is dead. This makes it all the more necessary to examine the situation, to find out what 'symphonic' really means, so that we can see whether it is an exhausted possibility, or whether it is something that can still fire the imagination. And even if we were to reach the conclusion that such a way of writing music is no longer possible, we must still try to discover what it is, for it has generated some of the greatest and most durable music in existence.

As Harold Truscott has admirably shown in the first chapter of this book, the origins of the symphony as we know it were in a new attitude to tonality, or key. In the third decade of the eighteenth century, tonality began to be felt in a new way, a change of key being an event that thrust the original key away over the horizon, so that it, for the time being at any rate, it disappeared. Tonality is a difficult thing to describe in words, impossible in fact. Yet few people fail to understand it instinctively or, partly, by unconsciously acquired habit. Only a tone-deaf person could remain undisturbed if a simple hymn tune were to end in the wrong key. The right tonic chord is expected, demanded by us all. We also feel the rightness or wrongness of the harmonies in the middle of the tune, as the different notes of the melody are supported by various related chords. Now imagine such a process greatly extended, so that instead of a simple tune we have a much larger composition whose intermediate harmonies are stretched out into periods, each containing all sorts of activity. We can hear that, like the hymn tune, the piece possesses a sense of tonal direction, and when we reach the end, we feel the same completeness and finality. Any characteristic Bach prelude will illustrate this. The extension is such that what was originally felt as a close succession of harmonies is now so much spread out, and so enlivened by figuration or contrapuntal invention, that it seems like a drift through a series of keys. But the whole has still as static a feeling about it as the hymn tune. When we get to the end we have the idea that we have not really moved at all, but simply stood looking in various directions.

Each key has its retinue of related chords that can be used placidly without disturbing the original one. Imagine now a Bach prelude in a particular key, say A major. Get a musician to transpose it for you to E flat, and you are in a different world altogether (nothing to do with so-called 'key colour'. The internal relations are the same, but the sound of E flat is dramatic and strange after the sound of A. The two keys are as remote from each other as possible, and there is no need to be a trained musician to receive the full impact of the sensation. E flat virtually blots out the original sensation of A, once the first wrench is over. Now it would be possible to thrust the original key over the horizon without a wrench, by means of a modulation – a raising of tension by means of various harmonies (some of them dissonances) that eventually relaxes into the new key. A modulation from A to E flat would be an extreme one, and one can more easily modulate to much nearer regions. We have seen that a Bach prelude more often than not sticks to related harmonies; its first point of rest is very likely to be on <u>dominant</u> harmony, that is to say the chord a fifth higher than the original tonic. The dominant demands a return to the tonic:

In this case, one tonic chord of C major is enough to satisfy the simple demand left by the unfinished quotation. The G major chord is merely a harmony in the course of a melody. If Bach arrives on it half-way through the course of an elaborate piece, the rest of the piece will find its way back, normally through an exquisite series of steps.

Suppose we treat this dominant not as a chord but as a key and we <u>modulate</u> to it, creating enough tension in the intervening process to thrust the original key out of earshot. This is what happened in the early eighteenth century, and it gave rise to a whole new world of music, essentially dramatic in feeling and dynamic in movement. The first great idea that arose out of it was the sonata principle, on which most new chamber and orchestral music was founded. If the original key is genuinely supplanted by a new one, the process of returning home again has to be pretty muscular; it gave rise to the so-called development section of a sonata movement, with its kaleidoscopic, restless changes of key. The return is itself a dramatic incident (even if it is quietly and smoothly effected), and the whole point of the recapitulation is that it has to insist upon the original tonality with much more weight than Bach would find necessary. Sometimes even the weight of the recapitulation is insufficient; then there has to be a <u>coda</u> to reinforce it.

Countless symphonies, quartets and sonatas begin with a movement of this type. The early quartets of Haydn do not differ in any fundamental respect from his early symphonies, and the gradual divergence of his chamber and orchestral music is no divergence of musical streams – it is a gradual realization of the essential difference between the capabilities of the small intimate group and those of the increasingly 'public' orchestra. Haydn and Mozart put their best into both; in the field of chamber music the string quartet and quintet proved to be the means of conveying the highest degree of concentration. The name 'symphony' became attached to orchestral works aiming at the same kind of density and significance. And not only density; variety within a required unity was always tacitly regarded as vital, variety both of movement and character. No really great symphony lacks this internal variety, achieved within the scope of a concentrated sense of unity. This is also true of great quartets; but the quartet is so-called by a purely utilitarian, statistical name. If it is a bad, loose, or rhapsodical composition, it is still undeniably a quartet. But a symphony cannot be called such if it wants certain qualities. The name itself, whatever its primitive origins, has come to mean a work for orchestra in which the composer has obeyed and mastered (a paradox that really does mean something, for once) not a set of rules but a body of principles, or standards.

The difference between the kind of musical thought in, say, Tchaikovsky's Francesca da Rimini and the first movement of his Fourth symphony is not merely one of degree; it is a basic difference in kind. The one is episodic, essentially static; the other is organic, and essentially dynamic. It is no use saying that this difference resides in the fact that the movement of the symphony is in sonata form. Rules are not the root of the matter; it is easy enough to find episodic, unsymphonic movements that stick haplessly to the sonata plan (there are some by Tchaikovsky). Few musicians nowadays would be so rigid as to insist that a symphony shall deploy sonata form – there are plenty of real symphonies that have little or nothing to do with it. But (and it is tremendously important to realize this) they live by the principles of which sonata form was the first great manifestation. The symphony and the sonata arose from a new revelation about tonality;

a 'breakthrough' (to use a currently fashionable word) that is as space flight is to gravity-bound air travel, and almost strictly analogous.

We cannot now put off any longer an attempt to list (however haltingly) those elements of music a composer must master if he is to write a true symphony. They must be put in the most general terms possible, for this is not, being an artistic phenomenon, a matter for the strait-jacket.

(1) The fusion of diverse elements into an organic whole. The composer must be able to create a wide range of movement and character, shape and colour, even mood and atmosphere, within severe and powerfully concentrated limits. A great symphony embraces all kinds of musical movement, from one extreme to the other. From this arises:

(2) The continuous control of pace. Even within a single movement the control of pace must be absolute; an abrupt change of motion that might be acceptable for itself in a ballet will require subsequent justification in a symphony. In a great master it will have the thrilling effect of imperiously commanding justification, as it does in the first E major outburst in the first movement of Nielsen's Fourth symphony (see Vol 2, Ex. 41). A movement in a single pervasive tempo must show a continuous mastery of <u>composed</u> flexible pace; the listener must have the sense that it is the composer and not the conductor who is controlling this. In the first movement of the 'Eroica', though it is an unbroken Allegro con brio, there is far more variety of motion than in, say, Liszt's Les Préludes, which requires the conductor to make crashing changes of gear from time to time.

(3) The reserves of strength necessary to achieve (1) and (2) are such as to express size. A true symphony is always big in its powers of suggestion, even if its physical dimensions are small. Consider any of Haydn's middle-period symphonies, Beethoven's Eighth, or Sibelius's Seventh. I regard this work as more genuinely symphonic than does Harold Truscott. A symphony may possess great dimensions, but these alone are not enough; Beethoven's Seventh is gigantic in its implications, which dwarf many a monster of sheer bulk. The mere fact of this special kind of mastery is enough to invest with a distinctive sense of power and stature even light and gay symphonies such as Mendelssohn's 'Italian', and there is more of such quality in Prokofiev's Classical Symphony than in his much more aggressive and expansive Scythian Suite.

(4) In the first place it was the dynamic treatment of tonality that made all this possible; it was a reaction against the tonal passivity of earlier music. The important thing to remember about it is that the revolt was vital and constructive, positive – it threw away nothing, not even counterpoint. In the introduction to Volume 2, I have to describe another kind of revolt, a negative one.

(5) Perhaps the basic observation one can make about true symphony is that it is active in all possible ways. That is to say that in creating it the composer must never allow any prime element of the music (rhythm, melody, harmony, tonality) to seem to die, so that artificial respiration becomes necessary. In a piece of ballet or purely picturesque music, temporary failure of one of these elements may not matter seriously – the effect may even be compelling or beguiling. But in a symphony such a failure amounts to a lapse; even when movement is temporarily denied to such an ingredient as, say, tonality (as is often imperative) there must always be an awareness that the movement can be restored at will, without disrupting the continuity. In such a case the composer, if for example he leaves the bass holding a long pedal note, must <u>know</u> what he is going to do with it, and that what he will do will be positive. No evasions are tolerable in the attempt to achieve the highest state of organization of which music is capable. In the orchestral field we have long applied the term 'symphony' to such an endeavour.

Questions of what should or should not be included in a book of this nature arise more in respect of the second than the first volume, and will be discussed in the other introduction. In the meantime I would like to make it clear that so far as individual contributors are concerned, I have left each free to tackle his subject in his own way, in the belief that the upshot would be livelier and more varied than the effect of a rigid format. The demands of different subjects cause different approaches. Hans Keller, for example, has commented upon every single one of Mozart's symphonies, for this is a subject not fully dealt with elsewhere. Basil Lam in his penetrating observations about Beethoven has largely dispensed with music quotations, knowing that the works are familiar and pocket scores and records easily obtainable, and he has concerned himself with those profound generalities that routine analysis precludes. Some of the chapters, indeed, are not light reading, although they are I think very readable. We have not assumed that our readers are children – rather that they wish to reach to the heart of the matter and are prepared for a burst of rewarding effort here and there. Only one chapter has been reprinted (though slightly revised) from the previous Pelican Symphony –Humphrey Searle's treatment of Liszt. To all the contributors I offer my thanks, and to Julius Harrison, who died before he could see his chapters through the press, this publication is dedicated in affectionate memory.

APPENDIX 5

THE SYMPHONY (2) ELGAR TO THE PRESENT DAY (PENGUIN BOOKS 1967)

INTRODUCTION

STRAVINSKY, HINDEMITH AND OTHERS

Robert Simpson

In the introduction to the first volume of The Symphony, I made an attempt to show the origins of symphony and tried briefly to define its essence. Now it is my task to indicate why some admirable composers have not found their way into the scheme of the book, even though they have published works called symphonies. Since some of these works are widely performed, their admirers will justly require some sort of apologia for my decisions. I must begin by reassuring my readers that none of these omissions is made with intent to disparage; so far as I am concerned, the matter is one of careful classification. No intelligent bat would take offence at the omission of his species from a book on birds; but he may well feel that his 'wings' entitle him to be mentioned, if only to show that he may deserve another book to himself. The title 'symphony' is in many cases even looser terminology than 'wings' in respect of a bat. To discuss this is valuable, so here goes.

Hans Keller's definition of symphonic music is 'the large scale integration of contrasts'. (See Vol. 1, p. 52). This is plausible enough, superficially, until one realizes that the word 'integration' begs a great many questions. The contrasts of Le Sacre du Printemps or Iberia may reasonably be thought integrated on a large scale in that their distribution produces a satisfactory balance (at any rate in the Debussy work). But such music is balletic, it is episodic, sectional. Why? Because all its elements are not functioning equally. When rhythm and melody are dominant, tonality marks time; when tonality changes, rhythm and melody wait. In a symphony the internal activity is fluid, organic; action is the dominant factor, through and through. At the end of a great symphony there is the sense that the music has grown by the interpenetrative activity of all its constituent elements. Nothing is ever allowed to lapse into aimlessness, or the kind of activity that needs artificially reviving. At times the activity of particular ingredients is abated – we can find passages in Beethoven's symphonies where nothing but rhythm is left, for instance – at such times, however, we always feel that the other things are merely latent. Often it is as if all the elements of the music have suddenly concentrated themselves into a rhythm or a harmonic progression, or a flash of pure tonality; but such moments are impossible in isolation. The great thing to keep constantly in mind is that no single element is ever abandoned, or deliberately excluded, that the composer must master them all and subordinate them to the demands of the whole. In this sense a symphony is profoundly inclusive. If a composer chooses deliberately to exclude, for example, a great natural resource like tonality, he at once excludes inclusiveness. He may bring off something expressive and individual, but he denies himself the kind of comprehensiveness that a symphony must have if we accept that it is to be the highest type of orchestral music (and, I think, history commands us to insist upon this).

If the term 'symphony, is to be the supreme challenge (and there does not seem to be any other accepted generic term of this sort), we must in composing symphonies ignore no basic response of the human mind, so far as elemental musical phenomena are concerned. The human sense of tonality has many times been modified, but cannot be abolished. To attempt to abolish it is to cease to be comprehensive, to be narrowly exclusive. If I appreciate the kind of expression that Schoenberg achieved,[*] my sense of tonality, though it may be deliberately anaesthetized for the time being, is by no means abolished. Since all my musical faculties are not being engaged, I cannot feel that such music is comprehensive. It is certainly concentrated, but that alone will not make it 'symphonic'; if you lose a leg, you have to concentrate in order to move about without it, but however hard you concentrate, you cannot escape the conclusion that it is better to have two legs. With these, you can forget problems of locomotion and concentrate on objects. With one leg you can hop about, but will find it difficult to invent new dance steps that have more than the temporary appeal of oddity.

[1]This is taking the extreme case of the abandonment of tonality; but the fact that it is tonality that is the deepest current in the river of true symphony, means that the flow of the whole depends upon it. The composer cannot forget it while he gives over his senses to the enjoyment of rhythm and harmony. In a ballet he can let the tonality stick while he makes a dance; the tonality then becomes the floor of a stage rather than the current of a river. This happens in the brilliant and original works that Stravinsky calls symphonies. Anyone who believes these to be real symphonies cannot be aware of the nature of symphonic thought. If Stravinsky himself is aware of it, he clearly does not wish to develop it here, in works so vividly balletic in character. Within their own circumscribed terms they are highly organized, but the motion of symphony is absent. They are exclusively concerned with rhythm and texture rooted in primitive monolithic tonality; when one (or a combination) of these has transiently performed enough of its function, it is replaced, and the total effect, however internally agitated, is as static as a stage upon which dancers are gyrating. Because so

---

[*] *I happen to dislike it, but that is irrelevant to my appreciation of its accomplishment.*

famous a composer has made use of the title 'symphony' we need not be over-awed into a fundamental denial of principle. The more characteristic a work of Stravinsky, the further it is from the symphonic idea; if this is not obvious to his admirers, they must surely admire him for other than his best features. The Symphony in Three Movements, a consistent and highly individual work, reveals its virtues most readily if one listens to it as one would approach a ballet score like Le Sacre du Printemps. It is no symphony; its episodic nature is disarmingly positive. It is interesting to compare Stravinsky's use of pedals with Sibelius's. The latter is very fond of long pedal-points, but they are in his mature symphonic works the background to an intense activity and create a vast slow motion of their own, like that of the sky as the earth rotates, while upon the planet's surface there is teeming human and animal movement. The pedals engender a new, larger dimension; they do not clog the symphonic flow, but throw it into relief against a sense of cosmic movement. In a slow majestic way, Sibelius's treatment of these pedals is as active as anything else in his music; they are drawn into the great current. Stravinsky, on the other hand, when he holds on to a pedal, allows the rest of the music to stick with it; a good example of this is the passage from Figs. 7 to 13 in the Symphony in Three Movements. The bass jogs in an ostinato, and the orchestra jogs with it; it is pure ballet music, and when the composer has had enough of this particular sort of jogging, he switches to another (see Figs. 13 to 21). These passages are not isolated examples, ripped from their context; they are entirely typical. The effect of the whole, though it is highly personal, is the opposite of comprehensive or symphonic.

Hindemith's is a different case. The basis of his art is nearer to that of Bach than to Beethoven's; his attitude to tonality is fundamentally like Bach's or Handel's, and he rarely treats it dramatically or dynamically. His splendid Symphony in E flat has the same kind of calm solidity as an early suite; the tonalities move round like the spokes of a wheel, rotating about a fixed centre that is never seriously in doubt. The so-called symphony based on the opera Mathis der Maler is another such work, not radically different from the magnificent ballet suite Nobilissima Visione. Although Hindemith can be sweeping and powerful, his action is more like that of a weight-lifter than that of a sprinter. He raises a massive object into the air, then puts it down again exactly as it was. This is impressive, but the music does not 'travel' like symphonic invention. His use of the term 'symphony' revives its ancient sense (as does Stravinsky in Symphonies pour instruments à vent) and these works have much in common with the Turmmusik of the seventeenth century; they are dramatic as wholes, dramatic as would be a great tower with trumpeters upon its turrets, not dramatic in their internal processes.

Omission of these composers from the book will also provoke questions about those actually included. A composer has been included if his prime intention, whether fully realized or not, is or has been to compose true symphonies; to omit him because of only partial success would have been really high-handed. We may argue for ever about the success of this or that symphonist as such (how about Shostakovitch, for example?) but the fact remains that his reputation may rest upon a body of such works, in which case we must include him. Neither Stravinsky nor Hindemith quite fits this category. Nor does Schoenberg, whose two tonal chamber symphonies would more than bear scrutiny. Here I hesitated longer, but finally decided that these are really chamber music; the full orchestration of No. 1, in my view, does no more than illuminate the chamber-musical sensitivity of the original. Again, Schoenberg's reputation can scarcely be held to rest upon these two compositions; further, they are adequately treated elsewhere. Some may aver that works like Benjamin Britten's Sinfonia da Requiem or his 'cello symphony should qualify, but this is music whose positive attributes do not depend upon the art of symphonic movement with all it implies - this composer's main achievement lies in other fields. His 'Spring' symphony shows this clearly, an enlarged song-cycle so unequivocal that it cannot be misunderstood as can some of Mahler's symphonies similarly (but adversely) commented upon. The number of composers that could be dealt with has also been limited by space; here it has been necessary to stop somewhere in our own time. This unfortunately meant the exclusion of gifted figures. To mention only some British composers, the symphonies of Malcolm Arnold, Peter Racine Fricker, Daniel Jones, Alan Rawsthorne, Humphrey Searle (a contributor to this publication) and William Wordsworth all deserve detailed consideration. The fact that there is still a notable body of music that, regrettably, has had to be crowded out is at least evidence that the idea of composing symphonies is far from dead. But I must leave the reader to speculate upon what he would have included here, or excluded; perhaps he will charitably observe that the two volumes cover a very wide range of music. If anything in them makes him cross, let us hope it will sharpen his enthusiasm as well as his temper.

APPENDIX 6
ON CONDUCTING ONESELF IN PUBLIC
Robert Simpson

In conducting his own work a composer has one initial natural advantage and another possible later one. From the start the orchestra will not expect him to be an accomplished conductor in the technical sense; this may be an advantage, however, only at the outset, before the orchestra has become acquainted with his music. On the music itself depends his possible second chance – if the players are at once aware that what they are playing is (on the lowest level) practical and practicable, that they are faced with a sound professional musician, the first advantage is confirmed. It may be thought that above these two factors is the ability of the composer to know how his music should be interpreted. This is not so, because there are a thousand ways of performing any worthwhile work; if the composer has produced what he should, he has provided a valid basis for projecting many different human reactions, all of which (provided they come within certain artistic limits, admittedly difficult to define) are true accounts of genuinely coherent experiences. That is why composers are less often dogmatic about matters of interpretation than musicologists, and it is why I am always interested in the spontaneous reaction of the performer when he is confronted with my own music.

To perform (or to direct performances of) one's own work is a valuable lesson in more ways than one. Its simplest value is purely practical: there is no better way of finding out what can or can't be done. I discovered, for example, that the beginning of my Second Symphony, where muted second violins are divided between B and A sharp in soft dissonance, was wonderfully easy to write down but enormously difficult to perform properly. How, when you give the beat, can you and all the players be sure that the two notes will be exactly equal in sound? They must be, or the opening loses its point. This is a problem I have not yet solved, and it is no consolation to me that no skilled conductor has solved it either. All music contains difficulties of this nature, and being compelled to deal with them is not only salutary in the practical sense – it may well spark the imagination to new adventures. It is surprising how many of a composer's best ideas come from grappling with practical problems.

In doubting the ability of a composer to give a definitive interpretation of his music and in feeling that there can be no such thing, I do not suggest the absurd extreme that he has no authority. As the originator of the work, he has in his mind a number of points he (better than anyone else) knows must be made; he is more aware, perhaps, than any other musician of the form of the work, the thing that can remain constant throughout a variety of interpretations, but which can become distorted if certain cardinal aspects of the piece are not perceived. The composer normally regards these as basic to his idea; a performance over which he has no control, or which he cannot influence at rehearsal, may well miss them and will fall outside the artistic limits defining an interpretation. If the work is new, only the unfortunate composer is likely to be aware of this, and one cannot blame the unsuspecting listener for thinking that what he hears is the composer's fault. I, for one, am always grateful for the chance to insist on these fundamentals in a performance, even though my own interpretation may never be twice the same. The attempt is of course not always successful.

These basic structural facts about a work do not depend on a 'correct' tempo. I am often asked 'What is the right tempo?' and can reply only that it is between this and that, depending on the performer's temperament, his present state of mind, the acoustics, the standard of the orchestra, and many other considerations. The composer himself will not always adopt the same tempo, but within limits he feels to be sensible, will react naturally. Beyond these limits the work can be misrepresented. A case in point is the finale of my own Second Symphony – it is the sort of music that tempts the speed merchant by its appearance on paper and by its obviously vigorous nature. But to rush it is to make impossible proper accentuation and to reduce the impression of pace. I became so exasperated by this tendency in conductors that I eventually added a footnote to the score – 'If this movement lasts less than eight minutes, it is too fast' – and have so far believed to find it effectual. Listeners with stopwatches will no doubt hope to catch me out here; if so, they will be disappointed.

A common fallacy is that composers (as performers) know their own scores better than anybody else. When you have composed a work, you have got it out of your system and rarely love it very much: they say that a woman quickly forgets the pains of childbirth; a composer as quickly forgets his child, and can look at it as at a stranger. I know the Eroica far better than any of my own symphonies: first because I have known it much longer, second because I did not suffer the composing of it, third because I love it much more, fourth (and obviously) because it is so infinitely more worth knowing. And there is no more difficult or unnatural process than the reabsorption, detail by detail, of what you have tried so hard to remove yourself from in the first place. It is like returning to – let us not pursue this analogy. This problem, I am sure, will always effectively prevent me learning my own scores with either the accuracy or even the enthusiasm I would apply to other music. To learn the score of the Eroica is (from the composer's point of view) to enjoy the journey back into Beethoven's mind without having experienced the original creative pain. Only a composer can appreciate the sheer delight and excitement, the glorious relief, of such a task.

If the composer cannot know and love his own work as he does the masterpieces that have driven him to compose, he must at least know his own ear. Disaster strikes if he cannot hear wrong things in his score during rehearsal. I think there are two things he must be absolutely sure of. He must never be satisfied until what he has written arouses genuinely in him the spontaneous excitement he hopes to arouse in the listener – without this sensation he cannot hope to produce a response in anyone else. He cannot do this without being sure that he hears everything he writes down: this is the second necessity, too often forgotten today. A famous conductor once told me a tale he swore was true (and he is a man whose word one does not question). He was rehearsing a concert of new works, and one of the composers approached him at the rostrum, hesitantly: 'Would you mind taking it a little quicker?' The amazed conductor knew that this was a situation in which tact could serve no purpose and replied: 'But this isn't your piece!' The 'composer' would have been spared this particular embarrassment had he been conducting his own work; at least he would have known whose piece it was when it was his turn to step on the rostrum. One should always be glad of the chance.

(First printed in The Listener 11th January 1968;c. BBC Enterprises 1968)

APPENDIX 7
LATE BEETHOVEN

Take a fascinatingly original composer like Stravinsky. His music can easily be divided into distinct periods; the early ballets that move away from the kind of thing most Russian composers had been doing, culminating in the violent outburst of the *Rite of Spring*. Then the so-called neo-classic period, where the surface mannerisms of the eighteenth century were used as new stylistic devices in works of crystalline inorganic construction. In that brilliantly witty and sometimes deep book *Music Ho*! Constant Lambert describes this phase:

"Like a savage standing in delighted awe before those two symbols of an alien civilisation, the top hat and the pot de chambre, he's apt to confuse their functions."

Stravinsky's a composer who had to keep changing course in order to maintain course. Rapid change is his brand of consistency. Most of his life he was consciously striving to be in front, and his very last period shows him striving not to be behind. If you dip into Stravinsky, like as not you'll hit some characteristic product of a tendency of the time, usually initiated by him, and soon dropped by him.

Or think of Bruckner. He spent the whole of his creative life trying to solve one vast problem, scarcely aware of what it was: how to cope with pure instrumental music on a Wagnerian time-scale. So we get one huge work after another, with revision after revision. The nineteenth century, in fact, became the time of the artist with a problem – usually one problem, when you boil it down. In the case of Berlioz, for instance, it was how to reconcile a supreme melodic gift with an irresistible urge for the spectacular: often he had to keep these things away from each other, though occasionally there's a miracle, and they live together.

Take almost any nineteenth-century composer and dip into him at random: what you'll find is a stage in his tussle with a central and usually definable problem, the result, among other things, of the artist becoming self-employed. Earlier, when artists were doing prescribed work for rich employers, including the church, the problem of so-called 'style' was the reconciliation of personality and prescription – inner and outer demands having to be met. The genius had his problems, but they tended to be resolved by sheer talent, as in Bach and Haydn, coupled with opportunism, as Handel's case. A composer like Mozart is perhaps the first case of radical disquiet. But if you dip at random into almost any composer from Machaut to Mozart, you'll hit something that shows what he was preoccupied with at the time, either technically, or from the requirements of his situation. Bach wrote nearly all his cantatas during a particular period, and works like *The Musical Offering* or *The Art of Fugue* belong to his latter years, when he was free to pursue abstractions.

Now, it's a common-place to say that Beethoven stands between these two periods. His music seems to strike a fine balance between classic discipline and personal intensity, but to say this isn't enough. After all, you could say the same about any perfect and deeply felt aria by Bach. Beethoven differs from most other artists in another way. If you dip into any very productive period of Beethoven's life - say the late 1790s, or 1804-8, or his last five or six years – you won't hit anything remotely stereotyped; assuming, that is, that you strike a masterpiece, which is more likely than not. Not only will you come across works in widely different media, but you'll find an extraordinary range of expression and character, all of it intensely personal, yet evenly mastered. In the three or four years before 1800 we find a strikingly comprehensive cross-section of Beethoven's nature, as it was at that time; more comprehensive and revealing than in anyone else's music, and rivalled only by what Schubert promised. And think of 1804-1808, the years of Leonore and the middle symphonies, quartets and trios and sonatas. The range and depth of the personality revealed by all these works is more than we can see elsewhere, yet the artistic discipline is as rigorous as in any narrower creator.

Well, this talk's supposed to be about Beethoven's late period, and what I'm getting at is this: there isn't one – at least in his terms, because he didn't live long enough. At every productive period of Beethoven's life we get a very full cross-section of all that he was – or rather, all that he felt didn't interfere with artistic integrity. He became <u>more</u> as he grew older; but he wasn't fifty-seven when he died; all we say is that each successive wave of creation reveals more because there <u>is</u> more; we can't say that the last period is some sort of final testament, because there's no sign of finality in it. Far from it, the energy and variety of those last works far outstrips anything before or since, and Beethoven's imagination reaches further into the past as well as into a future nobody has so far consolidated. The last thing Beethoven finished was the heroically merry and profoundly subtle second finale to Op. 130; nobody could suppose *that* to be any kind of last gasp. If Beethoven had lived another twenty years, what might have happened? That would have taken him to 1847, the time of The Damnation of Faust and Tannhauser, and both those works (and many others) might have been very different if Beethoven had been still alive and able to reveal still more of his developing consciousness.

But it's no use complaining that Beethoven didn't stay around to change the course of musical history: after all Beethoven's effect on musical history hasn't been all that beneficial as things stand. It's not his fault that the unprecedented power of his work was persistently and romantically misunderstood by most of his successors, who didn't see much more than revolutionary fury in him. There's no reason to suppose that if he'd lived longer he would have been any the less misconstrued by those with their own axes to grind. The people get the government they deserve – usually a bad one. Benjamin Britten's famous remark that 'The rot started with Beethoven' should really have been directed at those who would have started the rot if Beethoven had never existed. He was right about the rot, but wrong about Beethoven. When we think about the music that we're sorry to say was Beethoven's last, we should think about what it promises in its own terms, rather than what we imagine even later works might have caused in other, inferior, minds. In the last few years Beethoven was both refining and invigorating his art. He was clearing it of assertiveness, the assertiveness necessary in his earlier intensification of sonata. But even as I say this, I think of the G major Piano Concerto, the Violin Concerto, the F sharp-major Piano Sonata; and these aren't at all isolated examples of pervading contemplative gentleness in middle-period Beethoven.

It's dangerous to generalise: and yet there's more than a grain of truth in observing that the later works use accents, for instance, in a new way: not for assertion, but for a new rhythmic subtlety, and also for a new and delicate way of easing from one tonality into another. Formal outlines are unobtrusive: the exquisitely calculated recapitulation in the first movement of Op. 127 is a perfect example that must surely have had an effect on Schubert when he wrote the *scherzo* of his great B flat Piano Sonata. In this last period of Beethoven there's more subtlety than even before: that's only what you'd expect, but we shouldn't forget that the range is increasing too. The late works contain, if anything, more popular elements, as if Beethoven is more than ever concerned with immediacy. Yet these simple ingredients are put into contexts that make them appear mysterious; no, that show they <u>are</u> mysterious. Also mysterious is the extraordinary vehemence of some of this music; it's a vehemence beyond assertiveness – pure energy. Somehow I don't feel that the *Grosse Fuge* or the finale of the *Hammerklavier* are altogether the struggling things some commentators seem to think. The strife is that in nature, from which order emerges, which creates. I won't forget the experience of first hearing – on a record – the second finale of Op. 130 immediately after the *Grosse Fuge*. It was as if Beethoven, having with immense effort created a world of fresh clean air and glorious sunlight, said, "Now we can play".

If we say that Beethoven reveals the widest and deepest-known human awareness – certainly in music, and perhaps in any art outside the greatest Shakespeare – we mean no more than that it shows the extent of Beethoven's consciousness at the time it was written. Perhaps that second finale is a glimpse of the joy that might have flourished had he lived, but it any case, joy is already the sense that suffuses Beethoven's last works more deeply than any other. It remains to be said that in every way Beethoven's last music is *later* – that's to say more truly advanced – than anybody else's.

APPENDIX 8
AGAINST LIPSIUS
Robert Simpson

(first broadcast as 'The Ferociously Anti-Pessimist Composer' R3, 12 May 1971 and subsequently published in the Listener)

In a broadcast discussion not long ago between Deryck Cooke and Jascha Horenstein, I was described as an optimist and a humanist. The same thing, more or less, was said about Nielsen, whose music has greatly influenced mine. I'd like briefly to examine these concepts, at least as I think they apply to me and my work.

A composer can't see himself as others see him, but he's the only one who really knows what he's got to cope with. Edmund Rubbra, who heard the discussion, wrote in the Listener that he saw no necessary connection between optimism and a humanism, as he put it, 'devoid of religious faith'. I'd go further than that and say that I can see no necessary connection between optimism and humanism, or between optimism and religious faith, for that matter. I tend to think of religion (at least in its most common forms) as man's failure to recognise his own wholeness, pessimistically attributing those parts of himself he doesn't understand to the supernatural. To that extent I suppose I'm a humanist of sorts, though I don't have most humanists' faith in human nature, certainly not as it appears to have shown itself at large so far.

One of the worst features of humanity (perhaps the worst) is the inertia with which the vast majority allows the aggressions of the power-hungry minority to dominate; it has always been so, and much as I would like to, I'm not really able to share the Marxist optimism that it will ever be otherwise. This mass inertia, it seems to me, could well be the result of some basic flaw, such as the isolation of individual consciousness, perhaps. I'm not talking about 'original sin', but about a possible wrong turning in evolution. There are millions of life forms on this planet, and probably countless more in the universe. From what we know about the history of life on earth, all the various forms that have existed have either become extinct through inadequacy or changes of conditions, or reached a static state – the dinosaurs on the one hand and the ants on the other, for instance.

Man would not readily assume himself to be doomed in this way – but his behaviour is no warranty of exemption. The distinction he seems at times to be approaching is that of being the first creature to annihilate itself by means of its own ingenuity, perhaps by totally polluting his environment, by blowing himself to smithereens or (most likely) by besotting his own intelligence and sensitivity with the foul products of rampant commercialism. All these possibilities could be the consequence of inertia. The difficulty that faces any honest creative artist lies in the fact that at no previous time have these dangers seemed so imminent.

All this would seem to brand me as a pessimist, not an optimist. But if I can't cheerfully describe myself as an optimist, I must insist that I'm an anti-pessimist of the utmost vehemence – ferociously anti-pessimist, in fact, for there's no other realistic form my anger can take. Pessimism would allow all these fearful things to happen; it would do nothing. In Nielsen's music we can already find this kind of anti-pessimism, foreseeing a situation that did not quite exist in his time, though it was incipient, and reflected in the gloomy late romanticism against which he reacted so powerfully. Nielsen understood that things were going seriously wrong, but he hoped there was a chance. One of the most profound of his simple remarks was that music was the sound of life.

In a sense all art is optimistic; it's an optimistic act to write something down, since you presumably hope somebody will take some notice. In this sense the smallest artist is an optimist. But there is a great gulf between what I call 'Yes art and No art'; I prefer these terms to the more equivocal 'optimistic' and 'pessimistic'. The greatest art I know (and which I think most perceptive people will recognise) defies death by being organic. When Nielsen said that music was the sound of life he also meant that it was not the sound of death. And I don't think he meant just any music; he meant music of a certain organic vitality, such as he himself was aiming at.

Serious artists and lovers of art reserve their deepest appreciation for what they call organic; if they see in a work a convincing analogue of living processes, these they recognise as art that says 'Yes' to life, whether the expression is tragic or comic. All great art defies death. It resents and challenges it, even where it depicts it. When we call it organic we mean (as Nielsen meant) that it is the sound of life, that its processes are like living processes, informed by vital interactions that inwardly cause it to take forms that are superbly clear and energetic, the complexity of their inner forces inevitably resolved into outer forms that are unmistakably alive.

There's precious little such art today, and I think we must be very cautious about worshipping the gods that such an age as ours throws up. In a time when mental pollution is even more serious than physical, popularity is no commendation. In all periods of so called civilisation, most art has been worthless and I have had it put to me that the same is true now, that my depressing view of the appreciation of the arts today doesn't properly take this into account. But all mediocre (and even bad) art of the eighteenth century or any other period than our own aims at being art. This is the first age to produce anti-art, consciously and deliberately anti-organic, not defying death but playing with it. The abrogation of the artist's authority is the snuffing out of his life. He becomes a symptom of a sickness, the smell of the corpse. I don't want to be either of these things, even if I end up as useful compost. This makes me not so much an optimist as an anti-pessimist, and a humanist only insofar as I hope humanity at large might eventually emerge. It takes a Beethoven to demonstrate that humanity isn't merely a concept; the rest of us can only try, but it's important that we do. The moment I'm completely unconvinced of this I shall stop composing.

In the discussion I referred to, Jascha Horenstein remarked that what interested him in my work was 'the absence of any reference to the existence of people like Schoenberg, Webern, Bartók, Stravinsky – his behaviour as a composer is as if these people never existed.' If my dear friend had stopped to think about it, he wouldn't have said this about any serious composer, even if he meant it as a compliment, which I naturally think he did.

Schoenberg is far from being my favourite composer, but it so happens that the idea for a new treatment of tonality came to me from listening, not to Nielsen or any other composer I love, but to Schoenberg's Piano Concerto, many years ago. It struck me that in spite of the serial technique the work was fixed to a tonal centre, which loomed periodically behind the murk, and was deliberately avoided at the end – as if Schoenberg had finally made a fearsome effort to exorcise a ghost. I thought then, though I didn't know how, that it might be possible to make a positive use of this phenomenon. I didn't want, as Schoenberg did, to deny tonality – I wanted to find a way to make tonal centres react against each other, not make non-tonality react against tonality. I felt (and still feel) that to try to anaesthetise the listener's tonal sense was to deny oneself a powerful means of expression. So atonality was not for me.

But the fact remains that it was Schoenberg who started this train of thought, who, by making me react against him, had a positive effect. It was only later that I found confirmation of my own instincts in Nielsen, as if I had discovered a kind of music that I knew ought to exist somewhere – and there it was. Horenstein, incidentally, said that Nielsen wasn't an intellectual. Well, he met him, and I unluckily was born too late, but to judge by the music, and by Nielsen's beautiful prose style, by his comprehensive appreciation of literature, painting and sculpture, and his profound knowledge of philosophy, I'd say he was an intellectual of high distinction, and I can only assume that his quietness and modesty (to say nothing of a foreign language) wouldn't permit him on that occasion to indulge in conversational fireworks. After my encounter with Schoenberg had produced what Hans

Keller calls productive tension, Nielsen gave me the kind of intellectual and spiritual support I needed to help me go my own way.

As for the other composers Horenstein mentioned, Webern certainly had no influence on me at all, except the negative one of indicating to me in wonderfully precise terms exactly what I don't want to do. Bartók and Stravinsky have interested me in certain aspects of sonority, but I have reacted strongly against the inorganic nature especially of Stravinsky; I'm quite convinced that if there's ever a better age, he won't be its favourite composer.

All this goes to show that one doesn't need to reveal one's influences in any imitative way; negative influences are as important as obviously positive ones, of which (on the other hand) one shouldn't be ashamed – no-one born deaf could ever be a composer, though if it could happen, now is the time; only the fact that I've conversed with some so-called avant gardistes and they've heard what I said has convinced me that they are at least able to perceive sound waves. It's not impossible that one of these gentlemen might get the idea of getting hold of a congenital deaf mute, of somehow explaining to him that there was such a thing as music, and getting him to write some down – aleatoricism come full circle, the random achieved by deliberate and precise notation! I can only hope I haven't given someone an idea, though in this I'm no optimist. Not long ago a man came and showed me a score (or rather a diagram) and I jokingly said I didn't understand why no-one had thought of the idea of inviting the audience to go up and poke the musicians with umbrellas, to see what effect this would have on the sounds produced. To my horror he said with incorruptible sincerity and seriousness, 'Well, ye-es... maybe... interesting idea ... perhaps ... why not?" And, believe me, there are not a few critics who would write solemnly about it.

All this is only a symptom of the real pessimism which I'm ferociously anti. But it's not enough to be a merely anti. It may be platitudinous to follow this up by saying that something positive is needed. But it is! If I react against the situation into which I've been pitchforked through no choice of my own, I'm entitled to look for sustenance where I can get it. I find it in art and in people that in the profoundest sense defy death, perhaps above all in Beethoven, who does not belong merely to the past. In Beethoven I find more force of life than in any twentieth-century composer; his is still the most powerful heart, mind and voice in music. I'd rather try to learn from him than from anybody, and trust to luck and what talent, guts and scepticism I've got to pull me through the ordeal. Scepticism is very important – it should be taught in schools. We must try to write music for a better age; unless we try, no-one will ever succeed. Some people are trying. As for the rest, Laurence Sterne prophetically had them taped as long ago as the 1760s.

I'm extremely grateful to Mr Bernard Dunstan for quoting in a letter to the *Listener* this, from *Tristram Shandy*; his letter is about the similar situation in the field of painting:

You forget the great Lipsius, quoth Yorick, who composed a work the day he was born; they should have wiped it up, said my uncle Toby, and said no more about it.

APPENDIX 9

SYMPHONIES

by Robert Simpson

People who write symphonies usually do it because they feel able to: a lot of those who don't feel able tell everyone else the symphony is dead. If they think this, they are quite right not to attempt symphonies. I take leave, however, to question their right and even their common sense if they will insist on telling me (or anyone else who feels able to compose symphonies) that it is wasted effort. They had better get on with their work and let me get on with mine. The trouble is that the symphony as an abstraction does not exist: there may be exhausted symphonies and exhausted composers, but the response to a challenge to one's capacity for large-scale organisation and development - that can be exhausted only in individuals. There may be many such exhausted characters around nowadays, but that is no reason to collapse into conformity. There are also those whose talents genuinely lie elsewhere: they are usually too busy to tell other people what they ought not to be doing. The only relationship that matters is between the composer and his human audience: there is (or should be) no connection whatever between the artist and the trendist or professional opinionist, both of whom deal far too often in vague abstractions, the result of never having had to face the fearsome difficulties of actually making music. This leads inevitably to the stance of the critic who approaches everything with the disastrous awareness that his response has to be a plausible opinion – plausible, that is, to those prepared to swallow the same rickety system of general apprehensions.

So let's all get on with our jobs, provided they <u>are</u> jobs. The fact that a composer may not be interested in the 'relevance' of anti-this-or-that is no reason to accuse him of being out of touch: his lack of interest may be the result of his being only too well in touch. It would seem more than futile nowadays to charge Beethoven with having been out of touch with Hummel or Reicha, or J.S. Bach with Sammartini or young Gassmann.

Ultimately we can do only what we are constituted to do: whether we do it well or not is what really matters – and contact with durable human instincts is more vital than tagging onto fashions. Such thoughts arise not unnaturally in an atmosphere where constructive work is perforce difficult, where what is euphemistically known as 'counter-culture' is discussed by those who enjoy the game of abstracting ingenious meanings from the deliberately meaningless. Those who do not wish to join in the fun are dubbed conservatives: we are in fact conservationists, interested in trying to express human force by means of positive musical development. The crucial word is 'trying', and it is a worse than sad thought that so simple an aim, which should be an artistic axiom, can now be treated as pretentious. It should not be necessary to say such things, but saying them is now part of the trying. If we don't try, no one will ever succeed.

Another reason for this stream of generalities is the difficulty of specifically discussing one's own works, and it may be that those who share my views will find such generalities helpful in approaching the two new symphonies I have written: more helpful, possibly, than a thicket of analytical description, couched in the dry language that modesty dictates. Both these works aim at human responses, the Fourth more approachably, perhaps, than the Fifth. The dedication of No 4 'to my friend and fellow Beethovenian James Loughran' is not simply a reference to a common interest of the conductor and myself: it is relevant to the nature of the work, in which Beethoven's influence is pervasive. It is essentially a classical symphony, in four movements, even going so far as to have a main tonality (E flat) with the two middle movements in dominant and subdominant. The influence of Beethoven is, I feel, organic more than stylistic (in no sense is this symphony neo-classical), and the first and last movements are very freely constructed, having nothing to do with sonata, except in a very general developmental sense. The two inner movements, on the other hand, are more 'regular'; the scherzo comes second and is on a very large scale, with a trio that quotes literally an innocent passage from Haydn's Symphony No 76 in E flat, confronting it with problems that do not disturb it. After this, the return of the scherzo is completely recomposed, only the subject-matter being the same. The slow third movement is large and calm, and in straightforward ternary (ABA) shape; it leads directly into the active finale. The Fifth Symphony is entirely continuous, but falls into five divisions: an Allegro at each end, a brief Scherzino in the middle, and on either side of that a slow canonic section. The work opens with a soft sustained string chord that is basic to the symphony; it reappears sometimes unexpectedly, as its function is analogous to that part of your mind that coldly observes yourself no matter what disturbances, mental or physical, occur. When this symphony was half-written, I was taken seriously ill. Completing it some months later was no worse a problem that it would in any case have been, since the whole was more or less complete in my head. But the experience, though not pleasant, was salutary in confirming once and for all that there is indeed a part of the mind that, by remaining objectively detached, helps you to survive if you can hang on to it.

(Article published in The Listener, 19th April 1973)

APPENDIX 10

WHY COMPOSE?

by Robert Simpson

The passion for verbal explanations that grips many present-day composers interests me less and less; on occasions I have thought an explanatory programme note might possibly help to get the audience (which does not, for this purpose, include the critics) on my side. But this has always been a mistake, not because of any obvious consequent antagonism from the audience, but because explanations tend to distract rather than focus attention. They also offer journalists material to pervert. So in the long run it is far better to let the music speak for itself; if it needs explaining, it needs a prop. I don't believe that the most elaborate (and even lucid) programme note would have made the Grosse Fuge any more approachable for its first audience. Beethoven would have snorted at the idea. If this is my view, why do I agree to write here about my own work? The answer is – I do not. Instead, and perhaps with more relevance than any attempt to explain myself away in technical terms, there is something to be said about the situation in which an artist finds himself today, about the problems of creating anything at all.

A composer who has spent his whole life trying to discover and master his own skills (not the same as mere academic adroitness), whose natural inclination is to consider himself above all a musician, is faced with a situation unprecedented in history. He is inevitably disturbed by the spectacle of not only music but all the arts under attack by philistines that Schumann could not have conceived of, even as a joke. At present the very existence of art itself is consciously and deliberately threatened, not by mere incompetence, but by anti-artists who deny the value of all positive achievements of civilization, past or present. When I first joined the BBC in the early 1950s it was thought a matter for regret (and occasionally amusement) that some composers arrived to hear the first rehearsals of new works in a state of curiosity, unfortunately not knowing what they were about to hear, and certainly unable, most of the time, to tell whether what was being played was correct (i.e. as written) or not. We could not know then that this was a form of unconscious mental aleatoricism. I remember having a lively argument with a young composer who insisted that it was not necessary to imagine the sound of what you wrote down. Is it surprising that the random was soon and conveniently elevated to a principle by those whose faculties could not tolerate the rigours of the imagination? The anti-artists could not have stumbled on a more apt road to madness; they have not been slow to exploit it, for what could be easier? The recent broadcast by the European Broadcasting Union of two simultaneous phenomena (I forbear to call them compositions, as their authors would probably be offended) devised by two individuals without collusion is by no means the end of the road. What we used to suggest as a joke is now commonplace; I venture to propose (as a joke, of course) that the EBU should now attend to the possibility of simultaneously improvised works by deaf mutes, afflicted of course from birth, to ensure that the purity of their impulses should not be corrupted by the slightest experience of music. I once offered the organiser of a series of fashionable concerts a work in which the performers ate each other; his refusal no doubt sprang from a suspicion that he might not, yet, be able to get away with it. When he feels the climate of opinion has advanced enough, the offer is still open, though I shall stipulate that he is one of the performers, and the other a certain well known critic. To prolong the performance as long as possible they must start with each other's feet.

The anti-artists (and we must be clear that this is their own name for themselves) would not bother to call us musician composers conservatives. When Karlheinz Stockhausen was asked if he thought that all music would eventually be electronic or random, and if human performers would cease to exist, his answer was No – there would always be the complete spectrum, from the ape to the Holy Spirit. We must be grateful not to be condemned to annihilation, though a little apprehensive as to which end of the spectrum we are consigned. Conservatism apparently does not come into it, and for that I personally am thankful, being a fierce left-winger myself. In the face of the mental pollution to which we are all being mercilessly subjected I would rather describe myself as a conservationist composer, hoping that an attempt to achieve direct and disciplined human expression may still meet with a response somewhere. When one is in the thick of things one tends perhaps to attribute to small but strident factions more importance than they possess, for it is extremely difficult to think in a confused noise. A serious composer is also understandably distracted by sympathy for those who are alienated by this terrible world, who have allowed themselves to emit only squeals of helpless despair. All this makes it very hard to compose nowadays. Sometimes we are tempted to wonder if the human race is going to forget art in the future – in other words whether the species is going to fail in its struggle to become human. But there is Beethoven, among many other great artists, to prove that humanity is not altogether a forlorn hope, and there is the overwhelming fact that most intelligent and sensitive people show that they need this kind of stimulus. This knowledge makes it worthwhile to go on trying; and there are still artists who are convinced of this. To some such a view might seem arrogant, but it is not so much so as the contemptuously boring insults to human sensibility that trade on the fear of critics to be thought old-fashioned. Many of us who understand the situation may not succeed in our attempts to express a valid and durable humanity, held fast in concentrated, disciplined, deeply felt works of art; none of us can be absolutely sure that his talent is sufficient or his resolution strong enough. But if no one tries, no one can succeed.

There are many ways of making the attempt, according to experience and temperament. For myself, a great love of the classics, especially Beethoven and Haydn, is the strongest influence. This does not involve yet another form of "neo-classicism" along the lines first suggested by the works of Saint-Saëns and later more strikingly by Stravinsky. It means an attempt to recover classical energy rather than the mannerisms of classical styles, to attack the problem from the inside. It is a mistake to suppose there is nothing new to learn from the classic masters; wherever one can find deep excitement, there is something to learn. As a composer I wish to express in my own way the kind of excitement and enlargement of spirit I feel when I listen to Beethoven; this means accepting the challenge of the symphony when the stream is running the other way. By "the symphony" I mean the most highly organized and deeply energetic kind of composition, in which all elements increase each other's potency. Adopting classical forms is not necessarily the way to do this, though they need not be excluded. True form arises when a composer succeeds in productively disciplining his instincts, and his musical instincts are largely formed by his experience of music. I, at least, do not believe that one born deaf could ever become a composer, though there may be some who do. My first great musical experience occurred when I was Fourteen, hearing Beethoven's Sixth Symphony on the radio from a Promenade Concert; I didn't know what had hit me and went out of the house and walked around in a daze for hours. This experience has remained vivid ever since, and I cannot now hear a fine performance of Beethoven without recapturing some of that excitement, added to which, naturally enough, is a deeper understanding of its cause. Is it surprising that I should want to express something of this in my own efforts? It would be surprising (and abject) if I did not.

As a product of the Twentieth Century I cannot help being acutely conscious of my own time. So the music that emerges from attempts to express my own reactions to these great and humane works of the past is inevitably permeated by conflicts that, I hope, will eventually prove new because realistic. The present is the product of the past, and it is unrealistic to relegate vital and profound works to a museum; in creative work one must relate them to the here and now, not in any over-sophisticated self-conscious way, but instinctively. All the greatest artists have expressed in the languages of their time certain human truths that remain constant; if it were not so their works would have died with them. Why do we go on looking at Rembrandt and listening to Shakespeare and Beethoven, being impressed by the great Gothic cathedrals? It is because they represent all the most marvellous attributes that distinguish man from the inarticulate animals; we feel this, even at our most desperate, and are strengthened, though we may not always understand why. For the same reason our astronomers continue to pursue the quest begun by the ancients; mere curiosity of the kind that killed the cat is insufficient. We may have lost the euphoric Nineteenth Century romantic belief in the inevitability of Progress (the collapse of this, after all, led to romantic despair and the cynicism we now see) but we may still determine to do our best. Unless we do we are finished. It is possible, even probable, that not enough of us will try.

(from '20 British Composers', Chester, 1975)

APPENDIX 11

AFTERTHOUGHT: THE COMPOSER AND THE AUDIENCE

The Proms have always fulfilled a clear responsibility to contemporary music, a duty the more pressing because they are run on public money and because their audience has a certain stability, both in the Albert Hall and on the radio. No single planner, engaged even for a restricted period, could be expected to know the full spectrum of new music at any given time throughout the world. In this field a committee could be valuable, even necessary, a research committee made up of BBC personnel, using fully the BBC's wide contacts at home and abroad. Much of this work is already done through the regular score-reading process entrusted by the music department to a panel of substantial musicians, augmented in cases of doubt by the staff themselves. Works are also brought to the Controller's attention by various interested parties. Knowledge of what is going on in most areas of modern music is therefore extensive and up-to-date (Richard Howgill once remarked: 'We must have the means to represent what we are afraid is happening'). Directing research with a special eye to the Proms would be a simple and useful further step, since the BBC's present intake of new music for consideration depends largely on what is submitted, what may be picked up from foreign radio tapes, or what may be found in contemporary music festivals. This certainly provides a wide range of information. But if the BBC were able to make firm and cogent programmes for a whole Prom season well in advance, it would become even more important to carry out a positive search for new matter, rather than rely to a great degree on what presents itself. Provision must always be made, of course, for very new works, produced after the season has been essentially planned, felt to be striking enough to warrant early placing; this need not be a problem unless the music in question is for highly unusual resources – postponement in that case need neither surprise nor too severely disappoint the composer. The nature of commissioned works will normally be known in advance.

The Prom audience has already shown itself tolerant of nearly everything a contemporary composer can throw at it, and this demonstrates the range of material exposed at the Proms. It is right that the Proms should do what lamentably few public concerts will risk; most concert-promoters who depend on box-office takings will realistically avoid including present-day music that they know will halve the audience. Contemporary music tends to become segregated in heavily subsidised concerts, or in festivals devoted to it, and its audience becomes a coterie. This is an unhealthy climate for it, and the BBC itself is not guiltless of compounding the situation in studio programmes like 'Music in Our Time', which cannot avoid being a ghetto, unnecessarily so because there is no economic excuse for it. From time to time an established symphony orchestra will commission a new work by means of a grant from, say, the Arts Council of Great Britain; this it will perform at one of its regular concerts, usually for the first and last time. These performances are often under-rehearsed. They frequently illustrate the musicians' saying, 'The first performance is the last rehearsal', while at the same time showing off the astonishing speed with which British orchestral players can reach the point of being able to negotiate the most difficult scores. But there is no time for considered artistic achievement, and many a new work has been dropped after its first 'performance' because although it has been placed in a concert it has not been heard at all. Being acutely aware of all this, the unfortunate composer sitting in the hall is the last person to blame the orchestra for the fact that he is the only person in a couple of thousand (or maybe a few hundred thousand if the concert is broadcast) who knows that what is emerging is not what he heard in his mind. In such conditions the critics cannot truly assess what they imagine they are supposed to be hearing. Only several performances, each more confident and free than the last, can put matters right. The BBC is in a unique position to see that this happens, and I would advocate an extension of the occasional practice that the Prom performance (or the Festival Hall performance by the BBC Symphony Orchestra) is not necessarily the first – it should be the first public appearance of the work, which will have already been given several times on the air.

In Britain the BBC sponsors the only large-scale public music-making that does not treat the box-office as a crucial consideration. The Corporation is concerned to recoup expenses and even to reap a profit if possible, and we have seen how it could move further in this direction if it made rational use of its own resources. The Proms do not have a captive audience, but it is one whose loyalty dies hard, and it has proved possible to present it with fare that would empty the Festival Hall (as the BBC's own Wednesday concerts sometimes demonstrate!). So it is not necessary to exhort the Proms to adventurousness – only to say that when you can plan your adventures with real foresight they will become the more exciting and the audience the more discriminating. The Prommers have been called indiscriminate, and there is amongst them an element more demonstrative than discerning, an exhibitionist minority such as may be found in any large band of enthusiasts. But the whole audience, not counting the radio listeners, is considerably larger than that leaning on the rail in front of the orchestra. The opportunity to perform new music in public has been seized at the Proms as nowhere else, and a vital aspect of its presentation is the context in which it is heard. Only occasionally is there a 'fringe' Prom for a 'fringe' audience of the kind that will also frequent places where they display piles of bricks. The normal practice is to play new music in company with more familiar or traditional works, against which it must stand or fall, and this helps to bring it an audience as well as providing a perspective in which it can be perceived. The fact that this is noteworthy is disturbing, and raises the question of why contemporary music is often an audience deterrent, and why it is so often shovelled into a corner.

The composers themselves are not entirely blameless. One may fairly and sympathetically observe that audiences are apt to want to spend their money on what they know will give them satisfaction, but their unwillingness to face a new work is not always due to conservatism. Most music-lovers will grimace if the subject is broached, and the reaction reveals not caution but active hostility. Audience and composer have become alienated from each other, and it is only a small minority of concert-goers which experiences pleasurable curiosity at the thought of a first performance. The rest bases its response on what it regards as bitter experience, and this is not to be ascribed solely to a want of education in the matter. The bitterness of the experience is not altogether imaginary and it can evoke a proper reaction.

Why?

The reasons are inevitably complex and diverse. In the nineteenth century the so-called romantics, in response to a changed human climate and reacting against what had become in inferior hands a moribund 'classicism', sought increasingly to reflect and glorify a growing illusion of individual freedom and the western world's fascination with 'progress'. The would-be rationalism of the previous century was being supplanted by technical rather than abstract thought; instinctively resisting this trend, artists became inclined more to the subjective and were faced with a contradiction amounting to a predicament. The personal was more closely and defensively cultivated and cherished. As the working people became perforce trapped and stereotyped in the industrial revolution, the artist was more consciously determined to be different from his fellows, and the cult of individuality became an obsession, often coloured by a forced sense of pathos or tragedy. This was evident in many different arts, but the Austro-German musical hegemony made certain that in music its weightiest manifestation was in Central Europe. Where a Beethoven had had to grow up to an Eroica, a young romantic composer felt obliged to make it his Opus One. The cult of personality was in a sense the cult of immaturity, and the fatal looseness of structure common in that time was due to the failure to achieve mature grasp of the means to artistic integrity. There were also new discoveries, in part extensions of existing roots, in part their breakdown. As the desire for personal projection became more widespread and extreme, the elements of breakdown became more influential, and it was from Central Europe that most of them emanated. New and priceless enlargements of human consciousness, some highly disturbing but inescapable, were made possible. But the higher the degree of subjectivity, the lower was the potential for artistic integrity, which demands the power of detachment. Schoenberg must have sensed this in instinctively seeking to salvage order from a growing welter, and other composers at the turn of the century found themselves looking for systems, or cultivating sets of personal fingerprints by which they could be identified.

All this time, the rate of change in society was accelerating, with confusing effect on the sensitive artist who had always needed time for thought. We may object by remarking that Mozart or Schubert could compose so fast as to preclude any apparent pause for thought; but theirs was still a time of relative social stability and absence of obvious material change, when the language of music was not being rapidly and radically transformed. The objection also leaves out of account the fact that, apart from Mendelssohn in its first half, the nineteenth century possessed no Mozarts or Schuberts, though it is tantalising to try to imagine what might have happened if Schubert had lived into the 1870's. Even in Schubert, the only composer worthy to have followed Beethoven, we can find evidence of new and not altogether bracing influences, and it may well be significant that Mendelssohn, as he moved in his short life further into the century, seemed to lose something of the felicitous genius and perfection of taste that at first made him comparable to the two earlier composers. The historical – philosophical – sociological approach to artistic matters is often hazardous; but discernible general trends have to be explained in broad terms. There is some excuse for the idea that the late romantic composer, bent on the colossal, extruded his vast and sometimes prolix masterpieces with protracted grunts and snorts; high aspirations could prove no more than ambitions, and if imagined inspiration brought quick results, they were apt to want substance. Mahler wrote his enormous Eighth Symphony in a very short time; its first part is solidly composed, but its second, from the first solo baritone entry, is thrown overboard into an ocean of shameless 'kitsch' from which it is never rescued, least of all in the inflated ending, and it must be regarded as one of his weakest compositions. Such dangers were always liable to trap even the most gifted and intelligent musicians; the higher they aimed, the greater the risk of bathos.

Self-consciousness to the point of fixation, an obsessive urge to project the personality in a rapid vortex of change - these conditions saw the breakdown of norms; the process proved too often self-defeating, and only a few spirits felt obliged to resist it. The result was not fruitful diversification, but a gradual growth in uniformity. When all are making the same effort to be different, only the sameness of the effort characterises the majority. Genius is still distinguished, but more by its dependance on sharply identifiable hallmarks than on the breadth of its humanity or the organic nature of its processes. Among the less notable composers of the twentieth century the sameness is not of the kind that gave the eighteenth a lingua franca; it is a monotony born of haplessness, of a forced conformism at length compelled to the meaningless in pursuit of the singular. The pace of change in our world and the gigantic threat facing the species are dizzying to the artist; he may even declare himself the anti-artist, so contributing in his small way to the violence that is on the increase in society. Commercial pressures are such that the throwaway product becomes an object of contemplation and the artist, no longer the servant of patrons he can recognise, or conscious of a vitally receptive public, is victim to the pervasive mores methodically procured by the multinational corporations. Yet the public, ready enough to be hoodwinked by the advertisers of commercial goods, still retains a vestigial sense that music and the other arts ought to have more substance, more appealing humanity, some promise of permanence, a feeling constantly being confirmed by frequent encounters with the great masters. The average music-lover unsurprisingly suspects that something is badly wrong, although he cannot analyse it. He is intimidated into unreadiness to identify rubbish, and is not encouraged by a similar pusillanimity in the critics who, moreover, often disguise it by blinding him with pseudo-science. The result is an atmosphere in which for the first time in history it is possible to be thought a composer without being a musician. 'The Emperor's New Clothes' was never a more apt parable.

So composers cannot justly complain if the public regard them with plain suspicion; some are entitled to protest a little, but not against the public. Those who are sincerely and concentratedly striving to create mature work may fairly be angry at the trend that has bred an unreceptive and suspicious audience, mostly unwilling to risk the expense of concert tickets in these hard times. It is not surprising that promoters are equally unwilling to take their very much bigger risks, and it is a matter for relief and gratitude that something like the Proms exists to help restore the balance. The BBC'S present immunity from entrepreneurial infections must be jealously guarded; the encroachment of commercial interests, however it may stimulate altruism, must inevitably be a corrupting influence.

Another factor makes the composer's present situation different from any in the past. Imagine Haydn composing next week's symphony. He can see in his mind's eye every face in the audience that will hear it - there may be a few new ones, or some missing, but he is in the wonderful position of being able to say to himself: 'This is going to startle old So-and-so!', or, 'This'll kill 'em', or 'Whatsisname's going to be moved by this – he always reacts to a beautiful modulation', or 'I won't be able to play for laughing when this hits 'em!' This may have been a very real compensation for servitude, but the reality of human contact was more important; nothing could be more stimulating or rich in meaning than knowing, while you were writing it, who was going to be listening to your music in the near future. Think of Bach slogging away at next Sunday's cantata; he might be wondering which of the choirboys he would have to clout next, but he would also be thinking, not of a collection of aristocrats such as Haydn composed for, but of the ordinary folk he would meet in the street or their houses; they were not an audience of social superiors, and he must have known many of them intimately, on an equal footing. To them he would have been able to say: 'Sorry about all those da capos, but if you had to knock off a cantata every week, you'd be glad to get away with writing only two-thirds of every aria!' The ladies who clutched tear-sodden handkerchiefs while Beethoven improvised earned from him a contempt the more vigorous because he knew them only too well.

What of the composer of today? It is indeed rare that he can compose for a known audience, and the one precious thing he can sometimes do is compose for known performers – a joy denied to electronic operators! Even if he writes chamber music, aware that the numbers listening will be small, he is unlikely to know them as an audience, which may or may not contain a few friends, who may or may not be visible in the Queen Elizabeth Hall or even in the Wigmore Hall. If his orchestral music is being played, he sits in a huge hall among thousands of others, and if he goes on the platform afterwards he sees only a vast sea of anonymous faces. A gladiator in the Colosseum could not have felt less cosy. If he is himself an habitué of the Proms he will surely know some of the grins in the front row of the arena, though he will probably be unable to identify them in his mind as he composes – assuming he is writing something specially for the Proms, which is not a regular occupation of most composers. Far more new works are done on the radio than in the concert hall. Here the audience is invisible, and not only that – it is incalculable and seemingly immaterial; the music seems to go out on the empty air. There may afterwards be a letter or two from friends or even strangers who heard it, and the realisation that his music can be heard at great distances is for the composer a weird stimulus that Haydn could not have begun to imagine. But the composing of it cannot be enlivened by thoughts of So-and-so or Whatsisname. This is a most serious deprivation. One remedy I am at present trying is to get an articulate and intensely musical friend to describe the kind of symphony he would wish to hear, and then to try to oblige him. It is a little step towards Haydn's enviable condition, without the servitude.

ROBERT SIMPSON (Reprinted from 'The Proms and Natural Justice' Toccata Press, 1981)

APPENDIX 12

OUR SHY MASTERS

Robert Simpson

Hopes of escaping a nuclear holocaust could seem to hang on the inconvenience of such a catastrophe to the multi-national corporations which, as they grow bigger and fewer, seek to dominate and eventually control the world economy. They are still too diverse to have formed a coherent strategy, but their achievements are already alarmingly impressive, certainly more potent than most people understand. It is plainly in their interests to unify; this process is probably inevitable, and will entail the ruthless sacrifice of humanitarian considerations as well as the ambitions of many individuals within the corporations. Compunction will not be one of the salient virtues engendered in the process. The multinationals are even now deeply influential in the East as well as the West (a matter meticulously examined by Charles Levinson in his courageous book *Vodka-Cola* (1980); they work systematically to gain economic power in repressive regimes of both Right and Left, where they are assured of cheap, strike-free labour, enabling them to create convenient large-scale unemployment (in order to keep down wages) in the more advanced industrial countries. To this end they are much assisted by interested governments, including our own. Total destruction of these happy hunting grounds would clearly not be to their advantage; they will not be disposed to bring this about, though as will be seen they are not afraid to take risks in the pursuit of power. Moreover, by concealed infiltration of the political arena they are rendering national politics parochial, pliant and obsolescent, even in the largest and strongest states. This is a further method of safeguarding the gradually maturing strategy.

As the multinationals fuse together and concentrate themselves, increasingly able to circumvent contradictory national laws and regulations, they must be expected to form a faceless, clandestine world government, dedicated to its own power and profit. There are no strongly constituted, international monopoly commissions capable of preventing this. Many communication media, significant banking systems (including the International Monetary Fund), and most very large industries producing fuel, food, drugs, arms, machinery and advanced technology of all kinds, with research and development facilities, are already a part of this rapidly expanding organism. Giant entities tend to breed ingrowing inefficiency and possibly this one might at length break down, but not during the present dynamic formative stage or before it has become economically invincible.

This growing force obviously needs to avoid a nuclear world war, and although it is not yet fully able to dictate the course of events, it has a better chance of doing so than any other grouping. This does not mean that it is pacific. Its interests are effectively served by a constant and widespread succession of wars, large and small, in which some 30 million persons have been killed since the Second World War, conflagrations stoked by the arms trade, for which they are valuable proving grounds. The 17,000 million dollars spent on arms every two weeks would provide decent housing, food, education and health services for the world population in the same period (quoted by COPAT, Committee on Poverty and the Arms Trade). Most of the large-scale commerce in arms involves massively the corporations. By their activities and those of the US, USSR, French and British governments (the largest national participants) the Third World has been steadily made poorer and its regimes more oppressive, usually rich militaristic elites sustained by organisations into whose debt they have been manoeuvred. Their need to suppress protest means the purchase of more and better weapons, incurring greater debt, with increased subservience to the bodies that either initiated the process or simply exploited an existing situation.

So it is not advantageous to the corporations to expunge war; they benefit immensely from maintaining world tension. Their own extinction, however, is another matter; that would be involved with everyone else's in a nuclear conflict. But nuclear productivity is very much their business, and since (being still too many and too competitive) they are not yet able to control all the consequences of their activities, we cannot be completely hopeful that they will succeed in preventing disaster, precipitated by accident or by panic. Yet the spectacular arms race is at this stage necessary to them, and in fostering it they cannot be guiltless of inspiring the politicians, though they cannot stop some of these from uttering inanities that could never be ascribed to the cold rationalities of the calculating organisation man. But while political fanaticism might *seem* to father the chilling suggestion that a nuclear war could be both winnable and survivable, this may well be traced to covert industrial salesmanship aimed at governments all too willing to buy new types of 'strategic' devices. On the other hand, the terrifying Report of the *British Medical Association Board of Science and Education into the Medical Effects of Nuclear War* (April 1983) makes it perfectly clear that the British government's proposals for 'civil defence' are cynically preposterous. Where more sophisticated theories are concerned, many politicians still have to prove their disinterestedness; in some cases proof of honesty would be a certificate of madness. The BMA'S report, estimating a possible 38.6 million deaths and 4.3 million casualties in a nuclear attack on Britain, seems. to display a gaunt sense of humour in stating that it does not involve politics and could be used equally to justify massive armament or unilateralism. This disclaimer might have been better omitted, leaving the facts to speak for themselves.

The multinationals have grown from the capitalist system, but the physical destruction of the so-called communist bloc is not their object. They want rather to dominate it economically. In the not very long run the Soviet Union and its satellites will be unable to withstand this insidious pressure, and there is clear evidence that it is already coercive. Nuclear war is not needed for this purpose. Patience, unremitting assiduity and sustained, highly profitable terror – these will serve admirably, and the last is efficaciously assisted by aggressive political bluster on both sides of the Iron Curtain. A number of these mouthpieces have readily identifiable multi-national connections (see *Vodka-Cola*, cited above). Also helpful in this long-term cause are the predictably fruitless 'disarmament' or 'arms limitation' discussions at Geneva and elsewhere. The crazy spiral of expenditure, against a background of well-staged charades, is reaping untold profits for our shy masters, so skilled in exploiting the suspicion between rival blocs, while governments on all sides are increasingly in thrall to these unostentatious potentates.

In such a situation NATO and the Warsaw Pact are complementary. Without both, the strategy would be in some trouble – there can be no race without rivals. Capitalist the corporations may be, but they can scarcely be inclined to undermine militarily the Warsaw Pact while NATO exists. Technological 'secrets' pass to and fro – who knows by what mechanisms? These can always be shown to be various sorts of smuggling, and any accomplice whose cover is blown can always be dispensed into a handy jail by due process of law – or discreetly murdered. Krushchev may not altogether have been joking when he asked why everyone didn't employ the same spies, since we all knew the best ones. Ownership or control of much of the world's press and broadcasting makes it possible to represent whatever is desired; in dictatorships there is no problem, while in so-called democracies dissenting views may be allowed ephemeral outlet, virtually ineffectual against insistently and often subtly nurtured prejudice.

So what of the nuclear danger? It is now being proposed (at least in the US) that sole responsibility for peace should be put in the 'hands' of a sophisticated computer, programmed to fire on warning. This final attempt at intimidation has been rightly described as 'the ultimate madness'. Effectively forbidden objectives do not loom large in the history of nuclear armaments and if such a computer were to be employed it would constitute the extremity of risk. Because a technical hitch could mean catastrophe, the device would instantly abolish all human rights on earth, even if it never actually functioned. Such an apparatus would certainly have to be ordered from one or more of the multinationals. Human rights do not interest them.

But they do need a human population and could decide against the risk for amoral reasons. Rivalry between them, however, could ensure that if one group feigned altruism, another would be more 'realistic'. Those who propose that the deterrent should be retained because it purports to have prevented a major war for thirty-five years ought to be consistent enough to express satisfaction that both sides possess this great prophylactic. They should also realise that the opposing deterrents do not constitute some kind of reassuring status quo. And who is being deterred? All the information we receive in Britain about Soviet weapons and Soviet intentions comes from the US, either directly or through government channels. The man in the street cannot find out how much of this is truth, and its sheer volume is enough to soften his brain. Have no doubts about the oppressiveness of the so called communist regimes; it perfectly suits the aims of the multinational corporations which increasingly are propping them up. The economic weakness of these 'peoples' democracies' makes suspect the constant western harping on their military potential, which depends on vast loans from western banking systems owned or manipulated by the multinationals. While the political West tries to scare its poorer rival bloc into ever deeper expenditure and economic straits, the corporations pull it out of these into ever deeper debt.

This phenomenon adds significance to the fact that so far all talk of pre-emptive strikes or strategical nuclear devices has originated in the US. Sometimes rogue information slips embarrassingly out of America. A senior US weapons expert, Kosta Tsipis of the Massachusetts Institute of Technology, has recently revealed that US monitoring of Soviet missile tests has shown them to be 'not nearly accurate or reliable enough to destroy American missile silos in a first strike.' Tsipis estimates that Soviet missile accuracy is unlikely to improve dramatically in the foreseeable future. Unless one cynically interprets this as a green light for an American first strike, and even if one does not, it seriously compromises the persistent exaggerations of President Reagan and the Pentagon. And we should not forget that the Cruise missile is itself a first strike weapon. The British government's film against the peace movement, *A Better Road to Peace*, insists that the nuclear deterrent has kept the peace and that 'we just have to see that we keep it that way.' The Quaker Peace Secretary, Ron Huzzard, points out that 'this astonishing assertion implies an indefinite continuation of the nuclear arms race.' The 'keep it that way' mentality is creeping towards the sly totalitarianism exemplified recently by a small secret committee, permitting no public discussion, which contrived to turn Greenham Common into private land so as to be able legally to evict the Women's peace camp. This type of person is always the first to denounce the denial of human rights in the USSR (though they rarely mention Chile or South Africa).

If a nuclear war occurs between the super-powers it will be more likely by accident than by design. But the mere accumulation of such destructive power incalculably compounds the chances of an irreversible accident. It also advances the nightmare certainty of proliferation, which can hardly be forbidden or even discouraged by those clinging to their own arsenals. Advocates of the independent deterrent ignore both these perils. One cannot deter a mishap, nor can it be prevented for certain by any human or technical means. The longer this stockpile exists and waxes, the nearer looms inevitable global accident. The multinational corporations offer no plausible assurance of whatever sinister safety they have in mind for us. The sophistries that would risk the torment and annihilation of humanity cannot be defended and must be attributed to criminal intrepidity, cynical disregard or hapless gullibility.

In permitting political influences to affect its vote on the subject, the Synod of the Church of England betrayed not only its avowed faith but also the people who depend on it for moral guidance. That Jesus would have voted against the nuclear deterrent must be obvious to Christian and non-believer alike. In a letter to *The Guardian* (14 February 1983) Donald Matheson said crisply 'The Synod has voted. When do the Christians vote?' The Archbishop of Canterbury averred that the absence of a nuclear deterrent would make a terrible conventional war more probable. But it cannot logically be asserted that a war between the great powers would remain 'conventional', and if this argument is carried to its conclusion, the only sane policy is to get rid of all weapons; as a leader of Christians the Archbishop of Canterbury should have insisted on this as the only moral policy – indeed the only hope, now all guarantee has gone that the pursuit of violence will not end in our demise. The splendid and inimitable James Cameron might perhaps observe that this demise would not dismay the Christian sure of the delights of heaven, though he would no doubt wonder what could be done about the sudden overcrowding of that glorious place, and the even worse problems facing the administration in the other.

Here is the crux. For the first time in history it is possible for the human species to wipe itself out, almost at a stroke. It is not necessary to refute the thoughtless objection that there have always been bigger and better weapons, from the stone axe to the bomber, that nuclear bombs are simply worse bombs. Nor should it be necessary to point out that those insisting that it is better to be dead than red are somewhat presumptuously inviting everyone else, whatever their persuasions, to join them in oblivion. They really must include everyone else – it is no longer possible to defend what has to be destroyed in the process. If we do not wish to be a wrong turning in evolution we must determine that these Damocletian devices be dismantled before they dispose of us, by accident, by, human panic or by mere technical inefficiency. This insistence will have to come from every corner of the world if it is to have the least effect on the small number of obdurate and powerful people who have imposed the threat. Nothing would be more likely to start such a reaction than the courageous decision of one country to give up not only the most obscene option, but all armaments. If no other state followed this example the moral necessity would have been honoured. Whether or not there were any positive official responses, the consequent pressure from the common people of the world might well become irresistible, a possibility not less credible than the disaster that will surely follow its denial. The fact that there is now quite a large body of opinion in favour of this action is the one gleam of visible hope.

No one should believe the dissembling protestations of the present British government that it realistically serves the peace by hanging on to its own nuclear armoury and by harbouring a foreign power's offensive missiles, so rendering the UK a prime target in any conflict. Such talk serves only the arms race and those who profit by it; the arguments are fabricated and their recent intensifications reflect no more than a sneaking fear that the peace movement might become too influential in trying to save what remains of honest sanity. How much sanity does remain after the stultifying onslaughts of the media – East and West – the repressive terror in totalitarian states across the world, the unthinkable poverty, starvation and crippling diseases in the multinationals' vast guinea pig, the Third World – all terminally menaced (not deterred!) by a giant, mindless, precarious mechanism?

This is the moment in human evolution when it has become finally obligatory to give up violence as a means of settling differences. It has previously been possible to survive this flaw, at least physically; morally we have been diminished by every manifestation of it. It would be naive indeed to expect this chaotic and misdirected world to arrive at a practical solution of this or any other kind. But to relinquish violence is not only our last hope of climbing successfully out of the jungle – it is the one slim chance we have of survival. Its unlikelihood does not bar it from being the only realism; the Domesday clock ticks on remorselessly. If you are drowning there is no time for sophistical pragmatism. Can the world learn to swim so quickly? There is no lifeline in the prevarications of Church officials, the sophistries of politicians, the ingenuities of diplomats, the viciousness of terrorism or the machinations in multinational boardrooms. The voice of sanity is heard' but faintly through the roar of the big battalions. Are we, after all, Mother Nature's most disastrous mistake? Did Beethoven, Rembrandt and Shakespeare live for nothing? Were they no more than a fleeting glimmer of what might have been? And what about Mother Teresa and the uncountable kindnesses in the world from age to age? If all these wonders vanish, can there be any tiresome recriminations? Yes - there may still be a few of us left to gasp them out, but not for long.

From Unholy Warfare—The Church and the Bomb
(Edited by David Martin and Peter Mullen, Basic Blackwell, 1983)

APPENDIX 13

ON COMPOSING CHAMBER MUSIC

By Robert Simpson

There can be no greater challenge to a composer than a kind of music in which every detail must be heard with frightening clarity; in composing for a few instruments he is really up against it. I forget who it was who said, sharply: "There is no mercy in art" – but he might have been thinking of chamber music, and of string trios and quartets in particular. Indeed, there is no mercy in any art; if you aim at perfection in anything you are up against the nearly impossible. It is perhaps easier to create an effect if your resources give you a certain kind of scope. A not very good composer can sometimes get away with a blast from the brass or a few detonations from the percussion department if he doesn't know what to do next in an orchestral piece but he can't do that in a real symphony, and if he's the sort of composer who can't resist temptations like that, he's not really capable of composing proper symphonies, which are the most serious and demanding kind of orchestral music. There's no better training for writing symphonies than writing string quartets – or vice versa. Perhaps I should have said that chamber music, with its intimate quality and its natural transparency, is the ideal medium for the finest kind of musical thinking, and that composing symphonies for the orchestra means that you have to apply the same sort of discipline. If you want to do the very best you can in any medium, don't look for mercy!

There is of course good and bad chamber music. Those who play it are very much aware of what sort of part it is they have. Is it merely padding or does it feel like an individual voice? To play a great quartet by Beethoven is to feel part of a profound conversation, and the music exists for you whether or not there is an audience – you and the other players are engaged in an activity that absorbs you quietly, and you don't (or shouldn't) think about *projecting* yourself to an audience as you would, say, in playing a concerto. The music may have its periods of vehemence, even fierceness, but these are not attempts to stun the hearer with main force, as in some orchestral climaxes. There are times when the pressure of the thought or the feeling demands an extra intensity that the players must direct *towards each other* rather than towards an audience at a distance. There are a good many highly accomplished chamber ensembles (some of them very famous) that do not appear to understand this.

All music needs to reach a wide range of humanity if it is to survive, and if we say that chamber music is meant mainly for the players, we don't mean that it's exclusive of the audience. Audiences love listening to chamber music, and rightly, because there is nothing more illuminating than to eavesdrop on a marvellous conversation (that is, if you can't take part in it yourself!). But the more the music absorbs the players and makes them forget the audience, the greater it is, and the more it must naturally appeal to the listener. That is what the composer of – chamber music must remember all the time. As he writes each part, he must think of its contribution to a coherent conversation; it must be utterly individual as an instrumental part, yet it must never get out of hand and hog the limelight, unless there's some enormously compelling reason, as for instance in those remarkable recitatives for the violin in Beethoven's Op.132 quartet.

Normally there's no limelight in chamber music, and if one player gets temporary prominence, the balance has somehow to be restored before long. Since everything can be heard by players and audience with great clearness it is essential that the composer be sure that his own imagination hears everything with clarity and justice - clarity because he should in any case never write down anything he can't imagine (this happens all too often these days!), and justice because he must see to it that each player gets a just share of the argument. So composing chamber music is the finest possible discipline for sharpening the inner ear and for developing the power of sustained musical thought with the utmost precision.

Chamber music not only shows these basic necessities in a composer (or their absence); it ruthlessly exposes any tendency he may have to exaggerate. He won't be able to get away with extravagance. Just as in playing chamber music it is fatal to show off, so it is with composing it. Brilliant fireworks have to be justified by the current of the music; they can be thrown off only when the conversation reaches a pitch of excitement that infects all the participants, or when one member gains the exhilarated support of the others (how wonderful when this happens in the coda of the first movement of Beethoven's E flat quartet, Op.74!). Brilliance can erupt at the right time; emotional inflation never. Intensity isn't the same thing as emotionalism piled on for effect; real intensity of feeling comes when the music itself grows into it, when it is the inevitable consequence of real inner pressures. Nothing is crueller to the habitual emoter than chamber music, as we can see in more than a few late romantic works that try to sound like symphonic poems. If the feeling of the music is not also its substance we have disaster; this of course applies to any music, but the fact is never concealed by chamber music.

In writing individual parts the composer must take care to respect the natural qualities and possibilities of the instruments. Present-day composers don't do this often enough; players frequently complain that they are asked to force from their instruments things for which they were not evolved. It's true that instrumental techniques have evolved through the demands of composers, and many things that were once thought unplayable are now taken for granted. This is natural, and the composer who too often plays safe is as doomed as the one who thinks of nothing but inventing new tricks. But if a composer genuinely stretches the capabilities of an instrument, he does this by extending what is natural to it; it may at first seem strange or difficult, but time will show whether the extension is natural and whether the music justifies it. In chamber music the thought must justify everything, and as in all the other aspects of it, falsity is mercilessly revealed. I have often heard players say that in many new works they aren't conscious of playing different instruments – they merely make the same sort of sounds at different pitches. In this way all character disappears, and composers begin to sound nightmarishly alike, having forgotten, for instance, that string instruments are tuned in fifths (ask yourself why!), that they are played normally with the bow and can *sing*, that the natural sonority of intervals on the piano can have meanings far beyond the mere instant combination of notes, or that wind instruments have registers other than extreme top or bottom. The chamber music composer, now more than ever before, must learn the truth that this is the medium that more than any other will show what he is really made of.

APPENDIX 14

Chronological List of Compositions

The publishers of each work (where known) are indicated to the right of the compositions in square brackets.

For convenient navigation, this list is divided into decades:
1940-49, 1950-59, 1960-69, 1970-79, 1980-89, 1990-97, unclassified, unfinished

1940-49

Sonata for piano (1946) [Lengnick]

Variations and Finale on a theme of Haydn (1948) (for piano) [Lengnick]

1950-59

Symphony No. 1 (1951) [Lengnick]

String Quartet No. 1 (1952) [Lengnick]

String Quartet No. 2 (1953) [Lengnick]

String Quartet No. 3 (1954) [Lengnick]

Allegro Deciso for strings (1954) [Lengnick]

Symphony No. 2 (1956) [Lengnick]

Canzona for brass (1958) [Lengnick]

Violin Concerto (1959) *(withdrawn)*

Variations and Fugue for recorder and string quartet (1959)

(this piece, thought lost, was reconstructed in 2000 from parts found in the Dolmetsch Archive by John B. Turner)

1960-69

Symphony No. 3 (1962) [Lengnick]

Incidental music to Ibsen's play *The Pretenders* (1965)

Trio for clarinet, cello and piano (1967) [Lengnick]

Piano Concerto (1967) [Lengnick]

Quintet for clarinet and string quartet (1968) [Lengnick]

1970-79

Energy: **symphonic study for brass band** (1971) [Boosey & Hawkes]

Symphony No. 4 (1972) [Lengnick]

Symphony No. 5 (1972) [Lengnick]

String Quartet No. 4 (1973) [Lengnick]

String Quartet No. 5 (1974) [Lengnick]

Incidental music to Milton's play *Samson Agonistes* (1974)

String Quartet No. 6 (1975) [Lengnick]

Quartet for horn, violin, cello and piano (1975) [Lengnick]

Media morte in vita sumus **for chorus, brass and timpani** (1975) [Lengnick]
('In the midst of death we are surrounded by life!")

Symphony No. 6 (1977) [Lengnick]

Symphony No. 7 (1977) [Faber]

String Quartet No. 7 (1977) [Lengnick]

Sonata for two pianos (1979) [Lengnick]

Volcano symphonic study for brass band (1979) [Winwood]

1980-89

Symphony No. 8 (1981) [Faber]

Quintet for clarinet, bass clarinet, and string trio (1981) [Lengnick]

String Quartet No. 8 (1982) [Faber]

String Quartet No. 9 (1982) [Faber]

Variations on a theme by Nielsen (1983) (for orchestra) [Lengnick]

String Quartet No. 10 "for peace" (1983) [Roberton]

The Four Temperaments (1983) (for brass band) [Winwood]

String Quartet No. 11 (1984) [Lengnick]

Trio for horn, violin and piano (1984)

Sonata for violin and piano (1984) [Lengnick]

Michael Tippett, His Mystery (1984) (for piano)
[published in "Michael Tippett, O. M.: A Celebration", Edited by Geraint Lewis (l985, ISBN 9780859361408)}

Eppur si muove, **Ricercar e Passacaglia for organ** (1985) [Lengnick]

Symphony No. 9 (1985-87) [Faber]

String Quartet No. 12 (1987) [Lengnick]

String Trio (1987) [Lengnick]

String Quintet No. 1 (1987) [Lengnick]

Tempi, **for full mixed voice chorus a capella** (1987) [Roberton]

Introduction and Allegro on a bass by Max Reger (1987) *(for brass band)* [Winwood]

Symphony No. 10 (1988) [Lengnick]

Trio for violin, cello and piano (1988-89) [Lengnick]

Flute Concerto (1989) [Winwood]

String Quartet No. 13 (1989) [Lengnick]

Brass Quintet (1989) [Winwood]

Vortex, **for brass band (**1989) [Winwood]

1980-89

Symphony No. 11 (1990) [Lengnick]

String Quartet No. 14 (1990) [Lengnick]

Variations and Finale on a theme by Beethoven (1990) *(for piano)* [Lengnick]

Cello Concerto (1991) [Lengnick]

Variations and Fugue on a theme by Bach (Sarabande) (1991) *(for strings)*

String Quartet No. 15 (1991) [Lengnick]

String Quintet No. 2 (1995)

Unclassified

Die Kunst der Fuge, BWV1080, *Contrapunctus I-XIV***(Bach/Simpson)** *(for string quartet)* (Early 1960s)
Variations on Happy Birthday (for William Walton's Birthday) (for orchestra)

Transcription of Commotio (Nielsen/Simpson) *(for piano, four hands)* (1950)

Songs

The Cherry Tree – *song for high voice and piano (1946), text by Housman.*

Trocknet nicht, Tränen – *solo song, undated.*

Unfinished

(projects left unfinished at the time of Simpson's death; sources for this information are included where possible)

String Quartet No. 16

Violin Concerto
(withdrawn for revision)

Double Concerto for violin, piano and orchestra
(discovered in Simpson's papers after his death by Graham Melville-Mason – Dick Edwards, Leading Notes, December 1998)

Publisher Information for Simpson Compositions

The Publishers of each work (where known) are indicated to the right of the compositions in the chronological, categorised and discography lists and link to the publishing information below.

Boosey & Hawkes Music Publishers Ltd.

Aldwych House
71-91 Aldwych
London
WC2B 4HN
UK
Tel: +44 (0)20 7054 7200
Fax: +44 (0)20 7054 7290
E-mail: composers@boosey.com
Web: http://www.boosey.com

Published works:
Energy: symphonic study for brass band

Faber Music Ltd.

74-77 Great Russell Street
London
WCIB 3DA
UK
Tel: +44 (0)20 7908 5310
Fax: +44 (0)20 7908 5339
E-mail: information@fabermusic.com
Web: www.fabermusic.com

Published works:

String Quartet No. 8
String Quartet No. 9
Symphony No. 7
Symphony No. 8
Symphony No. 9

Alfred Lengnick & Company Ltd.

For Printed material:

Elkin Music International, Inc.
94 Merrills Chase
Asheville
NC 28803
U.S.A.
Tel: +18286519828
Fax: +1 828 651 9655
E-mail: elkinmus@lbellsouth.net
Web: www.elkinmusie.com

For Hire material:

Chester Music and Novello & Company
14-15 Berners Street
London
W1T 3LJ
UK
Tel: +44 (0)207612 7400
Fax: +44 (0)20 7612 7545
E-mail: promotion@lmusicsales.co.uk
Web: www.chesternovello.com

Published works:

String Quartet No. 1
String Quartet No. 2
String Quartet No. 3
String Quartet No. 4
String Quartet No. 5
String Quartet No. 6
String Quartet No. 7
String Quartet No. 11
String Quartet No. 12
String Quartet No. 13
String Quartet No. 14
String Quartet No. 15
Trio for clarinet, cello and piano
Quintet for clarinet and string quartet
Quartet for horn, violin, cello and piano

Quintet for clarinet, bass clarinet, and string trio
Sonata for violin and piano
String Trio
String Quintet No. 1
Trio for violin, cello and piano
Sonata for piano
Variations and Finale on a theme of Haydn (for piano)
Sonata for two pianos
Eppur si muove, Ricercar e Passacaglia for organ
Variations and Finale on a theme by Beethoven (for piano)
Canzona for brass
Symphony No. 1
Symphony No. 2
Symphony No. 3
Symphony No. 4
Symphony No. 5
Symphony No. 6
Symphony No. 10
Symphony No. 11
Piano Concerto
Cello Concerto
Allegro Deciso for strings
Variations on a theme by Nielsen (for orchestra)
Media morte in vita sumus for chorus, brass and timpani

Robertson Publications

Goodmusic
PO Box 100
Tewkesbury
GL20 7YQ
UK
Tel: +44 (0)1684 773883
Fax: +44 (0)1684 773884
E-mail: sales@goodmusicpublishing.co.uk
Web: www.goodmusicpublishing.co.uk

Published works:

String Quartet No. 10 "for peace"
Tempi, for full mixed voice chorus a capella

Winwood Music

Unit 7, Fieldside Farm
Quainton
Buckinghamshire
HP22 4DQ
UK
Tel: +44 (0)1296 655777
Fax: +44 (0)1296655778
E-mail: sales@winwoodmusic.com
Web: www.winwoodmusic.com

Published works:

Brass Quintet
Volcano: symphonic study for brass band
The Four Temperaments (for brass band)
Introduction and Allegro on a bass bv Max Reger (for brass band)
Vortex, for brass band
Flute Concerto

APPENDIX 15

Discography of Simpson's Works with Reviews

This is a categorised list of recordings. Albums that contain works in more than one category are listed in each category.

String Quartets

String Quartet No. 1 (1952)
String Quartet No. 2 (1953)
String Quartet No. 3 (1954)

Element String Quartet (Ernest Element and Sylvia Cleaver, violins; Dorothy Hemming, viola; Norman Jones, cello)

Recorded: 1953-4

Format: CD ADD (Mono 151)

Label: Pearl (Pavilion Records)

Catalogue No.: **GEM 0023**

Barcode: 0727031002321

Released: August 1988

Produced from tapes and acetates in the collection of Robert Simpson.

Review by David Fanning (Gramophone, September 1998)

String Quartet No. 1 (1952)

The Aeolian String Quartet (Sydney Humphreys and Raymond Keenlyside, violins; Margaret Major, viola; Derek Simpson, cello); Bernard Walton, clarinet

Recorded: August 1971 (with Clarinet Qintet, 1968)

Format: LP

Label: Unicorn

Catalogue No.: **UNS234**

This LP is no longer available. This performance of the Clarinet Quintet was later released on Unicorn-Kanchana UKCD2028 then later again on NMC Ancora NMC D109 (overleaf).

Review by Robert Layton (Gramophone, August 1971)
Review by Stephen Johnson (Gramophone, June 1990)

String Quartet No. 1 (1952)
String Quartet No. 4 (1973)

The Delmé Quartet (Galina Solodchin and John Trusler, violins; John Underwood, viola; Jonathan Williams, cello)

Recorded: February 1990
Format: CD DDD
Label: Hyperion
Catalogue No.: **CDA66419**
Barcode: 0034571164199
Released: November 1990

Audio extracts and sleeve notes (PDF) available at Hyperion.

String Quartet No. 2 (1953)
String Quartet No. 5 (1974)

The Delmé Quartet (Galina Solodchin and John Trusler, violins; John Underwood, viola; Jonathan Williams, cello)

Recorded: October 1989
Format: CD DDD
Label: Hyperion
Catalogue No.: **CDA66386**
Barcode: 0034571163864
Released: July 1990

Audio extracts and sleeve notes (PDF) available at Hyperion.

Review by David Fanning (Gramophone, October 1990)

String Quartet No. 3 (1954)
String Quartet No. 6 (1975) (with String Trio, 1987)

The Delmé Quartet (Galina Solodchin and John Trusler, violins; John Underwood, viola; Jonathan Williams, cello)

Recorded: July 1989
Format: CD DDD
Label: Hyperion
Catalogue No.: **CDA66376**
Barcode: 0034571163765
Released: March 1990

Audio extracts available at Hyperion.

Review by David Fanning (Gramophone, July 1990)

String Quartet No. 7 (1977)

String Quartet No. 8 (1982)

The Delmé Quartet (Galina Solodchin and Jeremy Williams, violins; John Underwood, viola; Stephen Orton, cello)

Recorded: November 1983

Format: CD AAD

Label: Hyperion

Catalogue No.: **CDA66117**

Barcode: 0034571161174

Released: August 1989

Audio extracts and sleeve notes (PDF) available at Hyperion. From LP A66117(S).

Review by Arnold Whittall (Gramophone, September 1984)
Review by David Fanning (Gramophone, February 1990)

String Quartet No. 9 (1982)

The Delmé Quartet (Galina Solodchin and John Trusler, violins; John Underwood, viola; Jonathan Williams, cello)

Recorded: March 1984

Format: CD MD

Label: Hyperion

Catalogue No.: **CDA66127**

Barcode: 0034571161273

Released: October 1989

Subtitled 32 Variations and Fugue on a Theme of Haydn. Audio extracts available at Hyperion. From LP A66127(S).

Review by David Fanning (Gramophone, February 1990)

String Quartet No. 10 "for peace" (1983)

String Quartet No. 11 (1984)

The Coull Quartet (Roger Coull and Philip Gallaway, violins; David Curtis, viola; John Todd, cello)

Recorded: June 1986

Format: CD

Label: Hyperion

Catalogue No.: **CDA66225**

Barcode: 0034571162256
Released: March 1988

Audio extracts available at Hyperion.

String Quartet No. 12 (1987)
String Quintet No. 1 (1987)

The Coull Quartet (Roger Coull and Philip Gallaway, violins; David Curtis, viola; John Todd, cello); Roger Bigley, viola

Recorded: May 1991
Format: CD DDD
Label: Hyperion
Catalogue No.: **CDA66503**
Barcode: 0034571165035
Released: April 1992

Audio extracts available at Hyperion.

Review by Stephen Johnson (Gramophone, July 1992)

String Quartet No. 13 (1989)
Quintet for clarinet and string quartet (1968)
String Quintet No. 2 (1995)

The Delmé Quartet (Galina Solodchin and John Trusler, violins; John Underwood, viola; Jonathan Williams, cello); Thea King, clarinet; Christopher van Kampen, cello

Recorded: February 1997
Format: CD DDD
Label: Hyperion
Catalogue No.: **CDA66905**
Barcode: 0034571169057
Released: September 1997
Audio extracts available at Hyperion.

Review by Martin Anderson
Review by David Fanning (Gramophone, October 1997)

String Quartet No. 14 (1990)
String Quartet No. 15 (1991)
Quintet for clarinet, bass clarinet, and string trio (1981)

The Vanbrugh Quartet (Gregory Ellis, violin (Quartets only); Elizabeth Charleson, violin; Simon Aspell, viola; Christopher Marwood, cello); Joy Farrall, clarinet; Fiona Cross, bass clarinet

Recorded: August 1992
Format: CD DDD
Label: Hyperion
Catalogue No.: **CDA66626**
Barcode: 0034571166261
Released: March 1993

Audio extracts and sleeve notes (PDF) available at Hyperion.

Review by David Fanning (Gramophone, September 1993)
Review by David Wright (MusicWeb International, July 1999)

Other Chamber Music

String Quartet No. 1 (1952)
Quintet for clarinet and string quartet (1968)

The Aeolian String Quartet (Sydney Humphreys and Raymond Keenlyside, violins; Margaret Major, viola; Derek Simpson, cello); Bernard Walton, clarinet

Recorded: August 1971
Format: LP
Label: Unicorn
Catalogue No.: **UNS234**

This LP is no longer available. This performance of the Clarinet Quintet was later released on Unicorn-Kanchana UKCD2028 then later again on NMC Ancora NMC D109 (below).

Review by Robert Layton (Gramophone, August 1971)
Review by Stephen Johnson (Gramophone, June 1990)

String Quartet No. 3 (1954)
String Quartet No. 6 (1975)
String Trio (1987)

The Delmé Quartet (Galina Solodchin and John Trusler, violins; John Underwood, viola; Jonathan Williams, cello

Recorded: July 1989
Format: CD DDD
Label: Hyperion
Catalogue No.: **CDA66376**
Barcode: 0034571163765
Released: March 1990

Audio extracts available at Hyperion.

Review by David Fanning (Gramophone, July 1990)

String Quartet No. 12 (1987)
String Quintet No. 1 (1987)

The Coull Quartet (Roger Coull and Philip Gallaway, violins; David Curtis, viola; John Todd, cello); Roger Bigley, viola

Recorded: May 1991
Format: CD DDD
Label: Hyperion
Catalogue No.: **CDA66503**
Barcode: 0034571165035
Released: April 1992

Audio extracts available at Hyperion.

Review by Stephen Johnson (Gramophone, July 1992)

String Quartet No. 13 (1989)
Quintet for clarinet and string quartet (1968)
String Quintet No. 2 (1995)

The Delmé Quartet (Galina Solodchin and John Trusler, violins; John Underwood, viola; Jonathan Williams, cello); Thea King, clarinet; Christopher van Kampen, cello

Recorded: February 1997
Format: CD DDD
Label: Hyperion
Catalogue No.: **CDA66905**
Barcode: 0034571169057
Released: September 1997

Audio extracts available at Hyperion.

Review by Martin Anderson
Review by David Fanning (Gramophone, October 1997)

String Quartet No. 14 (1990)
String Quartet No. 15 (1991)
Quintet for clarinet, bass clarinet, and string trio (1981)

The Vanbrugh Quartet (Gregory Ellis, violin (Quartets only); Elizabeth Charleson, violin; Simon Aspell, viola; Christopher Van Kempen

Recorded: August 1992
Format: CD DDD
Label: Hyperion
Catalogue No.: **COA66626**
Barcode: 0034571166261
Released: March 1993

Audio extracts and sleeve notes (PDF) available at Hyperion.

Review by David Fanning (Gramophone, September 1993)
Review by David Wright (MusicWeb International, July 1999)

Quintet for clarinet and string quartet (1968)
Symphony No. 3 (1962)

The Aeolian String Quartet (Sydney Humphreys and Raymond Keenlyside, violins; Margaret Major, viola; Derek Simpson, cello); Bernard Walton, clarinet; London Symphony Orchestra, conductor Jascha Horenstein

Recorded: 1971 (Quintet), 1970 (Symphony)
Format: CD ADD
Label: NMC Recordings
Catalogue No.: **NMC D109**
Barcode: 0675754906023
Released: April 2006

This performance of the Clarinet Quintet was previously released with String Quartet No. 1 played by the Aeolian String Quartet, on Unicorn LP UNS 234. This CD is a re-release of Unicorn-Kanchana UKCD2028 on the NMC Ancora series of re-issues.

Review by Stephen Jollnson (Gramophone, June 1990)
Review by Rob Barnett (MusicWeb International, April 2006)

Quartet for horn, violin, cello and piano (1975)
Trio for horn, violin and piano (1984)

Richard Watkins, horn; Pauline Lowbury, violin; Caroline Dearnley, cello; Christopher Green-Armitage, piano

Recorded: December 1993
Format: CD DDD
Label: Hyperion
Catalogue No.: **COA66695**
Barcode: 0034571166957
Released: June 1994

Audio extracts available at Hyperion.

Review by David Fanning (Gramophone, December 1994)

Sonata for violin and piano (1984)
Trio for violin, cello and piano (1988-89)

Pauline Lowbury, violin; Christopher Green-Armitage, piano (Sonata); Ursula Smith, cello; Elizabeth Burley, Piano (Trio)

Recorded: December 1993
Format: CD DDD
Label: Hyperion
Catalogue No.: **COA66737**
Barcode: 0034571167374

Audio extracts available at Hyperion.

Review by Martin Anderson (Fanfare Magazine)

Variations and Fugue for recorder and string quartet (1959)
John Turner, recorder; the Camerata Ensemble (Richard Howarth and Julia Hanson, violin; Tom Dunn, viola; Jonathan Price, cello)
Recorded: December 2000
Format: CD ODD
Label: Olympia
Catalogue No.: **OCD 710**
Released: January 2002
With other pieces for recorder and chamber ensembles by various composers.

Review by Hubert Culot. Colin Scott-Sutherland (MusicWeb International, January 2002)

Music for Keyboard

Sonata for piano (1946)
Variations and Finale on a theme of Haydn (1948)
Michael Tippett, His Mystery (1984)
Variations and Finale on a theme by Beethoven (1990)

Raymond Clarke, piano

Recorded: August 1995
Format: CD ODD
Label: Hyperion
Catalogue No.: **CDA66827**
Barcode: 0034571168272
Released: February 1996

Audio extracts available at Hyperion.

Review by Martin Anderson (Fanfare Magazine, 1996)
Review by Roderick Swanston (Classic CD Magazine, April 1996)
Review by David fanning (Gramophone, May 1996)

Eppur si muove, **Ricercar e Passacaglia for organ** (1985)
Canzona for brass (1958)
Media morte in vita sumus **for chorus, brass and timpani** (1975)
Tempi, **for full mixed voice chorus a capella** (1987)
Iain Quinn, organ; Corydon Singers; Corydon Brass Ensemble, conductor Matthew Best
Recorded: 1997-8
Format: CD ODD
Label: Hyperion
Catalogue No.: **CDA67016**
Barcode: 0034571170169
Released: November 1998

Audio extracts available at Hyperion. Texts included.

Review by Martin Anderson (Fanfare Magazine, 1999)
Review by David Fanning (Gramophone, February 1999)

Music for Brass Band

Energy: symphonic study for brass band (1971)

The G.U.S. (Footwear) Band, conductor Stanley Boddington

Recorded: 1972
Format: LP Stereo
Label: EMI Studio 2
Catalogue No.: **IW0379**

On The World Champions Play Test Pieces for Brass, with other music for brass band by Vinter, and Berlioz arr. Wright.

Review by Tim Mutum (4barsrest, April 2008)

Canzona for brass (1958)
The Locke Brass Consort, conductor James Stobart
Recorded: 1977
Format: CD ADD
Label: Chandos
Catalogue No.: **CHAN6573**
Barcode: 0095115657324

With other works by Bliss, Brian, Benjamin, Elgar, Walton, Tippett, Rubbra and Jacob. This CD was previously released as RSA Red Seal LP RL 25081.

Volcano: **symphonic study for brass band** (1979)

The John Foster Black Dyke Mills Band, conductor Major Peter Parkes

Recorded: 1979
Format: CD ADD
Label: Chandos
Catalogue No.: **CHAN4522**
Barcode: 0095115452226
Recorded live in the Royal Albert Hall, with other music for brass band by Vinter, Huber, Gregson and Calvert.

Energy: **symphonic study for brass band** (1971)
Volcano: **symphonic study for brass band** (1979)
The Four Temperaments (1983)
Introduction and Allegro on a bass by Max Reger (1987)

Vortex, **for brass band** (1989)

Volcano: **chandos recording** (1979)
John Foster Black Dyke Mills Band, conductor Peter Parks

The Desford Colliery Caterpillar Band, conductor James Watson

Recorded: August 1990
Format: CD
Label: Hyperion
Catalogue No.: **CDA66449**
Barcode: 0034571164496
Released: May 1991
Audio extracts available at Hyperion.

Canzona for brass (1958)

Kensington Symphonic Brass, conductor Russell Keable

Recorded: 6 May 1994
Format: CD
Label: Dunelm Records (Divine Art)
Catalogue No.: **DRD02S3**

Live recording, on Music for Brass and Percussion – 1, with other works by Copland, Britten, Glass, Rubbra, Frescobaldi, Gabrieli, Bliss, Grieg, Barber, David. Re-mastered December 2005.

Review by William Kreindler (MusicWeb International, February 2006)

The Four Temperaments (1983)
Kensington Symphonic Brass, conductor Russell Keable
Recorded: 31 March 1995
Format: CD
Label: Dunelm Records (Divine sill
Catalogue No.: **DRD02S4**

Live recording, on Music for Brass and Percussion – 2, with other works by Arvo Part, Gabrieli, Purceli, Mussorgsky, Elgar Howarth.

Review by Tim Perry (MusicWeb International, June 2006)

***Energy*: symphonic study for brass band** (1971)

Williams Fairey Band, conductor James Gourlay

Recorded: February 1997
Format: CD DDD
Label: Chandos
Catalogue No.: **CHAN4S47**
Barcode: 0095115454725

With other music for brass band by Jenkins, Alwyn, Rubbra, Elgar and Vaughan Williams.

***Eppur si muove*, Ricercar e Passacaglia for organ** (1985)
Canzona for brass (1958)
***Media morte in vita sumus* for chorus, brass and timpani** (1975)
***Tempi*, for full mixed voice chorus a capella** (1987)

Iain Quinn, organ; Corydon Singers; Corydon Brass Ensemble, conductor Matthew Best

Recorded: 1997-8
Format: CD DDD
Label: Hyperion
Catalogue No.: **CDA67016**
Barcode: 0034571170169
Released: November 1998

Audio extracts available at Hyperion. Texts included.

Review by Martin Anderson (Fanfare Magazine, 1999)

Canzona for brass (1958)

Cambridge University Brass Ensemble, conductor Philip Walsh

Recorded: April 2004
Format: CD
Label: Dunelm Records (Divine Art)
Catalogue No.: **DRD0226**

20th Anniversary Reunion Concert, King's College Chapel, with other works by Janáček, Barber, Grieg, Gabrieli, Alfred Uhl, Hindemith, Richard Strauss.

Symphonies

Symphony No. 1 (1951)
London Philharmonic Orchestra, conductor Sir Adrian Boult
Recorded: January 1956
Format: CD
Label: EMI Classics
Catalogue No.: **5757892**
Barcode: 0724357578929
Released: November 2002

This CD is a re-release of His Master's Voice BLP 1092, a 1956 33½ rpm mono recording that was previously reissued as HMV 20 Series HQM 1010 by EMI in 1966, with Fricker Symphony No. 2. The new CD includes the Fricker symphony along with Orr's Symphony in One Movement.

Review by A.P. (Gramophone, April 1957)
Review by M.M. (Gramophone, March 1966)
Review by Tony Haywood (MusicWeb International, December 2002)

Symphony No. 1 (1951)
Symphony No. 8 (1981)

Royal Philharmonic Orchestra, conductor Vernon Handley

Recorded: July 1996
Format: CD DDD
Label: Hyperion
Catalogue No.: **CDA66890**
Barcode: 0034571168906
Released: November 1996

Review by Martin Anderson (Fanfare Magazine)

Symphony No. 2 (1956)
Symphony No. 4 (1972)

Bournemouth Symphony Orchestra, conductor Vernon Handley

Recorded: July 1992
Format: CD DDD
Label: Hyperion

Catalogue No.: **CDA66505**
Barcode: 0034571165059
Released: October 1992

Review by Karl W. Nehring (The Sensible Sound)
Review by David Fanning (Gramophone, December 1992)

Symphony No. 3 (1962)

London Symphony Orchestra, condutor Jascka Horenstein (with Clarinet Quintet, 1968)

Orchestra, conductor Jascha Horenstein
Recorded: 1971 (Quintet), 1970 (Symphony)
Format: CD ADD
Label: NMC Recordings
Catalogue No.: **NMC D0109**
Barcode: 0675754906023
Released: April 2006

This performance of the Clarinet Quintet was previously released with String Quartet No. 1 played by the Aeolian String Quartet, on Unicorn LP UNS 234. This CD is a re-release of Unicorn-Kanchana UKCD2028 on the NMC Ancora series of re-issues.

Review by Stephen Johnson (Gramophone, June 1990)
Review by Rob Barnett (MusicWeb International, April 2006)

Symphony No. 3 (1962)
Symphony No. 5 (1972)

Royal Philharmonic Orchestra, conductor Vernon Handley

Recorded: May 1994
Format: CD DDD
Label: Hyperion
Catalogue No.: **COA66728**
Barcode: 0034571167282
Released: March 1994

Review by Karl W. Nehring (The Sensible Sound)
Review by Martin Anderson (Fanfare Magazine)

Symphony No. 6 (1977)
Symphony No. 7 (1977)

Royal Liverpool Philharmonic Orchestra, conductor Vernon Handley

Recorded: September 1987
Format: CD DDD
Label: Hyperion
Catalogue No.: **COA66280**
Barcode: 0034571162805
Released: April 1988
Review by Karl W. Nehring (The $ensible Sound)

Symphony No. 9 (1985-87)

Bournemouth Symphony Orchestra, conductor Vernon Handley

Recorded: February 1988
Format: CD DDD
Label: Hyperion
Catalogue No.: **CDA66299**
Barcode: 0034571162997

The final track is an illustrated talk on the work by the composer.

Audio extracts and sleeve notes (PDF) available at Hyperion.

Review by Karl W. Nehring (The $ensible Sound)
Review by David Fanning (Gramophone, December 1988)

Symphony No. 10 (1988)
Royal Liverpool Philharmonic Orchestra, conductor Vernon Handley
Recorded: February 1991
Format: CD DDD
Label: Hyperion
Catalogue No.: **CDA66510**
Barcode: 0034571165103
Released: September 1991

Symphony No. 11 (1990)
City of London Sinfonia, conductor Matthew Taylor
Recorded: December 2003
Format: CD DDD
Label: Hyperion
Catalogue No.: **CDA67500**
Barcode: 0034571175003
Released: August 2004

Audio extracts and sleeve notes (PDF) available at Hyperion.

Review by Hubert Culot (MusicWeb International, September 2004)

Review by Arnold Whittall (Gramophone, December 2004)

Interview with Matthew Taylor by Martin Anderson (Fanfare Magazine, Nov/Dec 2004)

Review by Guy Rickards (Gramophone, 2005)

Review by Paul Ingram (Fanfare Magazine, Jan/Feb 2005)

Symphony No. 1 (1951)
Symphony No. 2 (1956)
Symphony No. 3 (1962)
Symphony No. 4 (1972)
Symphony No. 5 (1972)
Symphony No. 6 (1977)
Symphony No. 7 (1977)
Symphony No. 8 (1981)
Symphony No. 9 (1985-87)
Symphony No. 10 (1988)
Symphony No. 11 (1990)

Variations on a theme by Nielsen (1983)

Royal Philharmonic Orchestra, Bournemouth Symphony Orchestra, Royal Liverpool Philharmonic Orchestra, conductor Vernon Handley; City of London Sinfonia, conductor Matthew Taylor

Recorded: 1987-2003
Format: Boxed set, 7 COS
Label: Hyperion
Catalogue No.: **C0544191/7**

Barcode: 0034571141916
Released: October 2006

Interview with Matthew Taylor by Martin Anderson (Fanfare Magazine, Nov/Dec 2004)

Review by Paul Ingram (Fanfare Magazine, Jan/Feb 2005)
Review by Rob Barnett (MusicWeb International, September 2006)
Review by Paul James (Paul James' Modern Music Review)
Review by Pliable (On An Overgrown Path, October 2006)

Concerti

Piano Concerto (1967)

John Ogdon, piano; Bournemouth Symphony Orchestra, conductor Constantin Silvestri

Recorded: 1967
Format: CD ADD
Label: Carlton BBC Radio Classics
Catalogue No.: **15656 91762**

With Rawsthorne Piano Concerto No 2, Concerto for Two Pianos.

Review by Keith Potter (BBC Music Magazine)
Review by Andy Jackson

Other Orchestral Music

Symphony No. 11 (1990)
Variations on a theme by Nelsen (1983)
City of London Sinfonia, conductor Matthew Taylor
Recorded: December 2003
Format: CD DDD
Label: Hyperion
Catalogue No.: **COA67500**
Barcode: 0034571175003
Released: August 2004

Audio extracts and sleeve notes (PDF) available at Hyperion.

Review by Hubert Culot (MusicWeb International, September 2004)

Review by Arnold Whittall (Gramophone, December 2004)

Interview with Matthew Taylor by Martin Anderson (Fanfare Magazine, Nov/Dec 2004)

Review by Guy Rickards (Gramophone, 2005)

Review by Paul Ingram (Fanfare Magazine, Jan/Feb 2005)

Variations on a theme by Nielsen (1983)

Royal Philharmonic Orchestra, Bournemouth Symphony Orchestra, Royal Liverpool Philharmonic Orchestra, conductor Vernon Handley; City of London Sinfonia, conductor Matthew Taylor

Recorded: 1987-2003
Format: Boxed set, 7 COS
Label: Hyperion
Catalogue No.: **C0544191/7**
Barcode: 0034571141916
Released: October 2006

Interview with Matthew Taylor by Martin Anderson (Fanfare Magazine, Nov/Dec 2004)
Review by Paul Ingram (Fanfare Magazine, Jan/Feb 2005)
Review by Rob Barnett (MusicWeb International, September 2006)
Review by Paul James (Paul James' Modern Music Review)
Review by Pliable (On An Overgrown Path, October 2006)

Vocal Music

Eppur si muove, **Ricercar e Passacaglia for organ** (1985)
Canzona for brass (1958)
Media morte in vita sumus **for chorus, brass and timpani** (1975)
Tempi, **for full mixed voice chorus a capella** (1987)

Iain Quinn, organ; Corydon Singers; Corydon Brass Ensemble, conductor Matthew Best

Recorded: 1997-8
Format: CD DDD
Label: Hyperion
Catalogue No.: **COA67016**
Barcode: 0034571170169
Released: November 1998

Audio extracts available at Hyperion. Texts included.

Review by Martin Anderson (Fanfare Magazine, 1999)
Review by David Fanning (Gramophone, February 1999)

Arrangements

Die Kunst der Fuge, BWV1080, *Contrapunctus I-XIV* (Bach/Simpson) (date unknown)

The Delmé Quartet (Galina Solodchin and John Trusler, violins; John Underwood, viola; Jonathan Williams, cello)

Recorded: November 1999

Format: CD DDD

Label: Hyperion

Catalogue No.: **CDA67138**

Barcode: 0034571171388

Released: September 2000

Robert Simpson's arrangement of the Art of Fugue for string quartet. Audio extracts available at Hyperion.

Review by Paul Shoemaker (MusicWeb International, April 2003)

APPENDIX 16

Books and articles by Robert Simpson

Note: If you know of any additional books and articles by Simpson, please send an e-mail or a letter to the Robert Simpson Society Archive.

"The Seventh Symphony of Bruckner: An Analysis", R. Simpson, Music Review (1947): 178-187.

"Carl Nielsen: Symphonist", R. Simpson, 1952, (revised 1979).
Taplinger Publishing Co. New York (1986), and Kahn & Averill, London (1986).
ISBN-IO: 0900707461, ISBN- 13: 9780900707469

"Janus Germinus: Music in Scandinavia", R. Simpson (1960), in "Twentieth Century
Music – an International Symposium of Essays on Current Trends in Music", Ed. R. Meyers.
Calder (1960), and Calder and Boyers (1968).
ISBN-10: 0028645812, ISBN-13: 9780028645810

"Bruckner and the Symphony", R. Simpson (1963). British Broadcasting Corporation, London, England (1963).
A PDF version of this booklet can be downloaded from the Anton Bruckner website.

"Sibelius and Nielsen: a Centenary Essay", R. Simpson (1965). British Broadcasting Corporation, London (1965).

"The Essence of Bruckner: An Essay Towards the Understanding of his Music", R. Simpson (1966). Gollancz, London, England (1967).

"Beethoven Symphonies", R. Simpson (1970). A BBC Music Guide,
BBC, England (1971), and Seattle, University of Washington Press, USA (1971)
ISBN-10: 0563204842, ISBN-13: 9780563204848

"The Symphony" (Two Volumes), R. Simpson (Ed.).
Penguin Books Ltd, Middlesex England (1966-67).
Volume 1: Haydn to Dvořák
ISBN-10: 0140207724, ISBN-13: 9780140207729
Volume 2: Elgar to the Present Day
ISBN-IO: 0140207732, ISBN-13: 9780140207736

Forward to: "Beethoven, Sibelius and the 'Profound Logic': Studies in Symphonic Analysis", by Lionel Pike, London [Atlantic Highlands,] NJ: Athlone Press; distributed in the USA by Humanities Press, (1978).
ISBN-IO: 0485111780, ISBN-13: 9780485111781

"The Prom and Natural Justice, a Plan for Renewal", R. Simpson, with a forward by Sir Adrian Boult (1980). Toccata Press, London (1981).
ISBN-10: 0907689000, ISBN-13: 9780907689003

"Beethoven Concertos", R. Simpson, in "A Guide to the Concerto",
Edited by Robert Layton. Helm, England (1988).
ISBN-IO: 019288008X, ISBN-13: 9780192880086

"Robert Simpson on Beethoven", Essays, lectures and talks by R. Simpson selected and edited by Uonel Pike, published privately by Dr. Pike's Aardvark Publishing.
ISBN-10: 0952815508, ISBN-13: 9780952815501

"Carl Nielsen Now: A Personal View", R. Simpson, in "The Nielsen Companion", Edited by Mina Miller. Amadeus Press, Portland, Oregon U.S.A. (1995).
ISBN-10: 1574670050, ISBN-13: 9781574670059

Forward to: "Experiencing Music", by Vagn Holmboe, edited and translated by Paul Rapoport, Toccata Press, London.
ISBN-IO: 0907689159, ISBN-13: 9780907689157

"Carl Nielsen: A Life in 6 Symphonies", S. Rattle and R. Simpson (with Musical Examples played by the City of Birmingham Symphony Orchestra, conducted by Rattle), BBC videocassette. The only information we have on this video came from a now defunct web page at the Dutch Media Center for Language and Culture. If anyone knows any further details, please send email to the Robert Simpson Society.

Program Notes for the Vanbrugh Quartet's Beethoven String Quartet cycle (on Intim Musik IMCD043-IMCD050).

Simpson's notes on Bach's Die Kunst der Fuge can be found in the booklet for the Delmé Quartet's recording (on Hyperion Records, CDA67138) of his own arrangement of the pieces.

Ed. D Martin and P. Mullen: "Our shy masters" – unholy warfare – the Church and the Bomb/Basil Blackwell 1983).

"More Reflections (After Composition)", R. Simpson, Tempo No 144.
The piano miniature **"Michael Tippett, His Mystery"** (1984) in
"Michael Tippett, O.M.: A Celebration", Edited by Geraint Lewis.
Baton Press, England (1985).
ISBN-l0: 0859361403, ISBN-13: 9780859361408
Many articles for various journals, especially 'The Listener' programme notes for his own and other music, record reviews for especially, the EMG Newsletter (unsigned).

Books, articles and talks about Robert Simpson

"The Symphonies of Robert Simpson", Edited by Robert Matthew Walker, Alfred Lengnick & Co Ltd. London (1991). ISBN-10 1873343043, ISBN-13 9781873343043.

"Robert Simpson, 50th Birthday Essays", Edited by Edward Johnson, Triad Press,
London (1971).

TONIC Vols 1-18. Journal of the Robert Simpson Society. Volume 11 is now available online as a PDF file.

"Robert Simpson's Symphonic Appetite", Callum MacDonald. Recorded talk with musical examples, Dunholm Publicity Ltd (1993). CDs (DRDOOll) or cassettes of this talk are available from Divine Art.

"Conflict, Momentum and the Will of the Tonalist", Simon Phillippo, M.Phil. dissertation, University of Cambridge, 1997.

"Robert Simpson's Third Symphony: Sources and Influences", Martin Ratcliffe, Ph.D. dissertation, Royal Holloway College, University of London (1998).

"The Symphonism of Robert Simpson", Simon Phillippo, Ph.D. dissertation, University of Cambridge, 2000.

Northcott on Simpson, Tempo, No 135.

"Robert Simpson's New Way (String Quartet No. 8)", Lionel Pike. Tempo, No 153, Jun 1985, p20-29.

"Robert Simpson's Ninth", Stephen Johnson. The Musical Times, Vol 128, April 1987, p196-199.

"Robert Simpson's Ninth Symphony", Lionel Pike. Tempo, No 170, Sept 1989, p19-23.

"Robert Simpson as Symphonist", Matthew Taylor. Music and Musicians International,
Vol 38 No 12, August 1990, p14-16.

"Robert Simpson: his Fifth Symphony at the Proms", Mark Doran. The Musical Times,

"Robert Simpson's Tenth Symphony", John Pickard. The Musical Times, Vol132 No 1775, Jan 1991, p703-705.

"Robert Simpson: our Major Symphonist", Robert Matthew-Walker. Musical Opinion, Vol114 No 1359, Mar 1991, p83-85.

"The Perpetual Striver", Simon Phillippo. The Musical Times, Vol 139 No 1865, Winter 1998, p25-30.

"Symphonic Momentum and Post-Tonal Dramas: Robert Simpson's First Symphony", Simon Phillippo. Tempo, No 209, July 1999, p2-6.

"An introduction to the String Quartets of Robert Simpson", Callum MacDonald. Recorded talk with musical examples, Dunelm Records Ltd (1999). COS (DRD0IIO) or cassettes of this talk are available from Divine Art.

"Robert Simpson" Lecture by Malcolm MacDonald, Wigmore Hall, 2000.

Articles written following Simpson's death on November 21 1997 may be found on the Obituaries and Tributes page

H. Ottoway: **'Robert Simpson: Symphony No. 1'**, Musical Times 1956

H. Ottaway: **'Robert Simpson, Symphonist'**, Musical Opinion, 1957-8

D. Gow: **'Robert Simpson: Music Portrait'**, Musical Times 1960

R. Angles: **'Dr Robert's Third'**, Music and Musicians, 10, 1962-63

D. Richards: **'Simpson's First'**, Music and Musicians, 9, 1969-70

A. Orga: **'A Champion for Simpson'**, Music and Musicians, 12, 1969-70

F. Barker: **'Simpson Four and Five'**, Music and Musicians, 1972-73

H. Ottaway: **'Simpson's New Symphonies'**, Tempo, no. 105, 1973, 53-4

B. Northcott: **'Recent Simpson'**, Tempo, no. 135, 1980, 43-6

L. Pike: **'The Robert Simpson Archives at Royal Holloway College'**, Brio, 1984, 11

J. Pickard: **The Symphonies of Robert Simpson**, (dissertation, University of Wales, 1989)

L. Pike: **'Robert Simpson's Tenth Quartet: Politics, Pacifism and the Language of Tonality'**, Music and the Politics of Culture, ed.

C. Norris, London and New York, 1989

L. Pike: **'Towards a Study of Musical Motion: Robert Simpson's Variations and Finale on a Theme of Haydn** (1948)', Music Review, 1993, 137-48

S. Philippo: **Robert Simpson's Rasumovsky Quartets**, (dissertation University of Cambridge, 1995)

G. Laybourn: **Robert Simpson's Dynamic Analogy: Techniques and Structural Re-Modelling**, (dissertation, University of London, 1996)

Robert Simpson; Composer. Essays, Interviews, Recollections. Editor Jurgen Schaarwachter (Georg Olms Verlag 2013

INDEX

A

Aarhus Symphony Orchestra, 123
Adams, Ivon, 121
Adler, Larry, 23
Aeolian Quartet, 71, 111
Albinoni, Tomaso, 80
Aldebaran (ensemble), 193
Alkan (Morhange), Charles Valentin, 245, 258
Allegri Singers, 177
Amis, John, 60, 217, 307
Anderson, Martin, 160, 163, 171, 223, 283, 308
Andropov, Yuri, 226
Antheil, George, 109
Aprahamian, Felix, 74, 88, 117
Arensky, Anton, 202
Arnell, Richard, 81, 145
Arnold, Malcolm, 80, 97, 113, 207
Arts Chamber Orchestra of Orange County High School, 135
Aylesbury Choral Society, 127

B

Bach, Johann Sebastian, 10, 32, 38, 43, 74, 101, 135, 152, 170–71, 178, 188, 195, 197, 236–39, 272, 298
Bacon, Francis, 9
Bacon, Pamela, 181–82, 228
Bain, Frances, 175
Baker, Allan Hawthorne, 49
Baker, Robert, 258
Ball, Eric, 112
Balsam, Artur, 258
Balshaitis, Fransiska. See Simpson, Fransiska (née Balshaitis)
Banda, Pal, 202
Bantock, Sir Granville, 56
Barbirolli, Sir John, 75, 103, 218, 255
Barker, Frank, 150
Barnes, Robert, 160
Bartok, Bela, 174, 209

Bax, Sir Arnold, 78–79, 146, 210, 247, 305
BBC Choral Society, 93
BBC Chorus, 93
BBC Concert Orchestra, 109
BBC Scottish Symphony Orchestra, 76
BBC Symphony Orchestra, 93, 117, 119, 147, 310
BBC Welsh Symphony Orchestra, 118
Beard, Paul, 260
Bebbington, William, 258
Beckett, Gwen, 260
Beecham, Sir Thomas, 36, 56, 65, 254–55
Beethoven, Ludwig van, 6–7, 25, 32, 38–40, 47, 49, 60–61, 72–75, 77–79, 83, 94, 101, 110–11, 113, 115–17, 123, 125–29, 131–32, 134, 136, 157, 162–63, 170–71, 173, 179–80, 183, 185–91, 198, 205, 207, 209–10, 215, 228, 233–34, 236–43, 247, 257, 265–67, 277, 281, 287, 290, 292, 294, 296, 298–99, 307–8
Belkin, Alan, 258
Bellini, Gentile, 9
Bellini, Giovanni, 9
Bendall, Peter, 5
Benians, Elisabeth Grant (née Matthews), 31
Benians, Martin, 42
Benjamin, George, 207
Bennett, Sir Richard Rodney, 108, 113, 146
Bentzon, Jørgen, 65
Berg, Alban, 245
Bergstet, Harald, 157
Berkeley, Lennox, 137, 144
Berkeley, Michael, 184
Berlin Philharmonic Orchestra, 271
Berlioz, Hector, 86, 93–95, 176, 207, 232, 236, 241, 255, 257, 282, 307
Bernard, Anthony, 75–76

Berners, Lord, 184
Bernstein, Leonard, 81
Berry, Rose, 11
Berwald, Franz, 240
Best, Matthew, 79, 128, 177, 193, 201, 204, 207, 227, 289
Binns, Malcolm, 291
Birkill, Frank, 38
Birtwistle, Sir Harrison, 248
Bishop (Kovacevich), Christopher, 141
Bizet, Georges, 168
Black Dyke Mills Band, 138
Blair, James, 123
Blair, Tony, 228, 306
Blake, William, 294
Bliss, Sir Arthur, 70
Bloch, Ernest, 146
Blom, Eric, 71
Blomstedt, Herbert, 114
Bluff, Susan, 209
Blyth, Alan, 60, 118, 121, 164
Boddington, Stanley, 113
Bohlke, Herr, 205
Bolton, Julian, 119
Booth, Bramwell, 12, 14
Booth, General William, 11
Booth, Miriam, 12
Borodin, Alexander, 79, 109, 241
Boulez, Pierre, 117, 311
Boult, Sir Adrian, 57–58, 84, 93, 103, 144–45, 254
Bourgeois, Derek, 144–45
Bournemouth Symphony Orchestra, 78, 156, 170–71, 218
Bowers-Broadbent, Christopher, 165
Brahms, Johannes, 39, 60, 66, 79, 83–84, 86, 109–11, 121, 124–25, 132, 163, 185, 209, 239–42, 270, 274, 283, 299, 304
Brand, Geoffrey, 185
Bream, Julian, 194, 233
Brecht, Bertold, 149
Breughel, Pieter, 9
Brever, Menachem, 201
Brian, Havergal, 20, 56, 85, 92, 94–95, 120, 146, 192, 205, 245, 256, 260–62, 270, 287, 300, 304
Brian, Hilda, 121, 262

Brittania B.S. Band, 178
Britten, Benjamin, 97, 113, 163, 174, 247, 283, 303, 305
Broadstock, Brenton, 258
Bronowski, Jacob, 149
Brookes, Simon, 195
Brooks, John, 160
Brooks, Sylvia, 160
Brown, David J., 155
Bruck, Axel, 201
Bruckner, Anton, 8, 38–39, 47–48, 62, 69, 79, 89, 92, 94, 100–101, 103–7, 113, 118, 127–28, 137, 156–57, 162, 168, 170–73, 180, 183, 199, 205, 238, 241, 246, 250, 254, 256–57, 263–64, 269–73, 275, 286–87, 298–99, 305, 309–10
Brymer, Jack, 153
Budden, Julian, 4, 217, 232–33, 235, 239, 245, 252–54
Burke, Edmund, 221
Burney, Charles, 189
Busch, Adolf, 271
Bush, Alan, 146
Bush, George Sr., 222, 228
Busoni, Ferrucio, 39, 85, 146, 245, 286, 295–96, 298, 304
Butterworth, Arthur, 258
Buxtehude, Diderik, 160
Byrd, William, 237

C

Cage, John, 253
Cairns, David, 88, 155
Calvert, Morley, 138
Cambrian Brass, 184
Camerata Ensemble, 81
Capell, Richard, 66
Caravaggio, Michelangelo, 9
Cardus, Sir Neville, 61, 105
Carewe, John, 173
Cargill, Simon, 100, 139, 221, 234, 245, 247
Carner, Mosco, 58, 67, 72, 76
Carpenter, Humphrey, 206
Carragan, William, 107

Carter, Elliot, 134–35
Casals, Pablo, 194
Cater, Percy, 59, 87
Celibidache, Sergiu, 106
Chabrier, Emmanuel, 75
Chadwick, Wilfred, 258
Chandler, Mary, 72
Chaplin, Charlie, 23
Chaucer, Geoffrey, 43, 184, 280
Chilingirian Quartet, 209
Chissell, Joan, 116
Chopin, Frederic, 77
Chung, Kyung-Wha, 157
Churchill, Sir Winston, 9
City of Birmingham Symphony Orchestra, 77, 84, 86
City of London Choir, 93
City of London Sinfonia, 159, 187, 197, 289
Civil, Alan, 129
Clark, Jeremiah, 49
Clarke, Raymond, 49, 52, 78, 109, 164, 189–90, 209, 248
Clarkson, John, 168
Classical Orchestra of St. Petersburg, 135
Clemens, Cyril, 143
Clements, Andrew, 150
Cline, William D., 204
Cole, Hugo, 79, 117
Concord Orchestra, 124
Conrad, Joseph, 294
Constable, John, 9
Cooke, Alistair, 78
Cooke, Arnold, 130, 146, 248
Cooke, Deryck, 23, 59, 87, 103, 105, 263–64
Cooper, Martin, 61, 66, 71, 114, 118, 122
Copland, Aaron, 146
Corydon Orchestra Singers Brass Ensemble, 79, 128, 177, 207, 289
Coull Quartet, 161–62, 174, 176, 191–92
Couperin, Francois, 80
Cox, Ainslee, 90, 112
Cox, David, 79
Craft, Jackie, 193

Craft, Professor Sir Ian, 7, 130, 193, 201, 258
Crichton, Ronald, 87
Croft-Jackson, Harry, 75
Crompton, Richmal, 25
Cross, Fiona, 154
Crossley-Holland, Peter, 78
Crowson, Lamar, 51, 60, 79
Crowther, Robert, 193
Croxford, Eileen, 109, 129
Crusell, Bernard, 76
CSR Symphony Orchestra Bratislava, 96
Cunningham, Brian, 258
Curzon, Clifford, 89

D

Dallapiccola, Luigi, 146
Danish Radio Symphony Orchestra, 65
Danish State Radio Orchestra, 58
Dann, Horace, 80
David, Mark, 194
Davies, Sir Henry Walford, 116
Davies, Sir Peter Maxwell, 114, 119, 248
Da Vinci Ensemble, 181–82
Davis, Peter G., 110
Davis, Sir Andrew, 117, 121–23, 131
Davis, Sir Colin, 5, 68, 76, 256
Dean, Stewart, 108
Dearling, Robert, 58, 109, 193, 213, 234, 244, 259
Dearnley, Caroline, 129
Debussy, Claude, 58, 109, 193, 213, 234, 244, 259
Delmé Quartet, 71, 127, 154–55, 175, 184, 190, 237
de Nevers, Bernard, 49
Dent, Edward, 65, 98–99
de Peyer, Gervase, 110
Desford Colliery Caterpillar (Dowty) Band, 113, 138, 178, 185
Devoyon, Pascal, 209
Diether, Jack, 105
Dimmock, Sarah, 5
D'Indy, Vincent, 98
Dixon, Dean, 100

Dobson, Peter, 112
Dodgson, Stephen, 145
Dohnányi, Ernst von, 176
Dolmetsch, Carl, 80
Donohoe, Peter, 180
Doran, Mark, 218
Dorrell, Anthony, 50, 149
Dorrell, Daphne, 7, 265
Dorward, David, 51
Douglas, James, 144, 153, 160, 192
Dowd, Ronald, 93
Downes, Sir Edward, 153
Drew, David, 87
Driver, Paul, 173
Drucker, Gerald, 153
Drummond, Sir John, 143, 207, 300
Duchamp, Marcel, 254
Duke, Brian, 214
Dunne, J. W., 214
Dvořák, Antonin, 57, 76, 88, 96–97, 131, 171–72, 176, 188, 191, 238, 240, 242, 305

E

Eastaugh, Kenneth, 261
Eben, Petr, 184
Eden, Bracha, 138
Edwards, Dick, 48, 50, 160, 190, 206, 269, 296
Edwards, Sydney, 87
Eggert, Irmelin, 65
Eisenhower, Dwight, 270
Element, Ernest, 73, 83–84, 163
Element Quartet, 55, 70–72
Elgar, Sir Edward, 9, 32, 58, 60, 67, 79, 88, 96, 98–99, 109, 123, 134, 174, 195, 197, 218, 243, 247, 270, 304
Ellis, David, 81
Emmanuel School Choir, 93
Emmett, Peter, 258
Enescu, George, 70
English Chamber Orchestra, 133
Ewazen, 207

F

Fairfax, Bryan, 100
Fallows, David, 159
Fanning, David, 132, 135, 174, 180, 188, 246
Farnaby, Giles, 160
Farrall, Joy, 154
Faulkner, William, 144
Fenby, Eric, 201
Ferber, Albert, 49
Ferneyhough, Brian, 214
Festival Trio of London, 163
Few, Ray, 148, 258
Few, Rosemary, 157
Finzi, Gerard, 305
Flaubert, Gustave, 6
Ford, Christopher, 57, 115, 234
Foreman, Lewis, 4, 25, 53, 85, 131, 133, 140, 142, 223, 232, 247
Forshaw, David, 81
Fortune, Nigel, 87, 308
Foulds, John, 109
Fowler, Michael, 207
Franck, Cesar, 79, 98
Frankel, Benjamin, 145
Fraser, Bessie (Squibs). See Simpson, Bessie (née Fraser)
Fredman, Myer, 258
Fricker, Peter Racine, 62, 80, 97, 144, 146, 216
Fürtwängler, Wilhelm, 61

G

Gabrieli, Giovanni, 79, 104, 237
Gabrieli Quartet, 126, 136–37
Galilei, Galileo, 164
Galtieri, General, 225
Garvie, Peter, 258
Gavin, Barry, 126
Gibbon, Edward, 261
Gieraczynski, Bogdan, 204
Gill, Dominic, 149, 162
Gillette, David, 50, 138, 144
Gilliam, Laurence, 65
Glock, Sir William, 56, 93–94, 145, 300
Goddard, Philip, 258

Goehr, Alexander, 146–47, 216
Goehr, Walter, 74
Goering, Hermann, 112
Goethe, Johann, 61, 92
Goldberg Ensemble, 197
Goldschmidt, Berthold, 145
Goldsmiths Choral Union, 191
Goldstone, Anthony, 187
Gollancz, Victor, 94, 100, 103, 105–6, 309
Gomez, Jill, 143
Gomme, Andor, 227, 258
Goodwin, Noel, 59, 76–77, 87, 108, 248, 250
Goossens, Sir Eugene, 93
Gorbachev, Mikhail, 228
Gordon, Douglas, 208, 258
Gordon, Sheila, 226
Govaars, Gerrit, 12, 14
Govaars, Helena Hendrika. See Simpson, Helena Hendrika (née Govaars)
Govaars, Mary Jane (née Wilson), 14
Grant, Fred, 25
Granville-Barker, Frank, 150
Gray, Cecil, 66
Green, Professor Edward, 233
Green-Armytage, Christopher, 129, 163, 209
Greenfield, Edward, 88, 108, 121, 129, 131, 173
Gregson, Edward, 138
Griffiths, Paul, 134
Grøndahl, Launy, 58
Groves, Charles, 88, 95, 111, 131, 256
GUS (Footwear) Band, 113

H

Hall, Barrie, 147
Hall, Michael, 160
Hallé Orchestra, 75, 116
Halliday, Amy, 13
Hampstead Choral Society, 93
Hancock, Harry, 51
Handel, George Frederick, 80, 136, 238

Handley, Vernon, 62, 78, 90, 95, 120, 124, 132, 135, 153, 172, 179, 195, 210, 215, 256, 291
Hanslick, Eduard, 62
Hardwick, Christine, 152
Harkness, Gordon, 223
Harrison, John, 193
Harrison, Julius, 97–98
Harrison, Max, 150
Harty, Sir Hamilton, 93
Hauer, Josef Mathias, 278
Haug, Halvor, 258
Haydn, Joseph, 38–39, 50, 52, 58, 73, 75, 88, 96, 108, 115, 117, 149, 154–55, 159, 162, 169, 182, 191, 202, 205, 207, 209–10, 233, 238, 257, 286–87, 295, 298, 300, 305
Haydn Orchestra, 286–87
Hazell, Terry, 5, 24, 31
Heath, Edward, 306
Heine, Heinrich, 236
Hemmings, Dorothy, 70
Herschel, Sir William, 136
Heyworth, Peter, 76, 147
Hickox, Richard, 183
Hildegard of Bingen, 288
Hill, Benny, 23
Hill, Bob, 115, 248, 258
Hill, Ralph, 97
Hindemith, Paul, 74, 76, 97, 160, 245
Hirsch Chamber Players, 237
Hoddinott, Alun, 153
Hoffnung, Gerard, 75
Holbrooke, Josef, 56
Holmboe, Vagn, 47, 67, 144–45, 152, 160, 251, 303
Holmes, Martin, 5
Holst, Gustav, 9, 41, 304
Honegger, Arthur, 146
Horenstein, Jascha, 77, 89, 103, 106, 112, 151, 252, 271–72, 277–78
Houlding, Christopher, 207
Howard, George, 147
Howells, Herbert, 40, 50, 145, 259, 279–80, 286
Hoyle, Sir Fred, 136
Huber, Paul, 138
Hudson, Gareth, 235

Hughes, Ian, 220
Hughes, Laurence, 210
Hughes, Rosemary, 67
Huntley, Alison, 258
Hussey, Dyneley, 60, 74, 76
Hutchings, Arthur, 289

I

Ibsen, Hendrik, 79, 90, 287
Iliffe, Barrie, 129
Ireland, John, 51, 216
Isaacs, Leonard, 55, 205, 223, 258
Israel Piano Trio, 180, 201
Ives, Charles, 98

J

Jacob, Gordon, 40, 58, 279
Jacobs, Arthur, 236
Jalas, Jussi, 256
James, Burnett, 89
Janácek, Leos, 10, 160, 242
Jeans, Lady Susi, 136, 192
Jeans, Sir James, 136
Jewell, Caroline, 51
Johannison, Grant, 209
John, Augustas, 9
John, Gwen, 9
Johnson, Arthur, 223
Johnson, David, 258
Johnson, Edward, 112
Johnson, Lyndon Baines, 144
Johnson, Stephen, 93, 96, 119, 132, 160, 183, 187, 203
Jones, Barbara, 70
Jones, Daniel, 97
Jones, Ken, 207
Jones, Kenneth V., 51

K

Kahn and Averill, 65, 310
Kantorov, 135
Karajan, Herbert von, 254, 271
Keable, Russell, 119, 132
Keane, Nancy, 184
Keane, Peter, 201

Keeley, Robert, 109
Keller, Hans, 93, 112, 144, 171, 216, 228, 245, 282–83, 285, 292
Keller, Milein (Cosman), 133, 282–83, 285
Kempe, Rudolf, 103, 117
Kennedy, Michael, 180
Kennedy, Nigel, 134
Kensington Symphony Orchestra, 119, 132
Kenyon, Sir Nicholas, 137, 155, 206, 252
King, Martin Luther, 161, 203, 220
King, Thea, 111
Kinsella, John, 168, 188
Kleiber, Erich, 112
Klemperer, Otto, 103, 205, 257, 271
Knussen, Oliver, 5, 248–50
Kodaly, Zoltan, 51
Kohl, Helmut, 226
Kok, Nicholas, 119
Korn, Peter Jona, 98
Kozinn, Allan, 163

L

Lam, Basil, 126, 213
Lambert, Constant, 76
Lane, Piers, 109
Larner, Gerald, 134
Last, Richard, 87
Laurel and Hardy, 23
Layton, Robert, 47, 71, 112, 132
Leew, Reinbert de, 124
Leicestershire Schools Symphony Orchestra, 94
Leighton, Kenneth, 130, 145, 248
Lenard, Ondrej, 96
Lengnick, 49, 196, 250
Leonard, Frankie, 223
Leonard, Laurence, 75
Lewis, A. J., 229
Lilburn, Douglas, 76
Lill, John, 116
Lindsay Quartet, 209
Liszt, Franz, 97, 99, 189
Llewellyn, Grant, 109
Locatelli, Pietro, 80

Locke Brass Consort, 79
Loftus, Tony, 87
Lom, Herbert, 165
London Chamber Orchestra, 75–76
London Double-Bass Ensemble, 153
London Philharmonic Orchestra, 88, 130–31, 173
London Symphony Orchestra, 89, 96, 113, 120
Loppert, Max, 116, 118, 122
Lord Byron, 174
Loughran, James, 94, 116, 208
Lovell, Sir Bernard, 136
Lowbury, Edward, 258
Lowbury, Pauline, 129, 163, 209
Lowbury Trio (P. Lowbury, Ursula Smith, Elizabeth Burley), 218
Lowengard, Manfred, 230
LSO Brass, 207
Ludd, Jack, 121
Lundquist, Torbjorn Iwan, 251, 258
Lympany, Moura, 258

M

Macdonald, Malcolm (Calum), 126
MacEwan, David, 25, 54, 220, 228
MacEwan, Miriam, 5
Maconchy, Elizabeth, 51, 143, 146
Maggini Quartet, 202
Mahler, Gustav, 8, 47, 92, 100–101, 119, 186, 204, 239, 242–43, 246, 263–64, 272, 300, 310, 312
Malipiero, Francesco, 145
Manduell, Sir John, 79, 190, 207
Mann, William, 74, 104, 108, 249
Manning, Jane, 5, 96, 192
Marshall, John, 258
Martelli, Carlo, 74
Marthinsen, Niels, 160
Martin, Frank, 145
Martin, Philip, 240, 245, 258
Martin Quartet, 80
Martinů, Bohuslav, 47
Marx, Groucho, 176
Marx, Joseph, 271
Marx, Karl, 224
Mason, Colin, 74, 76, 84
Mason, Frances, 129
Massey, Ron, 215
Mathias, William, 258
Matthews, David, 201, 210
Matthew-Walker, Robert, 138, 180
Maw, Nicholas, 248
Mawby, Colin, 176
May, Brian, 227, 258, 304
Mazzuca, Giuseppe, 107
McCabe, John, 78, 144–45, 184
Medtner, Nicholas, 47, 286
Mellers, Wilfred, 72, 77
Melos Ensemble, 110
Melville-Mason, Alex, 184
Melville-Mason, Graham, 184, 209
Mendelssohn, Felix, 9, 75, 89, 97, 112, 135, 186–87, 192, 240, 245–46, 297
Menuhin, Hepzibah, 61
Menuhin, Yehudi, 61
Messiaen, Olivier, 98
Meyer, Torben, 66
Milan, Susan, 182–83
Milhaud, Darius, 146
Milkina, Nina, 258
Miller, Glen, 160
Miller, John, 184
Milner, Anthony, 76, 145–46
Milnes, Ian, 258
Milton, John, 127
Minty, Shirley, 93, 96
Mitchell, Donald, 49, 73, 84
Mitchinson, John, 96
Moeran, E. J. (Ernest John), 305
Montagu-Nathan, M., 71
Monteverdi, Claudio, 88
Moore, Sir Patrick, 217
Moravian Philharmonic Orchestra, 234
Morris, William, 149
Mozart, Wolfgang Amadeus, 38, 47, 70, 72–73, 76–77, 83, 86, 89, 121, 123, 135, 153, 168, 173, 175, 197, 202, 236, 238–39, 241, 257, 282, 284
Musgrave, Angela Mary. See Simpson, Angela (née Musgrave)
Musgrave, Ethel May (Doris), 78
Musgrave, Percy Eric, 78

Musgrave, Peter, 5
Musgrave, Thea, 113
Music Group of London, 128–29
Mussolini, Benito, 228
Mussorgsky, Modest, 241, 246
Myers, Rollo, 216

N

National Symphony Orchestra, 173
Nelsova, Zara, 209, 258
Newbould, Brian, 116
New Philharmonia Orchestra, 95
Newstone, Harry, 34, 44, 77, 90, 94, 286–87
New York Philharmonic Orchestra, 271
Nielsen, Carl, 6, 47, 50, 57–58, 60, 65–69, 71, 75, 77, 96, 105–6, 113, 115, 119, 130–31, 134–35, 149, 152, 156–57, 159–60, 165, 170, 173, 179, 182–83, 185, 187, 189–91, 204, 207, 209, 232, 242–44, 247, 251, 255–56, 258, 265, 274, 286–88, 294–95, 297–98, 307–8, 310
Nielsen, Irmelin, 190
Nightingale, David, 127
Nohejl, Jaromir, 123, 234
Nord Deutscher Rundfunks Orchestra, 77
Northcott, Bayan, 126, 134, 173, 283, 303
Northern Sinfonia, 185
Nyman, Michael, 116

O

Oeser, Fritz, 105
Ogdon, John, 108–9, 123
Oklahoma City Symphony, 90
Oliver, Michael, 57
Oliver, Stephen, 184
Orga, Ates, 250
Orland, Desmond, 75
Ormandy, Eugene, 103
Orpington Junior Singers, 93
Orr, Buxton, 60
Orton, Stephen, 209
Orwell, George, 305
Ottaway, Hugh, 58, 71, 75, 111–12, 117, 122
Owen, (Lord) David, 227

P

Palestrina, Giovanni, 237
Palmer, Peter, 175
Palmer, Samuel, 9
Palmer, Tony, 304
Parikian, Manoug, 79
Parkes, Peter, 138, 207
Parkhouse, David, 109, 129
Parkin, Eric, 51
Parry, Sir Hubert, 9, 247, 304
Pattison, Jim, 116, 119, 206
Pavarotti, Luciano, 169
Payne, Anthony, 88, 162, 173, 210, 283, 303
Payne, Sarah Burney, 189
Peacock, Arthur, 129
Pearce, Edward, 206
Pellay, Paul, 258
Pérotin (Perotinus Magnus), 264
Perry, Simon, 187
Perry, Ted, 55, 178, 287, 290
Petrassi, Goffredo, 144
Pettitt, Stephen, 159, 163
Pfitzner, Hans, 119, 245
Philip Jones Brass Ensemble, 79
Phillippo, Simon, 258
Phillipson, Harold, 166
Pickard, John, 179–80, 193, 209, 258
Piggott, Patrick, 124, 258
Pike, Lionel, 21, 35, 59, 189, 218, 228, 238, 258
Pinkett, Eric, 94
Pissarro, Lucien, 9
Pizzetti, Ildebrando, 145
Pleeth, William, 110
Ponsonby, Robert, 94, 145, 147–48, 218, 300
Pope, Charles, 127
Pope, Stanley, 94, 133, 205
Poulenc, Francis, 244
Prague Chamber Orchestra, 77
Previn, André, 5, 113

Pritchard, John, 62
Prokofiev, Sergei, 47, 174, 246
Pryce-Jones, John, 160
Pugin, Augustus Welby Northmore, 220
Purcell, Henry, 49, 74, 80, 237

Q

Quinn, Ian, 165
Quinn, Matthew, 88

R

Rachmaninov, Sergei, 98, 131, 180, 189, 209, 250, 287
Rajna, Thomas, 49
R. A. M. Brass, 160
Ramsoe, E. W., 160
Rasmussen, Arne Skjold, 67, 119, 190
Rattle, Simon, 68, 172–73, 204
Ravel, Maurice, 129, 182, 244
Rawsthorne, Alan, 97, 109, 123
Raybould, Clarence, 58
RCM Sinfonia, 210, 279
Reagan, Ronald, 226, 229
Reed, Henry, 149
Rees, C. I. B., 234
Regan, Kenneth, 51
Reger, Max, 145, 177, 199, 236
Reid, Charles, 88
Reizenstein, Franz, 130, 145, 248
Rembrandt (Van Rijn), 215, 267
Rex Foundation of San Francisco (The Grateful Dead), 120, 173
Ricci, Ruggiero, 85
Richardson, David, 156, 170
Rickards, Guy, 300
Rigby, Cormack, 258
Rignold, Hugo, 77, 86, 108
Rihm, Wolfgang, 124
Rimsky-Korsakov, Nikolay, 61
Roberton, Kenneth, 12, 176
Roberton, Margaret, 176
Roberts, Eric, 74
Roberts, Rex, 5
Robson, William, 258
Roland-Adams, Gordon, 232
Ronan, Tamsin, 5

Rossini, Gioachino, 84, 235
Roussel, Albert, 146
Royal Danish Orchestra, 149
Royal Holloway Orchestra, 109, 132
Royal Liverpool Philharmonic Orchestra, 275
Royal Philharmonic Orchestra, 88, 90, 124, 153
RTE Choir, 177
Rubbra, Edmund, 9, 59, 128, 130, 138, 144, 146, 217, 232, 247–48, 282, 291–92, 300, 303–4
Runswick, 153
Russell, Christopher, 135
Rye, Matthew, 109

S

Sacramento Symphony Orchestra, 77
Sadie, Stanley, 98
Saint-Saëns, Camille, 61
Salzedo, Leonard, 51
Samale, Nicola, 107
Sammartini, Giovanni, 80
Sand, George, 6
Sargent, Sir Malcolm, 255
Sassoon, Siegfried, 149
Satie, Eric, 214
Scarlatti, Domenico, 51, 111
Schaarwëchter, Jurgen, 5, 401
Schafer, Murray, 216
Scheibe, 80
Schmidt, Felix, 172
Schmidt, Franz, 145, 245, 300, 304
Schmidt, Ole, 68, 96, 123
Schmidt-Isserstedt, Hans, 77
Schnabel, Artur, 61
Schnittke, Alfred, 247
Schoenberg, Arnold, 93, 97, 216, 244–45, 272, 278, 282, 309, 311
Schönzeler, Hans-Hubert, 74
Schreker, Franz, 271
Schubert, Franz, 38, 49, 72, 111, 132, 155, 175, 191, 202, 238, 240, 242, 289, 296, 300
Schuller, Gunther, 153
Schumann, Robert, 77, 97, 109–10, 149, 240, 283

Schurmann, Gerard, 145
Schwartzkopf, Elisabeth, 261
Schweitzer, Albert, 23
Scott, Cyril, 56
Seamarks, Colin, 300
Searle, Humphrey, 97, 144, 146, 216
Sedgewick, A. R. M., 148
Segovia, Andres, 194
Seiber, Matyas, 81, 145
Semkow, Jerzy, 149
Serafina, Gabriel, 204
Shakespeare, William, 6, 40, 61, 204, 280
Sharp, Cecil, 305
Shawe-Taylor, Desmond, 60, 66, 105, 116, 122, 134
Sheppard, Honor, 93
Sherman, Russell, 124
Shirley-Quirk, John, 153
Shostakovich, Dmitri, 47, 119, 135, 174, 246–47, 282, 298, 303
Sibelius, Jean, 32, 62, 65–66, 68–69, 71, 95, 109, 113, 132, 174, 180, 186, 195, 202, 214, 216, 242–44, 255–56, 273, 281, 293, 298, 300, 307, 310
Silvestri, Constantin, 393
Simon, Richard, 77
Simons, Charles W., 49
Simple, Peter (Colm Brogan / Michael Wharton), 66
Simpson, (Wilfred) Gordon, 12
Simpson, Angela (née Musgrave), 55, 78, 126, 156
Simpson, Bessie (née Fraser) "Squibs," 34, 44, 47
Simpson, Fransiska (née Balshaitis), 12
Simpson, Helena Hendrika (née Govaars), 13
Simpson, James Young, 10
Simpson, Nicholas, 258
Simpson, Robert Warren, 12–13
Simpson, Robert Wilfred Levick (Bob)
  birth, 10
  childhood (including band membership), 11
  Westminster City School, 22, 24
  discovery of classical music, 24
  holidays in Holland, 37
  holidays in England, 31
  pre-medical course (Chelsea Polytechnic), 31
  relationship with Elisabeth Grant Matthews, 31
  abandons medicine, 31
  conscientious objector, 35
  civil defence, 34, 279
  studies with H. Howells, 279
  marriage to Bessie Fraser, 34
  wife's nervous breakdown, 52
  Exploratory Concert Society, 100
  move to Grand Avenue, Muswell Hill, 52
  joins BBC, 54–55
  doctorate, 56
  Hoffnung Music Festival, 75
  meets Angela Musgrave, 156
  move to Cedar Cottage, Chearsley, 85
  produces Gothic Symphony, 92
  contributes to Great Musicians series, 111
  fiftieth birthday tributes, 266
  cerebral haemorrhage, 121
  diabetes diagnosed, 121
  exchange with Arts Council, 129
  resigns from BBC, 140–42
  refuses CBE, 224
  foundation of RSS, 144
  sixtieth birthday tributes, 144
  death of first wife, 154
  marriage to Angela Musgrave, 156
  move to Siochain, Killelton, County Kerry, 165
  disagreement regarding Cheltenham Festival, 190
  seventieth birthday celebrations, 190
  stroke and thalamic pain, 200–201
  death, 208
  memorial concert, 209
  ninetieth anniversary tributes, birthplace marked, 210
  on conducting, Appendix 6, 254
  character, 215, 230
  humour, 75, 230, 266, 271, 273, 287
  tastes, 214

astronomy, 217
philosophy, 218, 220
religion, 218
political views, 218, 220, 222, 224, 228
pacifism, 218, 220, 223
on conductors, 254–55, 259–60, 273
books
  Carl Nielsen, Symphonist (1952), 58, 310
  Symphony, The (1966–1967), 79
  Essence of Bruckner, The (1967), 92
  Proms and Natural Justice, The (1981), 54, 143–45, 149, 206, 254, 259, 304, 310
on composing, Appendix 3, 8, 10, 11,
  on symphonies, Appendix 9, 253
musical works
  first attempt, 24
  early works now destroyed, 38–39
  Piano Sonata (1946), 49
  Variations and Finale on a Theme of Haydn (1948), 50, 300
  1st Symphony (1951), 53
  First Quartet (1952), 70, 72, 110, 198
  Second Quartet (1953), 71, 209, 248
  Third Quartet (1954), 72–73, 109
  Allegro Deciso (1954), 72, 74
  Second Symphony (1955–1956), 60, 62, 67, 69, 75–78, 133, 160, 259
  Canzona for Brass (1958), 79
  Variations and Fugue for Recorder and String Quartet (1959), 79
  Violin Concerto (1957–1959), 233
  Third Symphony (1962), 7, 86, 90–91, 105, 163, 183, 261, 277
  incidental music to Ibsen's The Pretenders (1965), 287
  Piano Concerto (1967), 78, 108–9, 291
  Trio For Clarinet, Cello, and Piano (1967), 109
  Quintet for Clarinet and Strings (1968), 110
  Energy-Symphonic Study for Brass Band (1971), 112
  Tribute to Sir William Walton (1972), 113
  Fourth Symphony (1970–1972), 115, 120, 243, 303–4
  Fifth Symphony (1972), 65, 68, 77, 94–95, 121, 123, 195, 205, 210, 274, 302
  Fourth Quartet (1973), 71, 126, 137
  Fifth Quartet (1974), 72
  Sixth Quartet (1975), 175
  incidental music to Samson Agonistes (1974), 127
  "Media Morte in Vita Sumus" (1975), 79, 127, 207
  Quartet for Horn, Violin, Cello, and Piano (1975), 128
  6th Symphony (1977), 6–7, 62, 68, 107, 204, 258
  7th Symphony (1977), 133, 185, 191, 201, 207, 235
  7th Quartet (1977), 137, 192, 209–10, 258, 283
  Volcano-Symphonic Study for Brass Band (1978), 137
  Sonata for Two Pianos (1979), 138
  8th Quartet (1979), 7, 85
  8th Symphony (1981), 56, 62, 79, 144, 148–49, 155, 234, 266, 275, 285, 297, 310
  Quintet for Clarinet, Bass Clarinet, and Three Double Basses (1981), 153
  9th Quartet (1982), 50, 206
  Variations and Finale on a Theme of Carl Nielsen (1982), 156
  Four Temperaments for Brass Band, The (1983), 160
  10th Quartet (1983), 162
  11th Quartet (1984), 162, 191
  Trio for Horn, Violin, and Piano (1984), 163
  Violin Sonata (1984), 32, 50, 79, 163, 182, 209
  "Michael Tippett, His Mystery" (1985), 164

"Eppur Si Muove" (1985), 67, 79, 128, 164–65
9th Symphony (1985–1987), 103–4, 107, 156, 161, 164, 174, 187, 210, 215, 234, 240, 288, 298
12th Quartet (1987), 191
String Trio (1987), 175
1st String Quintet (1987), 175
"Tempi" (1987), 79, 128, 176–77
Introduction and Allegro on a Theme of Max Reger for Brass Band (1987), 177
Tenth Symphony (1988), 185, 191, 263
Piano Trio (1988–1989), 164
Flute Concerto (1989), 182–83, 190–91, 196, 202
13th Quartet (1989), 202, 237
Brass Quintet (1989), 184
"Vortex" for brass band (1989), 184–85, 192, 207
11th Symphony (1990), 159, 175, 186, 190
Variations and Fugue on a Theme of Beethoven (1990), 188
Cello Concerto (1991), 194–95
14th Quartet (1990), 220
Variations and Fugue on a theme of J.S. Bach (1991), 74, 195
15th Quartet (1991), 188
2nd String Quintet, 111, 199, 202
Simpson, Rose (née Berry), 11
Simpson, Sir James Young, 21
Simpson, Wilfred Levick, 11
Singer, Aubrey, 284
Skalkottas, Nikos, 145
Slatkin, Leonard, 114
Slovak Philharmonic Orchestra, 96
Small, Jonathan, 193
Smetana, Bedřich, 209
Smith, F. Graham, 136
Smith, Martin, 201
Smith, Ronald, 49, 144, 258
Snell, Howard, 178
Sommer, Raphael, 291
Sorabji, Kaikhosru, 73
Soutine, Chaim, 9
Spange, Annalise, 164

Spange, Svend Aage, 67, 164
Spooner, Joseph, 132
Stadlen, Peter, 89
Stalman, Roger, 93
Standford, Patric, 5, 124, 244
Stark, Peter, 210
Stephens, James, 258
Stevens, Bernard, 145, 258
Stevenson, Ronald, 130, 144, 146, 248, 295–96
Stewart, Michael, 224
Stobart, James, 79
Stockhausen, Karlheinz, 210, 252–53, 312
Stokowski, Leopold, 277
Strauss, Richard, 86, 89, 92, 94, 108, 174, 238, 242–43, 248, 270, 295
Stravinsky, Igor, 61, 97, 103, 108, 245, 247, 278, 283–84, 307–8
Sturt, Hilary, 135
Swann, Donald, 75
Sweelinck, Jan, 295
Symphony, 90
Szasz, Thomas, 284
Szell, Georg, 61
Szerying, Hendryk, 87
Szymanowski, Karol, 146

T

Tallis, Thomas, 237
Tamir, Alexander, 138
Tate, Phyllis, 110
Tavener, Sir John, 209
Taylor, Gordon, 5
Taylor, Matthew, 68, 74, 78, 109, 132, 135, 159, 177, 184–90, 194, 197, 201–2, 209, 218, 289–90, 297–98
Taylor, Robin, 210
Tchaikovsky, Pyotr Ilich, 47, 86, 99–100, 111, 149, 152, 173, 242, 282
Telmányi, Anne Marie, 65
Terroni Trio, 182
Thames Sinfonia, 78, 135, 258
Thatcher, (Lady) Margaret, 306
Thatcher, Sir Denis, 225
Thomas, Adrian, 190
Thomas, Dylan, 149

Thomas, Edward, 149
Thompson, Bryden, 118
Thompson, Dorothy, 203
Thompson, E. P. (Edward), 203
Tierney, Neil, 134
Tippett, Sir Michael, 145, 164
Tomkins, Thomas, 237
Tonderová, Petra, 4–5
Tortelier, Paul, 88
Toscanini, Arturo, 259–60, 270
Tovey, Sir Donald Francis, 100, 237, 287
Truscott, Harold, 49–50, 57, 205, 296, 300
Tryer, Stephen, 153
Tuckwood, Alan, 132
Turner, John, 81
Twain, Mark, 143–44
Twentieth Century Ensemble, 74

V

Vanbrugh Quartet, 153, 188, 196–97, 207
Van Kempen, Christopher, 202
Vansen, Frederick, 258
Varwig, Rudolf, 26
Vaughan Williams, Ralph, 9, 38, 51, 58, 66, 79, 95, 204, 217, 236, 247, 303–5
Vellinger Quartet, 209
Verdi, Giuseppe, 62, 150, 236
Vermeer, Johannes, 295
Vertavo Quartet, 209
Vetterlein, John, 258
Vicars, Mervyn, 60
Vignoles, Roger, 143
Vinter, Gilbert, 138
Voltaire, 295
von Karajan, Herbert, 254

W

Wagner, Richard, 94, 104, 118, 176, 229, 236, 241, 253, 264, 272
Wallfisch, Peter, 110, 201
Wallfisch, Raphael, 194–95
Walsh, John, 206
Walsh, Stephen, 89, 108, 116, 122
Walton, Bernard, 71, 109, 111
Walton, Sir William, 65, 113
Ward, Major, 39
Warlock, Peter (Philip Heseltine), 66
Warrack, John, 60
Waterhouse, J. F., 59, 70, 72–73, 76, 84
Watkins, Richard, 129, 163
Watson, James, 113, 160–61, 178, 185
Watts, Anthony, 127
Webern, Anton, 245, 278, 308
Wejchert, Alexandra, 208
Wellesz, Egon, 112
Westrup, Sir Jack, 98
White, Jillian, 175, 203
Widdecombe, Gillian, 89
Wigmore, Richard, 71, 80, 106, 153, 155, 162–63, 182, 191, 202, 209, 290, 296
Willcocks, Sir David, 5, 222, 228
Williams, Nicholas, 303
Williams, Stephen, 59
Willison, Sally, 85, 172, 174
Willoughby, George, 75
Wilson, Colin, 216
Wilson, Harold, 306
Wilson, Mary Jane, 14
Wilson, Peter, 178
Wilson, Thomas, 137, 258
Wind Music Society, 79, 93
Wiseman, Beth, 81
Wöldike, Mogens, 145
Wolf, Hugo, 62, 250
Wolff, Endre, 86
Wood, Gordon, 220–21
Wood, Henry, 24, 260
Wood, Hugh, 5, 248
Wood, Philip, 81
Wood, Professor Gordon, 220–21
Wood, Sir Henry, 24, 145, 260
Woods, Nicholas, 97
Woolven, Nicholas, 118
Wordsworth, William (composer), 97
Wright, Brian, 134, 193, 203, 235

Y

Yeats, William Butler, 149
Yorkshire Imperial Metals Band, 160, 185
Young, Hugo, 226
Young, John, 188, 220
Young Musicians Symphony Orchestra, 123

AUTHOR BIOGRAPHY

I was born in Cambridge in 1949. My father, who was originally from the Outer Hebrides, was a village policeman, and I grew up in the East Anglian countryside, a very different place then—quiet lanes and fields full of wild flowers and butterflies, now largely gone thanks to intensive agriculture and the growth of private car ownership.

I was educated at Newmarket Grammar School and the County Boys School in Cambridge; while at the latter, I discovered a passion for painting pictures which has stayed with me ever since. In 1968 I began a four-year course at Reading University, hoping to continue along the path I had already taken; alas, those who ran the place were modernists with no time for figurative work. Thus I graduated in Art History. On the positive side, two of the sympathetic lecturers and two fellow pupils (similarly looked down upon) have remained lifelong friends.

With a useless degree, I had to earn a living in various ways—farm worker, Christmas postman, porter, cleaner, bricklayer's labourer and (for two years) an auxillary in an operating theatre, while continuing to paint as much as I could. In 1979 I joined the Civil Service, and worked in government service until taking early retirement in 2005.

This gave me the freedom to pursue my own consuming interests. Although painting is my first love I have always enjoyed writing, and while still a civil servant I maintained my sanity by writing a polemical trade union journal successively entitled Thames News, North-West Passage and Red Kensington. This is my first book. It was written as a labour of love. I came across Robert Simpson at an early stage: after choosing his book The Essence of Bruckner as a school prize I began listening to his own music, and was greatly impressed. Later, I met the composer and spent several highly enjoyable holidays with he and Angela in their house in County Kerry, Eire. Some six years ago the then Chairman of the Robert Simpson Society, the late Terry Hazell, mentioned that he had been trying without success to persuade someone to write the composer's biography, and I volunteered for the task.

Since retirement, in addition to painting and writing, I have been attempting to fill some gaps in our family history discovering, for example, that two of my Hebridean relatives were killed in the First World War. I also believe that I have identified my English grandmother's father (previously un-named) although this has to be confirmed.

I am single and live in North-West London for the present. When not working I enjoy reading, solving crosswords, listening to music, drinking real ale and smoking tobacco. My paintings may be viewed on the website www.

donaldmacauley.com. If you sense a certain kinship with the work of the fifteenth century Flemish and Italian artists you are quite right—I admire many painters past and present, but as far as I am concerned this was the golden age.

Ingram Content Group UK Ltd.
Milton Keynes UK
UKHW011944210323
418953UK00012B/198/J